Praise for *The End of Wall Street*

"[*The End of Wall Street*] is a complex but imaginative book. . . . [Lowenstein] is able to identify the creative instruments of financial destruction with the directness that is all-important to a book like this." —*The New York Times*

"Think of Roger Lowenstein's *The End of Wall Street* as a tuition-free class in twenty-first-century U.S. macroeconomics. . . . *The End of Wall Street* debunks the notion that no one could have seen the economic catastrophe coming." —*USA Today*

"*The End of Wall Street* is a calm, reasoned, and often witty tour of the current financial landscape and how it got that way." —*The Philadelphia Inquirer*

"Over the past year, there has been a steady stream of books trying to make sense of the crisis. The latest, and perhaps the most accessible and even-handed, is Roger Lowenstein's *The End of Wall Street*." —*The Washington Post*

"Witty, well-written, heavily researched, and often dramatic." —Associated Press

"Lowenstein's strong knowledge of the source material and flair for the dramatic and doomsday title should draw readers who still wonder what went wrong and how." —*Publishers Weekly*

"Lowenstein does a great job of explaining. . . . in understandable terms that unobtrusively avoid the injection of emotion and politics." —*Booklist*

"A veteran financial/business journalist examines the past three years of economic collapse, chronicling actions and inactions from dozens of villains and a few heroes. . . . A well-delineated chronicle likely to cause readers to ask who put the clowns in charge of the circus, and why aren't they confined to prison cells." —*Kirkus Reviews*

PENGUIN BOOKS

THE END OF WALL STREET

Roger Lowenstein, the author of four previous books, reported for *The Wall Street Journal* for more than a decade. He is now a contributing writer for *The New York Times Magazine* and other publications, and a columnist for Bloomberg. He has three children and lives with his wife in Newton, Massachusetts.

THE END OF WALL STREET

ROGER LOWENSTEIN

PENGUIN BOOKS

PENGUIN BOOKS
Published by the Penguin Group
Penguin Group (USA) Inc., 375 Hudson Street, New York, New York 10014, U.S.A. •
Penguin Group (Canada), 90 Eglinton Avenue East, Suite 700, Toronto, Ontario, Canada M4P 2Y3
(a division of Pearson Penguin Canada Inc.) • Penguin Books Ltd, 80 Strand, London WC2R 0RL,
England • Penguin Ireland, 25 St. Stephen's Green, Dublin 2, Ireland (a division of Penguin
Books Ltd) • Penguin Books Australia Ltd, 250 Camberwell Road, Camberwell, Victoria 3124,
Australia (a division of Pearson Australia Group Pty Ltd) • Penguin Books India Pvt Ltd,
11 Community Centre, Panchsheel Park, New Delhi – 110 017, India • Penguin Group (NZ),
67 Apollo Drive, Rosedale, North Shore 0632, New Zealand (a division of Pearson
New Zealand Ltd) • Penguin Books (South Africa) (Pty) Ltd, 24 Sturdee Avenue,
Rosebank, Johannesburg 2196, South Africa

Penguin Books Ltd, Registered Offices:
80 Strand, London WC2R 0RL, England

First published in the United States of America by The Penguin Press,
a member of Penguin Group (USA) Inc. 2010
This edition with a new afterword published in Penguin Books 2011

1   3   5   7   9   10   8   6   4   2

THE LIBRARY OF CONGRESS HAS CATALOGED THE HARDCOVER EDITION AS FOLLOWS:

Lowenstein, Roger.
The end of Wall Street / Roger Lowenstein.
p. cm.
Includes bibliographical references and index.
ISBN 978-1-59420-239-1 (hc.)
ISBN 978-0-14-311872-5 (pbk.)
1. Financial crises—United States—History—21st century. 2. Wall Street
(New York, N.Y.)—History—21st century. 3. United States—Economic policy—2001-2009.
4. Mortgages—Government policy—United States. I. Title.
HB3743.L677 2010
332.64′2732—dc22
2009050864

Printed in the United States of America
DESIGNED BY MARYSARAH QUINN

To Judy, who saw me through this and more

CONTENTS

Cast of Characters

DAVID ANDRUKONIS, chief risk officer of Freddie Mac, warned that Alt-A loans were being abused

SHEILA C. BAIR, chairwoman of Federal Deposit Insurance Corporation, jousted with Paulson and Bernanke and pushed for help for homeowners

THOMAS C. BAXTER JR., New York Fed general counsel, directed Lehman to file for bankruptcy

RICHARD BEATTIE, storied chairman of Simpson Thacher & Bartlett, counseled Willumstad of AIG that bankruptcy was an option

BEN BERNANKE, succeeded Alan Greenspan as chairman of Federal Reserve on February 1, 2006; previously was a distinguished scholar who disputed that bubbles should be "pricked"; after the meltdown worked furiously to supply liquidity

DONALD BERNSTEIN, partner at Davis Polk & Wardwell, tackled the daunting task of separating "bad" Lehman assets from "good"

STEVEN BLACK, cohead of the investment bank of JPMorgan Chase and Jamie Dimon's right-hand man

LLOYD C. BLANKFEIN, soft-spoken CEO of Goldman Sachs, was too close to Paulson for his rivals' comfort

BROOKSLEY BORN, ran the Commodity Futures Trading Commission in the late '90s; her attempt to regulate derivatives was squelched by more powerful regulators

DOUGLAS BRAUNSTEIN, top JPMorgan investment banker, tried to piece together a rescue for AIG

WARREN E. BUFFETT, billionaire investor, frequently mentioned as potential savior of troubled investment banks

ERIN CALLAN, chief financial officer of Lehman

DAVID CARROLL, Wachovia senior executive, at a football game his BlackBerry fatefully buzzed

JOSEPH CASSANO, built AIG's financial-products unit into a powerhouse that was overexposed to credit default swap losses

JAMES E. (JIMMY) CAYNE, bridge-playing CEO of Bear Stearns, retired as the firm's troubles were mounting

H. RODGIN COHEN, Zelig-like partner at Sullivan & Cromwell, involved in numerous high-stakes Wall Street negotiations

CHRISTOPHER COX, chairman of the Securities and Exchange Commission

JAMES (JIM) CRAMER, television stock jock, went into a rant over Bernanke's slowness in cutting interest rates

GREGORY CURL, deal maker for Bank of America, tasked with negotiating with Merrill Lynch

ENRICO DALLAVECCHIA, chief risk officer of Fannie Mae, warned his superiors of portfolio risks

STEPHEN J. DANNHAUSER, chairman of the law firm Weil, Gotshal & Manges, feared a Lehman bankruptcy would be catastrophic

ALISTAIR DARLING, UK chancellor of the exchequer, insisted that Britain could not save Lehman

ROBERT EDWARD DIAMOND JR., CEO of Barclays Capital, urged the U.S. to guarantee Lehman's trades until the British bank could acquire it

JAMES L. (JAMIE) DIMON, CEO of JPMorgan Chase, coolly and methodically reduced his exposure to other banks to protect his own

ERIC R. DINALLO, New York State superintendent of insurance, approved a complex maneuver to get liquidity to AIG to keep its hopes alive

CHRISTOPHER J. DODD, chairman of the Senate Banking Committee, took a sweetheart loan from Angelo Mozilo as well as hefty campaign contributions from Fannie Mae and Freddie Mac

WILLIAM DUDLEY, chief of markets at the New York Federal Reserve (he was promoted to bank president in 2009)

JOHN C. DUGAN, Comptroller of the Currency, urged fellow regulators to toughen mortgage rules

LORI FIFE, Weil Gotshal partner, pulled all-nighters to save the carcass of Lehman

LAURENCE D. FINK, CEO of BlackRock, blunt-spoken Wall Street insider

GREGORY FLEMING, president of Merrill Lynch, frantically urged Thain to strike a merger with Bank of America

J. CHRISTOPHER FLOWERS, boutique private equity banker with a habit of surfacing at critical junctures on Wall Street

BARNEY FRANK, powerful Democratic congressman and ally of the mortgage "twins" Fannie and Freddie

RICHARD FULD, CEO of Lehman and the soul of the firm, by the fall of 2008 was Wall Street's longest-standing chief executive

James G. (Jamie) Gamble, Simpson Thacher partner representing AIG, asked the government to better its terms

Timothy Geithner, president of the Federal Reserve Bank of New York, more open to bank bailouts than, initially, was Paulson; succeeded Paulson as Treasury secretary in 2009

Michael Gelband, Lehman banker who warned Fuld to lower the company's risk level; later he feared that bankruptcy would unleash "the forces of evil"

Joseph Gregory, Lehman president, shielded Fuld but was slow to react to the firm's growing risk

Maurice R. (Hank) Greenberg, longtime CEO of AIG, forced out by New York State attorney general Eliot Spitzer in 2005 as a result of an accounting scandal, when AIG's risk was escalating

Alan Greenspan, chairman of Federal Reserve from 1987 through 2006, greatly eased monetary conditions and disputed that instruments such as derivatives needed government regulation

Edward D. Herlihy, partner at the law firm Wachtell, Lipton, Rosen & Katz, close adviser to Paulson, Ken Lewis, John Mack, and others

John Hogan, risk officer at JPMorgan investment bank; after Lehman ignored his advice, he restricted Morgan's trading with the firm

Dan Jester, one of numerous Goldman bankers tapped by Paulson for the Treasury, became the government's point person on AIG

James A. Johnson, Fannie Mae's CEO during the 1990s, he refashioned the mortgage financier into a political juggernaut

Colm Kelleher, Morgan Stanley chief financial officer, amid a panic urged investors to return to sanity

Pete Kelly, Merrill senior vice president, tried to dissuade O'Neal, his boss, from buying a subprime issuer

ROBERT P. KELLY, CEO of Bank of New York Mellon

KERRY KILLINGER, CEO of Washington Mutual, he fancied that peddling risky mortgages was no different than selling retail

ROBERT KINDLER, Morgan Stanley banker, offered to accept capital written on a napkin

ALEX KIRK, former Lehman banker who returned after the management shakeup in June '08, tried to reduce the company's risk

DONALD KOHN, veteran Fed governor, informal tutor to Bernanke

RICHARD M. KOVACEVICH, CEO of Wells Fargo, chose Stanford and a career in banking over professional baseball

PETER KRAUS, lavishly paid Merrill banker, formerly with Goldman, pursued selling a piece of Merrill to his former firm

JEFF KRONTHAL, head of Merrill's mortgage business; caution got him fired

KENNETH D. LEWIS, CEO of Bank of America, hungered to acquire Merrill Lynch but also entered the hunt for Lehman

JAMES (JIMMY) LEE JR., JPMorgan's star of high-yield banking, concluded that AIG would need an $85 billion bailout to survive

ARTHUR C. LEVITT, SEC chairman during the '90s, despite a reputation as a tough regulatory cop, joined with Greenspan, Rubin, and Summers to stop Brooksley Born

JOHN MACK, CEO of Morgan Stanley, battled hedge funds and refused to take an order from Washington

DERYCK MAUGHAN, Kohlberg Kravis & Roberts banker, tried to throw a life raft to AIG

BART McDADE, quiet Lehman banker promoted to president in June '08, as firm was careening toward the edge

HUGH E. (SKIP) MCGEE III, Lehman head of investment banking, bluntly told Fuld he needed to make a change

HARVEY R. MILLER, Weil Gotshal bankruptcy expert, assigned a team to work on Lehman under a code name

JERRY DEL MISSIER, president of Barclays Capital, sought eleventh-hour deal with Lehman

ANGELO MOZILO, CEO of Countrywide Financial and archetypal promoter, he epitomized the subprime era

DANIEL MUDD, CEO of Fannie Mae, struggled to satisfy both Congress and Wall Street

DAVID NASON, Treasury official involved in the effort to reform Fannie and Freddie, his visit to Senator Schumer was met with an insulting response

STANLEY O'NEAL, CEO of Merrill Lynch, stunned to learn of his bank's portfolio, he avidly sought to sell the firm

JOHN J. OROS, managing director of J.C. Flowers & Co., made a simple request of AIG

VIKRAM PANDIT, months after joining Citigroup was elevated to CEO, succeeding Prince

HENRY M. (HANK) PAULSON JR., secretary of Treasury from mid-2006 through January 20, 2009, a free-marketer turned fervent interventionist

LARRY PITKOWSKY, mutual fund investor who made a surprising discovery about the housing boom at a Dunkin' Donuts

STEPHANIE POMBOY, newsletter writer and consultant, forecast a "credit stink" late in 2006

RUTH PORAT AND ROBERT SCULLY, Morgan Stanley bankers who took on a near-impossible assignment: advising Paulson on Fannie and Freddie

CHARLES O. (CHUCK) PRINCE III, Citigroup chief executive and successor to Sandy Weill, resigned as bank began to rack up massive losses

FRANKLIN DELANO RAINES, CEO of Fannie Mae 1999–2004, vowed to push "opportunities to people who have lesser credit quality"

LEWIS S. RANIERI, Salomon Brothers trader considered the father of mortgage securities

CHRISTOPHER RICCIARDI, Merrill salesman who peddled CDOs from New York to Singapore

STEPHEN S. ROACH, Morgan Stanley chief economist, voiced the unmentionable: the people shorting Morgan Stanley's stock were its own clients

JULIAN ROBERTSON, hedge fund legend who turned foe of Morgan Stanley

ROBERT L. RODRIGUEZ, CEO of First Pacific Advisors, obsessively cautious fund manager whose nightmare prefigured grave misgivings about the health of credit markets

ROBERT RUBIN, chairman of the executive committee of Citigroup; the former Treasury secretary was famed for his cautious approach to risk but failed to apply it at Citi

JANE BUYERS RUSSO, head of JPMorgan's broker dealer unit, made a difficult call to Lehman

THOMAS A. RUSSO, vice-chairman of Lehman, saw credit storm coming but counted on Fed liquidity and overseas investors to bail out Wall Street

HERBERT AND MARION SANDLER, husband-and-wife coheads of Golden West Savings and Loan, highly regarded lender until it went overboard on option ARMs

BRIAN SCHREIBER, AIG's head of planning, frantically looked for credit as Wall Street backed away

CHARLES E. SCHUMER, Democratic senator from New York, rejected the need for a "dramatic restructuring" of Fannie and Freddie

ALAN D. SCHWARTZ, replaced Cayne as Bear CEO and reached out to Jamie Dimon for help

JANE SHERBURNE, Wachovia general counsel, coolly juggled competing merger offers

JOSEPH ST. DENIS, internal auditor at AIG; his reports were answered with profanity

ROBERT K. STEEL, undersecretary of the Treasury and close confidant to Paulson, left the government to become CEO of Wachovia

MARTIN J. SULLIVAN, replaced Greenberg as head of AIG but struggled to get a grip on CDO risk

LAWRENCE SUMMERS, as Rubin's headstrong deputy at Treasury, helped to thwart derivatives regulation; later, as Treasury secretary, was a skeptic of Fannie and Freddie; named White House economic adviser by Obama

RICHARD SYRON, chief executive of Freddie Mac as it accumulated massive mortgage portfolio

JOHN THAIN, former Goldman executive who replaced O'Neal as CEO of Merrill Lynch; after early stock sale resisted advice to raise more equity

G. KENNEDY (KEN) THOMPSON, CEO of Wachovia, acquired high-flying Golden West, even as he predicted it could get him fired

PAOLO TONUCCI, Lehman treasurer, prepared a list of assets that the Fed never asked to see

DAVID VINIAR, Goldman executive vice president and chief financial officer, became worried when the firm's mortgage portfolio lost money ten days running

MARK WALSH, commercial property banker for Lehman, struck risky deals in a frothy market

Kevin Warsh, Fed governor and colleague of Bernanke's, fretted over Treasury's support of Fannie and Freddie

Sanford I. (Sandy) Weill, architect of modern Citigroup, retired in 2003 with his dream of a synergistic supermarket unfulfilled

Meredith Whitney, Wall Street analyst, her report on Citi torpedoed the stock

Robert Willumstad, retired Citigroup executive, named CEO of AIG in June 2008; thought he had three months to fashion a plan

Kendrick Wilson, Paulson adviser and emissary to Wall Street, was stunned to learn the Treasury didn't have a plan

Barry Zubrow, JPMorgan risk officer, spread the word to Wall Street firms to cut their risk

INTRODUCTION

I N THE LATE SUMMER OF 2008, as Lehman Brothers teetered at the edge, a bell tolled for Wall Street. The elite of American bankers were enlisted to try to save Lehman, but they were fighting for something larger than a venerable, 158-year-old institution. Steven Black, the veteran JPMorgan executive, had an impulse to start saving the daily newspapers, figuring that historic events were afoot. On Sunday, September 14, as the hours ticked away, Lehman's employees gathered at the firm, unwilling to say goodbye and fearful of what lay in wait. With bankruptcy a fait accompli, they slunk off to bars for a final toast, as people once did in advance of a great and terrible battle. One ventured that "the forces of evil" were about to be loosed on American society. Lehman's failure was the largest in American history and yet another financial firm, the insurer American International Group, was but hours away from an even bigger collapse. Fannie Mae and Freddie Mac, the two bulwarks of the mortgage industry, had just been seized by the federal government. Dozens of banks big and small were bordering on insolvency. And the epidemic of institutional failures did not begin to describe the crisis's true depth. The market system itself had come undone. Banks couldn't borrow; investors wouldn't lend; companies could not refinance. Millions of Americans were threatened with losing their homes. The economy, when it fully caught Wall Street's chill, would retrench as it had not done since the Great Depression. Millions lost their jobs and the stock market crashed (its worst fall since the 1930s). Home foreclosures broke every record; two of America's three automobile manufacturers filed for bankruptcy, and banks themselves failed by the score. Confidence in America's market system, thought to have attained the pinnacle of laissez-faire perfection, was shattered.

The crisis prompted government interventions that only recently would have been considered unthinkable. Less than a generation after the fall of the Berlin Wall, when prevailing orthodoxy held that the free market could govern itself, and when financial regulation seemed destined for near irrelevancy, the United States was compelled to socialize lending and mortgage risk, and even the ownership of banks, on a scale that would have made Lenin smile. The massive fiscal remedies evidenced both the failure of an ideology and the eclipse of Wall Street's golden age. For years, American financiers had gaudily assumed more power, more faith in their ability to calculate—and inoculate themselves against—risk.

As a consequence of this faith, banks and investors had plied the average American with mortgage debt on such speculative and unthinking terms that not just America's economy but the world's economy ultimately capsized. The risk grew from early in the decade, when little-known lenders such as Angelo Mozilo began to make waves writing subprime mortgages. Before long, Mozilo was to proclaim that even Americans who could not put money down should be "lent" the money for a home, and not long after that, Mozilo made it happen: homes for free.

But in truth, the era began well before Mozilo and his ilk. Its seeds took root in the aftermath of the 1970s, when banking and markets were liberalized. Prior to then, finance was a static business that played merely a supporting role in the U.S. economy. America was an industrial state. Politicians, union leaders, and engineers were America's stars; investment bankers were gray and dull.

In the postindustrial era, what we may call the Age of Markets, diplomats no longer adjusted currency values; Wall Street traders did.

Just so, global capital markets allocated credit, and hordes of profit-minded, if short-term-focused, investors decided which corporations would be bought and sold.

Finance became a growth industry, fixated on new and complex securities. Wall Street developed a heretofore unimagined prowess for securitizing assets: student loans, consumer debts, and, above all, mortgages. Prosperity in this era was less evenly spread. Smokestack workers fell behind in the global competition, but financiers who mastered the intricacies of Wall Street soared on wings of gold. Finance now was anything but dull; markets were dynamic and ever changing. Average Americans clamored to keep pace; increasingly they resorted to borrowing. By happy accident, Wall Street had opened the spigot of credit. People discovered an unsuspected source of liquidity—the ability to borrow on their homes. With global investors financing mortgages, ordinary families were suddenly awash in debt. The habit of saving, forged in the tentative prosperity that followed the war, gave way to rampant consumerism. By the late 2000s the typical American household had become a net borrower, fueled by credit from less-developed countries such as China—a curious inversion of the conventional rules.

Paradoxically, the more license that was given to markets, the more that Wall Street called on bureaucrats for help. Market busts became a familiar feature of the age. Notwithstanding, it was the doctrine of the experts—on Wall Street and in Washington—that modern finance was a nearly pitch-perfect instrument. A preference for market solutions morphed into something close to blind faith in them. By the mid-2000s, when the spirit of the age attained its fullest, the very fact that markets had financed the leverage of banks, as well as the mortgages of individuals, was taken as proof that nothing could be wrong with that leverage, or nothing that government could or should try to restrict. Financiers had discovered the key to limiting risk, and central bankers, adherents to the cult of the market, had mastered the mysterious art of heading off depressions and even the normal ups and downs of the economic cycle. Or so it was believed.

Then, Lehman's collapse opened a trapdoor on Wall Street from which poured forth all the hidden demons and excesses, intellectual and otherwise, that had been accumulating during the boom. The Street suffered the most calamitous week in its history, including a money market fund closure, a panic by hedge funds, and runs against the investment firms that still were standing. Thereafter, the Street and then the U.S. economy were stunned by near-continuous panics and failures, including runs on commercial banks, a freezing of credit, the leveling of the American workplace in the recession, and the sickening drop in the stock market.

The first instinct was to blame Lehman (or the regulators who had failed to save it) for triggering the crisis. As the recession deepened, the thesis that one firm had caused the panic seemed increasingly tenuous. The trouble was not that so much followed Lehman, but that so much had preceded it. For more than a year, the excesses of the market age had been slowly deflating, in particular the bubble in home loans. Leverage had moved into reverse, and the process of deleveraging set off a fatal chain reaction.

By the time Lehman filed for bankruptcy, the U.S. housing market, the singular driver of the U.S. economy, had collapsed. Indeed, by then the slump was old news. Home prices had been falling for nine consecutive quarters, and the rate of mortgage delinquencies over the preceding three years had trebled. In August, the month before Lehman failed, 303,000 homes were foreclosed on (up from 75,000 three years before).

The especial crisis in subprime mortgages had been percolating for eighteen months, and the leading purveyors of these mortgages, having started to tumble early in 2007, were all, by the following September, either defunct, acquired, or on the critical list. Also, the subprime crisis had fully bled into Wall Street. Literally hundreds of billions of dollars of mortgages had been carved into exotic secondary securities, which had been stored on the books of the leading Wall Street banks, not to mention in investment portfolios around the globe. By September 2008, these securities had collapsed in value—and with them, the banks' equity and stock prices. Goldman Sachs, one of the *least*-affected banks, had lost a third of its market value; Morgan Stanley had been cut in half. And the Wall Street crisis had bled into Main Street. When Lehman toppled, total employment had already fallen by more than a million jobs. Steel, aluminum, and autos were all contracting. The National Bureau of Economic Research would conclude that the recession began in December 2007—nine months ahead of the fateful days of September.

On the evidence, Lehman was more nearly the climax, or one of a series of climaxes, in a long and painful cataclysm. By the time it failed, the critical moment was long past. Banks had suffered horrendous losses that drained them of their capital, and as the country was to discover, capitalism without capital is like a furnace without fuel. Promptly, the economy went cold. The recession mushroomed into the most devastating in postwar times. The modern financial system, in which markets rather than political authorities self-regulated risk-taking, for the first time truly failed. This was the result of a dark and powerful storm front that had long been gathering at Wall Street's shores. By the end of summer 2008, neither Wall Street nor the wider world could escape the imminent blow. To seek the sources of the crash, and even the causes, we must go back much further.

THE END OF WALL STREET

PROLOGUE:
EARLY WARNING

IT WAS EARLY IN 2006, on Lincoln's Birthday, that Bob Rodriguez had the dream. In the fog of his sleep, he saw himself in a courtroom. Rodriguez was in the dock; an attorney was firing questions at him. Was Mr. Rodriguez the manager of the FPA New Income Fund, a mutual fund that invested in bonds? Yes, sir. Did he represent it to be a high-quality fund? Yes again. The attorney leaned closer. Had he purchased obligations of Fannie Mae and Freddie Mac, the bankrupt government-sponsored enterprises? *Bankrupt* government-sponsored enterprises? Rodriguez turned fitfully in his bed. He did own them—yes. The lawyer motioned to his client, an elderly woman investor evidently rendered destitute by Rodriguez's reckless stewardship (though Rodriguez, in his somnolent state, could not recall that he *had* been reckless) and continued. Did Mr. Rodriguez agree that a *prudent* fund manager would always read a company's audited financial statements before committing to invest? He did. Was Mr. Rodriguez aware that neither Fannie nor Freddie even had an audited financial statement? Rodriguez awoke with a start, perspiring heavily. It was a little after midnight.

His first feeling was relief: it was only a dream. He was not in court, and Fannie and Freddie were not bankrupt. But the sense of unease lingered. In the morning, the dream still vivid in his mind, Rodriguez dressed quickly and drove from his home in Manhattan Beach, a seaside community near Los Angeles, to the office of First Pacific Advisors, where he ran a top-performing stock fund as well as a highly rated bond fund. Rodriguez told his colleagues about the dream.

FPA was not in the business of interpreting dreams. It was interested in facts. But Rodriguez's dream was not without foundation. The fact that had evidently troubled his subconscious was that neither Fannie nor Freddie had been able to produce a clean set of books for more than a year. Very few investors seemed to care. Accounting problems or no, the mortgage giants Fannie and Freddie were the bulwarks of the American housing industry. Thanks to them, millions of Americans got mortgages at, it was supposed, lower interest rates than they otherwise would have. The companies had the implicit backing of the U.S. government, which allowed them to borrow at cheaper rates than other financial firms. Every fixed-income manager in the business owned their bonds. From Washington, D.C., to Beijing to Rome, a vast array of investors including top-drawer institutions and many national governments owned $5 trillion of their paper.

The implicit government backing satisfied most investors, but it did not satisfy Rodriguez, who scrutinized securities with the same care that his father, a jeweler who had emigrated from Mexico, had exercised in picking over gems. While other investors professed to be careful about risk, Rodriguez actually went to great pains to avoid it. And as a free market purist, he took little comfort in government promises, implicit or otherwise. Rodriguez had been subscribing to the bulletins of the U.S. Federal Reserve since the tender age of ten. As far as he could tell, the country had been adding to the list of what it was willing to guarantee for as long as he had been a subscriber, without ever figuring how it would pay for it all.

The dream reminded Rodriguez that, in a general sense, he had been worried about U.S. credit markets for some time. Over a period of many years, American society had become increasingly reliant on debt. This had occurred at every level: the household, the corporation, the federal government. After World War II, families still living in the shadow of the Great Depression had kept their borrowings to, on average, only about a fifth of their disposable income. Even as late as 1970, households' debts were significantly less than their earnings. Now, though, the average family owed one third *more* than it earned. Financial companies such as banks and Fannie and Freddie had become similarly hooked on credit. Indeed, the total debt of financial firms was slightly greater than the gross domestic product—that is, more than the value of everything the United States produced. In 1980, it had been equal to only a fifth of the GDP.[1] Some of the reasons for the country's credit binge were cultural. Americans' lifestyles had evolved toward spending rather than saving; they became, in stages, less anxious and then quite comfortable with deploying the plastic cards in their wallets for any conceivable purpose.

The very accessibility of credit made it appear less menacing. After all, the borrower who could not repay his loan in cash could usually refinance it. Lenders lost sight of the distinction, as if liquidity and solvency were one and the same. The tide of interest rates, generally falling during the last quarter of the twentieth century, encouraged people and firms to relax the wariness of credit forged in earlier generations. Rates were guided in their downward path by the person of Alan Greenspan, the economic consultant and Ayn Rand disciple turned interest-rate guru who served as Federal Reserve chairman from 1987 to February 2006 (he retired a fortnight before Rodriguez's bad dream). It would be an oversimplification to credit (or blame) Greenspan for everything that happened to interest rates over that period, but it was his unmistakable legacy to stretch the boundaries of tolerance, to permit a greater easing of credit than any central banker had before. Greenspan made a particular habit of cutting short-term rates whenever Wall Street got in a mess, which it periodically did. It was a central tenet of the Greenspan worldview that market excesses—"bubbles"— could not be detected while they were occurring. This stemmed from his faith in the seductive doctrines of the new finance, a core element of which was that financial markets articulated economic values more perfectly than any mere mortal could. People might be flawed, but markets were pure—thus "bubbles" could be ascertained only after markets themselves had identified and corrected them. Greenspan's was a Rousseauean vision of markets as untainted social organisms—evolved, as it were, from a state of nature. (It overlooked the obvious point that markets were also human constructs—made by men.)

If central bankers could not be trusted to say that markets were wrong, neither could they be trusted to interfere in them—to prick the bubble before it burst on its own. It is of more than passing interest that Greenspan was emboldened in this view by the scholar who was then the foremost academic expert on monetary policy, the Princeton economist Ben Bernanke. Considering the question in 1999, when the prices of dot-com stocks were close to their manic peak and when, it was later said, the existence of a bubble could have been detected by a child of four, Bernanke insisted that until a bubble popped, it was virtually impossible to say for certain that prices weren't fully justified.[2]

Just so, Greenspan was inclined to let financial markets run to excess and intervene only, on an as-needed basis, the morning after. After the stock market break of 2002, the Fed lowered short-term interest rates to a hyperstimulative level and continued to abide low rates even when—and after—the economy shifted into recovery. This had its intended effect: it spurred the economy, especially the housing market. Most investors, and probably most Americans, supported Greenspan's policies. The economy grew smartly during his tenure, as did the stock market. With stock prices rising and inflation quiescent, the Fed chairman continued to be widely praised in the most laudatory fashion. Even in 1999, when under the Fed's approving eye Internet fever had infected the public, Phil Gramm, chairman of the Senate Banking Committee, had saluted Greenspan with this admiring prophecy: "You will go down as the greatest chairman in the history of the Federal Reserve Bank."[3]

A minority of market watchers, Rodriguez among them, worried that the Greenspan boom was based on too much credit, and that cheap money would lead to reckless lending, inflation, or both. Rodriguez obsessed about risk. He regarded a small dose of financial risk the way an epidemiologist would examine a small swab of microbes. Though he raced sports cars as a hobby, professionally he was loath to take chances, which often cost him profits in the short run. His round, owlish glasses disguised his most salient trait, which was his ferocity in resisting the crowd and in holding firm to his beliefs. Though the same could be said for a minority of other investors, few went on record with their convictions so fervently or so early—actually, five years early. In 2003, in a letter to investors of the New Income Fund, Rodriguez announced that he was going on a "buyer's strike." Specifically, he would not be buying obligations of the federal government of longer than one year, because he did not have faith in what Washington—and in particular Greenspan—was doing. "We have never seen the magnitude of liquidity that is being thrown at the system," he wrote. "We believe that this is a bond market bubble"—one similar in scale to the dot-com bubble.[4]

Since announcing his strike, Rodriguez had continued to invest in the obligations of Fannie and Freddie, which had been created by the government but operated (mostly) as private concerns. However, the mortgage market was looking ever more frothy. In October 2005, a few months before his nightmare, Rodriguez told his investors that his staff had been "combing through our high-quality mortgage-backed bond segment and"—lo and behold—"we found two suspicious-looking mortgage-backed CMOs." CMOs are bonds that are supported by pools of mortgages. The two dubbed suspicious by Rodriguez were backed by so-called Alternative A mortgages, which differed from conventional loans in that the prospective borrowers were not required to supply information to document their income. Securities like these, based on unconventional—and risky—mortgages, were the rage on Wall Street. Banks and institutional investors were overloaded with mortgage securities, the more "alternative" (and thus higher-yielding) the better. It was only to Rodriguez and a few others that they looked "suspicious." He sold them both.

Rodriguez's partner noted worriedly in the same letter that too-easy monetary policy had stimulated a "run-up" in real estate prices, and that higher prices, combined with "loose lending standards," had caused the volume of home equity loans to soar by 80 percent in only two years. Supposedly, rising home values had been making Americans richer; in reality, Rodriguez and his partner noted, people with home equity loans were withdrawing that wealth and spending it. In the common parlance, they were treating their homes like piggy banks.[5]

The authors commented on two further troubling developments. A much higher percentage of mortgages than before were adjustable, meaning that borrowers would be on the hook for much bigger monthly payments if interest rates were to rise from their present low levels. Second, banks had greatly increased the volume of mortgages issued to "subprime borrowers," or those with low credit scores.

Rodriguez's concerns sharpened his unease about Fannie and Freddie, which were hugely exposed to the U.S. mortgage market; the two either guaranteed or owned nearly half of the country's approximately $11 trillion in mortgages. Although Rodriguez's portfolio was considered conservative by most of his peers, his dream made him wonder whether he had, in fact, been too daring. After he and his staff reviewed the matter, Rodriguez reached a decision. Fannie Mae and Freddie Mac, two of the most trusted companies in the world, were to be put on FPA's restricted list. All their bonds were to be sold. By Valentine's Day, 2006, they were.

1

TO THE CROSSROADS

I do not want Fannie and Freddie to be just another bank. . . . I do not want the same kind of focus on safety and soundness.

— REP. BARNEY FRANK (D-MASS.),
SEPTEMBER 25, 2003[1]

M OST OF THE BOOMS of recent decades were financed by private sector companies such as technology promoters, or Wall Street banks, or oil drillers. The U.S. housing boom of the early twenty-first century was different, thanks to its intimate relationship with the U.S. government. The government has supported home ownership in one way or another since the Homestead Act of 1862, which gave deeds to farmers willing to improve the land. Modern housing policy was grounded in a similar premise—that individual home ownership would strengthen democracy. While the goal of government policy was to help people own their homes, its effect, over time, was akin to that of a giant accelerator in the housing market. And though other industries—defense contracting, say, or public transportation—also depended on the government, only in housing did the government so greatly disturb the natural supply and demand. Public transportation, for instance, was a natural monopoly. No one was going to invest in a rival subway system no matter how much the government subsidized fares. And in the case of defense contracting, the U.S. government didn't influence the prices paid by private buyers, because private buyers don't exist. (Only governments buy F-16s). But millions of Americans buy and finance homes. The government's housing policy had a big effect on what people could afford to pay, which made it hugely influential over the largest sector of the U.S. economy. The principal agents of the government's policy were the two giant mortgage companies, Fannie Mae and Freddie Mac.

Fannie Mae was created in 1938, in the midst of the Great Depression, to provide citizens with mortgage financing and, it was hoped, stem the tide of foreclosures that had plagued communities during those difficult years. As an agency of the federal government, it didn't lend to homeowners directly; instead, it purchased mortgages from savings and loans, replenishing their capital so they could issue more loans. Fannie operated according to strict standards, purchasing only those mortgages that met tests of both size and quality. For many years, for instance, no mortgages were approved if the monthly payment was more than 28 percent of the applicant's income.[2] Fannie thus exerted a constructive influence on thrifts (the technical term for savings and loans), which were wary of writing loans that did not conform to Fannie's guidelines and would thus be less marketable.

After World War II, as Americans flocked to the suburbs and bought new homes, Fannie's balance sheet swelled. Every mortgage purchased was recorded as a government outlay, which put a sizable strain on the federal budget. In 1968, President Johnson—doggedly trying to balance the budget—moved to get Fannie off the government's books. Promptly, the company sold shares to the public, which allowed the government to take Fannie off budget. Relocation to the private sector added to Fannie's public agenda another, not necessarily consistent, goal: earning a profit. Fannie managed these disparate aims by sticking to its conservative guidelines; however, it was assumed that—if needed—the government would come to its aid. In the 1980s, volatile swings in interest rates devastated the savings and loan industry, as thrifts were burdened with low-interest mortgages on which the yields were less than the cost of their funds. Fannie came close to failing;

moreover, Freddie Mac, a sibling company that had been founded in 1970 to give Fannie competition, briefly wound up as a ward of the Treasury Department.

Thus, by the early '90s, the government had ample evidence that guaranteeing private housing markets was a risky business, and it was forced to think about how its offspring should be run. The question of whether the mortgage twins should retain some government backing was a sticky one, especially as their business was now considerably more complex than it had been when they left the nest. Fannie and Freddie not only owned mortgages outright, they also served as the guarantors for huge collections of mortgage securities owned by investors.

Their role as guarantor implied a daunting federal obligation. What if large numbers of homeowners defaulted and one or both companies had to make good on their guarantees? Would taxpayers be forced to make up Fannie's and Freddie's losses? At a minimum, the situation called for federal regulation, which the mortgage twins had so far avoided.

Robert Glauber, the Treasury Department's undersecretary of finance under the first President Bush, was charged with designing a policy. Glauber would have preferred that the federal umbilical cord be cut, since this would have eliminated the risks to the taxpayer associated with a government guarantee. But since this was a nonstarter politically, he drafted legislation to put the mortgage twins under the strict supervision of the Treasury Department. Fannie, led by its chief executive, Jim Johnson, a former banker and Democratic Party stalwart, mightily resisted. In the bill Congress ultimately sanctioned in 1992, the government link was anything but cut. Fannie and Freddie were assured of a line of credit from Treasury, as well as exemption from state and local taxes. Owing to their privileged position, the twins continued to be able to borrow at below-market interest rates. This assured healthy profits for Fannie and Freddie's shareholders, with plenty of gravy left over for their executives. In return, Congress insisted that Fannie and Freddie commit a portion of their portfolios, specified by the secretary of Housing and Urban and Development, to lower-income housing. And Congress all but ignored the issue of their safety and soundness; against the advice of Undersecretary Glauber, it handed the task of regulation to a toothless new subagency of HUD, the Office of Federal Housing Enterprise Oversight (OFHEO), which had zero expertise in financial supervision.

Unusual as their situation was—the twins were neither fish nor fowl, neither wholly private nor public—the housing industry heartily embraced it. To mortgage financiers, private capital was always preferable to federal control, but private capital with federal support was the best alternative of all.

Jim Johnson, who had become Fannie Mae's CEO in 1991, built the company into a powerhouse. He was said to attend a different black-tie Beltway function nearly every night, hobnobbing with the likes of President Clinton and Robert Rubin, the treasury secretary.[3] The twins poured money into political campaigns, and helpfully opened "partnership offices" in the districts of influential congressmen. Over a decade, they spent $175 million on lobbying, and when need be, they bullied opponents into submission.[4] The result was a political grotesquerie, in which Fannie and its smaller sidekick used public leverage to buy the sympathies of elected officials. In the face of this effort, OFHEO, the regulator, was virtually powerless.

The twins did elicit concern in high quarters. Larry Summers, who succeeded Rubin at Treasury in 1999, was troubled by the twins' perceived government tie. Another high-placed critic was Alan Greenspan, who, like many free-market apostles, saw Fannie and Freddie as examples of state-sponsored corporatism at its worst. But neither of them was able to slow the twins' juggernaut. From the Clinton years to the early 2000s, Fannie's stock soared, mirroring rapid growth in the mortgage industry. Many new mortgage lenders were not banks in the traditional sense (they didn't take in deposits) but, rather, were financial firms that borrowed at one rate, lent mortgage money at another rate, and quickly unloaded their loans rather than hang on as had traditional savings and loans. Since these lenders lacked a fount of capital, the twins supplied it. Fannie purchased loans by the bushelful from Countrywide Financial, the fast-growing California lender, which it regarded as a vital new loan channel. Johnson, the Fannie CEO, unashamedly courted Countrywide's chief executive as a business partner and golfing chum.[5]

Johnson retired in 1999, but Fannie did not miss a beat under his successor. Franklin Delano Raines was, like Johnson, an investment banker versed in the political arts. The son of a Seattle parks department worker and a cleaning lady, Raines had a sixth sense for placating constituents. He bragged of managing Fannie's "political risk" with the same intensity that he handled its credit risk. For the twins, massaging politicians was just as important as packaging loans. Their secret sauce was the political appeal of home ownership. The subtext of the twins' ceaseless lobbying was that anyone who deviated from its agenda was an enemy of home mortgages—in effect, of the American dream. Rep. Barney Frank bluntly admitted that Congress and the twins had struck a bargain—support for affordable housing in return for "arrangements which are of some benefit to them." By arrangements, the congressman meant Congress's turning a blind eye to the fact that government support was stoking shareholder profits and executive bonuses. In a single year, Raines rewarded no fewer than twenty of his managers with $1 million in pay—an extraordinary haul at a company enjoying taxpayer largesse.[6]

For the twins, the downside of the bargain was that they had to tailor their business to suit politicians—even financing pet projects in some of their districts.[7] Both Congress and the second Bush White House, which trumpeted a goal of increasing minority home ownership, leaned on them to do more for affordable housing. Raines duly promised to "push products and opportunities to people who have lesser credit quality." Plainly, this meant lowering Fannie's credit standards. Meanwhile, he vowed to double shareholder earnings in five years. Struggling to meet two agendas, the twins stretched their balance sheets. In effect, they became mortgage *traders*—publicly sponsored corporations attached to private hedge funds. Fannie's mortgage portfolio ballooned alarmingly from 1990 to 2003, rising from $100 billion to $900 billion.[8]

In 2003 and 2004, two serious accounting scandals—first Freddie and then Fannie had to restate its results, and in each case senior management resigned—seemed to hand a weapon to their critics. The United States charged Raines with manipulating Fannie's earnings (and thereby fattening his bonus). The case was settled out of court. The Bush administration and other critics on the right beseeched Congress to create a stronger regulator. John Snow, the treasury Secretary, warned in 2005 that a default "could have far reaching, contagious effects."[9] He pushed for limits on the twins' portfolios.

The default talk was only hypothetical—Fannie's shares, at the time, were valued in the stock market at $50 billion. But the concern was real. What alarmed Snow was that Fannie and Freddie, with all their assets, held less than half the capital of similar-size banks. Greenspan was even more alarmed. Abandoning the Delphic prose for which he was famous, the Fed chief bluntly warned the Congress that systemic difficulties are "likely if GSE [government-sponsored enterprise] expansion continues." Congress did nothing.[10]

Rep. Frank, among other Fannie and Freddie supporters, continued to put intense pressure on the companies to do more for affordable housing. His brief was not without merit; thanks to soaring home prices, the United States *did* have a dearth of affordable homes. However, extending credit does not render a house affordable to a borrower unless he or she has the income to repay it. Nor did Frank's good intentions erase the twins' growing vulnerability to a downturn in housing. The congressman attempted to bluff—"I am not going to bail them out," he declared in open session in 2005, as if he could dictate the twins' mission without bearing responsibility for it.[11] The administration was similarly conflicted. While Treasury lobbied for a tougher regulator, HUD repeatedly increased its mandate for support of low-income housing. And though it was more typically the Democrats who supported the twins' political agenda, in this case the Bush cabinet lined up behind HUD as well.

In addition to these pressures, in the early 2000s Wall Street began to present the twins with a serious competitive threat. Investment banks such as Lehman Brothers were securitizing mortgages—that is, turning groups of mortgages into securities. This meant the underlying risk was held by disparate investors rather than the issuing banks. In the past, Fannie and Freddie had kept the securitization business mostly to themselves. With Wall Street investment banks now in the game in a major way, mortgage lenders had a viable alternative. They could bundle loans for Fannie and Freddie or they could shop them to a "private label" firm such as Lehman. Though the twins, with their government backing, still had the advantage of being able to issue guarantees, investors were no longer so concerned with whether their mortgage securities were guaranteed. With home prices persistently rising, housing was looking like a risk-free game.

In 2004, private-label firms for the first time claimed a greater share of the market than Fannie and Freddie combined. Fannie's share, previously 40 percent, collapsed by half.[12] Each of the twins thus felt severe pressure to accept more of the new, riskier loans that Wall Street was packaging. David Andrukonis, Freddie's chief risk officer, was so concerned that he prepared a memo to his bosses elaborating on the rapid rise of NINA loans, a subset of the Alt A loans that worried Rodriguez. (NINA stood for "no income, no asset," and referred to loans for which the borrower did not provide documentation of either.) "The NINA mortgage was created over twenty years ago as a way of servicing borrowers with inconsistent income patterns (actors, the self-employed, etc.) but strong credit profiles and down payments," Andrukonis noted. This former niche product, he warned, was being marketed to a wider swath of the population and toward a dubious purpose—essentially, to people who needed to mask their income lest the true picture disqualify them. Andrukonis recommended that Freddie "withdraw from the NINA market as soon as practicable." He was overruled.[13]

Fannie was experiencing similar strains. A new CEO, Daniel Mudd, had taken over in late 2004, and in a presentation given to him in the middle of the following year, Fannie's managers observed that the company stood at a "strategic crossroads."[14] Essentially, it faced a choice between endorsing riskier mortgages, which were driving Wall Street's growth, or seeing its market share erode further. Especially worrisome was the steady loss of business from Countrywide, Fannie's most prized customer.

Like Freddie, Fannie decided to increase its share of Alt A loans and of subprime loans. It also began to guarantee loans on which borrowers had little equity. Though Fannie had been purchasing mortgages for seven decades, it had little experience in how these new mortgages performed. Nor did anyone else.[15]

This new business represented a significant amplification of Fannie's charter, and Mudd encouraged it warily. A soldierly ex-Marine and one-time executive with GE Capital, Mudd was not a political acrobat like his predecessors Johnson or Raines, and he felt intensely the pressure from Congress. Compounding the pressure, Wall Street pushed him even harder. One hedge fund manager, irate because Fannie's stock had hit a wall, chastised Mudd for failing to relax the company's mortgage criteria even more than it had. The investor arrogantly demanded, "Are you stupid or blind? Your job is to make me money."[16] Since Mudd, who was earning $7 million annually, ultimately worked in the service of shareholders, he could scarcely refuse. As his managers warned him, the company faced two "stark choices." It could stay true to its principles and continue to lose share or—the higher risk option—"meet the market where the market is."[17] And the mortgage market was going where it had never been before.

2

SUBPRIME

*These mortgages have been considered more safe
and sound.*

— DAVID SCHNEIDER, WASHINGTON MUTUAL
HOME-LOAN PRESIDENT, TO FEDERAL
REGULATORS, 2006[1]

FOR THE FIRST HALF of the twentieth century, mortgage banking
adhered to strict standards, and the savings banks that provided
mortgages were prudent institutions. Bank presidents tended to be
pillars of their communities—faithful Rotarians and cautious financiers. Thrifts did not give mortgages to people with spotty credit, and
borrowers were generally required to put up a third of the purchase
price. Adjustable-rate mortgages were prohibited. (To most Americans
of the time, for a lender to raise the interest rate on a homeowner in
midstream would have smacked of loan sharking.) Second mortgages
were likewise out of the question. To the customer who demanded a
flexible rate, a more generous allocation of credit, or a permissive wink
at debts unpaid, the mortgage banker had a four-letter response: rent.

In about 1960, however, the Beneficial Loan Society began to issue
second mortgages to folks with weaker credit. Beneficial was not a
bank (it did not take deposits) and was therefore outside the purview
of bank regulators. In the years before 1960, it had financed kitchen
appliances, furniture, and the like. Service was on a personal basis.

When customers were late to pay, its loan officers made friendly house calls and, if need be, carted off the collateral. With mortgages, too, Beneficial relied on its knowledge of the individual customer. Not only did it lend up to 80 percent of the purchase price—a level that thrifts found shocking—it made credit available to troubled borrowers. Thus was the invention of what was to be called the subprime mortgage.

In the 1970s, and more rapidly in the '80s, the banking system was deregulated. Capital poured into thrifts, and in the new, competitive environment, applicants with substandard credit scores began to get a second look. Home equity loans proliferated and, as banking rules loosened, applicants were permitted to finance a larger share of their homes. Even people with credit blemishes could qualify. More borrowers defaulted than on conventional mortgages, but the bank compensated by charging higher interest (which, thanks to deregulation, it now was permitted to do). It also insisted on a healthy down payment. In short, a subprime credit rating was a signal to the lender to exercise greater-than-usual care in the approval process. As with, say, a college applicant with low SAT scores, rejection was not automatic, but the applicant was clearly at a disadvantage.

In the late '80s, buoyed by this modest experiment, a wave of California thrifts (and also some nonbank lenders such as the Money Store) sought to focus specifically on subprime borrowers. They insisted on hefty collateral, yet in the '90s, when the California real estate boom went bust and home values fell, the collateral was found to be insufficient. Most of the new breed of subprime specialists either failed or had to be acquired. In retrospect, the reasons were clear. Banks that had gone looking for subprime customers had reversed their former emphasis on caution. It was hardly surprising that default rates had surged. Elbowing one another for borrowers who were behind on their credit card debt or car payments, lenders had ditched selectivity for an open admissions policy. Despite the carnage, some of these lenders (and their staffs) retained a palpable hunger for selling subprime mortgages. Many reemerged under new labels marketing the old wine. For instance, Long Beach Financial became the subprime department of a bigger thrift, Washington Mutual. Despite the risks, from the lender's point of view, credit-challenged customers offered two clear advantages. If a mortgage company wanted to expand in a hurry, it had to look for customers who did not already have a mortgage. And since they were a greater risk, they could be charged higher interest.

Public officials also warmed to the subprime industry, because (so the thinking went) it was helping the poor. President Bush trumpeted a vision of an "ownership society"—one in which union members and public servants would, through the blessings of small, individual investments, mutate into fervent capitalists. Increasing home ownership (also privatizing Social Security) was part of the pitch. Though subprime was not precisely synonymous with affordable housing, it seemed close enough. The business took off in states, like California, where housing was *least* affordable. Subprime catered, if not to the poor, then at least to the emergent middle class, the striving middle, and the upwardly covetous middle.

Eager lenders such as Countrywide and New Century were hailed as suburban Johnny Appleseeds, planting a mortgage in every backyard. Countrywide's cofounder, Angelo Mozilo, son of an Italian immigrant, was feted for helping to democratize credit. In Mozilo's view, every citizen was entitled to a mortgage. In this, he was echoing Michael Milken, who had earlier preached the gospel that every corporation—not just sniffy blue chips—should have access to Wall Street. The Mozilos and the Milkens answered to a distinctly American yearning for a capitalism that was egalitarian, or at least broadly accessible. It was a cross between the Puritan ideal of self-improvement—uplift through work—and the more forgiving siren of populism: uplift (or adjustable mortgages, at any rate) as an unlabored entitlement. Mozilo, especially, espoused a prettified version of capitalism that was stripped of its raw but inescapable truth: one needed capital to pursue it.

In 2003, in a speech cosponsored by Harvard University and the National Housing Endowment, Mozilo proclaimed, "Expanding the American dream of homeownership must continue to be our mission, not solely for the purpose of benefiting corporate America, but more importantly, to make our country a better place." Among Mozilo's suggestions for national betterment was that mortgages should be available to people who made no down payment.[2] This no doubt struck some listeners as fair-minded, but it had little basis in economics. For capitalism to function, credit must be rationed on the basis of balance-sheet soundness. Mozilo based creditworthiness on something else—not on soundness but on faith. For what else could justify giving a home to someone who put no money down?

As subprime lending underwent a resurgence, David Andrukonis, the risk manager at Freddie Mac, saw troubling signs of predatory lending—that is, unsavory lending practices aimed at unsophisticated clientele. A high proportion of NINA loans were being peddled to Hispanics. If mortgages issued without supporting documentation were sound, why were so many being issued to the largest socioeconomic group with significant numbers of immigrants and non-English speakers? "The potential for the perception and the reality of predatory lending with this product is great," Andrukonis noted.[3]

Enrico Dallavecchia, his counterpart at Fannie Mae, was similarly troubled. To Dallavecchia, targeting unsophisticated residents of borderline neighborhoods smacked of exploitation. One mortgage shop in Baltimore worked 4 P.M. to midnight, the better to catch customers at home. Salespeople cajoled would-be clients, assuring them of the ease with which they could finance and—if their rates adjusted—refinance. Were such lenders helping customers or luring them toward disaster? Mudd, the Fannie CEO, was torn. Some of his team thought subprime was a borderline criminal enterprise. But just because you had a credit blemish, or because you lived in working-class Lynn, Massachusetts, instead of on Beacon Hill, did that mean you weren't entitled to a home?

There was always that tension latent in subprime: If you helped more folks—especially the disadvantaged—to get mortgages, more would default and more would be foreclosed on. The risk was apt to increase over time, because bankers signed up the most attractive customers first. In a growing market, each vintage would be less credit-worthy than the one before, because mortgage salesmen were forced to dig deeper into the barrel for acceptable fish. And the business was indeed growing. In 2002, subprime issuance totaled $200 billion. By 2004, it was over $400 billion. As a percentage of annual volume, sub-primes now topped 16 percent—up from a mere 8 percent a couple of years earlier and hardly anything in the '90s.[4]

The subprime onslaught was part of a broader and no less remarkable mortgage wave. Over those same two years, following the dot-com crash in 2001, total outstanding mortgage debt grew from $6 trillion to nearly $8 trillion—an extraordinary rise in a stable population.[5] The most plausible explanation for this sudden surge lies in the country's remarkably forgiving credit markets. Starting the week after New Year's, 2001, the Fed lowered short-term interest rates thirteen times until, finally, in June 2003, rates touched 1 percent—their lowest level since the John F. Kennedy era. Not until the middle of 2004, the third year of the economic recovery, did Greenspan begin to raise rates, which he did at a painstakingly deliberate pace. Even as late as June 2005, the Fed funds rate was only 3 percent. Since that was equal to the rate of inflation, banks were effectively borrowing for nothing. As with any commodity, money is used wisely only when it is rationed—that is, when its price prevents its overuse.

The plenitude of credit encouraged people to borrow. Just as importantly, cheap money fostered an expectation of liquidity—a sense that one could borrow any amount because the sum, if need be, could always be repaid with fresh borrowings. On Wall Street, investment banks became obsessed with earning the "spread": the difference between their own ultralow borrowing costs and the return on any investment that yielded a trifle more. There was a boom in buying companies on credit. So-called private equity buyers put up little cash, acquiring familiar companies such as Hertz, Toys R Us and Burger King much as ordinary people purchased their homes—on credit. The more they could borrow, the higher prices went. Cheap credit thus inflated Wall Street profits and fostered the illusion that the buyout firms were genuinely improving their corporate charges.

Ordinary Americans, if they could, borrowed even more. Consumers exhausted their savings and kept on spending (the total of household savings plummeted from 4 percent of the GDP when Clinton took office to negative 4 percent of the GDP by the end of Bush's first term). Whatever the purpose—a home, a car, a lifestyle enhancement—credit sustained it.

If this blissful-seeming period had a downside, it was that investors, who were penalized by low interest rates, which lowered their returns, struggled to find higher-yielding securities. Not just professional investors and corporate CEOs, who routinely complained of a lack of opportunities, but hospital funds, school boards from remote Whitefish Bay, Wisconsin, to those in big cities, university endowments from Harvard's on down, state pension funds such as California's— all reached for securities that offered a smidgeon of extra yield. Investors did not think of themselves as "reaching," a term that implies a degree of incaution. They were assured that loans to private equity deals were safe and, certainly, that mortgage pools were safe. But when interest rates are low, the only way for investors as a group to earn more is to assume more risk.

The phenomenon of low interest rates was worldwide, but in the search for yield, investors tilted west. China, Japan, Germany and various oil-exporting nations spent less than their income and thus had money to lend. It was their dollars that fueled the credit binge. The United States, the United Kingdom, Spain, and Australia absorbed more than half of the world's surplus capital; at the manic peak of its borrowing, in the late 2000s, the United States alone sopped up 70 percent.[6]

The U.S. current account deficit was a perpetual source of worry in international financial circles. (The current account records the payments coming in and out, principally from trade, and is a barometer of financial health.) Ben Bernanke, one of the seven governors who oversaw the Federal Reserve, of which Greenspan was chair, presented a benign explanation that seemed to absolve Americans of either worry or blame. While the world chided America for borrowing so much,

Bernanke suggested that the fault lay equally with the lenders. As he elaborated in a much-quoted 2005 address, the decline in U.S. saving might in some part be "a reaction to events external to the United States. . . . My own preferred explanation focuses on what I see as the emergence of a global saving glut in the past eight to ten years."[7] In short, America was borrowing because others were lending. The "others" were China and other countries, many from the Third World— once profligate but lately transformed into paragons of thrift. Bernanke argued that their dollars had to flow somewhere, and the United States was merely an attractive destination.

The curious financing of rich nations by poor ones reversed a long tradition. During previous eras, the U.S. had loaned money to developing nations, and had often come to rue the day. This time, as two professors, Carmen Reinhart of the University of Maryland and Kenneth Rogoff of Harvard, put it, "a large chunk of money had been recycled to a developing economy that exists *within* the United States' own borders [emphasis added]."[8] Surplus credit was flowing not to weak borrowers overseas, but to a Subprime Nation inside the United States.

Generally, it is the job of the Fed to mitigate potentially destabilizing financial currents. And Bernanke was well aware that the global savings glut was making its presence felt in the bubbly market for real estate— in particular, he noted, "as low mortgage rates have supported record levels of home construction and strong gains in housing prices." In other words, foreigners were lending cash that, via a network of financial intermediaries, was fueling home buyers and inflating prices potentially beyond the level warranted by supply and demand. In particular, Chinese exports of everything from toys to computers were fueling U.S. mortgages. Nonetheless, neither Bernanke nor Greenspan were much unsettled by these trends. As Bernanke emphasized, "I am not making a value judgment about the behavior of either U.S. or foreign residents or their governments."

The key to understanding the global flow of credit was the remarkable "sophistication," to use Bernanke's admiring term, of America's capital markets. In the late 1970s, "private label" firms began to purchase pools of mortgages and sell them to investors. Lewis Ranieri, a trader at Salomon Brothers, is credited with devising mortgage bonds. Ranieri focused on investment-grade mortgages, and carved them up in such a way as to appeal to institutions that previously invested in corporate bonds. Wall Street had suddenly met Main Street. Mortgage banks obtained an additional source of capital, meaning they did not have to hold as many of their loans for the full thirty years.

Though this made life easier for thrifts (indeed, it helped to avert a reenactment of the S&L crisis of the 1980s) the "cure" introduced subtle, and profound, changes in the allocation of credit. Investors who bought into pools of mortgages did not have a sense of the individual borrowers, as the loan officer on Main Street did. They relied for assurance on a credit rating. The rating agency dealt in volume, and volume required economies of scale. The risk involved in any *particular* mortgage came to matter less than the *average* risk assigned to the group. In this sense, Ranieri's revolution—turning mortgages into bonds—altered the very basis of credit.

The early securitizations were of prime mortgages, but in 1997 ContiMortgage assembled hundreds of riskier loans. As was typical of Wall Street firms, Conti financed the mortgages through the sale of securities to the public. The investors got bonds—actually, various classes of bonds—which were secured by the underlying mortgages. Even though the mortgages were high-risk, about 85 percent of the bonds were rated triple A. In other words, ContiMortgage had assembled a pool of junk mortgages and convinced the rating agencies that the pool, as a whole, was primarily investment grade. This was not black magic, or not entirely. It was a deft use of the concept of subordination. Although the checks from mortgagors were deposited in undifferentiated fashion into the pool, the money flowed out to bond holders according to a carefully tiered structure, so that the lowest rank of bondholders—in this case, the bottom 15 percent—absorbed all prospective losses before the next class lost a cent.

Any one of these risky mortgages might default, and none of them individually would be considered safe. But what ContiMortgage asserted, and what investors accepted, was that losses on the *pool* would not be greater than 15 percent. Such deals opened a universe of possibilities, for they allowed the multitudinous organizations (pensions, mutual funds, corporate treasurers) that insisted on investment grade to dip their toes in subprime.

Of course, sponsors of such deals also had to find buyers for the riskier layers of bonds at the bottom. In the exemplary ContiMortgage case, 15 percent of the bonds were lower rated, all the way down to BBB, the lowest grade above a "junk" rating. Investors in the BBB-rated paper were compensated with higher interest rates; however, they stood first in line to suffer losses if mortgagors defaulted. Only extremely savvy investors—those with the expertise to assess the risks—would touch the BBBs, and these savvy investors served as watchdogs for everyone else. If an investment bank assembled a package that, in its totality, was too risky, the investors would balk, and the bank would be stuck holding the BBB paper itself. This the bank did not want. Therefore, the presence of discriminating investors served as a check on the entire process.

In the early 2000s, this delicate equilibrium was upset by a new, less-discriminating class of investor. These investors were collateralized debt obligations. CDOs were dummy corporations—legal fictions organized for the purpose of buying and selling bonds. Engineered by Wall Street banks and similar operators, the CDO introduced a second level of securitization. Instead of buying mortgages directly, the CDO was a security that invested in other, first-order securities that themselves had acquired mortgages. The CDO thus introduced an additional layer into the process, with the result that the ultimate investor was further removed, and less equipped to scrutinize, the quality of the underlying mortgages.

One naturally recoils from such complexity and, indeed, these convoluted machinations were a sign that serious mischief was afoot. Within limits, Wall Street performs a useful service; it aggregates the country's savings and deploys them where (one hopes) investment is warranted. The skill with which investment bankers perform such feats is impressive. Imagine, for instance, the difficulty of taking a company such as IBM and dividing the capital into various classes—common stock, preferred, bonds, and even distinct classes of bonds—so that IBM has the funds it needs, with appropriate levels of dividends and interest due, and each investor assumes just the level of risk and potential gain that he or she desires. This is a performance worthy of society's applause. But when financial structures become too complex, they subvert the underlying object, like a dashboard whose inner circuitry is so overrun with memory slots and connectors that it becomes a flashy distraction from the primary task of driving the automobile.

The mortgage-backed security was a useful innovation; by pooling a group of mortgages it achieved the benefit of collective security. Duly marketed to investors, such first-order securities channeled public capital into a socially useful purpose. But the CDO was a rarer and more suspect breed of cat. It was a secondary construct, more abstract, detached, mathematical. By 2004, they were a major and perhaps *the* major investor in mortgage securities. As CDO investors became willing to pay higher prices, they pushed aside the savvy investors who had served as watchdogs. It may be asked, how did the CDOs get money? Simply, they also sold bonds to the public, luring them with interest rates that were a bit higher than those on less risky securities.

Investors in CDOs were distant enough from the underlying mortgages to gloss over the risk, and being dissatisfied with prevailing low interest rates, they flocked to securities that offered only a marginally higher return. Thus, they removed an important check. Previously, when a company such as ContiMortgage assembled a pool of mortgages, it had to exercise some care in selecting them, or else it would not be able to finance the pool by selling bonds. Now the only restraint was the global supply of capital that was hungry for a higher yield. And since the world, as Bernanke noted, was glutted with capital, the demand for CDOs was almost limitless.

So the U.S. housing market, instead of responding to the supply of homes, or to the incomes of home buyers, was hijacked by the whims of global investors. Actually, the trend was international, with prices soaring in many countries, including Britain, Ireland, and Spain. United States home prices in the early 2000s rose roughly 10 percent a year and even faster in hot markets—an unprecedented rate. By 2005, the press was rife with articles debating whether housing was in a "bubble."[9]

A mere rise in the price of an asset does not in itself constitute a bubble. It could be that changes in either supply or demand warrant a much higher price. A bubbly market is one that has lost its connection to supply and demand. In such cases—as in the late '90s, when fundamentally worthless Internet stocks claimed valuations of tens of billions of dollars; or in the 1630s in Holland when, at the peak of a mania, twelve acres of land were offered for a single bulb of Semper Augustus tulip—prices are floated on sheer froth.[10] During the tulip mania, Dutch traders met at taverns and contracted for the future delivery of bulbs of a flower regarded as a luxury and a status symbol. Precipitously, the bubble collapsed, and tulips once more were merely tulips. The question posed about bubbly markets has been the same ever since: What is the real price, or the price justified by supply and demand? In 2005, to get a fix on the housing market, Fannie Mae's managers overlaid a graph of prices with that of incomes over the previous generation. From 1976 to 1999, the two lines tracked each other—each blip in income growth reflected in a corresponding change in home prices. Then, suddenly, the lines diverged. In the new century, median household income tailed off, with an annual growth rate of only 2 percent or so. Meanwhile, home prices rocketed ahead. In Boston, for instance, the median home, which had sold for a reasonable 2.2 times median income in the mid-'90s, soared to 4.6 times income a decade later. Similar leaps were tracked in other high-growth and coastal cities.[11]

By mid-decade, with housing prices rising at double-digit rates, the public began to believe that home-price inflation would continue, and the rise continued on a self-perpetuating course. People bought homes as they once had bought stocks—not to live in but to sell. Conferences on how to buy real estate with little or no money down drew audiences of thousands. Lay people with no training in real estate were schooled at seminars in how to "invest" in real estate—by which was meant how to flip properties like fast-food burgers. Exploiting the leverage supplied by cheap mortgages was the entire purpose of such sessions, for leverage greatly magnified the potential profits. For a couple with an 80 percent mortgage, a home price that doubled in value translated to fivefold rise in equity. Not even tulips went up that fast. Books with titles such as *Real Estate Debt Can Make You Rich* appeared by the truckload and duly assaulted the bestseller lists.[12] The total of real estate commissions as a share of the GDP doubled almost overnight[13]—a bizarre, anomalous statistic, for what could be more stable than the rate at which people move and seek new homes? And if not to actual home dwellers, to whom were the mortgages going?

Larry Pitkowsky, comanager of the Fairholme Fund, a mutual fund based in New Jersey, wondered, like a few other investors, what was beneath the housing boom. Like a very few others, Pitkowsky went to investigate. He was curious not so much about mortgages as about the businesses of various construction companies, whose stocks had retreated sharply in the latter half of 2005. Thinking they might be due for a rebound, Pitkowsky decided to check out some properties at ground level. The developments all seemed to have British-sounding names; they spoke of foxes and manors and knolls, as if to cloak their newness with images of pastoral Victorian husbandry. Pitkowsky chose a typical subdivision called Royal Oaks, in Burlington Township, a suburb northeast of Philadelphia.

Royal Oaks, under development by MDC Holdings, a Denver-based company, was so new Pitkowsky couldn't find the location on his GPS. When he got to the area he stopped at a Dunkin' Donuts and, ordering a cup of coffee, asked the aproned woman at the counter if she had heard of Royal Oaks.

A man in line interceded. "I know that place. I own three units." Pitkowsky bought him a doughnut and listened to the man's story. The man turned out to be a local Realtor in his late thirties. He had decided he could make more money buying and flipping homes than working for commissions. For a prospective investor (or lender) this was alarming news, as speculators are more likely than actual home dwellers to abandon their mortgages. Pitkowsky thanked the man and, armed with directions, drove to Royal Oaks. Dormered homes—as yet unbuilt—were priced at up to half a million dollars. The developer required $5,000 on signing and $15,000 when ground was broken. That was it.

At the model house, which was brightened by a trim lawn, an agent was distributing flyers and showing customers around. Pitkowsky asked how the developer ensured that the buyers would live there and weren't just speculators. The woman said, "We have a very serious process." Pitkowsky probed further, and she explained that the process consisted of requiring buyers to "check a box." Pitkowsky began to think that the real estate market was frothier, and perhaps more transitory, than it seemed.

3

LENDERS

In the real world, what goes up also can go down.

—JOHN C. DUGAN, COMPTROLLER OF THE
CURRENCY, APRIL 2006.[1]

S PECULATION IN REAL ESTATE worked on lenders like an opiate. The
largest mortgage company, and the one emblematic of the breed, was
Countrywide. Its boss, Angelo Mozilo, had started in mortgages at age
fourteen, when he left his father's butcher shop to work as a messenger
for Lawyers Mortgage and Title, on West 43rd Street in Manhattan—a
leap for a first-generation Italian-American kid from the Bronx. He
worked there while attending night school at New York University, paid
his dues in the mortgage industry, and cofounded Countrywide in 1969.
Perhaps thanks to the Salomon Brothers trader Lewis Ranieri, a friend
and fellow Bronx native, Mozilo appreciated earlier than most the potential benefits of linking up with mortgage securitizers.[2] In the '80s,
even as conventional thrifts were suffering through the savings and loan
debacle, Countrywide was a burgeoning source of volume for Fannie
and Freddie. By the early '90s, it had overtaken long-established lenders such as Chase Manhattan. Though Countrywide owned a bank, it
shrewdly did much of its business through its less-regulated nonbank
subsidiary. Luring managers with high salaries and even higher bonuses,
Mozilo built a nationwide network of branches. He was a powerful
motivator—visionary and determined but possessed of a relaxed, easy

manner. His ambition seemed a part of his charm, as if attached to his perpetual tan and his Gucci loafers.

Mozilo did not enter subprime in a big way until 2000. Then, sensing an untapped market, he moved fast. He prodded his branches to open the credit spigot, and Countrywide quickly forged a reputation as a first stop for troubled borrowers. It also set up its own, in-house securitization department, giving it another channel to unload product. Falling interest rates provided a strong tailwind, stoking its volume. By 2003, Countrywide was originating (or servicing) 13 percent of mortgages nationwide, a huge chunk of such a competitive market. Mozilo proclaimed that his goal was nothing short of a 30 percent share.[3] Having come so far, he seemed to think the future limitless.

Countrywide's strategy, as it stated in SEC filings, was to ensure ongoing access to the investment market by producing "quality mortgages."[4] In fact, it gravitated toward increasingly risky ones. Over just two years, from '02 to '04, subprimes vaulted from 4 percent of its portfolio to 11 percent. Meanwhile, adjustable loans surged from a seventh of its book to half. Countrywide even realized Mozilo's dream of full financing, writing first mortgages for 80 percent of the home value and, often, simultaneous "piggyback" loans for the balance, so that the "buyer" was not out any cash. Thanks to these sundry concessions to weaker underwriting, in 2005 Countrywide's loan volume reached $500 billion, double that of three years earlier.

By far its riskiest product was the option ARM, an appealingly affordable mortgage with a diabolical twist.* Borrowers had the option of reducing their monthly payments at will; if they did, though, their loan balances would be increased by the equivalent amount. Thus, instead of steadily reducing their indebtedness, as in traditional mortgages, the homeowner was month after month sinking deeper into the morass. Or, to put a different shade on it, buyers—some quite sophisticated— could speculate on homes while starting with low initial payments and

---

* Lenders used various terms for this product. Though Countrywide's was "pay option ARM," for consistency the term "option ARM" is used throughout.

putting very little money down. It was typical for the interest rate on option ARMs to start at something like 4 percent and jump to 9 percent, meaning that when the loan adjusted the payment would double. However, some teasers were set at artificially low rates—even as low as 1 percent. Customers who got $150,000 mortgages could start with monthly payments of $125—subject, after the first year, to an astronomical leap to $876 a month. Countrywide brokers were incentivized to peddle such loans with free trips for volume producers to Las Vegas and Hawaii. They were trained to court customers with a seductive pitch, beginning, "I want to be sure you are getting the best loan possible." In fact, brokers sold whatever was the highest-commission product—even when it left the borrower short of funds for food and clothing. Many of the borrowers failed to grasp that the option ARM was a trap in which they could end up owing more than they had borrowed.[5]

When Countrywide stockholders began to ask questions about the obviously worsening standards in the mortgage industry, Mozilo smoothly reassured them. While he was concerned about other lenders relaxing their standards, he said on repeated occasions, he would never allow such a thing at Countrywide.[6]

In fact, Countrywide was leading the way. As a senior vice president bluntly stated in an internal e-mail, "the bottom line is that we expanded our guidelines in order to allow more loans to be approved without requiring an exception approval." Countrywide also relaxed the terms for granting "stated" loans, on which borrowers stated their income but were not asked to document it. Another loosening, late in 2005, was almost comically reckless. Countrywide had previously enforced a two-year waiting period before stated-income borrowers who had filed a personal bankruptcy could qualify for credit. Now the waiting period was shortened to a single day.[7]

It was widely believed among the staff that stated borrowers brazenly lied (employees referred to these loans as "liar loans"). But underwriters were discouraged from scrutinizing their applications. A company manual stated plainly, "We always look for ways to make the loan rather than turn it down."[8] It is hard to escape the conclusion that Countrywide preferred not to know.

Underwriters believed they were supposed to "paper the file" to give the appearance of scrutiny. This paper trail was necessary for Countrywide to sell the loan in the secondary market—and as long as the loan could be sold, its mission was fulfilled. In one case, a borrower applied for a jumbo loan for what was purportedly a primary residence. A Countrywide trainee, not yet versed in company procedures, pointed out that the borrower also owned three other homes, all of which were financed by Countrywide as well. Perhaps they should check to see if this residence were truly "primary"? The supervisor shot the suggestion down, noting, "We don't try to investigate."[9]

Remarkably, customers who had been rejected after documenting their income were urged to re-apply, this time on a no-doc basis. According to former employees, Countrywide loan officers would "assist" them—in short, coach them to lie—whereupon the loans were approved. One highly productive loan officer in Massachusetts simply cut and pasted files from the Internet to concoct a fraudulent verification of an applicant's employment.[10]

Whatever he knew of such practices, the cocky Mozilo was likely convinced that housing prices would continue to climb. California had not experienced a down market since the early '90s; New York City, not since the late '80s. A similar picture prevailed across the country. Home appreciation was an elixir that seemed to turn subprime borrowers into solvent ones. Perhaps as a form of insurance for some cataclysm to come, Mozilo granted sweetheart mortgages (on preferred terms) to a host of political and business luminaries.*[11] But his company appeared to be thriving. From '00 to '04, Countrywide's share price nearly quadrupled, and over the ensuing few years Mozilo personally reaped $474 million in stock sales.[12]

Mortgage banking inevitably produces a race to the bottom. Thanks

---

* Senators Chris Dodd and Kent Conrad, along with a California judge, two former secretaries of HUD and two former Fannie Mae CEOs (Johnson and Raines), were among the "friends of Angelo" who got sweetheart mortgages.

to competitive pressures, bad loan practice drives out good, and Mozilo's influence on the industry was considerable. The only way for rivals to compete was to go after the same business as Countrywide. Washington Mutual, a century-old Seattle-based thrift, had more conventional banking bloodlines, but in the new century it experienced a rebirth. WaMu had been run since 1990 by Kerry Killinger, a Des Moines music teacher's son who, as a student at the University of Iowa, had fixed up houses to build his capital.[13] He parlayed his profits into a career as a securities analyst with a small investment firm, which WaMu acquired in 1982. Eight years later, when Killinger was forty, he was named chief executive. He built the bank through acquisition, gobbling up Great Western in California, Dime Savings Bank in New York, and a raft of others. By 2002, WaMu was the country's biggest thrift. Revealingly, Killinger told an interviewer, "I view this business as more retail than banking. That's where the big payoff is." In New York, his tellers wore hip-looking black, like salespeople at a SoHo boutique.[14]

Unconventional lending excited Killinger no less than it did Mozilo. He pushed aside more-cautious bankers, replacing them with gunslingers. In 2001, he went so far as to try to buy Countrywide, but Mozilo rebuffed him. Killinger redoubled his commitment to a growth strategy that focused on adjustable rate mortgages. ARMs were the hot product, and WaMu—such was Killinger's conceit—was merely the store. Retail is concerned with a single, transactional moment (when the sale is made). But banking is different. A bank's harvest isn't truly reaped until years later, when its loans are repaid. This distinction did not overly trouble Killinger. By 2003 he had grown his store to 2,200 outlets in thirty-eight states.[15]

WaMu's branch managers were, if anything, more pressured to write loans than Countrywide's. Employees were grilled on the details of loans that failed to close and rebuked for making inquiries of applicants—even though these inquiries were indispensable to protecting the bank's equity, not to mention its government-insured deposits. When one WaMu mortgage screener discovered, with a single telephone call, that an applicant had $5,000 in the bank—not, as claimed,

$150,000—the presiding loan officer was furious. "We don't call the bank," the screener was told. Client information, as if in some alternate universe, was detrimental to the goal. A company flyer actually urged loan officers to keep interviews brief with the catchy and revealing motto "a thin file is a good file." In its advertisements, casually attired WaMu employees poked fun at staid bankers in suits—as if the prudent banking style that had maintained WaMu as a solvent institution since 1889 were not only antiquated but a minor embarrassment.[16]

Like Countrywide, WaMu offered a smorgasbord of exotic loans—subprime, piggybacks, and option ARMs—and each innovation incrementally weakened credit. As home prices rose, fewer people could afford to buy with conventional loans. Thus, traditional mortgages gave way to adjustable loans. Fluctuating interest rates enabled banks to charge a little less at the outset, making mortgages a tad more affordable. Adjustables were followed by interest-*only* loans—more affordable still—on which the customer need not repay principal for years. Most permissive of all, option ARMs deferred a portion of the interest as well as the principal *and* affixed an adjustable rate. Option ARMs became WaMu's most popular product, eventually constituting half or more of its residential portfolio. The bank's profits grew at double-digit rates, and Killinger, even if not in Mozilo's league as a Croesus, raked in $19 million in 2005 and $24 million the next year.[17]

With success coming so easily, WaMu was deaf to the need to monitor its risk. The entire organization, even employees tasked with risk control, was strong-armed into helping to close loans. In October 2005—when the option ARM book topped $70 billion—Melissa Martinez, WaMu's chief compliance and risk oversight officer, circulated a memo, allegedly to all risk personnel, including those in senior management. Far from warning of WaMu's exposure, the memo advised that the bank's risk management functions were being adapted to a "cultural change" and that, in the future, the risk department would play a "customer service" role and avoid imposing a "burden" on loan officers.[18]

With similar disregard for banking principles, not to mention economic reality, WaMu leaned on appraisers to puff up estimates of home values. Though appraisers were nominally independent, WaMu maintained a preferred list, and it was known that a disappointing appraisal would mean exclusion from the list in the future. As a tactful hint, WaMu penciled a suggested number on the file.[19]

By the mid-2000s, banking regulators were becoming concerned about such abuses, but mortgage executives repeatedly reassured them they had nothing to worry about. Regulators were slow to take action because banking regulation is highly fractured.[*] Some agencies worry about consumer protection; others about risk to institutions. Some oversee federally chartered banks and others state banks. No one regulator could see the entire mortgage bubble, much of which was occurring at nonbanks—lending operations that did not take deposits and thus were relatively shielded from scrutiny. Even banks under the federal government's authority, such as Citigroup, were escaping supervision by using nonregulated subsidiaries to write subprime loans.

Nonetheless, in the latter part of 2005, the Office of the Comptroller of the Currency began to push for restraint. The OCC regulates so-called national banks (those that the federal government, rather than the states, charter) and has authority over two-thirds of the assets and about 60 percent of the mortgages in the banking system. When the agency was created, in 1863, money existed only as banknotes; thus the banking regulator was literally a "comptroller of currency."

John Dugan, a lawyer and former Treasury official who became comptroller in the summer of 2005, was horrified by what he heard from his examiners—especially about no-doc mortgages and option ARMs.[20] The mortgage industry, Dugan realized, had become obsessively focused on offering loans with the lowest possible initial payment—with the expectation that each mortgage would be refinanced before it adjusted. This had elements of a Ponzi scheme, for the old loans were to be redeemed not from income but with new borrowings. Dugan began to push aggressively for regulatory guidance that would instruct banks

---

[*] Responsible authorities include the Federal Reserve, the Comptroller of the Currency, the Office of Thrift Supervision, the Federal Deposit Insurance Corporation, the Treasury, and state regulators.

to evaluate mortgage applicants on the basis of their ability to pay the *eventual adjusted rate*—not just the teaser.

But Dugan needed the cooperation of the Fed, as well as the Federal Deposit Insurance Corporation and the Office of Thrift Supervision (OTS), which proved slow going. His fellow regulators—in particular the OTS, which supervised highfliers such as Countrywide and WaMu—worried that if they shut down or even narrowed the loan channel, they could precipitate a credit crunch. And Greenspan was philosophically, perhaps reflexively, opposed to restricting credit.

By the end of 2005, Dugan had coaxed the group into issuing tentative rules, but these were subject to a comment period, and the mortgage industry was hotly opposed. For one, they said, if federally chartered banks were subject to tighter guidelines, applicants would seek out state banks and nonbanks. Also, banking executives reiterated that they were quickly selling the loans, removing the risk (or rather, transferring it to investors outside the OCC's domain). "If a willing buyer is taking these loans," the banks, in substance, replied to Dugan, "what do you care?"

The ability of lenders to offload mortgages to Wall Street greatly contributed to the mortgage bubble. Indeed, almost all the growth in mortgage volume was accounted for by loans that the Street securitized.[21] It is a dictum of classical economics that people respond to incentives and that, therefore, bouts of otherwise foolish lending must have a rational basis. Orthodox free marketers cannot explain why bankers would throw money away. But if they are losing money for *other people* (in this case, for investors in mortgage securities), the theory of the invisible hand remains untarnished.[22] Plainly, though, more than rational incentive was fueling this spree. After all, no bank could hope to sell its entire portfolio. Golden West Savings and Loan was a prime example.

Golden West was an Oakland-based California thrift long thought of as a model of prudent lending practices. It was run by Herbert and Marion Sandler, a married couple originally from New York (he was a lawyer, she a Wall Street analyst).[23] In 1963, the Sandlers bought Golden

West, a humble institution with twenty-five employees and two offices, for a total of $3.8 million. Over the next four decades, the couple served as co-CEOs, and Golden West flourished. In the 1980s, it branched into option ARMs, which the Sandlers marketed mostly to professionals whose incomes varied, and who, therefore, had use for flexible payment schemes. By the 2000s, Golden West was a dynamo with more than 250 branches. The Sandlers were still CEOs (Marion sometimes knitted during executive meetings); however, as competition intensified, their standards underwent a softening. Option ARMs were restyled as "Pick-A-Pay" loans, a name more evocative of lottery tickets than mortgages, and they were marketed to people who were simply unable to pay the full, "non-option" rate.

Perhaps Herb Sandler, who had grown up on New York's Lower East Side, the son of a gambler whose income was devoured by loan sharks, had some empathy with subprime borrowers—or perhaps, as with Killinger, the rising tide of risk tolerance loosened his moorings. The search for growth led Golden West inland to new developments in the California desert, where cookie-cutter homes and no-doc mortgages were the standard. By 2006, they had written more than $100 billion in ARMs,[24] and though the Sandlers continued to insist on a margin of collateral, home values were so inflated, and loan applications so rife with fraud, that the quality of their book was as suspect as WaMu's.

The Sandlers differed in just one important respect: Golden West did not securitize its loans; it held onto every one. The Sandlers must have believed in their loans, or at least they suspended the disbelief with which, in the past, they had scrutinized unworthy borrowers. This too was a feature of the bubble.

The lenders, like the Wall Street securitizers, were driven by more than reasoned incentive. It was some conjunction of incentive and belief. The very word "credit" derives from the Latin verb for "believe," and the greatest delusions in finance have always been based on the time-honored act of extending credit. One thinks of the South Sea Company in the eighteenth century, a British company organized to trade in the New World and to retire England's national debt. Its shares, financed largely with credit, rose tenfold in a single year in 1720. Then they collapsed, triggering bankruptcies and ruin. Or the Wall Street crash of 1929; stock speculation on credit helped to make the collapse so devastating. In the 1980s, corporations like Federated Department Stores palmed off junk bonds on which the interest due was far greater than their earnings.[25] The utter implausibility of their promises did not deter investors—until Federated and a wave of others filed for bankruptcy. It was not so much belief as a *desire* to believe. As long as the market is liquid, open to fresh injections of credit, the day of reckoning need never come, or such is the hope. In the '00s, mortgage bankers and investment bankers believed that there would always be another lender, another loan, to relieve them of the bad coin. One would have imagined that, at the very least, banks would not have needed coercion from regulators to take measures to safeguard their own precious capital.[26] Such was the central tenet of Greenspanism: people are rational; markets reflect the sum of many participants' rational decisions. In fact, lenders, like the victims of a Bernie Madoff, engage in a willful self-delusion.

By 2004, the number of Americans who "owned" their homes had climbed to an unprecedented 69 percent. By then, more than $2 trillion subprime and Alt-A no-doc loans were outstanding, and fully a third of new financings were for risky mortgages of one type or another— loans that, a short while ago, had been either unavailable or highly restricted. Among subprime loans, two-thirds were adjustable; thus, the borrowers would be vulnerable to a rise in interest rates, to a change in their own, already modest fortunes, and to a drop in home values. Even among prime borrowers, more than half were reaching for second mortgages, as if real estate proffered an endless bounty. The investor Rodriguez considered this to be exceptionally risky.[27] To investors of his temperament, real estate was at best a slowly appreciating asset, for what could be more stable than the demand for shelter and the wherewithal of a population to pay for it? Real estate was the country's bedrock. But for many families the home had become something else: a casino.

Economics alone cannot explain such dizzying speculation, or the stupendous weakening of standards that permitted it. The lenders, whether on Main Street or Wall Street, were swept up in the gale of mass hallucination. All that the banks—and the investors in the mortgage bonds, and the investment firms who structured the securities— needed was a soupçon of verification, some symbol or sign, some at least semiofficial authentication. The investors themselves were scarcely capable of checking on the individual underlying mortgages, nor would they have had any interest. Most investors seek reassurance rather than dissenting views. What the crowd desired, with regard to mortgage-backed securities, was a green light from some recognized expert: a seal or imprimatur. That could only come from the agencies that rated them.

4

NIAGARA

*I firmly believe that Moody's stands on the "right side
of history."*

—RAYMOND W. McDANIEL JR.,
MOODY'S CORPORATION CHIEF EXECUTIVE,
2006 *ANNUAL REPORT*

FOR MOST OF THEIR EXISTENCE, the virtue of rating agencies was their
impeccable objectivity. John Moody, a Wall Street analyst, hit on
the idea of selling independent bond ratings in 1909 and was soon
joined by three competitors: Standard Statistics, Poor's Publishing, and
Fitch.[1] (Standard and Poor's, it will be no surprise to learn, later
merged.) Then as now, Moody's graded bonds on a scale with twenty-
one steps, from Aaa to C; investors, banks, and others relied on these
ratings to gauge the probability of default. Rated corporations had a big
stake in the outcome but little ability to affect it. Moody's was working
for its subscribers, not for the issuers.

Unfortunately, this model didn't last. In the 1970s, the Securities
and Exchange Commission, in its effort to ensure that Wall Street
brokers had sufficient capital, decided to penalize brokers for holding
bonds that were less than investment grade. The SEC then faced the
question: Investment grade according to whom? The agency decided
to create a new category of *officially* designated rating agencies, and

grandfathered the big three—S&P, Moody's, and Fitch. In effect, the government outsourced its regulatory function.

By the '80s and '90s, many classes of investors, including banks and insurers, were similarly restricted to bonds that were rated by one of the three. Corporations thus were forced to seek credit ratings, without which their bonds would not be marketable. The agencies, realizing they had a hot product, now started to charge the very issuers whose bonds they were rating. In other words, if Ford Motor Company wanted to sell debt, it paid Moody's to issue an opinion. For Moody's, this was more efficient than charging subscribers, but it put the agencies in a conflicted position. Rather than selling opinions to investors, they were selling "licenses" that enabled very self-interested borrowers to operate in credit markets.*

The conflict became more serious when, in the 1980s, Wall Street invented structured finance—the general term for securities such as mortgage bonds and other pools of assets that it turned into ready investments. When Ford issued a traditional bond, the information necessary for investors to form an opinion about it already existed, in the balance sheet. But in the case of a mortgage security, if Lehman Brothers had tried to market a bond backed by, say, 1,400 mortgages—even supposing Lehman had been kind enough to provide the names and the addresses of the borrowers, and even their incomes—the typical investor would have stumbled away in stunned confusion. What is an investor to make of 1,400 mortgages? What Lehman and every underwriter did, therefore, was to retain Moody's, Fitch, or S&P. Once the bond had a rating, the investor was happy to take Lehman's call. Indeed, if Moody's said the security was triple-A, the investor was interested in little else. If the backside of American home ownership was

---

* The "license" metaphor was suggested by Frank Partnoy. The case of Enron is illustrative. For much of 2001, while Enron's fortunes were sharply deteriorating, Enron's credit rating remained triple-A. However, late in November, S&P lowered Enron's debt to subinvestment grade. To investors, this was a signal that Enron was locked out of credit markets: it had lost its "license" to borrow. Four days later it filed for bankruptcy.

a vast assembly line for packaging mortgages, rating agencies occupied the pivotal choke point.

Though the agencies were in a powerful position, Wall Street had considerable leverage as well. For one thing, the business was highly lucrative for the rating agencies. The fee for rating a mortgage pool was on the order of $200,000, and the business was concentrated among a relative handful of securitizers, meaning that (in this business) Moody's and the rest had relatively few clients. Given that the agencies' profits were soaring (from 2002 to '06, Moody's haul nearly tripled), it paid for them to stay on good terms with Wall Street. Moreover, when Lehman took a mortgage pool to Moody's, it paid the fee *only* if it was pleased with the rating. Otherwise, it could try its luck with S&P or Fitch. To understand the threat to the integrity of the process, imagine the big rating agencies as three competitive saloons standing side by side, with each free to set its own drinking age. Before long, nine-year-olds would be downing bourbon.

Predictably, the agencies began to bend their standards. In 2004, a thirty-four-year-old up-and-comer at S&P wrote despondently to the head of ratings, after Moody's had snatched away an assignment: "We just lost a huge RMBS [residential backed mortgage security] deal to Moody's due to a huge difference in the required credit support level." He made a plea for S&P to loosen its requirements: "the only way to compete is to have a paradigm shift in thinking." Even Ray McDaniel, the Moody's CEO, admitted in an e-mail missive that the market penalized agencies for strictness, dryly observing: "ratings quality has surprisingly few friends."[2] As the mortgage business grew, so did the temptation to relax the criteria.

Mortgage securities, remember, were sold to finance investment vehicles that purchased actual mortgages. In simplified form, the scheme resembled a swimming pool with one hose (delivering the payments from homeowners) flowing into the pool and another (distributing checks to bondholders) flowing out of it. The incoming hose needed to carry a little more fluid—both because the bankers wouldn't have bothered to structure the deal if funds hadn't been left over to pay their ample fees, and because one had to assume that some water would leak as a few homeowners defaulted. The trick for the banks was to gather enough subprime or otherwise suspect mortgages—on which the interest rates, and therefore the size of the homeowners' payments, would be higher—without jeopardizing the bond ratings. Higher interest rates on the mortgages meant more money flowing into the pool. But if the bonds were rated too low, more money would flow out, and the pool would drain.

This writer was allowed a peek at an actual pool, given the pseudonym Subprime XYZ. Issued in the spring of 2006, Subprime XYZ included 2,393 mortgages with a total face value of $430 million, or about $180,000 for the average loan. The mortgages had been issued by a "nonbank lender" (possibly Countrywide) on the West Coast. The lender took the loans to a New York investment bank, which assembled the pool and brought the package to Moody's.

XYZ typified the exuberance of the age. Every one of the mortgages was subprime, and three-quarters of the mortgages were adjustable. Moreover, according to the spreadsheet that the investment bank supplied to Moody's, 43 percent of the borrowers did not provide written verification of their incomes; Moody's would have to rate the mortgages on faith. Its analyst took comfort in the fact that most of the loans in XYZ were—so the borrowers said—for primary residences. However, Moody's did not make house calls in Southern California (where the mortgages were concentrated) to verify such points. Nor did it have access to individual loan files. Instead, it made a statistical analysis of the pool at large. Although the loans were for first mortgages, a point that favorably impressed the Moody's analyst, almost half the borrowers had taken out second loans as well. With their two loans combined, many had little or no equity.

The bank proposed to finance these mortgages with twelve layers of bonds from Aaa to lowly Ba1. Thus, rather than a single pool, the structure resembled a waterfall cascading over tiny millponds at successive levels. At the top, funds were siphoned to pay the triple-A bonds;

money that remained flowed to the next tier of the falls to pay the next-highest bond and so on. This dizzying financial Niagara depended on the fulfillment of two conditions: (1) about 80 percent of the bonds would be rated triple-A, and (2) even the lowest-rated bonds would merit an investment grade.

For the bank to obtain those ratings, it (or a client) had to invest what Moody's deemed an appropriate cushion of capital. The bank naturally wanted to minimize this investment; the rating agencies, then, were in the role normally reserved for governments or banks: determining the appropriate capital level. The agencies had models that calculated how much of a capital cushion a given pool of mortgages required, and these models were available to Lehman and the other issuers. Wall Street became adroit at assembling a mix of loans that the computer would bless. The banker on Subprime XYZ ran the numbers until he or she got a favorable result and sent a (proposed) package to Moody's *that stipulated the intended ratings.* Then, the bank and Moody's talked it over. Though Moody's had the final say, the process was collaborative. Wall Street's skill at working the system (combined with the fact that it paid the tab) contributed to an increasingly forgiving ratings environment. In the frenetic mortgage climate of 2006, Moody's took only a single day to process the data. In the case of Subprime XYZ, its analysts deduced that losses would be no greater than 4.9 percent; as the deal provided a 7¼ percent capital cushion, the ratings were approved.

The manager of XYZ still needed a way to dispose of the bonds, particularly the lowest tier, and this is where CDOs were so vital. By 2005, CDOs were buying (and selling) virtually every low-rated mortgage bond in sight. CDOs, it will be recalled, were secondary securities; they bought the securities (such as XYZ) that bought the actual mortgages. The CDOs were also financed by selling bonds, and their securities also required a rating—indeed, they would have been quite worthless without one.* Just as Subprime XYZ fashioned high-rated

---

* It is painful to report, but there were also third-order instruments, known as CDOs squared, that bought bonds issued by other CDOs. Hyperactive bankers even floated fourth-order derivatives: "CDOs cubed."

bonds from junk mortgages, the CDOs took low-rated mortgage bonds and turned them into triple-As. It was through the vehicle of the CDO that Wall Street truly engaged the mortgage bubble. What Countrywide was to home loans, Merrill Lynch would become to CDOs. Once the individual mortgages had been turned into a generic, rated security, they were, seemingly, just another Wall Street product, the sort of instrument that a Merrill dealt in every day.

Though the analyst on Subprime XYZ had some familiarity with mortgages, the analysts assigned to rate CDOs had virtually none. CDO analysts were pure quants—statistical animals who lived on numbers. They rated CDOs by extrapolating from previous securities. How often did a Ba1 default? How often did two in a row default? What about under conditions of stress? The math was extremely difficult. S&P built a 150-person CDO department, part of a priesthood of PhDs that stretched from firm to firm. Virtually no one among the unordained—not government regulators, not the banks' executives—could decode these arcane models.

But the CDO modelers had a secret. Because of the profound changes in mortgages, they had virtually no relevant data to input. In 2001, when CDOs were taking off, S&P examined the historical "correlations" of mortgage bonds. In statistical forecasting, correlations are the all-important key; they help analysts determine whether there is just a random chance or a better-than-random one of bonds defaulting in tandem. However, among the thousands of mortgage bonds for which a record existed in 2001, S&P found only forty-five that had defaulted—ever. It clearly wasn't enough of a sample to even guess at the correlations. But left with no option, guess was more or less what S&P and its competitors did.

As housing markets had, in the past, been regional, correlations were assumed to be modest. The New England market did not rise or fall with California's or Georgia's. Housing prices hadn't fallen on a national basis in any year since the early '60s (some promoters distorted this fact, preferring to claim that they had *never* fallen[3]). However, the mortgage industry was evolving fast. The same lenders were active, and offering the same new products, coast to coast. Common sense suggested the correlations were growing. And financial history is replete with examples of unexpected correlations when diverse assets and seemingly unlinked markets crash in unison.

Indeed, history is a very unreliable guide to the risk of financial calamities. It is tempting to calculate the odds from past experience, as if one were deducing the odds in a card game. In cards the risk can be quantified; we know for certain that the queen of spades appears once in every fifty-two draws. But our knowledge of the cards in history's deck is incomplete. Before 1929 a computer would have calculated very slim odds of a Great Depression; after it, considerably greater odds.[4] To CDO analysts, rising home values suggested that the mortgage deck was filled with aces. Freddie Mac stress-tested its portfolio for a scenario in which home prices fell 4 percent per annum for up to three years. That was the worst case they could imagine; a sharper drop was outside the scope of their models.

At the heart of Wall Street's thinking (and its models) was the assumption of randomness: events uncorrelated in the recent past were assumed to be random at all times. The credit rating agencies actually used a gambling metaphor to describe their methodology. It was known as the Monte Carlo method, because it evaluated future defaults as random accidents subject to the laws of casino games. Wall Street banks fully embraced this approach and so, more surprisingly, did federal regulators.[5] Historical data, such as stock prices and mortgage default statistics, were seen as evidence of immutable truths: the stock market is relatively stable; the housing market doesn't crash; home mortgages default at a rate of 1 percent per annum. Wall Street adopted quantitative strategies because they afforded more precision than old-fashioned judgment—they seemed to convert financial gambles into hard science. Investment banks stocked risk departments with PhDs. The problem was that homeowners weren't molecules, and finance wasn't physics. Merrill hired John Breit, a particle theorist, as a risk manager, and Breit tried to explain to his peers that the laws of Brownian motion didn't truly describe finance—this wasn't science, it was pseudoscience. The models said a diversified portfolio of municipal bonds would lose money once every 10,000 years, but as Breit pointed out, such a portfolio had been devastated merely 150 years ago, during the Civil War. With regard to Merrill's portfolio of CDOs, the firm judged its potential loss to be "$71.3 million."[6] This was absurd—not because the number was high or low, but because of the arrogance and self-delusion embedded in such fine, decimal-point precision.

Quants could compute the precise odds with dice or with naturally occurring phenomena such as height dispersions. Mortgage default patterns, though, do not necessarily conform to the bell curve. People default for reasons, usually because their income or other circumstances suffer an adverse change, or because the bank miscalculated to begin with. The factors that buffet one family's mortgage might be independent of those affecting their neighbor—in other words, random. But they might be related. It was no coincidence that millions were foreclosed on during the Great Depression. In the CDO era, the rating agencies ignored the vast changes in lending patterns, which might, in a uniform sense, affect the general propensity to default. The character of loans written by Countrywide and WaMu was so different from those of earlier eras that the statistics on which their models were based were virtually useless—like forecasting auto accidents using data from the era of the horse and buggy.

Why did CDO managers buy such risky mortgage paper? Mark Adelson, a structured finance expert at Moody's who left the firm just before the CDO craze heated up, thought it was because managers didn't have to bear the risk; the investors in the CDOs did. Also, knowing little about mortgages, the managers saw subprime bonds only as an abstraction. In a report on subprimes, Adelson wrote, "They ascribed mathematical properties to the underlying sub-prime mortgage. . . . They should have been focusing on the actual loans and on the lending process."[7] Investors, in any case, wanted to buy them—even though these investors knew nothing about the underlying product. In the view of the law professor Frank Partnoy, "High ratings replaced independent judgment."[8]

Even Mark Zandi, the chief economist at Moody's independent fore-casting division, was becoming deeply concerned. In May 2006, a month before Moody's rated Subprime XYZ, Zandi wrote that credit standards were becoming dangerously lax. "A healthy majority" of loan officers were easing underwriting standards for all types of consumer loans. Even as his colleagues were pushing more subprime sausage through the ratings machine, Zandi zeroed in on substandard mortgages—in particular, the "razor-thin" level of equity that underlay them. What would happen, he fretted, if the foreigners who held some $3 trillion of U.S. mortgage securities decided to sell? If they did, it could mean trouble in the mortgage market—in which the Wall Street banks, cour-tesy of CDOs, were becoming deeply invested. "The environment," Zandi concluded, "feels increasingly ripe for some type of financial event."[9]

5

LEHMAN

*[T]he banking system was metamorphosing into an
off–balance sheet and derivatives world—the shadow
banking system.*

—GARY GORTON, "THE PANIC OF 2007"[1]

NO COMPANY ON Wall Street was more implicated in mortgages than Lehman Brothers. Founded in 1850, Lehman was a scrappy firm with a tribal culture. Even as it had grown into a prestigious investment bank, its proud bankers had remained insular and suspicious of outsiders. If the firm had a personality, it was incarnated in the figure of Richard Fuld, who had joined Lehman in the days when it was a private partnership, remained there his entire career and, since 1994, been its boss. Though remote and taciturn, Fuld nurtured a familial dedication to the firm. At his insistence, executives took much of their pay in stock, reinforcing the sense of a shared fate. Lean and sinewy, he resembled the actor Al Pacino, whose character in *The Godfather* (a movie Fuld watched repeatedly) he vaguely emulated, most famously in the brutal stares with which he responded to subordinates' entreaties. His darting eyes seemed ever on the alert, as if for predators. Perhaps he had cause, for Lehman suffered a near-death experience almost every market cycle. In 1998, when the hedge fund Long-Term Capital Management imploded, seeming to imperil Wall Street, Fuld valiantly went on the road to keep Lehman's creditors from withdrawing their lines of credit; his efforts saved the firm. He had the daring of a gambler who believes, deep down, that he will always be able to play the last card—that if down markets or a credit crunch ever swamped his firm, he would find a way to steer it home.

Fuld had attended the University of Colorado, and his middling education left him deeply insecure among polished Ivy League investment bankers. In other respects, he was a typical Wall Street CEO. His trader's gruffness, his guttural barking, had been moneyed over. His ambition had been answered with a growing reputation, and with eight-figure paychecks and all they provided: his wife's auction-quality art collection and board seat at the Museum of Modern Art; homes on Park Avenue and in Greenwich, Connecticut, Sun Valley, Idaho, and Jupiter Island in Florida. The Fulds even bought a property in Vermont for use as a landing pad when they traveled by helicopter to visit their son, a hockey player at Middlebury College.

Like many Wall Street CEOs of his generation, Fuld was a former bond trader (he cut his teeth trading "three-year treasuries"). There were other similarities, too. Chuck Prince, Citigroup's chief executive, was once said not to know a CDO from a "grocery list,"[2] and Fuld was likewise of too early a vintage to grasp the nuances of newer, exotic securities. He relied on younger, mathematically trained traders to sort them out, but mostly, he took comfort in the knowledge that in a liquid market, securities were readily saleable. In Wall Street parlance, Lehman was not in the "storage business" of collecting assets to hold for keeps, but in the "moving business" of accumulating tradable tokens that it could unload at will. That way, in theory, it would never be stuck with a losing trade.

From its public stock offering, in 1994, through the end of 2005, Fuld's company had seen its stock rise sixteen times. In the mid '00s, it boasted record profits nearly every quarter. Though Lehman's prestige depended on its investment bankers, its profits derived from real estate—both residential mortgages and commercial property loans.

Not so very long ago, Wall Street was a place where aristocratic firms made money catering to big corporations and wealthy individuals.

Improbably, at the dawn of the new century, it had become a collection of mortgage factories whose profitability was based on loans to middle-class Americans and even subprime customers the likes of which would have appalled the blue-blooded bankers of yore.[3] Capital was so democratic, so broadly accessible, that investment banking no longer commanded a premium. Issuing stocks and bonds had become drudge work; legendary firms had been forced to seek new profit lines. For most, this meant taking more risk: not just collecting a fee for serving clients but becoming a principal in trading. Even at Goldman Sachs, perennially the leading adviser to Fortune 500 corporations, trading provided twice the revenues of investment banking—testimony that the traditional, client side of banking had been relegated to second string.[4]

Trading required consummate skill; it also required capital, and the easy credit of the mid-'oos was a great equalizer. Banks leveraged up, piling ever more trading risk on smaller slices of equity. Real estate was attractive because it seemed to temper the risk with predictability; while every corporate borrower had its own hazards, unique to the particular business, mortgage pools seemed generic, steady and safe. Also, the mortgage business was wide open. Rivals could scarcely dream of muscling Goldman aside on mergers and acquisitions, but Bear Stearns, Lehman, and the like had no trouble acquiring mortgages to feed their securitization machines.

Some banks merely traded mortgages, but Lehman handled every aspect of real estate finance, from issuing consumer loans to fashioning complex securities. It originated as many as $40 billion in mortgages per year,[5] and the subprime loans issued by one branch of Lehman were conveyed along a virtual assembly line to other units, which sliced them into bonds and reassembled them into CDOs. Since Lehman retained a portion of each of these securities, its investment in mortgages steadily mounted. It also assisted corporate clients in buying commercial properties—shopping malls, apartment buildings, and so on. To bring such deals to fruition, Lehman often extended some of the financing—either on a permanent basis or until it could sell its interest to investors.

This strategy entailed some risks. Obviously, real estate prices could go down. And Lehman was financed in part with short-term capital. Thus, it was using money it had borrowed for as little as thirty days to buy mortgage assets with terms of up to thirty years. If its creditors should ever walk, Lehman would need to convert assets to cash in a hurry. Of course, with credit in such bountiful supply, Fuld did not think this was likely.

By the mid '00s, Lehman's prowess in mortgage securitization was stirring the Street's envy. One subprime lender confided that the Wall Street banks "all want to be like Lehman Brothers." Lehman, he continued, "has a huge pipeline and everyone is coveting it." True enough, banks of pedigree low and high were striving to match Lehman's franchise. In 2006, Bear Stearns knitted together 2,800 Alt-A mortgages and devised an impossibly complex structure—with thirty-seven layers of bonds—against it. According to a confidential memo authored at Fannie Mae, investment banks seemed to be building permanent platforms in the mortgage industry. The Street's share of the business had tripled from 10 percent to 30 percent, virtually overnight, and its growth showed no sign of slowing. Credit Suisse First Boston had "ambitious goals," the Fannie memo noted. Bear was a rival to Lehman, and even the venerable Morgan Stanley, realizing that manufacturing CDOs was more lucrative than underwriting stocks and bonds, was furiously committing capital in a bid to extend its lustrous and formerly snooty brand to middlebrow mortgages.[6]

The banks tended to keep the senior-most layers of CDOs, which were triple-A rated and supposedly secure, on their books. For added security, they purchased insurance. Part of the conceit of the new finance was that every risk could be laid off—that is, transferred to some other party. Insurance could not *eliminate* the risk, which, in the U.S. mortgage market, was vast. But insurance emboldened the Wall Street firms to go further. The biggest purveyor of CDO insurance by far was the financial giant American International Group. AIG was based in Manhattan, its Art Deco skyscraper sprouting defiantly from behind the squat fortress of the New York Federal Reserve Bank. However, it sold CDO protection out of its derivatives unit in London, AIG Financial Products, a corporate satellite that employed a squadron of highly trained quants. Not unlike Long-Term Capital Management, the ill-fated hedge fund, Financial Products was an obscure, little-known trading outfit whose tentacles wrapped around the world of high finance. It didn't offer "insurance" in the traditional sense of writing policies; rather, it entered into derivative contracts known as credit default swaps, under which a counterparty—Goldman, say, or Merrill Lynch—paid an upfront fee for AIG to guarantee the value of a CDO, or some other security. If the value of the CDO faltered, AIG had to offset the loss. Thus, it was a guarantor for a considerable portion of American mortgages.

In an era of cookie-cutter corporations, AIG was a strange and unlikely beast.[7] It was founded after World War I by Cornelius Vander Starr, whose mother had run a boardinghouse in Fort Bragg, California, and had peddled liquor to the patrons of nearby bordellos. Starr had found his way to Shanghai where, in 1919, he opened a small insurance office. He hit on the novel idea of selling policies to Chinese nationals (other foreign-based insurers dealt only with Western clients) and expanded, in reverse fashion, from Asia to Latin America, Europe, and, lastly, the United States. But AIG's American operations did not really ignite until Starr entrusted them to another self-starter, Maurice "Hank" Greenberg, the son of a candy store owner on New York City's Lower East Side. Greenberg's father died when Hank was five years old, and at seventeen, Greenberg went into the army on a faked birth certificate—eventually landing at Omaha Beach on D-day and, in the war's final days, helping to liberate the Dachau concentration camp. Named by Starr as a successor in 1968, Greenberg boldly took risks that other insurers shunned—for instance, barging into Communist-ruled Russia and China well before competitors. Over several decades, he turned AIG into the world's biggest insurer. Though he was a visionary businessman, his autocratic style harked back to the days when companies were the playthings of landed tycoons. He was secretive and lordly, flouting the conventions of modern management as though AIG were his personal fiefdom. Divisions operated in cordoned silos, with the empire visible only to Greenberg and a few close lieutenants. He shrugged off the usual corporate controls and (with smallish items, anyway) seemed to take license with disclosure and reporting requirements.[8] He was brilliant but often abusive. Though two of his sons, both senior executives, fled the company—one when Hank lost confidence in him, the other because his father was so difficult—the staff held him in terrified awe. His diminutive stature seemed to heighten his aura, as though his power emanated from an invisible source.

In 2002, just as the mortgage boom was heating up, Greenberg tapped Joseph Cassano, a tough-talking son of a Brooklyn cop and a former colleague of Michael Milken's, to run Financial Products. Under Cassano, revenue soared, ultimately topping $3 billion a year.[9] The street-smart Cassano, who had joined AIG in 1987, when the trading unit was formed, had an instinct for finance. He used the parent corporation's triple-A balance sheet to procure cheap credit for the derivatives operation in London—a business that, had it stood alone, would have been regarded as highly suspect. Thus, the stellar ratings AIG had gained from its long experience in insurance were put at the service of hothouse derivatives traders. The credit agencies did not much notice or at any rate object; AIG was a vast conglomerate with insurance operations in 130 countries and assets as diverse as aircraft leasing, solar energy, and a ski resort in Vermont. The London unit was a tiny and remote offshoot, hardly viewed by S&P or Moody's as a threat.

Financial Products wrote swaps to guarantee a raft of diverse bonds, corporate loans in particular. But its signature deal was insuring CDOs. Cassano, a salesman given to mercurial outbursts, touted AIG's credit default swaps as easy money, like selling insurance for "a catastrophe that would never happen." AIG charged between seven and fifteen cents for each $100 of CDO value that it guaranteed (each contract was highly customized and individually negotiated, but the fees, reflecting Cassano's high confidence level, were invariably modest). His swap trades were based on models designed by Gary Gorton, a Wharton School finance professor. Gorton, who had written elegant papers on corporate finance, supplied assurances that the models were "robust" enough to withstand adverse economic conditions.[10]

Backed by Gorton's models, Cassano believed that AIG would not lose a single dollar on its swaps.[11] Though he did not have advanced mathematical training (he received an undergraduate degree at Brooklyn College), Cassano was an aggressive trader with a lofty self-regard. In the age of derivatives, to seamlessly transfer risk across corporate lines and national boundaries was to play in the sweet spot at which intellect and finance converged. AIG Financial Products occupied a hallowed perch, consecrated by employee bonuses that amounted to 30 percent or more of its revenues each year. Nor was the unit assessed a charge for future losses—for losses were not foreseen. Its bonuses spawned a gross mismatch between risk and reward, typical of the Street in periods when animal spirits ran unchecked. Cassano netted tens of millions a year while encumbering AIG with a long-term commitment to backstop much of Wall Street.[12]

Greenberg extended Cassano's outfit surprising license. The boss had a weakness for clever quants, and he was enamored with the group's seemingly easy profits. His greatest flaw was his obsession with reported earnings, which caused him to overlook underlying and longer-term risks. However, he was no naïf. Greenberg at least tried to rework the group's bonus arrangement.[13] And his instinctive wariness exerted a modest check on Cassano's trading.

Then, early in 2005, Greenberg was humbled by an accounting scandal and, just shy of his eightieth birthday, forced to resign.* The new CEO, Martin J. Sullivan, a former insurance underwriter, was as trusting as Greenberg was skeptical. Also, he was unfamiliar with

---

* AIG's board forced Greenberg to quit at the insistence of the New York State attorney general, Eliot Spitzer, who accused him of sham transactions with outside parties and of improper accounting. No criminal charges were brought, and Greenberg always maintained his innocence. However, in 2009, he settled related SEC securities charges, without admitting or denying guilt, for $15 million.

CDOs. In a matter of months, AIG's exposure to subprime-backed CDOs doubled.[14]

To his credit, Cassano reversed course at the end of 2005, and Financial Products belatedly stopped writing swaps on subprime CDOs. By then, it had guaranteed some 420 of the riskiest CDOs, through which its exposure was on the order of $80 billion. His group was effectively underwriting some 20,000 individual securities and millions of underlying subprime mortgages, as well as car loans, credit card receivables, and the like.[15] Given the complexity, and the innate fallibility, of human forecasting, no model could hope to master it. Very few observers were paying attention to AIG's risks—certainly not the rating agencies, and not the stock market either. However, Rodriguez, the investor, was watching. As Wall Street had turned to structured finance, the investor had begun to wonder about the quality of assets underneath the alphabet soup of newfangled securities, including credit default swaps. In a letter to his fund investors, in 2006, Rodriguez fretted that "default insurance [is] being priced very cheaply. . . . In our opinion, the CDO market has not been adequately stress tested to determine how it will behave under adverse circumstances."[16]

Even though AIG had stopped insuring subprime CDOs, Wall Street firms continued to mint CDOs at a torrid pace, now bearing the risk (or most of it) themselves. Demand from investors was insatiable. CDO prices soared—meaning, of course, that investors were accepting a far less attractive return.* In 2006, CDO production reached $225 billion (up from $50 billion in 2003). Since a record 20 percent of mortgages that year were subprime, the underlying asset quality was deteriorating even as the price was rising.[17]

So fierce was the demand for CDOs that investors wanted more of them than the supply of mortgage bonds permitted. Wall Street responded to this shortage with an arguably fantastic solution. Why not manufacture *synthetic* CDOs that, if they couldn't own actual mortgage

---

* The early CDOs yielded roughly three percentage points more than Treasury bonds—a gap that at least paid homage to the former's relative riskiness. By 2005–06, the spread had narrowed to one percentage point.

bonds (since all of these were spoken for), would at least mirror the performance of CDOs that did? By 2005, the Street was doing a booming business in CDOs that, also via credit default swap agreements, were "linked" to the performance of actual mortgage bonds. An investor bought, instead of the actual bonds, a promise from some other investor to provide the same return; if the real-world bonds lost money, the buyer took a similar loss. By 2006, half of all CDOs were said to be synthetic.[18]

Synthetic CDOs did not add to the country's economic output any more than did a bet at the track or, for that matter, a wager on the direction of the stock market. They were a mere—though a massive—side bet. To paraphrase the financial journalist Michael Lewis, synthetic CDOs had as much to do with real estate as fantasy football had to do with the NFL.[19] They built no houses and painted no walls; they simply multiplied the Street's gamble. Thanks to these derivative ventures, far more money was wagered on mortgage debt than the total of such debt in existence. In some cases, a single mortgage bond was referenced in dozens of synthetics.[20] It was as if Wall Street, in all its mad, Strangelovian genius, had a found a way to clone armies of securities from a single strand of mortgage DNA.

The subsurface multiplication of CDO exposure fooled many a forecaster. Even the Federal Reserve, with its scores of economists, underestimated the subprime threat. The Fed simply counted mortgages. But thanks to derivatives, the whole of the banking sector or a goodly part thereof was poised on the subprime high wire.

D ERIVATIVES ARE financial contracts usually tied to (that is, "derived" from) some underlying index or price, be it the price of corn, the difference between two interest rates, the value of a CDO—anything. Since the range of such contracts was limited only by the inventiveness of Wall Street, they vastly increased the set of opportunities for investors. This is why free marketers were so enthusiastic. Not only was the scope of risk-taking enlarged, but the mechanics were easier and the instruments themselves were more supple and plastic than traditional stocks and bonds. In pre-derivative days, a bank could ditch a toxic asset only by selling it; now it could contract with a counterparty willing to bear the risk of default. Derivative commitments did not require as much capital as did traditional lending; a bank could simply *assume* the risk and potential rewards of a loan without extending any cash. In short, banks could take more risk. Bankers were enamored; they glimpsed a world of seamless transactions, fungible risks, efficient portfolios. A shadow banking system developed, producing almost magical profits for the bank.

In the shadow system, solvency was assured not by capital in the vault but by agreements with third parties—each of whom was linked in a chain of other such agreements. In the eyes of each individual firm, risk was reduced. But systemic vulnerability—the danger that a failing firm could bring down a host of others—slowly and stealthily accreted. Though invisible to the public, derivatives enabled speculators to circumvent virtually every rule designed for the safekeeping of markets. They effectively voided limits on leverage and rendered disclosure practices woefully inadequate. More subtly, derivatives turned financial risk, once discrete and contained, into a liquid, amorphous element. Bank loans formerly were potted—ergo, a bank with a bad loan was stuck with it. This naturally encouraged prudence. Now risk had the changeable aspect of mercury. The utter ease with which risks were offloaded by one firm to another ensured that more suspect loans, more dicey mortgages, would be written in the first place.

In the modern era, no financial crisis erupted that did not have derivatives at its heart, beginning with the stock market crash of 1987 ("Black Monday"), in which derivative instruments led to chain-reaction selling. Yet academics and practitioners continued to sing their praises. The leading troubadour was Alan Greenspan, who held that "regulation of derivatives transactions that are privately negotiated by professionals is unnecessary"—and indeed was harmful to market efficiency and the standard of living.[21]

Nonetheless, a series of troubling and in some cases destabilizing derivative blow-ups occurred in the mid-1990s.* All involved the "privately negotiated," or over-the-counter, derivatives that Greenspan extolled—basically, custom-tailored agreements to swap cash flows that were linked to some market or price. These instruments functioned in a regulatory vacuum, and by the middle of Clinton's second term, with swaps volume rising into the trillions of dollars, the Securities and Exchange Commission was wondering out loud whether they should be regulated. Unexpectedly, the Commodity Futures Trading Commission, a weaker rival agency, inserted itself into the debate, arguing that swaps were pretty much like the exchange-traded contracts for pork belly and wheat futures that the CFTC already regulated. (Except, of course, that swaps traded in opaque markets and were screened from government oversight.) Banks who were pioneers in swaps, such as J.P. Morgan, were discovering how lucrative the field could be and were terrified that the CFTC might intervene. The bankers bluntly warned the CFTC to butt out.[22]

Though the CFTC did not back down, its response could hardly have been expected to trigger alarm. In the spring of 1998, the agency issued a "concept release," an exploratory document intended to spur discussion, generally read only by Beltway insiders. The CFTC release—actually, it was a *draft* release—was a lengthy tome reasserting the agency's jurisdiction over what was now a $13 trillion market and floating the idea of increased supervision. In the spirit of open government, Brooksley Born, the CFTC chair, circulated the draft to other interested agencies. The draft inquired whether the basic regulatory tool kit (disclosure and capital adequacy rules, margin requirements, antifraud enforcement, and so on) could be applied to the swaps market.

The reaction was immediate and enraged. Every banker in Wash-

---

* Orange County, Bankers Trust, Barings Bank, Metallgesellschaft, and Sumitomo Corporation each suffered horrendous and unexpected losses from derivative transactions. In the case of Orange County, the treasurer, hoping to enhance the county's income, borrowed money to invest in interest-rate derivatives. However, in 1994, when interest rates rose, the scheme failed and the county filed for bankruptcy.

ington complained about the upstart CFTC. Following Wall Street's urging, Treasury secretary Rubin, a former cochairman of Goldman Sachs, was extremely hostile. A posse of regulators scheduled a meeting for late April, for the purpose of persuading Born to bury the release. Before the meeting, Larry Summers, Rubin's top deputy at the Treasury Department, called Born and berated her. Summers huffed, "There are thirteen bankers in my office. They say if this is published we'll have the worst financial crisis since World War II."

At the meeting, Greenspan, SEC chairman Arthur Levitt, and Rubin took turns pressuring Born—who was, lest we forget, head of an independent federal agency. The gist was that regulation of derivatives was not fit for discussion; to even breathe the phrase would create uncertainty, put a damper on trading, cause markets to teeter. Greenspan got in Born's face, blowing and blustering until he reddened. Rubin, always more politic, spoke with controlled fury, as if Born's proposal were unsuited to his society. He repeated that the CFTC was out of its jurisdiction and asked if Born (who had been elected president of the *Stanford Law Review* in 1963, when most of the women in law firms were still pouring coffee) would like an education in the applicable law from Treasury's general counsel.

Rubin figured he had quashed the release. But in May, Born published it. Though it merely proposed to *study* the question of derivatives regulation, Rubin, Greenspan, and Levitt jointly announced they would seek legislation to stop Brooksley Born.[23] This was arguably the greatest show of political firepower that has been turned on a concept release in Washington history.* It became, now, the earnest intent of the

---

* Curiously, of the four officials ganging up on Born, only Greenspan was a full-fledged partisan for deregulation. In their first meeting, Greenspan told Born [as she later recounted to *Stanford Magazine*] that he did not agree with her on the need, even, for laws against fraud—which Greenspan said the market would patrol on its own. Levitt, a pro-business Democrat, was far more liberal. He had taken on Wall Street in several controversial battles, including ones on shareholder suits and stock-option reporting. When he challenged Born, he was in the midst of a fight over auditor independence, battling Enron chairman Kenneth Lay, among others. With congressional Republicans chafing to downsize his agency, and Levitt already weakened politically, he was unwilling to antagonize the powerful Rubin-Greenspan duo. Rubin was the most articulate spokesman for the Democratic Party's newfound ideological flexibility on matters economic—which is to say, its break from its "big government" past. But his flexibility was not always distinguishable from expediency. In

Republicans in the U.S. Congress to ensure that no regulator would claim the authority to supervise derivatives. Temporarily, they enjoined the CFTC from moving ahead.

In the fall of 1998, the hedge fund Long-Term Capital Management lost $4.5 billion in a matter of weeks. This sudden loss destabilized markets and prompted the New York Federal Reserve Bank to organize a private-sector bailout. The LTCM debacle profoundly shook investors. It was the first time in the modern era that markets had seized up—that the new financial architecture was seen to pose systemic risks. That an obscure, privately controlled hedge fund could rock global markets was especially chilling, and most of its trades had been in derivatives. Born (who would testify on the issue seventeen times) argued that opaque derivatives trading could threaten the economy.[24] There was much public discussion of whether LTCM had exposed a latent systemic weakness, and a few voices wondered, once again, whether derivatives should be subject to scrutiny.

Though Greenspan was momentarily jolted by LTCM, his view on derivatives regulation did not materially change from 1994 when, with breathless faith, he had told a congressional hearing, "Risks in financial markets, including derivative markets, are being regulated by private parties."[25] By the following spring, the urgency of the post-LTCM period was receding and Greenspan was again calling for a less-burdensome regulatory regime.[26] In mid-1999, the powerless Born resigned. The following year, at the urging of now-Secretary Summers, Greenspan, and Levitt, and to the delight of bankers, the antiregulatory Commodity Futures Modernization Act was passed by the House of Representatives.

The bill would have died in the Senate but for the tireless advocacy of Phil Gramm, Republican of Texas, the powerful chairman of the

---

his 2003 book [published after the events described above] Rubin advocated "comprehensive" margin requirements for derivatives, and in pronouncements throughout his career, Rubin was generally a proponent of sensible, if moderate, regulation. In practice, he was often a deregulator. Simultaneous to his opposition to Born, he advocated repeal of the Glass-Steagall act—a cause championed by Citigroup, which Rubin would shortly join. Summers, probably the most liberal of the group, was generally open to the case for regulation. Yet when Born proposed some market supervision, Summers, too, tried to bully her into submission.

Senate Banking Committee. Gramm and his wife, Wendy, were each conservative economists and apostles of deregulation. Wendy had served in the Reagan administration, where Reagan had dubbed her "my favorite economist." As head of the CFTC (the position later occupied by Born) she earnestly promoted deregulation of swaps. In one instance, the agency approved a request from an influential corporation—Enron—that it exempt some energy derivatives from regulation. Subsequently, Wendy Gramm resigned and joined Enron's lavishly compensated board.[27] Meanwhile, Senator Gramm became one of the largest recipients of Enron's political contributions. The Gramms did not have to tailor their beliefs to satisfy these constituents; each was, wholeheartedly, a champion of unrestricted markets. The collapse of the Soviet Union had bolstered the extreme-right view that—total government having failed—any government presence in markets was undesirable. Wendy Gramm had established a policy of keeping regulatory hands off derivatives, but, absent legislation, the policy was subject to change.[28] And Born *had* tried to change it. This is what motivated Senator Gramm as well as his wife, who was now at a free-market think tank.

The bill was enacted by the Senate at 7 P.M. on December 15, 2000—it was the Congress's last act, three days after the Supreme Court decision deciding the presidential election. The law declared that swaps—now an $80 trillion market—were outside the purview of the CFTC and, save for very specific cases involving fraud, exempt from SEC regulation as well. As if to emphasize the degree of protection extended to derivatives dealers, the act specifically exempted swaps from century-old bucket shops laws. (Bucket shops were gambling parlors where investors went to make side bets on the stock market; states banned them in the early 1900s.) Congress was recognizing that dealers such as J.P. Morgan had become the bucket shops of the modern era, and it was making sure their business stayed legal.[29]

The onslaught against Brooksley Born was merely one skirmish in a generation-long war to unshackle the economy from the regulatory thicket of the New Deal and postwar era. Many of the reforms were wholly appropriate. To take an obvious and easy case, controls on energy prices up until the 1970s had discouraged investment in oil reserves and encouraged consumption, neither of which was in the public interest. Similar arguments applied to deregulation of airlines, trucking, and other industries.

Even in financial markets, some slackening of the rules was appropriate—as in, for instance, the liberalization that permitted interstate banking. But deregulators made two mistakes. One was failing to recognize that financial markets were more fragile than others, more vulnerable to panics and, indeed, more vital to the economy overall. Airline failures are rarely front-page news; bank runs are.

The other mistake was failing to see that the relative financial stability of the postwar era was largely a result of the regulation put in place during the New Deal and after. With the turn toward market-driven economies in the 1980s, it was thought that markets had outgrown the ancient perils that arise from speculative frenzy, excessive borrowing, and greed—when in fact, Washington had been holding them in check. As financial exotica from ARMs to credit default swaps sprouted outside of the regulatory walls, Washington's instinct was to let them bloom unrestricted. Regulators became so infatuated with the new finance as to believe that markets could fully police themselves. As Greenspan put it in 2002, "regulation is not only unnecessary in these [derivative] markets, it is potentially damaging."[30]

Such enthusiasms infected the SEC in 2004, when the investment banks, led by Goldman and its then-CEO, Hank Paulson, pleaded for a new regime to govern capital requirements. Instead of focusing on leverage or capital as a means of assessing risk, the banks wanted to use a financial tool known as Value at Risk. Under the banks' proposal, their "riskiness" would be measured according to the historical fluctuations in the *market prices* of their assets. By analogy, this was like evaluating mortgage risk not by the level of a homeowner's equity but by the variation in home prices in their neighborhood—or the correlation between prices in multiple neighborhoods. When the SEC acceded, it was a stunning adoption of the new finance. It imputed to historical prices a future prescience—all the more shocking because the toxic hedge fund LTCM had relied on just such an approach for calculating its risk.[31]

The SEC, in its wisdom, allowed investment banks to adopt Value at Risk only for securities in liquid markets. The agency, like the firms it regulated, believed that liquid markets were safer, because in liquid markets traders can get out of troublesome assets. The agency had no problem letting firms gauge their CDO exposure using Value at Risk, precisely because, in 2004 at least, the mortgage market was so liquid. But when markets run to extremes, liquidity inevitably evaporates and traders suddenly find themselves exposed. Wall Street has learned this lesson countless times.

The SEC did get something in return: investment banks agreed to submit to voluntary oversight of *non*-regulated activities (that is, the operations outside their broker-dealer units). This barely restrained them, and in the regulated parts of their operations, as a result of the switch to Value at Risk, leverage would surely rise—as the SEC anticipated.

A similar evolution was occurring in commercial banking. Banks were off-loading assets onto structured investment vehicles (SIVs)— nominally separate entities financed almost wholly with debt, for the purpose of keeping risky operations, and their associated debts, off the balance sheet. Even within the banks proper, management was evolving toward a "risk-based" model in which the focus was on credit ratings and market prices.* In determining a bank's safety and sound-ness, the emphasis was less on the old-fashioned metric of assets and liabilities, and more on the mix of assets, their expected volatilities, and so forth. It was market dependent. The banking regulators—the resi-dent examiners who look at bank balance sheets every day—were deeply divided over this trend. The more prudent examiners argued that models break down in extreme conditions—precisely the condi-

---

* Basel II, a multilateral pact to create an international banking standard, published in 2004 and yet to be fully adopted, aimed to ensure that capital allocation was "more risk sensitive." Incredibly, Basel's preferred approach for measuring market risk was Value at Risk—the selfsame technique that had led to the LTCM disaster.

tions for which risk models were designed. But when the momentum swung toward the new paradigm, these examiners were derided as old-fashioned. As a rule, regulators relied on case-by-case credit evaluation less and on models more.

This was also the approach adopted by the credit-rating agencies. The Enron scandal (which caught the agencies napping) prompted the SEC to consider reforms. But the SEC ducked, and let the rating agencies continue as they were.

By the mid-'oos, three core pillars of American finance—mortgages, banking, and investment banking—had arrived at a perilous state of semiregulation. No one agency concerned itself with maintaining sanity in the mortgage market. No Washington bureau was charged with the solvency of the investment banks—only with their broker-dealer units, and even then, only according to highly fallible models of market "risk." The Fed and other agencies still patrolled the banks, but with an indulgent eye, increasingly swayed by the confident nostrums of the new finance. Even in a fourth realm, insurance, risky contracts executed by a remote London unit of AIG had sidestepped the efforts of regulators. By turns, one financial realm and then another, some by design and others by natural evolution, was escaping from the protective sphere of government supervision. Protection, or control, was left to the market itself.

6

DESPERATE SURGE

*The most dangerous delusion today is that the banking
system is the picture of health.*

—STEPHANIE POMBOY, CEO OF CONSULTANT
MACROMAVENS, APRIL 7, 2006

THE EARLY STAGES of an investment bubble are patient and pleasant.
The rise is gradual, and is usually associated (if not entirely supported) by some logical development—a wonder drug or a new invention. In support of rising real estate values, brokers pointed to low
interest rates and a perceived housing shortage. Speculation was generally benign; prices went up, but brokers knew they could just as easily
come down. When investors start to count on a continuation of the
trend, however, prices depart from reason, and the situation becomes
more dangerous—doubly so if the buying is done on credit. Often this
occurs in the bubble's ultimate stage: fearing that the opportunity is
slipping away, investors become gripped by a kind of fever, as they were,
say, in Phoenix when home prices rose 42 percent in the year of 2005
alone.[1] By then, the original logic of the bubble is irrelevant, and the
consequent harm can be serious. This pattern is age-old. Popular memory recalls the entirety of the 1920s as "roaring," but for most of the
decade stocks merely yelped and pawed their way forward. In the years
after World War I, the Dow Jones Industrial Average hovered around
100, gaining little ground. Then, buoyed by the theory that industry was

entering a "New Era" of efficiency, organization, and mass production, it gradually picked up steam, and by early 1928, the Dow had reached 200. Had it halted then, it is doubtful that the aftermath would have been so brutal. However, over the next year and a half a true mania took hold, and the market surged an additional 90 percent. In the end, more than half of the market's eventual losses were set up in the final eighteen months of the boom.

Roughly in the spring of 2006, the end of the housing bubble was coming in sight, yet the big Wall Street banks maniacally raised the stakes. Citigroup had already ramped up its production of CDOs from $6 billion worth in 2003 to $20 billion in 2005.[2] In the latter year, in an effort to bolster sagging profits, the board decided to increase its risk even more. As an institution, Citigroup resembled AIG: a sprawling financial concern that had been stitched together by a charismatic, ambitious, and flawed architect. Sandy Weill, though tireless and possessed of keen instincts for a deal, was wedded to a quixotic vision of a financial "supermarket"; moreover, he was emotionally overinvested for a public CEO, incapable of distinguishing between his own fortunes and those of the bank.[3] He retired in 2003 with the company under an ethical cloud and his record of success tarnished. In naming a successor—perhaps a CEO's most important decision—Weill characteristically tabbed a close ally, his longtime general counsel and later senior executive, Charles Prince.

Prince tried to create a more professional organization. What he lacked was a background in banking. He had to trust in lieutenants and advisers, especially Bob Rubin, who had joined the board upon leaving the government in 1999 and assumed a murky but senior executive role as "a member of the office of the chairman." Rubin was also anointed chairman of the executive committee—giving him, in effect, veto power over decisions by both the management and the board. Cautious and cerebral, he seemed a perfect choice to steer Citi past whatever pitfalls. The handsome, graying banker, exceptionally well regarded at Goldman and later as Treasury Secretary, seemed more distinguished as he aged. Usually overlooked was the fact that he had led Goldman for only two years, and then only as co-chairman.

Temperamentally, Rubin was less equipped to be Citi's guardian than it seemed. Though a superb listener, he was better at hearing unwelcome counsel than giving it. He avoided conflict and confrontation, and tended to let others assume the active role in decision making. His influence was invariably—at times, almost comically—rendered in the passive voice. Even Rubin, in his memoir, described himself as "not manifestly aggressive"—as though he were afraid to take a stand even on the question of his own ferocity. He reveled in his role as a pragmatist in a sea of uncertainty, and fairly boasted to *Fortune*'s Carol Loomis that he believed that *nothing*, not even the day of the week, could be stipulated with "provable certainty."[4] However, his portfolio was less risk averse than his character. If nothing was provable, nothing was disprovable, either, so Rubin leaned with the odds. Unlike some senior execs, he understood what a CDO was, but not at the level of detail that might have aroused his concern. This half-knowledge was potentially lethal. Though not a troubadour for the new finance, he was enamored with the brainpower and mathematical elegance of academically trained financiers. When backed by calculable probabilities, Rubin was willing to roll the dice. Even as he made worried proclamations in public about the level of Citi's exposure, in private, in his deferential way, he was pushing the board to ramp up the company's risk.[5]

Citi's mortgage operation was cautious about issuing subprime and Alt-A loans. However, the bankers in its trading and investment realms were far more aggressive. In a relatively short time, Citigroup accumulated $43 billion in super-senior securities, the most protected pieces of CDOs. Citi's bankers viewed CDOs (thanks to their higher yields) as an easy way of generating additional revenue. Citi's risk managers, like AIG's, believed that they were risk-free—but they did not consult the mortgage specialists at their own affiliate, who had come to a contrary conclusion about the underlying mortgages.[6]

While its position in mortgage securities mushroomed, Citi layered risk upon risk by extending big loans (totalling some $30 billion) to highly leveraged corporations—the subprime borrowers of the corporate world. Corporate loans, no less than CDOs, were employed to juice profitability. Essentially, the bank used borrowed capital to manufacture loans, earn a fee, and collect a spread. It blithely assumed that the corporate borrowers would be able to service their debts—presumably, because Citi did not foresee a recession. To leverage its capital further, Citi spirited some of riskier assets off the balance sheet into obscure SIVs.

Regulators were watching Citi, which was the biggest bank under the purview of the New York Fed. Tim Geithner, the New York Fed's boyish, forty-five-year-old president, commissioned a review of the biggest banks' abilities to handle stress and concluded that banks were not taking into account the possibility of a nightmare scenario such as a severe economic downturn. Officials suggested more stress testing—how, say, would banks fare in a credit crisis?—but industry executives sloughed it off as remote, even implausible. The questions to Citi were a bit more pointed, the concern more acute, because Citi's capital cushion was thinner than that of others. Geithner continued to prod, but stopped short of taking remedial action.[7]

Even as Citi was adding CDOs, the housing market was weakening. In certain cities—Boston and San Diego in the fall of '05, San Francisco in May of '06—housing prices had peaked. With prices starting to fall, homeowners had less equity. Nationwide, one-third of borrowers who had gotten adjustable mortgages in 2005 entered the next year with zero or negative equity in their homes—an alarming figure, for if home prices were to cool further, many more homeowners would find themselves underwater.[8] On a national basis, prices kept rising, but the increase from April to June of '06, less than 1 percent, was the smallest of any quarter during the boom. Also, inventories of newly built homes were rising and prices of newly built homes were actually falling—a dark omen for the overall market.[9]

Clouds were also gathering on the financial horizon. Investors' appetite for mortgage securities appeared to be cooling.[10] And the Fed, long the ally of mortgage investors, was beginning to change direction. Having finally realized the need to reverse its cheap-money policy, the central bank was raising interest rates, gradually but inexorably. In the spring of 2006, it jacked the Fed funds rate to a restrictive 5 percent. Effectively, Ben Bernanke was pricking the bubble.

At Golden West, the Sandlers' West Coast mortgage emporium, the volume of loan applications took a worrisome dip. At the same time, Golden West was coming under pressure from banking regulators who had belatedly concluded that option ARMs were "untested" under conditions of stress. Although the regulators, moving slowly as usual, had issued only nonmandatory "guidance," they were pushing lenders to evaluate option ARMs on the basis of whether the borrowers could afford the eventual monthly payments and not just the teaser rate.[11] Such pressure would be expected to lead to a slackening in loans—and a concomitant slowdown in housing, perhaps even a contraction. It was, in short, a moment to retrench.

Instead, the banks—the Wall Street and big commercial banks in particular—opted to redouble their investment. Next to take the plunge was Wachovia, a banking behemoth headquartered in Charlotte, North Carolina. Wachovia had been formed in 2001 from the merger of two old Carolina banks, Wachovia National (banker to R. J. Reynolds Tobacco) and Union National (later First Union).[12] Since then, Wachovia had grown into a national institution by acquiring banks and financial service companies in a succession of new territories. This was a quick and seemingly easy way to expand—but one that carried substantial risk. For what is it that the purchaser of a bank acquires? The visible assets consist of Greek Revival–style buildings and brass-lined vaults. Perhaps, too, there is a worthy franchise, an esteemed name. But essentially, the buyer is acquiring a source of funding (deposits) and, of course, loans. It is extremely difficult for an outsider to assess the quality of a bank's lending operation, and in a market permeated by overly permissive lending, acquisitions are especially risky.

Most of the scores of mergers Wachovia had executed had been successful. Still, it had made slips. In 1998, it purchased the Money Store, one of the original subprime lenders; two years later, amid heavy losses, the unit was closed. Moreover, it had to keep making bigger acquisitions to maintain its growth rate. The banking industry as a whole grows only 1.5 times as fast as the GDP (say, about 5 percent a year). Since Wachovia's growth rate had been in double digits, it was clearly destined to slow down. Nonetheless, its CEO, a native North Carolinian named G. Kennedy "Ken" Thompson, was publicly committed to maintaining its growth. Acquisitions were the only route.

In the spring of 2006, Lehman Brothers suggested that Wachovia might want to acquire one of its clients. The client was Golden West. Wachovia knew all about Golden West's option ARM business. It also was aware that the subprime market could be at a peak. And Thompson, the CEO, had not forgotten his dreadful experience with the Money Store.

But California was the prize that had eluded him. And the Sandlers, one heard everywhere, were such good bankers, so highly regarded. Knowing that Golden West had hung onto its loans rather than securitize them, Thompson could not believe that it had not exercised proper care in their issuance. According to Golden West, its customers had sizable equity in their homes. The calculation of that equity, of course, depended on the accuracy of appraisal values, but to Thompson, that was a detail.

Wachovia and Golden West hastily agreed to a deal. In May, just before the merger closed, Thompson presided at the Wachovia Championship, a golf tournament in Charlotte. Waiting at the eighteenth green to present the winner's trophy, Thompson exclaimed, with a flash of insight, "I have to go to California to close this deal. This will either cement my reputation or get me fired."

A similar desperation had seized Merrill Lynch. Stan O'Neal, the CEO, was one of the more inspiring stories of American business. Perhaps, having overcome long odds, he couldn't bear to fall behind the pack, even as it plunged into subprime mortgages. And doubtless, he believed that he was smart enough to get out in time. The son of a farmer and the grandson of a freed slave, O'Neal grew up in Wedowee, a town of eight hundred people in northeastern Alabama. As a child, he occasionally picked cotton, but he preferred to spend his time reading.[13] When O'Neal was twelve years old, the family moved to Atlanta, where his father became an assembly line worker at General Motors. Stan attended a newly integrated high school, where racial incidents were frequent. As a senior, he applied to the GM Institute (now Kettering University), in Flint, Michigan, and was accepted on a work-study scholarship. He graduated and became a foreman on the 4 P.M. to midnight shift at a GM plant in Georgia. After two years, he was accepted to Harvard Business School, where GM gave him a merit scholarship, and where he received stellar grades. After getting his MBA, O'Neal returned to GM, working in the treasury department. In 1986 he joined Merrill, and by the early '90s he was running its leveraged finance unit. O'Neal was exceptionally smart and coolly—at times brutally— ambitious. He excelled in business lines such as junk bonds, demonstrating his tolerance for risk, and was a perceptive critic of Merrill's failings, pointing out how it could cut costs. He became CEO in 2003, accelerating his ascent by forcing the early departure of his predecessor and former mentor. Even after he reached the top, there remained in the tall, graying O'Neal something of the perpetual outsider. Subordinates found him remote, difficult, and intimidating. He squeezed out potential rivals and kept a small circle of confidants. He frequently left the office to play golf, often not as a social or professional outing but by himself.

O'Neal was obsessed with Goldman's success (underlings preferred not to be near him when Goldman released its earnings). He was forever pushing Merrill to emulate Goldman and its nonpareil traders, but this was not so easily accomplished. More realistically, O'Neal set out to emulate Lehman by building a mortgage operation. Earlier in the decade, Merrill had studiously, and carefully, avoided buying a subprime originator. By 2006, though, O'Neal could no longer resist, and doggedly pursued an acquisition. Even amid worries that the housing market was peaking, he repeatedly demanded of lieutenants, "Why haven't we bought a mortgage originator?"

In the spring of '06, Pete Kelly, a Merrill senior vice president, was dispatched to Irvine, California, to explore an acquisition of New Century Mortgage, a high-flying subprime firm.[14] Kelly was dubious. Subprime was a dirty business, and Kelly, a lawyer who was responsible for Merrill's operating businesses, didn't think a white-shoe firm like his should put itself in a position of having to foreclose on people's homes. A broad-shouldered native of the Bronx with a distinctly Irish-looking mien, Kelly felt his suspicions growing when he arrived at New Century's laid-back suburban offices. After meeting the CEO, Kelly asked to see the executive parking lot—a sly way of checking on the firm's culture. A moment later, he was staring at a row of Maseratis and Porsches.

Next, Kelly sat down with New Century's three top executives. "Let me ask you," he said congenially, "what keeps you guys awake at night?" All three responded that they slept like babies. This was not what Kelly wanted to hear from the officers of an eleven-year-old firm that specialized in no-money-down loans. Prudent bankers worry about everything—and they do not, at least not before the business has been tested, drive Maseratis. Kelly thought New Century would not outlive the next downturn, whenever it came. Subverting O'Neal's wishes, Kelly found a way to derail the deal.

Meanwhile, Merrill's production of CDOs was soaring. This was thanks in part to Christopher Ricciardi, a thirty-something innovator in building and bundling these complex securities.[15] Though a clever designer, Ricciardi's true gift was his talent for working clients. He peddled CDOs at exclusive redoubts such as the Sleepy Hollow Country Club in Westchester County, and the oak-paneled rooms of the Harvard Club in New York. He sold CDOs to a pair of hedge funds run by Bear Stearns and to global investors in Australia, Singapore, and Europe. Always, he stressed that CDOs paid a higher yield than similarly rated corporate bonds. Meanwhile, Ricciardi leaned on Moody's and on the other credit agencies to make sure the ratings were generous.

To Ricciardi, CDOs were more than a security; they were a calling—like subprime loans for Mozilo. Ricciardi once urged a group of salesmen to peddle CDOs with the exhortation, "These are the trades that make people famous!" He was a familiar Wall Street type, brilliant in his grasp of the latest financial exotica yet so smitten that he promoted it without regard to the underlying economics. In 2002, the year before Ricciardi joined Merrill, the firm underwrote $2 billion worth of CDOs. By 2005, the total had jumped to $35 billion—making it Wall Street's top producer.[16]

Jeff Kronthal, who oversaw Merrill's mortgage business, came under intense pressure to retain the senior-most slices of CDOs in Merrill's own account. Kronthal refused. Having cut his teeth in mortgage securities in the 1980s with Lew Ranieri, one of the pioneers in the industry, Kronthal had his doubts about subprime. Thanks largely to him, Merrill owned no more than a few billion dollars' worth of subprime-backed CDOs. Kronthal was also battling to keep Merrill from buying a subprime originator. Those efforts were cut short in July, when Kronthal was fired.

In September, O'Neal got his wish: Merrill bought First Franklin, a West Coast subprime issuer. It also bought stakes in a series of smaller subprime firms. Like Lehman, Merrill could now supply its own pipeline. And Merrill continued to mint CDOs at a record clip. In 2006, it underwrote $54 billion worth. Of those, $44 billion were backed by subprime mortgages—a threefold leap from the previous year.[17] However, as investors were becoming sated, Merrill could find few buyers. Therefore, most of its CDOs went into "inventory," which is to say, Merrill kept them. Incredibly, as its balance sheet ballooned with billions of potentially toxic securities, O'Neal and his immediate underlings remained unaware. O'Neal's policy was to review any single commitment of over $500 million. He regularly reviewed big loans to corporations, but bundles of mortgages, seemingly generic and triple-A rated, passed under his radar.

The head of Merrill's bond department assumed that its CDO portfolio was simply held for a trade—that it could unload securities when the market strengthened. In the meantime, he saw no reason not to keep minting CDOs. And O'Neal was increasingly withdrawn. Moody and restless, he was thinking about selling the company and spent, according to the estimate of a colleague, one hundred days that year on the links. One aspect of management to which he should have paid more attention was compensation. Wittingly or not, O'Neal managed an incentive system that rewarded the troops for gambling the franchise. Traders' bonuses were paid at year-end, but the "profits" on which the bonuses were based derived from trades whose true profitability would not be known for many years. In 2006, Merrill's bonus pool amounted to more than $5 billion—two-thirds as much as the firm's net income—and traders knew that regardless of what happened to its CDOs, those bonuses were for keeps.

Although CEO compensation drew the bigger headlines, in terms of the effect on risk-taking, compensation was more harmful *beneath* the level of senior management, which is where the bets were placed. Merrill employees referred to $1 million as a "buck," and in 2006, more than one hundred of them took at least a buck home with them. At Goldman, more than fifty employees—all of them, no doubt, expert in the art of slicing and dicing securities, trading bonds, merging companies, rejiggering capital structures and otherwise shuffling paper— earned more than $20 million each.[18] Such astonishing sums were the result not just of the mortgage bubble but of a steadily increasing disconnect on Wall Street between risk and reward. Inflation in banking compensation was aided, too, by gradually declining interest rates, which widened profit margins. As investment banks grew wealthier, their employees grew proportionately richer.

Bankers had always been well-compensated, but before the 1980s, they had no special call on privilege—no rank above surgeons, top-paid lawyers, or corporate executives. They were among the ruling class, but did not, in themselves, comprise it. One investment manager who attended an exclusive school in Manhattan during the 1970s recalled a diverse collection of parents—professionals and business people with only a single banker-father among them. By the '00s, that had changed.

Bankers (with their offshoots in hedge funds and private equity funds) were pervasive in the ranks of philanthropic and private school boards; they were kingpins of political campaigns and were politicians themselves, with the more prominent of their number having put their vast wealth toward winning the mayoralty of New York and the governorship of New Jersey.

Compensation was most inflated at the top. CEOs generally received more of their pay in stock, but enough was in cash (or in soon-to-vest shares) that their incentives were also biased toward maximizing short-term "profits." O'Neal, in 2006, received $48 million, much of it thanks to Merrill's lofty revenues in CDOs. It is unlikely that O'Neal consciously put Merrill at risk, for he had more to lose—his expected future salary, his reputation, and probably his career—if Merrill went down. But his eight-figure swag established a destructive example for the troops. It dulled his sense of urgency—the fear of failure that drives a manager to worry about the downside.

Bankers who took home these enormous paychecks were crafty financiers, but their cleverness served their personal interests first, their clients and shareholders second, and the economy barely at all. The bankers learned to fool the system: to game the rating agencies, to bundle deadbeat mortgages into paper that was triple A and foist it on trusting clients. They fooled their compensation committees and they fooled society, collecting astronomical pay for products (such as synthetic CDOs) that made only bankers richer. In the meantime, they led gilded lives; they shuttled in private jets, they nested in baronial mansions and weekend country homes. Their pay engendered a false sense of entitlement and invincibility. Ultimately, the bankers fooled themselves. If their personal fortunes were guaranteed, how could the fate of their institutions be otherwise? In 2006, Ken Thompson earned $18 million for his handiwork in acquiring Golden West; Daniel Mudd netted $15 million from Fannie Mae; Angelo Mozilo, $43 million at Countrywide; John Mack, $41 million at Morgan Stanley; Lloyd Blankfein, $55 million at Goldman; Richard Fuld, $28 million at Lehman; and James Cayne, $40 million at Bear Stearns.[19] Such sums reflected a suave self-assurance and remunerated arrogance. Their profits were at a record, their status exalted, their corporate palaces bedecked in Asian rubbings and polished wood. How could the banks' foundations be anything but solid?

In fact, their profits were dependent on their billowing leverage. Lehman was levered 26 to 1 (that is, it was using $26 of borrowed capital for each $1 of its own). At Bear Stearns, leverage was 29; at Morgan Stanley, 32.[20] The bankers were almost unaware of these numbers. They didn't keep close tabs on their leverage; they simply took what credit was available. Consciously or not, they were pursuing a strategy (endorsed by the SEC) of using a dollar of their own money and roughly twenty-nine dollars of other peoples' and wagering it on a truly manic market. And the money they borrowed was increasingly short term.

Commercial banks were scarcely any better. The share of their assets exposed to real estate had vaulted from a historic level of 15 percent to more than 50 percent. Yet even as their loans grew riskier, they were reserving less for future charges.[21] And their funding was shakier, because banks were relying less on ordinary depositors, who were relatively stable, and more on potentially volatile credit markets.[22] UBS, the giant Swiss holding company, was emblematic of the banks' late-cycle desperation. Early in 2006 it began to acquire tens of billions of dollars of CDOs, with its managers looking no further than the credit rating and the price history of the asset (as though yesterday's price would guarantee tomorrow's sale). Incredibly, its managers—raking in their skewed rewards—did not even distinguish between first-order mortgage bonds and second-order CDOs. They continued to commit billions even as the market chilled, believing that prices would inevitably recover. CDOs were "always treated as trading book," according to a report on UBS's eventual losses written after the fact. Liquidity was simply assumed.[23]

By mid- to late '06, various observers were becoming alarmed about the stability of the banking system. Stephanie Pomboy, a consultant and maverick newsletter writer, opined that the industry "looks remarkably similar to the run-up to the S&L crisis. Just as then, banks have record exposure to an asset bubble." Mark Zandi, the Moody's economist, said publicly that pressures in the subprime market (which the ratings division of his company had enabled) could precipitate "a global financial event."[24]

Angelo Mozilo was also alarmed, as his confidential e-mails showed.[25] In March '06, he alerted Countrywide's head of mortgage banking that their popular 100 percent mortgages (no down payments) were "the most dangerous product in existence . . . there can be nothing more toxic." In April, Mozilo stated in another e-mail, "It is just a matter of time" before Countrywide suffered "much higher delinquencies" on option ARM loans.

Such admissions were private, of course; in public, Mozilo remained implacably bullish. At an investor forum in September, Mozilo upheld Countywide as a "role model to others in terms of responsible lending." Soon after, with Countrywide shares above $40, Mozilo cynically stepped up his sales of the company stock.

Though the public had no access to Mozilo's alarums, the evidence of a developing disaster in real estate was plain. Delinquency rates on subprime mortgages had notched up sharply, to 7¾ percent, by the fourth quarter of 2006. Tougher mortgage rules were finally a fact, though the market tightening probably did more to close off credit than Washington did. The default rate was soaring in former boom towns such as Las Vegas, and it was highest on the most recent vintage of mortgages, when standards had been the most lax. By October, 3 percent of subprime mortgages written earlier that year were *already* delinquent. Buyers were halting payments within months of closing loans (or never paying at all). Zandi correctly suspected that many had lied about intending to move in and, with the market turning, abandoned their speculations.[26] Nationwide, in the third quarter, real estate prices fell—the first such drop in thirteen years. Knowing full well that if the trend continued, millions of homeowners faced the prospect of negative equity, a CDO analyst at Standard & Poor's—which, of course, had been affixing triple-A ratings to mortgage securities—blithely e-mailed his colleagues, "Let's hope we are all wealthy and retired by the time this house of cards falters."[27]

Yet even as banks reported sharply higher totals of past-due loans and restructured loans, they were pouring capital into risky assets—real estate and, in no small measure, highly leveraged corporate loans.[28] Lehman, pushing its commercial property franchise, lent more than $2 billion to a land developer in California. It was too speculative to entice investors, so Lehman kept the loans for itself. Similarly, Wachovia and Merrill Lynch financed the sale of Stuyvesant Town, a multibillion-dollar apartment complex in Manhattan.[29] Once these banks had played the part of middlemen, but now they acted as principals, committing large sums to pricey deals in a speculative market. On the residential side, a similar ethos prevailed: galloping commitments even as default rates ticked higher. Over the summer, Morgan Stanley bought a mortgage servicer to expand in what it euphemistically referred to as the "non-prime" market.[30] Fannie Mae convened a strategy session for its senior managers, off-site in Cambridge, Massachusetts, where the executives could loosen their collars and stretch their horizons. The result was a ringing decision, as the firm chronicled, to "say 'yes' to our customers by increasing purchases of sub-prime and Alt-A loans." The strategy, or at least its execution, shortly provoked a wounded cry from Fannie's risk officer, who complained to Mudd, the CEO, that Fannie was ignoring its control process.[31] What it really was ignoring was the worsening economics in the housing and lending markets. It was using good money to chase bad. Such trends presented what Karl Marx might have called a capitalist contradiction. The question was: When would someone other than a gadfly or a risk manager notice? In October, somebody did.

William King, who had built the portfolio of subprime securities at JPMorgan Chase, was in Rwanda when the red flag went up. King was there on a philanthropic mission to help rebuild the local coffee industry, which had been devastated during the country's genocidal war. At his hotel, he got a call from his assistant in New York, who said, "Jamie's looking for you." Jamie was Jamie Dimon, the JPMorgan Chase CEO. King did not think he had called to discuss the coffee business.

Though only fifty and still boyish, Dimon was arguably the country's most powerful banker. He had been famous first as an understudy to Sandy Weill, the two of them building a brokerage juggernaut that eventually merged with Citigroup and placed them at the pinnacle of Wall Street. When Dimon grew restless, even intemperate, Weill fired him. The second act of Dimon's career seemed almost fated. He was hired to run a large but ailing bank in Chicago, delivered strong returns, merged with an also-weakened JPMorgan, and was installed as CEO of the country's most storied bank. Though more authoritative than during his years as Weill's protégé, Dimon remained youthful, intense, informal, and relentlessly focused on risk. In 1998, when loans to Russia were the rage on Wall Street, Weill and Dimon, fearing that Russia was overextended, had ordered their traders to sell. Months later, Russia defaulted.[32]

Similar credit worries prompted Dimon to call King. Not only were subprime defaults rising but, Morgan's analysts noticed, people who were current on their credit card debts and auto loans nonetheless were defaulting on their mortgages. That was not supposed to happen. It looked as though people were *voluntarily* defaulting—perhaps because the equity in their homes was negative. If that was the case, there was no telling how high defaults could go. Dimon told King to sell or hedge whatever he could. Meanwhile, Morgan froze the accounts of a client, a subprime lender called Ownit Mortgage Solutions. In November, Ownit defaulted. Weeks later it shut down.

Similar flags were being hoisted all over. In December, Goldman lost money in mortgage securities for ten days running, and though the amount it lost wasn't great, this kind of rough patch was unusual. David Viniar and Gary Cohn, the firm's chief financial officer and chief operating officer, received a profit-and-loss report from every Goldman business every day; after two weeks of losses they had seen enough. At the same time, issuance of corporate junk bonds was falling fast, suggesting a general retreat from risky credits. Viniar, the heads of

Goldman's mortgage business, and various of its financial operatives, about twenty bankers in all, were summoned to a top-level powwow. The consensus was that mortgage values would get worse before they got better. The Goldman execs decided to get "closer to home," meaning to pare back their position in CDOs and other mortgage bonds. The firm immediately began to sell.[33]

Lehman also heard the warnings. Late in the year, one of the firm's senior bankers told Fuld it was time to cut back on risk. Though profits were booming, he pointed out, much of Lehman's success had stemmed from rising asset prices: it would be foolish to bet on such trends in the future. Fuld did not appreciate the advice—it suggested that luck, rather than Fuld's leadership, had been responsible for Lehman's success—and so he ignored it. Wachovia was similarly cavalier. Trying to reignite its new Golden West unit, it began to push option loans with monthly payments based on interest rates of 1 percent, a desperate attempt to spur volume by lowering rates to the floor.[34] It also integrated Golden West's risky product line into the rest of the bank. The zeal of bankers to pile on risk was both remarkable and reckless.

Mortgage traders would admit to a lull—nothing more—in the glorious securitization pipeline that had stoked so many profits. Citi, UBS, and Merrill continued to add to CDO positions. Employing a metaphor from the roulette table, a Merrill executive admitted, "We were betting on red." By the end of '06, most of Wall Street was in too deep to contemplate an exit. And if such an exit were needed, whence would the capital come? If investors already neck-deep in mortgage securities opted to sell, who was left to buy? Pomboy, the newsletter scribe, could see but one source. "The credit 'stink' has already begun," she wrote in December, just as Fuld was shrugging off his banker's warning. "The Fed will assume a new role—lender of last resort." Envisioning a heightened government role in mortgages, Pomboy issued a snarky prophecy: "We positively cringe in anticipation of the bevy of Homeowners' Assistance, Distressed Debtor, and other programs to come."[35]

ABSENCE OF FEAR

*At this juncture, however, the impact on the broader
economy and financial markets of the problems in the
subprime market seems likely to be contained.*

—BEN BERNANKE, TESTIMONY BEFORE THE
JOINT ECONOMIC COMMISSION,
MARCH 28, 2007

EARLY IN 2007 THERE appeared two annual letters that testified to the continued capacity for denial in American banking. They were published in the annual report of Citigroup—one signed by Chuck Prince, the CEO, the other by the chairman of the executive committee, Robert Rubin. Juxtaposed was a third, and separate, corporate letter, from Jamie Dimon to the shareholders of JPMorgan Chase. Such annual letters are generally exercises in public relations, usually the work of ghostwriters. Nonetheless, they convey a kind of inadvertent truth. Even if by omission, they communicate what the CEO is thinking or, at least, what issues and risks the CEO thinks warrant a presentation to the public.

Dimon's letter, which he wrote himself, focused on the risks in the subprime market and, to a lesser extent, the overall credit environment. He admitted that JPMorgan had been greatly surprised by the steepening pace of subprime defaults. While its underwriting had not been as lax as other banks'—Morgan had never issued option ARMs, for instance—Dimon faulted it for not having been more conservative than it was. And while Morgan had recently sold much of its subprime book, it was by no means insulated if, as he feared, credit markets turned "ugly." In such a case, lending standards would tighten, foreclosures would increase, and home values would suffer. Not least, Morgan's losses could rise considerably—by as much as $5 billion.[1]

Morgan's lawyers advised Dimon to stop there. However, the CEO thought it important to provide specific numbers—"not to worry you," he added, "but to be as transparent as possible about the potential impact of these negative scenarios." Dimon disclosed the percentage of assets that Morgan had charged off, or taken losses on, in 2006 in each of nine lines of business: home equity, subprime, auto finance, and so forth. Next to the charge-offs for '06, there was an estimate of how high losses could rise, in each category, if the environment worsened. These were only projections, of course, and, as Dimon admitted, "We do not yet know the ultimate impact of recent industry excesses." Shareholders, at least, had evidence that the chief executive was analyzing—in granular detail—the potential effects of a serious downturn.

Prince's letter to Citigroup shareholders was rather more upbeat. He focused on the bank's achievements for the year—adding ATMs in 7-Eleven stores and, notably, winning an Aaa rating from Moody's. He devoted precisely two sentences to credit markets, which, he forecast without elaboration, would likely suffer "moderate deterioration" in 2007. Presumably to humanize his letter, he described (with considerably more detail) his trip with his wife, Peggy, to Laishui County in China, where the CEO taught a class on credit and Peggy helped paint a school. He did not mention Citi's investment in subprime; he didn't mention subprime at all. Rubin's adjoining letter was even skimpier on detail. He focused on the outlook for the world economy, which he described as being in the midst of "transformative change." Such high-flown phrases abounded. He declared the global economy to be "strong . . . despite serious financial imbalances, geopolitical risks, and multiple other issues."[2] However, Rubin did not burden his readers by enumerating what those "issues" might be. Substantively, the letter was weightless.

Patronizing as they were, the Citigroup letters were highly (if unintentionally) revealing. The stewards of America's largest bank waxed optimistic about Citi's prospects, but paid no attention to the individual business lines, much less to the emerging stresses to those businesses. Neither Prince nor Rubin betrayed any awareness of excesses in the mortgage market, or in credit markets broadly. What their correspondences signaled, most of all, was an abject lack of focus on, and perhaps understanding of, the specific risks to the bank.

Clearly, Dimon was the one breaking ranks. Prince's and Rubin's guarded optimism was reflective of the prevailing economic consensus. Even the Federal Reserve, with its 220 staff economists, did not forecast a recession, or even a serious credit storm. The subprime problem was well in view, but generally, that is where the perceived problem stopped. Bernanke testified in February 2007, and again in March, that he did not expect difficulties in housing to spill over to the general economy.[3] Henry M. Paulson, Jr., the garrulous Treasury secretary, did not think so either.

Independently wealthy (his fortune was estimated at $700 million), Paulson was the first Treasury secretary who could hold his own with the neoconservative Cabinet members who had long held purchase on the president's ear. With his bald dome, gold-rimmed spectacles, and forceful style, the former Goldman chief was faintly intimidating, almost reminiscent of the cartoon villain Lex Luthor.

Paulson was sworn in in July 2006. His first guidance to the president, offered at Camp David, was to expect some stress in financial markets—which, he warned, had been preternaturally calm for too long. Paulson had no idea where the stress would occur; he imagined it might be a hedge fund.[4] Almost as if waiting for the storm to burst, he busied himself with an effort to streamline financial regulations and relieve some of the burdens on Wall Street. His decades at Goldman had imbued him with a deep reverence for the ways of the private sector.

However, Paulson was no free-market ideologue. He was appalled by the war (he referred to it as a "jihad") that orthodox Republicans were waging against Fannie Mae and Freddie Mac, and tried to broker a peace. He was headstrong but not self-important. A Christian Scientist, a devoted bird-watcher, and an energetic conservationist, he was, unlike some people who rise to high places, fundamentally decent. (Bernanke was another.) He had been raised on a farm in Illinois, and didn't go in for ski chalets, country club memberships, or expensive cars; instead, he and his wife shared a Prius. Paulson believed reflexively in unrestricted markets, but he had not thought deeply about the alternatives since serving a brief term in the Nixon White House after Harvard Business School. His management style, as befitted a deal maker, was tactical: he responded to provocations. Surprisingly for a CEO, he was not especially articulate. Words escaped him in guttural thrusts, his conclusions bursting forth in unrehearsed eruptions. As a two-hundred-pound tackle on the Dartmouth football team, he had been known as the "Hammer," and his speaking style still recalled his physicality.

Bernanke, by contrast, was a quiet and somewhat awkward professorial type eight years younger than Paulson. He took office in February 2006, shortly before Paulson, and the country greeted him as a welcome change from Greenspan, his overbearing predecessor. Where Greenspan was flashy, Bernanke tended toward a dull monotone. Less a guru than a technician, plainspoken rather than oracular, he might have disappeared beside the formidable Paulson save that he had the considerable advantage of having studied economic policy all his life.[5] Raised in Dillon, South Carolina, an agricultural town where his father was the pharmacist and his family was among the only Jews, he was the sort of boy who learned calculus on his own (it wasn't taught in his high school). He entered Harvard a year after Paulson departed, earned a doctorate from MIT, and won a name as a brilliant and self-effacing scholar. At Princeton, where the economics department was split in two warring factions, Bernanke, on the strength of his collegiality, rose to become the chairman. As Fed chairman, he was similarly democratic, giving fellow governors more of a say in monetary policy. He was cautious and deliberate; he measured his words as though injecting droplets into the river of his reputation. He was too modest to reveal even his elementary tastes to associates. When it was announced that he had been nominated to replace Greenspan, a colleague asked in surprise, "What's Bush doing appointing a Democrat?"

"Actually," Bernanke replied, "I'm a Republican."

Much of his life's study revolved around the Great Depression, its causes and the lessons it might provide. Bernanke was an acolyte of the seminal free-market economist Milton Friedman, and he believed along with Friedman that the Federal Reserve had brought on and then aggravated the Depression, by "pricking the bubble"—that is, tamping down stock market speculation before the crash—and by failing to stimulate the economy once the Depression was under way. In a speech to honor Friedman's ninetieth birthday, Bernanke famously "apologized" on behalf of the Fed, to Friedman and his cowriter Anna Schwartz:

> I would like to say to Milton and Anna: Regarding the Great Depression. You're right, we did it. We're very sorry. But thanks to you, we won't do it again.[6]

What is notable was Bernanke's assumption that the academy now understood perfectly the dynamics of one of the most complex economic eras in American history. Real life is messy and admits to doubt. Bernanke's research was steeped in econometrics, which offers the certainty of computer models.[7] He analyzed the Depression not as a historian grappling with conflicting actors and interpretations but as a social scientist in the lab. He seemed allergic to anecdote; his 2000 book, *Essays on the Great Depression*, contains only a handful of references to President Roosevelt. For Bernanke, the Depression was a monetary event, decoupled from the people who were unemployed or the banks that failed. The breadlines and soup kitchens were merely a response to the policies of the central bank. His was a highly Fed-centric view, in which the institution was capable of creating either disaster or miracle. In one paper, again citing his hero Friedman, he argued that the Fed could revive a moribund economy by dropping, in a figurative sense, bundles of cash from a helicopter. (This earned him the sobriquet "Helicopter Ben.")[8]

Happily, he believed the Fed was fully up to the job. For all his cautious instincts and consensual approach, he saw modern central banking as a realized, accomplished science rather than an evolving craft. Indeed, he chalked up the absence of serious recessions from the mid-'80s to the mid-'oos mainly to the improvement in monetary policy that was his life's work.* He agreed with Greenspan that the Fed was correct in not interfering with bubbles. In his writing, Bernanke often pinned disputative quotation marks around the word, implying doubt that such a thing as a "bubble" even existed.[9] Paulson shared Bernanke's moderately conservative worldview, but as a matter of instinct rather than theory. Though each was the product of a small-town religious family, was happily married and faintly moralistic (Paulson was an Eagle Scout), one was pensive, the other impulsive, one mild-mannered and wry, the other gregarious and impatient. Bernanke had studied the causes of economic crises his entire life, but mostly from the sanctuary of the campus; Paulson was steeped in Wall Street but hadn't pondered it from afar. Despite their contrasting styles, they became a comfortable Potomac pair, breakfasting weekly and talking often. Bernanke focused on big ideas; Paulson pulled the discussions back to policy. Yet Bernanke had greater interest in (and patience for) detail. The Fed chief relied on Paulson to anticipate the market reaction, or the political reaction, to their every move. Each came into office expecting the housing market (or at least the subprime sector) to cool, and each believed that the economy could negotiate a soft landing.

Wall Street was not so sanguine. By 2007, subprime firms were rapidly closing, and investment bankers knew that the trail of mortgage

---

* Bernanke may have been right to credit central bankers, who became better at resisting political interference after the inflationary debacle of the '70s. But other factors also helped to tame the cycle, such as the rise of the service economy (services are less volatile than manufacturing), and expanded world trade, which checked inflation and, thus, the need for monetary tightening.

debts led right to their doors. In February, New Century, the West Coast subprime issuer, revealed worse than expected default numbers and also fessed up to having improperly booked its prior earnings—a sign that subprime was not as healthy as had been believed. Only the previous summer, New Century's executives had boasted to Merrill that they slept like babies. Now the company was on the brink. The cochief of Merrill's markets and banking group assured an increasingly worried Stan O'Neal that their own holdings looked fine. He anticipated a break-even year on mortgages at worst. Such rosy forecasts notwithstanding, trading in mortgage securities was drying up.

In March, the trouble spread to the mother of all originators, Countrywide. Realizing that the window for refinancing was closing, Mozilo's bank abruptly stopped issuing "piggyback" loans. As if to arouse a final orgy of excess, an internal e-mail urged Countrywide loan officers to hurry before the policy changed: "Please get in any deals over 95 LTV [95 percent loan-to-value] today!"[10]

By month's end, New Century was out of business, and so were more than two dozen other subprime lenders. A similar number had been taken over in distress sales.[11] (There were just over two hundred subprime lenders in 2005, the last year that HUD kept track.) An alarmed White House analyst presented charts to administration officials suggesting that housing prices were dangerously inflated and quite possibly headed for a collapse. Home prices had *already* fallen; indeed, they had fallen for three straight quarters. The proportion of subprime mortgages that were at least ninety days past due and in the process of foreclosure, considered "seriously delinquent," had notched up to $8\frac{1}{3}$ percent. Paulson reckoned the market should be near a bottom. Many investors concurred. Through May, an index of mortgage-backed securities was down only 5 percent.[12]

The investing public still took comfort in ratings, and despite rising delinquencies, mortgage securities were still highly rated. Late in March, Fitch, the number-three service behind Moody's and S&P, held a conference call, presumably to soothe the Street's anxieties. Thomas Atteberry, Rodriguez's partner at FPA New Income Fund, listened as

Fitch reiterated that its models forecast smooth sailing for mortgage securities.

To analysts such as Rodriguez, this made no sense. Homeowners were falling behind on payments—even being foreclosed on—barely nine months into their loans. Sooner or later, the missed payments would necessarily have an impact on the bonds sold against them. Moreover, the delinquencies were not limited to subprime borrowers; Alt-A customers and others with good credit scores were defaulting as well.[13] Rodriguez thought the rating agencies were misreading their own data.

Fitch's model assumed that housing prices would rise, as they had during the boom, by an annual percentage in the low-to-mid single digits. During the question-and-answer period, Atteberry asked what would happen to the model if housing prices were, instead, flat. Fitch admitted that their model would start to break down.

"What would happen if housing prices fell by 1 percent or 2 percent?" Atteberry wondered. In that case, Fitch replied, the model would break down completely.

When Atteberry briefed him on the call, Rodriguez was stunned. Fitch was acting as though home price depreciation were impossible; in fact, it was already well under way. "The potential of a breakdown in the rating-agency models has serious implications for various types of financial institutions and debt origination structures," Rodriguez warned in his April shareholder letter. Indeed, the "implications" went far beyond the arcane world of mortgage securities. Rodriguez foresaw rising unemployment and predicted that the Fed would be forced to start lowering interest rates to counter economic distress, "likely around September." Rodriguez, however, wasn't waiting. Having already cleaned the larder of mortgage debts, FPA New Income pared its holdings in the only risk class it had left: junk bonds.[14]

Whatever the rating agencies were saying in public, in private they were acutely worried by the rising tide of delinquencies, which far outstripped their predictions. By the spring, 13 percent of the mortgages in Subprime XYZ (the Moody's-rated pool discussed in chapter 4) were delinquent—a shockingly high number for a bond of such recent vintage. When Moody's made inquiries with the lender, the news was even worse. Some properties lacked sod or landscaping, and keys remained in the mailbox; the buyers had never moved in. The implication was that people had bought homes on spec, and as the housing market turned, they had simply walked away.[15] Mortgage servicers around the country were discovering that these subprime speculators were an ornery bunch. They abandoned homes with taxes owed, resulting in greater losses to the lender. Some trashed homes and ripped out the lighting fixtures. Some defecated on the floor before they left.

In April 2007, Moody's revised the model it used to evaluate subprime mortgages. This belated decision (the model was five years old) was the first acknowledgment that the agencies had been selling pieces of a world that no longer existed. In the past, for example, homeowners who had borrowed substantially less on their first mortgage than the value of their home had been unlikely to default. Thus, the size of a first mortgage was thought to have predictive value. No longer. With the prevalence of piggyback loans, what mattered now was the size of *both* mortgages. Even borrowers with good credit scores were defaulting. There was "a shift in mentality," Moody's realized, coming to the same conclusion as had Rodriguez. Now "people are treating their homes as investment assets."[16] Homeowners who owed more than their homes were worth were indeed abandoning them. And due to inflated appraisals and, in some cases, fraudulent applications, this was becoming common.

As Moody's was undergoing a crash course in the new mortgage math, the subprime crisis claimed its first serious casualty on Wall Street. In 2004, Bear Stearns had set up a hedge fund to appeal to high-net-worth types who wanted, as such types often do, higher-than-market returns. The fund invested in CDOs, procuring much of its portfolio from Christopher Ricciardi at Merrill Lynch. For the next two years, the fund prospered. Results were so good that in August of 2006—the very peak of the housing market—Bear launched a second fund. Combined, the two funds purchased some $20 billion in investments.[17]

What distinguished the Bear funds was, first, they invested almost exclusively in mortgage securities and, second, they did so on margin. In the spring of '07, as the value of its securities began to plummet, the funds' investors demanded their money. Bear responded by freezing redemption requests. In turn, the funds' creditors—JPMorgan Chase, Citigroup, and Merrill Lynch—demanded collateral. (It was a sign of the times that Bear had not prepared for the day when Merrill, which had so eagerly supplied it with CDOs, might insist that it be paid.) Desperate, Bear pledged several billions in an attempted rescue. However, the hedge funds' losses mounted, wiping out their investors' equity (the funds eventually filed for bankruptcy).

Essentially, the funds had lost their entire net worth—approximately $1.5 billion—because the managers had been forced to liquidate. The assets were simply not worth stated value. This was alarming news. Given that most every financial institution in the country had been accumulating the same sorts of assets, the damage was unlikely to be limited to a pair of hedge funds. Since 2000, an estimated $1.8 trillion had been floated in securities backed by subprime mortgages, and investors were starting to realize that the actual value of those securities—the same ones that a year before seemed to have no upper limit—might have no limit on the downside.[18]

As the Bear funds were imploding, J. Christopher Flowers, head of a small and well-capitalized private equity firm that bore his name, paid a visit to Alan Schwartz, Bear's president. Flowers, a former Goldman partner, had a way of popping up at critical junctures on Wall Street. He was unusually bright and a trifle arrogant, a combination that tended to awe his peers as well as potential investors. "We have a bit of advice for you," Flowers told Schwartz. "We think what you need to do is to raise as much equity as you can." No executive wants to sell stock when the stock is off its high, and Bear's had fallen from 170 that January to less than 140. Flowers knew this. However, capital is a funny thing. "You don't *think* you're going to need it," Flowers continued. "But this is a problem that looks like it's not going to go away soon. And if you wait until you need it, you won't be able to get it."[19] Bear dithered.

It had an audited net worth, as well as a stock market value, in the tens of billions of dollars—many multiples of the hedge funds'. It did not occur to Bear that their mortgage assets were similarly suspect, and that—like the unfortunate hedge funds—they would also be vulnerable if forced to sell.

Bear's competitors seemed oblivious as well. A disconnect between top executives and front-line traders served to blunt the Street's understanding. O'Neal, still in the dark about Merrill's mounting CDO position, boasted in a press release in mid-May that Merrill was "performing extremely well."[20] Though prices of mortgage bonds were slipping, Merrill's traders assured O'Neal the quoted prices were "wrong" and would soon snap back.

Lehman was still busily originating mortgages. A few of its managers were becoming concerned, but Fuld was unwilling to intervene while profits were rolling in. Executives who felt otherwise found him utterly inaccessible. The chief was increasingly aloof and short with critics. He spent his time outside the firm, hobnobbing with elite bankers such as Henry Kravis. Within Lehman, he adopted a regal air. For years, Fuld had sided with fellow traders, the backbone of the firm, against the high-caste bankers. Now, grown comfortable in his thirty-first-floor perch, with its sweeping views of the Hudson River, he identified with the bankers and showered them with princely bonuses.* Fuld had tapped an operative with administrative experience, Joseph Gregory, to be Lehman's president, and while Fuld courted clients, Gregory ran the company's day-to-day operations. Though Gregory was a former trader, his main qualification was that he reinforced and shielded Fuld. If Fuld was kinder under the surface than his macho persona suggested, Gregory was the reverse: effusively outgoing yet inwardly power hungry. He did not have a businessperson's sensitivity to risk; the subject appeared not to interest him. Gregory viewed Lehman as a growth machine to be run at full throttle. He ordered an overnight expansion

---

* In *Greed and Glory on Wall Street*, a book about Lehman's last days as a private partnership in the 1980s, Ken Auletta wrote that Fuld "was almost defiantly antisocial toward bankers."

in commodities and bought an investment firm that specialized in selling CDOs in Australia. He pushed to issue more loans to highly leveraged corporations. Not so many years ago, Lehman had been a private
firm that guarded its partners' capital and mainly brokered deals for
clients. Now it deployed its capital while barely seeming to notice.

Gregory and Fuld each viewed dissenters as disloyal. Both were irritated by Michael Gelband, a twenty-four-year veteran who ran the
fixed-income division. Gelband tried to brake the flow of leveraged
loans and also opposed the Australian deal. Gregory told him he needed
to take more risk, but it became clear that the Fuld-Gregory duo
and Gelband had differing visions of the future. In May '07, Gelband
left the firm, depriving Lehman of its most outspoken advocate for
reducing risk.

Bankers within Lehman quickly understood that doubters would be
punished, which helps to explain why there was no internal debate
when, later in May, Lehman bought a half interest in Archstone-Smith
Trust, which owned 360 luxury apartment buildings across the country.
The price was a sky-high $22 billion—more than could be justified
given the rental rates on the apartments. Lehman, acting for a client,
won this dubious prize because it was willing to put up $8 billion or so
of debt and another $2 billion of "temporary" bridge equity until it
could find a permanent investor.[21] This was Lehman's signature tactic
in commercial property transactions—risking capital on the premise
that the market would stay liquid. Mark Walsh, who oversaw these
investments, was a clever financier, and each deal he engineered whet-
ted Fuld & Co.'s appetite for the next. The deals got steadily bigger.
The equity Lehman committed to Archstone amounted to 10 percent
of the capital that the firm had retained in the previous 150 years of its
existence.

With Walsh on a roll, no one within Lehman was of a mind to stop
him. In June, Lehman bought a partial interest in ten office buildings—
notable because the seller was the Blackstone Group, a private equity
firm, which had bought them only the previous fall as part of the most

expensive leveraged buyout ever. When you are buying from a seller who has paid a record price, caution is the watchword, but Walsh immediately struck again, acquiring a portfolio of warehouses valued at $1.85 billion—with Lehman, again, supplying most of the equity.[22]

Lehman's dealmakers did not seem to notice the spate of doleful tidings. The proportion of subprimes that were seriously delinquent rose another point during the second quarter, to 9¼ percent. Home prices continued to slide. Securities markets were starting to register alarm: prices of mortgage-backed bonds fell 7 percent in a month.[23] Things were getting bad.

At the end of June, Rodriguez presented his critique to a broader public, in a speech to the Chartered Financial Analyst Society of Chicago.[24] His address, which he called "Absence of Fear," was intended to sound an alarm to markets and regulators alike. Rodriguez was concerned by the still-high price of financial assets; investors were not being compensated for the tremendous risk inherent in mortgage securities and other bonds—and in the institutions that held them. He was also worried by the seeming lack of concern in Washington. Just a month earlier, also addressing a group in Chicago, Bernanke had commented, "We believe the effect of the troubles in the subprime sector on the broader housing market will likely be limited, and we do not expect significant spillovers from the subprime market to the rest of the economy or to the financial system." A month earlier, Paulson had described subprime as a contained issue, adding, "I don't see [subprime mortgages] imposing a serious problem."[25] Rodriguez, on the other hand, saw that Wall Street was intimately and inextricably involved. America's banks, he pointed out, had invested approximately 10 percent of their assets (an amount far greater than their equity) in CDOs. Even in the first half of 2007, the Street had churned out close to $175 billion of mortgage-type CDOs.[26] Contrary to Bernanke's belief, Rodriguez thought the financial system was up to its neck in subprime. Rodriguez worried, too, about the false sense of security permeating junk bond and private equity markets. But mortgage securities were "leading the way." He ended with a warning to the many who were counting on being able to exit in time: "We believe this liquidity safety net can be withdrawn without any notice."

The very next day, it was. Prices of mortgage bonds fell 3 percent, and throughout July they continued to plummet. An index of mortgage bonds that started the year at 100 was trading at 52 at month's end.[27] Demand for such bonds was suddenly nil; any bank that held mortgage securities now owned them for keeps. The market for securitizing mortgages slammed shut.

At Merrill Lynch's July board meeting, O'Neal asked for a presentation on the firm's exposure to subprime. A pair of senior bankers disclosed that Merrill owned $48 billion worth of CDOs. Whatever he had known, or imagined, before, O'Neal finally heard the truth. In addition to its CDOs, Merrill also owned billions in other subprime credits. Kelly, the lawyer who had balked at the idea of buying New Century, thought to himself, "It's over." O'Neal was stunned. Returning to his office, he asked the staff whether Merrill could hedge its position. The answer: too late. What about selling some of its CDOs? Answer: the market was "backed up." O'Neal, to his credit, knew when a cause was no longer worth fighting for. Through an intermediary, he placed a call to Ken Lewis, the CEO of Bank of America, inquiring whether Lewis would be interested in a merger.

Fannie Mae's board also met that month. Daniel Mudd was more sanguine, and even declared that Fannie could support *more* credit risk. Dallavecchia, the risk manager, angrily protested in a post-meeting e-mail that his budget was being cut even as the risks were mounting. Losing his cool over what he claimed were Fannie's insufficient risk controls, he demanded of the CEO, "Do I look so stupid?"[28]

Lehman had its come-to-Jesus moment later in July. The top executives were gathered at Fuld's sprawling home in Sun Valley for a strategic review. Suddenly, their stock price started to get hit. As the share price slid, the tone at Fuld's darkened. The execs knew they would have to shrink their mortgage unit—what Fuld had been advised and refused to do six months earlier.

One by one, the mortgage kingpins teetered. Over the summer, Moody's downgraded nearly one thousand mortgage securities worth $25 billion. S&P and Fitch did likewise. The downgrades were a bit of a joke, because the market had stopped believing in the ratings; bonds were plummeting regardless of what the agencies said they were worth. But the seizing up of the securitization business had grave implications for the mortgage market. Now that Wall Street was no longer hungry for loans, Main Street bankers had no choice but to tighten their lending criteria. After seven years of easy credit, the window for mortgage money was closing.

Countrywide's report for the second quarter, released in July, disclosed soaring delinquencies. Of its subprime loans, 10 percent were three months in arrears, and a staggering 20 percent were at least one month behind. Ominously, it admitted that it had previously classified as "prime" some loans that the rest of the industry would have regarded as subprime—a possible securities violation. To set matters right, Countrywide had "recalibrated" its underwriting standards—nudging them back toward responsibility. Even if Mozilo did not say so, it was clear that the rating agencies' sudden dose of religion had gotten to him. If Moody's was no longer blessing junk securities, Countrywide could no longer manufacture junk mortgages.[29]

As the market shriveled, American Home Mortgage, the country's tenth biggest lender, announced on August 2 that it was laying off six thousand employees. Four days later it filed for bankruptcy. On August 3, the chief financial officer of Bear Stearns, whose stock was plummeting, said credit markets were tighter than at any time in twenty years. The Dow fell three hundred points, and Jim Cramer, a hedge fund trader turned television personality, went into a rant on CNBC, pleading for an interest-rate cut and screaming that the Fed was asleep. "We have Armageddon. . . . Bernanke is being an academic," Cramer hollered, visibly embarrassing his co-anchor. "He has *no* idea how bad it is out there!"

Four days later, with Bernanke presiding, the Federal Open Market Committee (FOMC) convened a scheduled meeting. Despite the chaos in markets, the members voted to keep the interest rate constant at 5¼ percent. The real debate concerned what to say in its statement. The Fed's recent stance had been that (as is customary when the economy is growing) inflation was the paramount risk. Some members wanted to say that they now considered an economic slowdown to be a bigger potential problem. That would signal that the Fed was worried about the mortgage crisis, and ready to intervene. Bernanke maintained that inflation was still the greater concern, and he prevailed. The committee released a terse statement, acknowledging only that financial markets had been "volatile" and that the housing "correction" was "ongoing"—a modest description of the recent turmoil.[30] What is inarguable is that the Federal Reserve, led by Bernanke, did not see a crisis.

Two days later, on August 9, 2007, France's biggest bank, BNP Paribas, was forced to freeze three investment funds that were holding U.S. mortgage-related CDOs. The bank cited "a complete evaporation of liquidity."[31] With trading in mortgage bonds ground to a halt, European banks were short of cash. The European Central Bank was forced to open the spigot—that is, to lend unlimited funds to continental banks. When Bernanke awoke in the United States, the pleasant illusion that subprime was a contained problem had vanished. The Fed chief canceled plans for a vacation to Myrtle Beach, South Carolina, and huddled with advisers in Washington and New York. At age fifty-three, he was finally confronting a financial implosion of the sort he had so often written about.

Bernanke, who did not have hands-on market experience, sought a quick tutorial from two Fed officials who did: Kevin Warsh, a governor of the Federal Reserve, and William Dudley, the New York markets chief. He also counseled with Donald Kohn, the Fed's vice-chairman and a thirty-two-year veteran of the central bank. However, Bernanke's principal agent on Wall Street was Geithner, the New York Fed president. Geithner blended sharp wits with conventional instincts. He was raised largely in Japan, and followed his father, who worked for the U.S. Agency for International Development and the Ford Foundation, to

Dartmouth. He married a classmate and opted for a career in public service, in which he progressed rapidly.[32] After various lower-level posts at Treasury, he was picked by Larry Summers, then undersecretary for international affairs, to be his special assistant, which sparked his career. By 2007, Geithner had lived through several cross-border financial crises. This time as well, stocks were plunging on both sides of the Atlantic. In the United States, although the Fed funds rate was officially 5¼ percent, banks were paying as much as 6 percent for overnight money. This was a sign that banks were refusing to lend to banks—a signal feature of a depression. The New York Fed injected $38 billion in loans into the markets, while in Europe, where a similar panic raged, the ECB patched in even greater amounts.

The specter of American, French, and, now, German banks reporting subprime problems terrorized the market. Mortgage assets simply stopped trading. Secretary Paulson called O'Neal to solicit his view of the crisis, and the Merrill chief said darkly, "I'm taken aback. Secured lending between banks has failed." O'Neal thought markets were eerily still; they reminded him of being on a sailboat on Lake Michigan when the wind went flat. His Wall Street peers—champions of free markets all—suddenly were demanding help from Washington. The government *had* to do something. A week into the crisis, Bernanke did. The FOMC, meeting by telephone, decided to reduce the interest rate at the Fed's "discount window" for lending to banks. It also lengthened the term of such loans. The idea, novel in its particulars, was to make it easier for banks to borrow directly from the Fed, and thus prevent the problems of specific banks from infecting the system.

Later in August, Bernanke convened a war council of Fed colleagues in Jackson Hole, Wyoming, at the foot of the Grand Tetons. Gathered in a conference room upstairs at Jackson Lake Lodge, the assembled bankers agreed they were facing a "liquidity crisis": banks were hoarding their capital rather than lending it.[33] If this condition persisted, consumers and businesses would not get the credit they needed. The officials decided on a two-pronged approach. First, they would begin to lower interest rates in September—exactly when Rodriguez had forecast.

Second, they would become more creative in extending loans to troubled banks. The Fed historically had played the role of lender of last resort to institutions in distress. Bernanke wanted to do more. One thing he *had* learned about the Great Depression, particularly its early years, was that doing nothing didn't work. If there was a fire, Bernanke would be the fireman.

The diagnosis of a "liquidity" problem presumed, of course, that the banks remained solvent. It was a question not of whether they had enough capital but of whether they would lend what they had. A senior banker at JPMorgan was not so sure. Every day a different institution admitted to a problem. Countrywide disclosed that its finances were in jeopardy; then the two top executives of Bear Stearns nervously visited Morgan, almost begging for their support. "It was like watching popcorn," the Morgan banker said. "You didn't know where it would pop next." August set a record for home foreclosures. With each additional foreclosure, not only was a family dispossessed and a neighborhood disrupted, but a pool of bonds would suffer—some CDO nonchalantly acquired by an investment bank would depreciate, and the bank's capital position would fall. What if the problem were not just liquidity? What if the mounting mortgage losses led to mass insolvencies? O'Neal, for one, was worried. The time had come—he abruptly decided—to sell Merrill Lynch.

8

CITI'S TURN

*When the music stops, in terms of liquidity, things
will be complicated. But as long as the music is
playing, you've got to get up and dance. We're still
dancing.*

— CHUCK PRINCE, CEO OF CITIGROUP,
INTERVIEWED IN THE *Financial Times*,
JULY 2007

S TAN O'NEAL HAD one eager suitor. Ken Lewis, the chief executive of
Bank of America, had been interested in acquiring Merrill Lynch
for years. Bank of America lacked a premier Wall Street brand, and
Lewis, like O'Neal a Southerner and something of an outsider among
the financial elite, dearly wanted entrée into the club. Merrill's investment bank would complement Bank of America's retail and commercial bank, and the prospect of a merger plainly excited him. O'Neal was
motivated by the same synergies, and by opportunism as well. Fate
having dealt him a balance sheet laden with CDOs, he was—at the
right price—a willing seller.

After meeting Lewis in August 2007, O'Neal thought he could get
as much as ninety a share in a merger—twenty points above Merrill's
current stock price. But he would need to sell the deal to his board.
This could prove problematic. Jill Kerr Conway, the longtime senior
director and a former president of Smith College, was an O'Neal ad-

mirer. But Conway had retired from the board the previous April, and the new lead director, Alberto Cribiore, a private equity banker, was considerably more disposed to challenging O'Neal. When O'Neal informed him of his talks with Bank of America, Cribiore replied that Merrill Lynch was an "iconic brand" and that they shouldn't sell it. O'Neal didn't think Merrill's plight was urgent (during August and September, while credit markets were in turmoil, he managed to play twenty rounds of golf). Also, the personal chemistry between him and Lewis had not been easy. For the moment, O'Neal put his merger plans on hold.

During the autumn of '07, the crisis seemed to have abated, giving way to problems that were at least manageable. Bernanke had made good on his intention to lower interest rates, and bankers began to think they would muddle through. The stock market rallied in September, and by early October the Dow reached a new record, just above 14,000. True, the rate of mortgage delinquencies was rising even faster. More than 11 percent of subprime loans were now seriously delinquent—an alarming figure, and up by two percentage points from the spring. Even the delinquency rate among prime loans was rising. Wall Street was still nervous, its optimism tempered by caution. But Main Street was humming—the economy expanding, job totals rising, unemployment down to a meager 4.4 percent. In a sign of the still-optimistic times, the Blackstone Group acquired Hilton Hotels for $26 billion. Like the $7.4 billion leveraged buyout of Chrysler completed in August, it was a confident, almost insouciant, move, a record-setting deal with its success entirely predicated on the economy's remaining strong.

Lehman's Archstone deal, inked the previous spring, was another in the string of optimistic acquisitions. The $22 billion real estate deal was scheduled to close in October but, given the jitters in credit markets, there were rumors Lehman would pull out. Before August, Lehman had been able to borrow freely, at competitive interest rates, in every market. Now it was less able to pledge assets—in particular, mortgages— for financing. Fuld's lieutenants were carefully watching the company's cash levels. Over a period of months, they also closed the firm's subprime unit and laid off 2,500 employees involved in mortgages.

Nonetheless, optimism persisted among Lehman's ebullient property bankers. They argued that since rental apartments were distinct from owner-occupied homes, Archstone's rental units would be shielded from the mortgage fallout.[1] Fuld gave his OK to Archstone; the deal caused the balance sheet to swell at a delicate moment.

Lehman was also increasing its exposure in residential mortgages. Though subprime was shut down, Lehman continued to issue Alt-A and other mortgage products. Since the securitization market was closed, each new loan went on the balance sheet—a violation of the core Lehman principle that it should stick to the "moving" business, not the "storage" business—that is, not take on assets it could not quickly unload. (A banker said in retrospect of the firm's mortgage pipeline, "We should have turned everything off.") But the pipeline stayed open. Lehman's recklessness was noticed even in Washington. Paulson, who had long respected Fuld, had been following the progress of the Archstone deal. For the first time, he questioned his friend's judgment.[2]

Paulson and Bernanke were each worrying about bigger problems, the so-called systemic issues that could lead to a crisis in banking or funding and even a panic. Neither was sure how one might arise, and predicting such events is nearly impossible. In 1998, the one-two punch of Russia's debt default and the collapse of the hedge fund LTCM had caught markets and ministers by surprise. Yet the following year, when Greenspan had injected liquidity into the market to ease the much ballyhooed fear of a Y2K computer collapse, no crisis manifested.

Still, there is a logic to why crises strike financial markets. Markets function on credit, and when investors become concerned about a cessation of credit, they are liable to panic.* Even a single investor's panic

---

* In the 2007 JPMorgan annual report, Jamie Dimon observed that financial crises had been occurring (roughly) every five to seven years, to wit: the severe recession of 1982, the 1987 stock market crash, the S&L and commercial real estate bust of 1990–'91, the LTCM collapse (1998), the Internet bubble burst (2001) and, now, the mortgage crisis.

can have a bearing on the group. Each investor worries whether the fear will be contagious and naturally considers taking preemptive action (i.e., selling). The two factors, confidence and credit, are mutually reinforcing. Since events affecting borrowers are certain to affect lenders, and since institutions simultaneously borrow and lend with multiple parties, credit results in a complex network in which every financial participant is dependent on the rest. Given that even a single bond issuer may have thousands of lenders, the potential for a chain-reaction panic is clear. Lenders not only fear for the borrower, but for the borrower's borrowers—and for how a panic would affect them all. (Industrial markets, by contrast, are far less interconnected.)

Several issues in the fall of '07 gave Paulson and Bernanke reason to worry about systemic risk. In September, Northern Rock, one of the biggest mortgage banks in England, failed and was forced to avail itself of a government bailout; meanwhile, its depositors rushed to get their money out, reenacting the seminal drama of the Great Depression. "The bank is not short of assets," the BBC pronounced rather optimistically, "but they [the assets] are tied up in loans to homeowners." The same plight that had struck the Bear Stearns hedge funds now had felled a large British bank. Who would be next?

Bernanke told Paulson they should prepare for the day when some sort of intervention might become necessary stateside. Paulson had reinvigorated a body known as the President's Working Group on Financial Markets, basically the top economic officials in the government. By the summer of 2007, when 200,000 homeowners were being foreclosed on every month, the Working Group was focusing on mortgages.

The Working Group's fear was that when ARMs reset, people would not be able to afford the higher interest rate and even more would default. Sheila Bair, chair of the Federal Deposit Insurance Corporation, the agency that insures bank deposits, was the first to suggest a systemic remedy. While the administration was focused on the risk to banks, Bair, a Bush appointee with an independent streak, was concerned about the plight of homeowners. She proposed a freeze on the interest rate applied to adjustable mortgages—a remedy that would help all mortgagors, not just individual borrowers or banks. However, suspending resets would have violated the contractual rights of the banks. That horrified Paulson, for whom contract rights were holy ground. Given the secretary's faith in markets, federal intervention seemed too big a leap. The administration began to talk, instead, about a program by which individual banks could voluntarily forgive debt.

In Paulson's view the key to curing the mortgage industry was restraining Fannie's and Freddie's license, which required finally creating a stronger regulator. Though legislation to do so was perennially in the hopper, the obstacles in Congress were daunting, and Paulson had had little luck. He couldn't get a bill past Barney Frank, the ranking Democrat on the House Financial Services Committee, unless the legislation also created a fund for affordable housing. Paulson didn't like it but reluctantly agreed to Frank's condition.

In the upper chamber, the twins enlisted powerful friends who, even at this late date, saw political gains to be had from championing subprime. Senator Charles Schumer (D-NY) was urging Fannie and Freddie to invest $100 billion in "affordable" loans. Paulson was aghast at the prospect of the twins taking on additional risk. He sent Robert Steel, his former partner at Goldman and now his undersecretary at Treasury and the adviser he trusted most, and David Nason, another Treasury official, to pay Schumer a call and convince him of the need to subdue the twins' appetite for mortgages. The senator greeted them by demanding, "Why can't you do more for low-income Americans?" When Steel, who considered himself a pragmatist, explained they were worried about credit quality, Schumer made a show of clasping his hands and accused the officials of being ideologically "handcuffed" to the far right—which the officials found highly insulting. The Treasury could not even get an appointment with Senator Chris Dodd's staffer. Dodd, chairman of the all-important Banking Committee, was a recipient of big contributions from Fannie and Freddie and in any case was busy campaigning in Iowa for the Democratic presidential nomination. Without Dodd's active support, the legislation stalled. Frustrated,

Paulson took matters into his own hands and lobbied the twins to strengthen their balance sheets by raising capital. Each resisted, arguing they had all the capital they needed.

Paulson was at the time preoccupied with a meltdown occurring in structured investment vehicles (SIVs). These ungainly entities, one recalls, had been created by commercial banks to shunt off their least attractive, and least transparent, assets. SIVs were problematic from several standpoints. They were financed almost entirely with debt, making them experiments in (virtually) pure leverage. Indeed, their reason for being was to circumvent capital rules that restricted debt. They were inherently unstable because, while they invested in long-term assets such as CDOs, their own funding was short-term. And they violated the spirit, and perhaps the letter, of disclosure regulations. Though the banks' shareholders were told nothing, there remained a real possibility that if SIVs failed as independent entities, the sponsor banks would have to (re)assume their liabilities.

In the late summer and into the fall of '07, investors realized that the SIVs to which they had lent owned problematic (or inscrutable) mortgages and other assets. The emperor was now unclothed, and SIVs could no longer borrow. As roughly $500 billion—a huge pool—of SIVs existed, and could not survive without credit, a funding crisis developed.

Paulson and Steel dove deep into the mess, hoping to isolate the assets within each SIV that were causing the problem. This proved difficult. A Treasury official likened the disease to mad cow; some portion of each portfolio was contaminated, and it (or the fear of it) spread until, he analogized, "there is no price at which you buy hamburger."[3] Paulson ordered aides to develop an emergency plan, under which the government might buy distressed assets from banks or—a frightfully radical step—invest in them directly. They called it the "break the glass" plan, to be activated only in the most dire crisis.

What exacerbated the problem was that the SIVs had funded themselves by selling short-term IOUs ("commercial paper," in the parlance of Wall Street), often to money market funds. Money funds, regarded as the least risky of investments, were owned by millions of ordinary savers. In other words, financial engineers had contrived to connect safety-minded moms and pops to the mad cow of the financial world—exactly the stuff of which systemic crises are made.

As the value of SIV paper plunged, the money market funds themselves became imperiled. Roughly a dozen of them were on the verge of "breaking the buck"—that is, the net asset value of these funds was about to fall below the par value of $1 that investors had come to assume was guaranteed.

The funds' sponsors were left with little choice: either they made good the losses, or their own investors would lose money and probably sell, creating a liquidity crisis among money funds and possibly an all-out panic. The sponsors of the funds, at least temporarily, averted a panic by contributing capital to paper over the losses (most investors never knew how close they had come to being burned). Some of the sponsors, such as Wachovia, spent hundreds of millions of dollars to shore up their funds.

Although the money funds were for the moment safe, the failure to inform investors, save for in some hard-to-decipher fine print, was a huge failing, of which the SEC was strangely tolerant. With fuller disclosure, Wall Street would have realized a sobering truth: the financial system had dodged a bullet. Had investors realized how narrowly they had averted danger, the market would have forced the Street to rein in risk and start raising capital.

Moreover, rescuing the money funds did not solve the still-festering problem of the SIVs. Paulson tried to orchestrate an industry "super fund"—essentially, a joint rescue by the big commercial banks. In October 2007, the *Wall Street Journal* reported, in rather breathtaking prose, "The new fund is designed to stave off what Citigroup and others see as a threat to the financial markets world-wide."[4] The super fund proved difficult to establish, partly because the assets in question were devilishly complex, but also because Jamie Dimon, the JPMorgan CEO, resisted. Morgan had little exposure to SIVs and little desire to take care of other banks' problems. (In his year-end shareholder letter,

Dimon noted that "SIVs served no business purpose";[5] perhaps he meant no *valid* purpose.) As the SIV mess spread, Morgan's relative strength was proving to be a boon. Customers who preferred to deal with a stronger bank were transferring billions of dollars its way. It became increasingly clear that the super-fund idea was doomed. Thus, the responsibility of cleaning up SIVs fell to the banks that had sponsored them. By far the biggest of these was Citigroup, which at year-end was forced to take $49 billion of SIV assets back onto its balance sheet, and to provide the necessary financing.

When Citi's board met in October, the directors were already anxious about the bank's portfolio of CDOs. Chuck Prince, the chief executive, had been assured by his traders in September that the bank was not exposed to major losses, but recent hits to its mortgage portfolio had left those assurances in tatters. Only the size of its loss was in doubt.[6] At the board meeting, Prince divulged that in addition to the CDOs, Citi was also the country's biggest sponsor of SIVs. His chief financial officer tried to explain to the board the details of SIVs, and how Citi had gotten involved. The directors met him with blank stares. Having failed to prepare, or to properly inform, his board, Prince was now on shaky ground.

When Citi reported sharply falling earnings—off 60 percent—Wall Street awoke to the fact that the bank was facing serious trouble. Yet Prince still showed no sign that he understood the gravity of his situation. During a conference call in mid-October with Wall Street analysts, Michael Mayo of Deutsche Bank boldly called for a change at the top:

> Chuck [Prince] said this was the year of no excuses. You guys
> say the results are disappointing. So what are the repercussions
> at the level of the office of the chairman?

Prince, in seeming denial, insisted that the bank was on track.

> Well, Mike . . . if you look at our results this quarter, no one can
> be happy with the results in our fixed-income business or with

the results that relate to that. But I think if you are able to look at the other parts of our business, if you look at the strategic plan that we are executing on, I think any fair-minded person would say that strategic plan is working.[7]

In another striking display of optimism, Ben Bernanke proclaimed, in a speech in mid-October, that "the banking system is healthy." Bernanke said this at a time when financial firms were showing severe stress (WaMu was the latest to come clean with large provisions for mortgage losses), and mortgage securities, after a period of calm, were plunging again. The rating agencies had also embarked on fresh rounds of downgrades. A distressing pattern had emerged: every apparent respite in the mortgage storm was followed by worse turmoil. In his speech, the Fed chief attempted to resolve a conundrum: Why was the impact of the subprime disaster seemingly so out of proportion to the relatively small number of subprime loans? He concluded that subprime was a "trigger" more than a cause. The subprime collapse, which Bernanke gingerly referred to as "the episode," led investors "to become more uncertain about valuations of a range of complex or opaque structured credit products, not just those backed by subprime mortgages."[8]

Bernanke continued to underestimate the breadth of subprime and related problems, which were surely more than a "trigger." As a macroeconomist, even a brilliant one, he was slow to appreciate the grim tidings that could be gleaned only from microeconomic analysis—that is, by peering under the hood of specific banks, many of which were in decidedly bad repair. Bernanke's solution was to lower interest rates, which he did repeatedly that fall. That addressed "liquidity," but not the fact that bank capital was eroding. Within weeks after Bernanke referred to the banking system as healthy, the investor Rodriguez noted, in an investor letter, that Citigroup had on its balance sheet $135 billion in complex, structured-type securities for which it was difficult, if not impossible, to obtain any precise value. The only calculable value for such assets was what someone could be persuaded to pay for them. And the market for such credits was dead. In October alone, the value of an index of mortgage securities fell 43 percent—a bloodletting almost without parallel in modern markets.[9] Countrywide, ever a leader of trends in subprime, reported its first quarterly loss in twenty-five years.

In the same letter to FPA shareholders, penned in early November, Rodriguez warned that Citigroup's troubles had grave implications for the economy, owing to its "importance to the financial services industry."[10] Bernanke's confidence notwithstanding, Rodriguez did not view the banking system as healthy, nor did he think lower rates would do the trick. Rodriguez had recently moved to a spread on Lake Tahoe, where, from a lakeside deck, he had a view of snowcapped mountains. He was still managing the FPA funds in Los Angeles, but had relocated to Nevada to escape taxes in California (the ruination of the state's government was another of his worries). He was instinctively suspicious of government, and occasionally hyperbolic, but Rodriguez had the rare ability to anticipate how specific economic and financial problems could blossom into broader distress. In the fall of 2007, his principal concern was the credit cycle, which appeared to be held hostage to falling asset prices. No one would lend against assets whose prices were in free fall. Rodriguez had tried to immunize FPA New Income, his bond fund; in contrast to Citi, the fund held no investments in hard-to-value structured credits, and no subprime assets or CDOs.* But quite possibly, no investor—no citizen of any kind, no matter how careful—would escape the collateral damage. Downward-spiraling mortgage securities begat losses for banks; with the erosion of capital they had less capacity to lend. Thus, credit would be constricted. "For several years," Rodriguez warned, "U.S. economic growth has been driven by high credit growth and the development of the structured finance industry." If credit were to shrink, what for the economy then? "Many 'experts' are saying that the worst of the credit crisis is over and that 2008 will be just fine. We disagree!" In Rodriguez's

---

* Ironically, many shareholders were dissatisfied with Rodriguez's conservatism and redeemed their shares. Redemptions were even higher at FPA Capital, the equity fund he managed. Owing to Rodriguez's fears about the financial sector, he had kept more than 40 percent of the fund's assets not in stocks but in cash.

opinion, investors who had purchased securities that had suffered repeated downgrades would not return to those markets soon. And banks
that owned mortgage assets were, in many cases, unable to sell lest
they be forced to own up to losses. In short, potential buyers were
on the sidelines and potential sellers were in hiding. For markets to
work again, "additional pain" must be suffered. Rodriguez predicted at
least twelve to eighteen months more before the "cleansing of toxic
investment securities" was complete.

As the values of their portfolios plummeted, banks were forced to
recognize losses in CDOs and other loans. Merrill wrote off a staggering $8.4 billion—fully 22 percent of the company's net worth.
Meanwhile, O'Neal hastily resumed his efforts to sell the firm. His
earlier talks with Bank of America having been less than satisfying,
O'Neal and a senior Merrill executive felt out Wachovia, also a
Charlotte-based financial titan. Since Wachovia was not a nationally
known brand, O'Neal envisioned that a combined firm might retain
the Merrill name—and perhaps even be headquartered in New York.
Wachovia was receptive. The price, perhaps in the low seventies, would
be lower than what O'Neal had envisioned over the summer, but would
still salvage value for the stockholders.

Merrill's board met a few days later, the last Sunday of October, for
dinner at the St. Regis hotel in Manhattan. A formal meeting would
follow on Monday. O'Neal imagined that the directors would be glad
to hear of his overtures to Wachovia—which would give them, at very
least, a viable alternative to going it alone. The board reacted coolly.
Leaning over the table laden with fancy china, Alberto Cribiore, the
lead director, snapped, "We don't want to move our company to
Charlotte." O'Neal protested that relocating would not be necessary.
Although there was nothing extraordinary about a CEO's feeling out a
merger possibility and reporting the results to the board, Cribiore was
irked that O'Neal, after being warned not to pursue a deal with Bank
of America, had stitched together a second plot. The tension was palpable: an unspoken mistrust permeated the dinner. The directors acidly
questioned why O'Neal was so eager to sell. The chief, standing on

weakened ground, said the current crisis reminded him of the one in '98, a scorching experience in which Merrill had suffered massive losses and been forced to lay off thousands. O'Neal added that merging with a commercial bank would put Merrill on a sounder footing. Banks, he noted, had deposits—a more reliable source of funding. This was a prescient point, but one the board did not appreciate.

The group reconvened Monday in the Merrill boardroom on the thirty-third floor, overlooking the Hudson River. The independent directors had their own counsel, the white-shoe firm of Cravath, Swaine & Moore, specifically to advise it on O'Neal's merger proposal. That should have sent a worrisome signal to the chief. The meeting now acquired the trappings of a trial, with O'Neal in the dock. What undid him were not Merrill's losses or his carelessness in managing the firm, but that the reclusive and diffident banker had, in the directors' view, spurned the board's authority, even if in pursuing a merger that might have salvaged some of the value they had lost. O'Neal was allowed to resign; the larger truth was that the board fired him.

S IMILAR TENSIONS WERE brewing at Citigroup. Two months earlier, it had claimed to be immune to the subprime virus; now it admitted it would have to write down $8 billion to $11 billion in mortgage securities and corporate loans in the fourth quarter—in addition to a $6 billion charge for the third. Meredith Whitney, a Wall Street analyst, issued a blistering report that neutralized Prince's attempts to spin the bad news. Whitney reckoned that the bank would need to raise $30 billion of new capital to return to health.[11] By highlighting the underlying illness—a capital deficit—Whitney provoked a run on the stock. This, the board could not abide. Prince was forced to resign on November 4, five days after O'Neal.

Like O'Neal, Prince would leave with an unthinkable fortune in company stock. O'Neal's package was worth, at the time, $161 million, Prince's about $80 million. The payments sparked a wave of public revulsion. If American capitalism was a supposed meritocracy, vast pay-

offs for failed executives exposed it as a fraud at its uppermost reaches.*
Prince's departure also marked the end of the Sandy Weill era, and of
his vision of the financial "supermarket." The difficulty of managing
such a sprawling empire had outweighed the supposed benefits of
synergy—which had never materialized.

What each of the two firms needed now (aside from capital) was a
more focused organization, and a CEO with a more realistic, more
hands-on assessment of its risks. Robert Rubin, the power on the board
at Citi, made a surprising choice: Vikram Pandit, an Indian-born university professor turned securities executive turned hedge fund operator. Pandit was new to Citigroup and to commercial banking; Prince
had obtained his services earlier that year by purchasing his hedge
fund, for the exorbitant sum of $800 million. Pandit was the brainy type
that appealed to Rubin. He had a daunting intellect (and four degrees
from Columbia University) and was known for giving lucid tutorials on
complex financial topics. But he was awkward in large groups, and it
was uncertain whether the introverted trader could lead a multifaceted
and now deeply wounded organization.

Merrill hired John Thain, a former senior executive at Goldman and
head of the New York Stock Exchange. The tightly wound, fifty-two-
year-old banker was a seemingly inspired choice. He was no stranger
to corporate upheavals, having returned the stock exchange to normalcy
after a furor over the giant pay package of the previous chief, Richard
Grasso. And he had started his career as a mortgage trader. Thain was
politically ambitious and a friend of Senator John McCain, who was
running for president and thinking of Thain as a potential Treasury
secretary. Salvaging Merrill would burnish Thain's chances.

Thain's first move at Merrill was to raise equity by selling stock—a

---

* Technically, O'Neal's payment was not an "exit" package; it was an acceleration of stock already be-
stowed. The board's mistake was not rewarding him for failure, but sorely overpaying him during his
employ. Showing they had learned nothing, the directors gave the new CEO, John Thain, a signing
bonus worth more than $40 million. Prince was overpaid for working *and* for quitting. Upon leaving
Citi, he got $12 million "cash incentive" as well as free office space, secretarial and driver services,
and the taxes thereon, for five years, all worth an estimated $10 million and all in addition to his accu-
mulated stock.

promising step. A number of other Wall Street firms, including Morgan Stanley and Citi, also raised capital in November and December, drawing on Asian and Middle Eastern investors who jumped at the chance to purchase a stake, at depressed prices, in prestigious Wall Street names. Fannie and Freddie, succumbing to Paulson's entreaties, each raised $6 to $7 billion in preferred stock—which they were able to do, the *Wall Street Journal* noted, "because investors assume that the U.S. government would bail them out in a crisis."[12]

AIG was also experiencing mortgage-related agita, though nothing so public as the executive hangings at Citi and Merrill. From late summer on, AIG had been subject to incessant collateral calls from Goldman Sachs. Goldman, a counterparty with AIG on swap trades, was worried that the troubled insurance giant wouldn't be able to make good on its promises to offset losses on CDOs, and it wanted cash up front. As the CDO market slumped, the size of Goldman's demands grew. By November, Merrill Lynch and the France-based bank Société Générale were demanding collateral as well. Though AIG could haggle, contractually it had little choice but to fork over billions of dollars. Joseph Cassano, the aggressive and volatile maestro of AIG's swaps unit, kept assuring the brass that the demands for collateral were merely a temporary response to a weakened market. AIG had insured only the highest-ranking "super senior" level of CDOs, and Cassano insisted that lesser-rated bonds would absorb whatever damage.

But the collateral calls made AIG's auditors nervous, in particular an earnest young employee named Joseph St. Denis. St. Denis had been an auditor since the early 1990s, and had spent years with the enforcement division of the Securities and Exchange Commission. He joined AIG in 2006 and received excellent reviews from Cassano and others.[13] However, over the summer of '07, as mortgage securities plummeted, Cassano became unusually volatile, and his treatment of St. Denis bordered on abusive. In August, St. Denis found errors in the way AIG had accounted for hedging transactions (relating to natural gas, not mortgages). Cassano flew into a rage. "I've bent over backwards for this [expletive deleted] and I still get these [expletive deleted] lists,"

Cassano stormed. When St. Denis heard that AIG had received collateral calls on CDO contracts, he became extremely worried about the potential for a cash drain on AIG's reserves.

Cassano, though he should have elevated St. Denis's concerns, was only interested in hushing them up. He must have sensed that St. Denis would spell trouble for him, because he exploded at him again, concluding his tirade by shouting—whether in accusation or admission—"I have deliberately excluded you from the valuation of the Super Seniors because I was concerned you would pollute the process!" St. Denis resigned the next month.[14]

However, Cassano could not so easily dispose of AIG's board. As the directors read of Merrill's and Citigroup's losses, they naturally wondered whether AIG was in for the same. Cassano frequently attended committee meetings of the directors, in whose company he was, naturally, charming and genteel. He emphasized to the board that, regardless of what was happening to the market value of CDOs, the instruments were safe, and would remain so barring a catastrophic recession. The directors, understanding little about CDOs except what Cassano told them, were reassured. In November, AIG did write down its CDO position—but by a mere $352 million: for AIG, little more than a rounding error.

Unfortunately for Cassano, PricewaterhouseCoopers, AIG's outside auditor, also had questions about how AIG valued its swaps. Using red-letter language for an auditing firm, the auditor informed AIG that it might have a "material weakness" in its risk control process.[15] This was a potentially grave turn. Though the auditor's warning wasn't public—nor did AIG disclose it—investors were now becoming worried, as evidenced by the stock, which had slid from 70 into the mid-50s.

AIG was scheduled to meet with professional investors at the Metropolitan Club in New York, the first week of December, and the company decided to shelve its prior agenda and talk just about CDOs. They drew a crowd of two hundred mostly worried investors. The CEO, Martin Sullivan, and Cassano both spoke with great assurance. "We are confident in our marks and the reasonableness of our valuation methods," Sullivan said. AIG's mathematical models gave him "a very high level of comfort."[16] The executives went into elaborate detail, yet managed to sidestep AIG's biggest concern: regardless of what its models said the CDOs were worth, as long as prices kept falling AIG would be hit with continuing margin calls. As investors had no idea that AIG had received any collateral calls, and certainly had no independent means of assessing its CDO contracts, once again they were reassured.

Not for the first time, there was a feeling on Wall Street that the crisis was, if not quite over with, then at least past its worst. The Street divided naturally between equity professionals and credit analysts. While the latter worried about default risk, stock traders, by nature and trade, were more bullish. In early December they lifted the Dow into the upper 13,000s, within 5 percent of its all-time peak. Why such renewed enthusiasm? Traders believed or hoped that Merrill, perhaps even Citigroup, would prosper under new leadership. As for Lehman Brothers, it had thus far escaped with only a modest write-down. The crisis in money market funds had passed, and Citi and other banks had retrieved some of their orphaned SIV assets—a sign to the hopeful that the market could cure itself.

The trouble, which bond traders saw more clearly, was that banks were not manufacturing fresh credits; they were refusing to lend. The cycle described by Rodriguez—falling securities prices leading to losses and thus lessened capital ratios—was, inexorably, putting a damper on credit. Since the start of 2007, mortgage securities had fallen for nearly three quarters. Yet institutions such as Merrill and Citi still held billions in mortgage assets; they were vulnerable to more markdowns if the mortgage market deteriorated further. And it *was* sinking. In the fourth quarter, 14 percent—one out of seven subprime loans—was seriously delinquent. A year earlier, the rate had been 8 percent. Moreover, the decline in housing prices was accelerating.[17] Economists had worried for years that if housing, the so-called engine of the economy, ever cooled, the average American would suffer. And in December, job creation was nearly stagnant—the first sign that the financial storm was hurting Main Street.*

I N MID-DECEMBER, a week after AIG had dazzled investors, Bernanke cut the Fed funds rate for the third time in as many months. This was a normal response to a slowing economy, but Bernanke also did something unusual. Straining to restore liquidity, he set up currency exchanges with Europe's Central Bank so that foreign banks could lend in dollars. More novel still, Bernanke created a new facility so that banks could bid (via an auction) for credit from the Fed. The details mattered less than the fact that Bernanke was thinking, and acting, creatively to add liquidity to banks. Banks could already borrow from the Fed, at the discount window, but due to the common perception that only distressed banks sought discount loans, few of them did. The new facility was a patent attempt to snap the banks out of their stupor or, as the Fed described it, to alleviate "the strains arising from a generalized reduction in the willingness of sound depositary institutions to lend to one another."[18] (In other words, banks weren't lending to other banks.) Bernanke was now deeply concerned. As he knew from his studies of the Great Depression, if banks didn't lend, money didn't flow and the economy stopped.

By January, the stock market had internalized these anxieties and was falling sharply. On January 22, Bernanke cut the Fed funds rate by an unprecedented three-quarters of a percentage point; a week later, he cut it again. The rate at which banks could borrow overnight was now down to 3 percent. Until the previous September it had been 5.25 percent. Yet neither lower rates nor the Fed's repeated tonics stirred bankers out of their torpor. Banks lacked capital and confidence, and were chary of lending at any rate. Firms were shrinking payrolls; January would show a net loss in jobs. Bernanke had once

---

* A year later, the National Bureau of Economic Research would declare December 2007 the start of the recession.

written that in a crisis he could drop bundles of cash from a helicopter. Now, through the Fed's novel lending programs and repeated rate cuts, he was doing it.

For his part, Paulson was working on his former peers—the heads of the investment banks—to raise capital, always his preferred prescription. The banks' recent losses had depleted their capital, raising their leverage sharply.* The SEC, meanwhile, was monitoring the banks' liquidity, which was also a concern. Some of the banks had alarming totals of debt set to mature within the next year. Jamie Dimon picked up on this theme in his annual letter to JPMorgan Chase stockholders, observing: "Problems occur when there is too much short-term financing funding long-term assets. *There is one financial commandment that cannot be violated:* Do not borrow short to invest long—particularly against illiquid, long-term assets [emphasis added]."[19] This was an apt description of what the banks had been doing.

Dimon's sermon came with a veiled warning. JPMorgan was one of the two banks (Bank of New York was the other) providing intraday collateralized funding to much of Wall Street. In his letter, the CEO intoned, "Bad financial practices, like equity bridges or excessive leverage, are not good for us or, ultimately, for our partners." It sounded as though Morgan were preparing to tighten the credit spigot. This lent urgency to the investment banks' mission of raising capital. Ultimately, as Paulson had been saying, capital is the only inoculation against a crisis. Unlike liquidity, it does not depend on confidence or whim, and it does not disappear overnight.

However, the CEOs were reluctant. Many of them had just sold stock—at higher prices—and to print more shares now would be like cheapening their currencies. They still believed the worst was past.

---

* The figures are striking. As of year-end 2007, Merrill Lynch's leverage (the ratio of total assets to underlying equity) had risen from 22 to 32. Put differently, each $1 of equity was supporting $32 of assets. Over comparable periods, Lehman's leverage rose from 26 to 31, Morgan Stanley's inched up from 32 to 33, Goldman's increased from 23 to 26, and Bear Stearns's rose from 29 to an industry-high 34 (per company filings).

Citigroup and Merrill had each raised an amount equivalent to their recent write-downs. This provided a bulwark—assuming that their capital was not further eroded by new losses. With Merrill's stock sliding into the mid-50s, one investor met with Thain and urged him to sell more, just as a defensive measure. Thain replied that Merrill had all the equity it needed. Bear Stearns raised only a token sum.

The human temptation was to think that each new drop in home prices and mortgage securities was the last. Even Jamie Dimon succumbed to it. In 2006, Dimon would recall a year later, "we thought we focused early on the subprime issue. . . . Even so, we found ourselves having to tighten our underwriting of subprime mortgage loans six times through the end of 2007. (Yes, this means our standards were not tough enough the first five times.)" Even with that experience and awareness, by early 2008 Dimon still believed that a lot, if not all, of the losses had been taken. In fact, JPMorgan was increasing its share in mortgages.[20] Ken Lewis of Bank of America, in a rasher display of optimism, provided a life raft to the desperate Angelo Mozilo, head of Countrywide, whose stock had collapsed to single digits, and which was rumored to be on the verge of bankruptcy. The two agreed to a merger. In Countrywide's portfolio an incredible 27 percent of subprime loans were delinquent; 5½ percent were pending foreclosure.[21]

The hope for recovery in mortgages, Rodriguez observed three weeks into 2008, was that the Fed would come to the rescue.[22] The credit crisis, he noted, was not a function of restrictive monetary policy. It was a function of a credit bubble that had spawned high asset prices. Yet faith in the Fed was so reflexive, the consensus forecast of economists (including those at the Fed) continued to be for growth—slow growth during the first half of 2008 and faster growth thereafter. Rodriguez found such forecasts "totally unbelievable." He did not expect the crisis to ease until housing prices fell to realistic levels and banks rid their balance sheets of excess leverage. Deleveraging meant lending less and investing less; inevitably, the process would choke the economy. He reckoned that "large financial institutions" were sitting

on a knife's edge; some would be gone already had it not been for outside infusions of capital. And more such infusions would be necessary.
Rodriguez put the odds of a recession at "nearly 100 percent."

The investment banks were beginning to look like retailers with
inventories of unsaleable goods. In a perceptive article, which he presented at the annual gathering of financial heavyweights in Davos,
Switzerland, Thomas A. Russo, vice-chairman, chief legal officer, and
intellectual eminence of Lehman Brothers, observed that "bank balance sheets are backing up with assets," a trend, he added, that "significantly reduces banks' capital ratios."[23] Russo, who had a formidable
knowledge of Wall Street, forecast two million home foreclosures over
the next two years and the worst drop in home prices since the Great
Depression.

Russo, whose boss, Richard Fuld, was a celebrity at Davos for having weathered the storm so well, did not mention that one very backed-
up balance sheet belonged to his own firm. Ever since the Archstone
acquisition, Lehman had been furiously trying to sell some of its portfolio of commercial property loans—but as these loans were large, and
each for a distinctive property, it was slow going. Lehman still retained
some $49 billion in commercial assets, and some $32 billion in residential mortgages and securities. Lehman was also stocked with loans
to highly leveraged companies such as Chrysler, and sundry other assets, nearly $800 billion in all; this compared with only $25 billion in
equity.[24]

Yet Lehman entered 2008 feeling, if anything, chipper. It had just
completed a year of record profits. True, its franchise was in real estate
and real estate was suffering a contraction. But, confident the market
would rebound, it was adding more mortgages.[25] Russo believed that
the banks would be bailed out by investors, presumably from overseas,
and by aggressive actions by the Fed.[26] It was the old faith in liquidity,
and Lehman saw no need to taper its risk now. Michael Gelband, the
Lehman banker who had worried about risk, was gone; others who
sensed the firm straying from its mission stayed silent. Joe Gregory,
Lehman's president, seemed to regard the firm's finances as a distrac-

tion from sundry other subjects such as employee diversity, or his newly built, $32 million oceanfront home in the Hamptons. Gregory installed a new chief financial officer, Erin Callan, a tax lawyer turned investment banker, not for her experience in corporate finance but for her supposed prowess in marketing. Gregory acknowledged that promoting the forty-two-year-old Callan was a "leap"[27]—as if managing a $700 billion balance sheet were a sport. With Callan at the helm, Lehman did not sell equity until early February—and then, only $1.9 billion worth. Responsibility for its finances, of course, did not ultimately rest with Callan, nor with the cipher Gregory, but with Lehman's boss, Dick Fuld. More than any other CEO on the Street, Fuld internalized his company's successes and failures. He called it "da firm"—seeing bankers enter a restaurant he would ask "Do you work for da firm?" as if there could only be one. For a long time, this strong sense of identity had helped Lehman to outpunch its weight. But it turned discussions about stock sales into metaphysical debates. For Fuld, selling equity when the stock was at 60—25 percent below where it had been a year earlier—went against his every instinct. The only thing worse would be selling the firm in toto. A friend predicted he would never sell when he should—only when he had to.[28] Fuld had bitterly resisted the sale of Lehman's private partnership in the '80s,[29] and still considered himself the guardian of its independence, no matter how dark the cloud over its real estate assets. When the subject was raised at the end of 2007, he snarled, "As long as I am alive this firm will never be sold. If it *is* sold, after I die," he added, "I will reach back from the grave and prevent it."[30]

9

RUBICON

The Federal Reserve was not founded to bail out Bear Stearns.

—JIM ROGERS

THE WEEK BEFORE Martin Luther King Jr. Day, 2008, Eric Dinallo, New York State's top insurance regulator, got a series of frantic telephone calls. Among the callers were Vikram Pandit, the new Citigroup chief; H. Rodgin Cohen, the dean of Wall Street lawyers; Timothy Geithner at the New York Fed; and Robert Steel, Paulson's undersecretary at Treasury. Dinallo also heard from officials at MBIA and Ambac—a pair of bond insurance companies. Just as Allstate insured homeowners against fires, MBIA protected bondholders against defaults. Historically, such companies had written policies on sewer and water bonds and other municipal issues. In the boom, though, they turned to a seemingly more lucrative trade: underwriting mortgage-backed bonds issued by Wall Street. The thrust of the calls to Dinallo was that the insurers might not be able to pay their claims—the mortgage bust was simply too big—and that the burden of such policies would cause their credit to be downgraded. Banks with sagging fortunes had taken comfort that, at the very least, their *insurers* were triple-A rated. But now, the insurers were facing a crisis as well.

After the holiday weekend, Dinallo gathered the key players, some in his downtown Manhattan office and others by phone. Pandit, who was still learning the ropes, was stunned to hear that Citigroup's insurance did not entitle it to payments as the prices of its CDOs declined. Jay Brown, the former CEO of MBIA,* corrected him. "No—you have insurance on defaults, not on market value." This was a huge distinction. Since CDOs are long-dated instruments, no default was likely to occur soon. Thus, Citi (and every other bank with insurance) would have to wait for years to file claims, at which point the insurers could be out of business. Dinallo urged the banks to negotiate a settlement with their insurers, though it was clear they would have to settle for a fraction of their policies' face values. The upshot was that, from any near-term perspective, their insurance was meaningless.

The Street still had protection in the form of CDS contracts with AIG. But AIG had never reserved for losses. Its models had treated swaps like an all-win, no-loss business—violating every tenet of sound insurance. In February, PricewaterhouseCoopers, its auditor, concluded that AIG suffered from a flaw—a "material weakness"—in the way it valued its CDO positions. The issue was complicated, but in essence, AIG's accounting had reflected what its mathematical models said its swap contracts *should* be worth. It did not account for the fact that AIG's trading partners were marking such assets down and that, in the real world, mortgage-backed securities were sinking like a stone. Subprime securities had collapsed some 75 percent in 2007, and were falling even faster in 2008. AIG's counterparties, led by Goldman, were demanding more cash. Yet to judge from its books, AIG had barely been scathed.[1]

Still, Martin Sullivan, AIG's chief executive, was reluctant to mark the assets down—he knew the resulting loss would devastate the stock, and might also impair AIG's credit rating. Sullivan viewed the auditor's claims as almost on the level of a nuisance, more of an accounting technicality than a substantive concern.

Appropriately, PricewaterhouseCoopers brought its concerns to the board. AIG had several savvy directors who, in fact, had more financial

---

* Brown was reappointed as chief executive the following month.

expertise than Sullivan. The chief of the board's audit committee was Michael Sutton, the former chief accountant of the SEC.* After hearing the auditor's concerns, the directors realized that AIG had to revise its forthcoming earnings report. Sullivan's instinct was to blame the accounting rules, but Sutton told him, "Accounting is not your problem. The *market* is your problem." He meant the collapse in mortgage values should be treated as enduring and real, not as a momentary tremor.

With the support of the directors, PricewaterhouseCoopers forced AIG to revise the values at which swaps were carried on its books. This resulted in a $5.3 billion quarterly loss. At the end of February, when the loss was disclosed, along with the damning finding of "material weakness," the stock surrendered a fifth of its value in two weeks. The board called for the head of Joseph Cassano, the swaps chief, and Sullivan dismissed him.

The board, though, let Cassano keep a $34 million bonus; it also approved a $1 million-a-month consulting contract for him going forward. This was in addition to the $280 million that Cassano had garnered over the previous eight years.[2] That even a well-intentioned board could dole out such plums testified to the moral disconnect that obtained with regard to executive pay. Which of the directors, had he been asked to explain this compensation to the shareholders—or even to one of his own children—would have said Cassano deserved it?[†]

Perhaps worse, Sullivan dared to ask that in calculating his own bonus, the board disregard the impact of AIG's derivative losses. This was rather like a ballplayer asking that the owner consider only his hits, not his outs. The board refused. Sullivan did get a bonus—and, even less defensibly, a lucrative parachute in the event of termination. But now, he wore his crown uneasily. The board members began to ponder the unavoidable question of Sullivan's own responsibility.[3]

---

* The board also included Robert Willumstad, a retired Citigroup president who had lost out to Prince for the top job; Frank Zarb, former chairman of Nasdaq; and Stephen Bollenbach, the retired chairman of Hilton Hotels.
†Unlike Cassano, Joseph St. Denis, the concerned internal auditor, forfeited his bonus when he resigned. On Wall Street, the best intentions are not necessarily the best-rewarded.

With the bond insurers trembling, AIG under strain, the subprime lenders gone, and Wall Street gushing red ink, was there any institution that could rescue the tottering mortgage industry? Hank Paulson, improbably, began to see Fannie Mae and Freddie Mac as saviors, if only because nearly everyone else had quit the game. By the first quarter of 2008, they were handling 80 percent of the mortgages purchased by investors.[4] Though Fannie's and Freddie's balance sheets were larded with a total of $700 billion in subprime and Alt-A mortgages, Paulson hatched a plan for the twins to buy even more mortgage securities.[5] This might, he imagined, revive the market, pep up prices, and bolster the banks that were sagging under the weight of marked-down CDOs. The trouble was that Fannie's and Freddie's books were no better than those of the banks they were meant to rescue. Fannie Mae's leverage was on the order of 110 to 1; Freddie Mac was leveraged 170 to 1.[6] By comparison, Lehman and Bear were pikers.

The Fed was aghast at the Paulson plan. Since the Greenspan era, the Fed had viewed the twins as an exemplar of liberal intentions gone horribly awry, proof that entities endowed with government guarantees will sooner or later take on too much risk. If Bernanke was not as dogmatic as his predecessor, he and his colleagues still thought Fannie's and Freddie's risk levels should be reduced, not raised. Kevin Warsh, Bernanke's fellow on the board of the Fed, vehemently argued the point with Treasury. A former Morgan Stanley technology banker, Warsh had become a Fed governor at thirty-five. He was a lively, charismatic presence in an institution known for gray suits. Warsh thought letting the twins buy more assets could push them over the edge, perhaps trigger a systemic crisis. Along with the New York Fed's Geithner, Warsh wanted to rein in the twins—perhaps even seize them—before they did real damage.

Paulson (unlike the central bankers) was a political appointee, and could not risk such an inflammatory stance, nor did he have the patience for what he regarded as a moralistic, anti-twins crusade.[7] Though in his heart he did not believe the government should be so involved in the housing market, in practice, he felt, the twins had worked in the past and could be part of the solution now. The implicit guarantee had become his best asset. Since investors believed that the Treasury would not allow Fannie and Freddie to fail, the twins could borrow freely, allowing them to tap new funds for mortgage securities. That this would make taxpayers the mortgage industry's silent partner was a point the secretary chose not to emphasize. And though the twins' capital was maxed out, Paulson was determined to coax their regulator into bending the rules. Let Fannie and Freddie rescue the market first, Paulson suggested; then they could raise capital to shore up their own finances.

Characteristic of strong-willed CEOs turned public servants, the secretary had excessive faith in his ability to control events. Simultaneous with his effort to get the twins to buy mortgages, he was working on Congress to create a stronger regulator—still believing that, in some imagined future, they would be put on sounder footing. The House had passed a reform in 2007 but the Senate was stalled, partly because Senator Dodd, whose presidential hopes had ended after a single primary, had alighted on foreclosure relief as a means of political rehabilitation and was eager to make it the centerpiece of the housing bill. For the moment, it was the Paulson plan or nothing.

Working through Steel, Paulson cajoled Fannie and Freddie to sign on to the idea of greatly upping their commitments. The hope was that the twins could raise capital by selling stock faster than they lost it in mortgages. OFHEO, the regulator, grudgingly gave its OK. But the market didn't cooperate. By February 2008, Fannie's stock was in the 30s, down by half from the autumn of '07. Freddie's had suffered a similar hit. At month's end, they reported massive losses, a combined $6 billion, which pummeled their stocks further. Daniel Mudd, the chief executive of Fannie, and his counterpart at Freddie were increasingly powerless—forced to mediate between the demands of Paulson, OFHEO, Congress, and their shareholders.

The regulators' efforts to get Fannie and Freddie to sell stock had an unintended, and counterproductive, effect on their shares. Fearing a deluge of new stock, investors hurried to cash out. On March 4, Bernanke called for a new round of capital raising. Two days later,

Geithner amplified this theme, telling an audience in New York he favored "new equity capital raising" for financial firms at large.[8] This scared Wall Street stiff. From the day before Bernanke's address to the following Monday, March 10, Fannie's stock skidded from 27 to under 20. Other financial stocks were routed as well. Over the first six trading days in March, the twenty largest financial stocks lost $120 billion in value. Lehman plunged from 51 to 43; Merrill Lynch an almost identical 50 to 43.[9]

Worst hit was Bear, the smallest and most leveraged of the major investment banks. Ever since the previous summer, when its hedge funds had blown up, traders had nervously eyed its connection to mortgage securities. Then, its stock had traded at 130; by the end of February 2008, Bear was at 80. Over the next ten days, despite a virtual absence of news, it dropped to 62. Stan O'Neal, licking his wounds in retirement, wrote to Cribiore, the director who had pushed him out, that he could envision a panic in which Bear toppled and other firms would follow.

Bear's longtime chairman and chief executive, James Cayne, had retired from his executive post in January of 2008, after embarrassing reports that he had neglected the firm during crises to play bridge and golf. He was succeeded by Alan Schwartz.[10] But Bear continued to suffer from three, perhaps four, liabilities: it was highly leveraged; it had more than $10 billion in overnight borrowings that had to be replaced every day; many of its assets were mortgage securities of uncertain value; and, finally, Bear was not so much an integrated bank as a collection of brokerage and investment activities squeezed under one roof. The firm's balance sheet showed a net worth of $12 billion, or $92 a share; nonetheless, beginning roughly on Monday, March 10, it was engulfed in rumors that it was suffering a critical shortage of cash.

Bear denied the rumors and at first did not regard them as serious. But the chatter increased, and Schwartz felt compelled to appear on television to affirm that the business was running smoothly. Some of the rumormongers doubtless had a financial interest, having shorted the stock.[11] The role of CNBC in airing unverified gossip was also a factor. By Wednesday afternoon, though, the rumors had proved true: Bear's customers were pulling accounts, its reserves were shrinking. Finally realizing it might need cash in a hurry, that night, Bear called its banker, JPMorgan. Rodgin Cohen, a partner in the prestigious Wall Street law firm Sullivan & Cromwell, took the early shuttle to Washington Thursday and warned Steel at Treasury that Bear faced "real challenges." By day's end, Bear was $1 billion short of cash, a number certain to mushroom as creditors withdrew support on Friday. Incredibly, Bear was in danger of bankruptcy.[12]

Thursday evening, Schwartz desperately reached out to Jamie Dimon, the Morgan chief. Dimon answered the call with irritation; it was his fifty-second birthday, and he and his family were having a quiet dinner at Avra, a Greek restaurant in midtown Manhattan.[13] Schwartz said he needed an emergency loan—possibly as much as $30 billion. Darting outside the restaurant, Dimon said that was more than even JPMorgan could handle—moreover, Dimon noted, he could never authorize such an outlay without his board. Dimon offered to help though. First, he dialed Geithner at the New York Fed and briefed him on Bear's plight. Next, he called Steve Black, cohead of Morgan's investment bank, who functioned as Dimon's partner. Black was vacationing at Cap Juluca, a resort on the Caribbean island of Anguilla; Dimon told him to come home. Hurrying out of his pool clothes, Black fell and cracked a rib. He flew home in excruciating pain.

Meanwhile, Fed officials in Washington conducted an overnight conference call with Geithner in New York and Paulson and Steel at Treasury. It centered on a single question: should they help Bear Stearns? Failure could be grievous for money market funds that had invested in Bear, also for derivative markets. Geithner feared a broader panic, as had occurred during the LTCM meltdown. Warsh, the Fed governor, did not want the federal government in bed with a crippled Wall Street bank. He and Steel leaned against intervention. Chris Cox, head of the SEC, was also opposed, but carried little weight. Bernanke and Paulson were skeptical but noncommittal.

Geithner was closest to Wall Street and he knew that executives at the other Wall Street firms thought it would be catastrophic if Bear failed. The New York Fed was a hybrid institution—created by Congress (like the other regional banks) to implement policy for the Fed, but retaining some aspects of a private institution. Though an arm of the government, the New York Fed operated in close coordination with the for-profit banks that it regulated. Thus, Geithner was a colleague of Ben Bernanke, but Dick Fuld sat on his board. Just as important, Geithner was a career public servant who did not instinctively recoil from the idea of government intervention. His mentor at the Treasury, Robert Rubin, had championed the American bailout of Mexico, and as undersecretary for international affairs in the late 1990s, Geithner himself was a key player in the government's response to the pan-Asian financial crisis. Now he argued that the government had to save Bear Stearns or risk a systemic collapse—exactly what Paulson and Bernanke had been fearing. Since the Treasury couldn't act without Congress's authority, it had to be the Fed.[14]

Early Friday morning, the bankers and the bureaucrats reached a consensus. The New York Fed would loan money to Morgan, which would extend a secured line of credit to Bear. (The Fed did not have authority to lend directly to investment banks. However, Morgan was a conduit; the Fed was the party at risk.) Though the loan seemed to give Bear some breathing space, on Friday the stock plunged from 57 to 30. The Fed made it clear the loan was temporary, and invited take-over bids. Only two firms responded: JPMorgan and J.C. Flowers & Co., the private equity firm that had urged Bear to sell stock the previous summer—advice that Bear had spurned. Flowers's people spent the weekend camped in Bear's offices, poring through its books and smoking Cayne's expensive cigars.[15] They sent out to Brooks Brothers for clean shirts.[*]

Morgan's bankers operated in their accustomed comfort; their offices were across from Bear's, on the other side of 47th Street. But as

---

[*] John Oros, a Flowers executive, would later recount to a business school audience: "This is what Brooks Brothers lives on, investment bankers who don't go home, just sitting in offices getting new shirts."

they reviewed their neighbor's assets, particularly the mortgage portfolio, they grew more and more uneasy. By Sunday, Morgan was on the verge of dropping out.

Though Flowers was willing to bid unassisted, the government thought markets would react better if Bear landed with a well-known brand. Paulson and Geithner implored Dimon to reconsider. Geithner played on the CEO's sense of responsibility and on Morgan's historic role as a savior of Wall Street.[16] Such requests from the central bank are difficult to refuse. But if Dimon were to do the deal, he wanted the government to help. On the speakerphone to Paulson and Geithner, he indicated that—with their assistance—he was willing to offer, perhaps, $4 a share. This for a firm that traded at 62 at the start of the week!

Paulson had a surprising response: The price should be lower.[17] The secretary was hypersensitive to the charge that Washington was helping Bear's shareholders, cushioning the impact of failure and thus dulling the perceived incentive of other banks to monitor their risks. (In the language of economists, policies that weaken such incentives and encourage excessive risk-taking create a "moral hazard"; it was a charge that had often been leveled at Greenspan.) Morgan settled on $2 a share, prompting howls of protest from Bear. Critically, Morgan agreed to provide a backstop—to guarantee Bear's trades—so that Bear could remain in business until the deal closed, and the Fed agreed to finance, and absorb any losses on, $29 billion of Bear's most problematic assets.* Essentially, the taxpayers would cover Jamie Dimon's downside. The deal was announced shortly before 6 p.m. Sunday. For the first time in its ninety-six-year history, the U.S. Federal Reserve had intervened to rescue an investment bank.

Bear's collapse had immediate and worrisome implications for other banks. The Fed shifted its focus to the next weakest firm, Lehman, and ordered it to make a presentation the following week on its liquidity and, presumably, its solvency. Fears for Lehman were widespread. Wes

---

* A month earlier, when asked in public whether JPMorgan might consider acquiring an investment bank, Black had replied, "Over my dead body!" Though it got Bear on the cheap, the impression remains that Morgan's executives were less than thrilled with their purchase.

Edens, a former Lehman partner, strongly urged Fuld to sell the firm. With characteristic confidence, Fuld replied, "We'll be fine."

But in the post-Bear world, bankers were not so sure. And the problem of leverage was not confined to Lehman. Immediately after the Bear rescue, Barry Zubrow, Morgan's chief risk officer, began to rein in Morgan's exposure to other firms. He called David Viniar, Goldman's chief financial officer, and John Thain, the CEO of Merrill. (Zubrow knew each from his days at Goldman.) His message was directed at the whole of Wall Street. He bluntly told them that the business model of investment banks had changed, and they would have to operate with dramatically less leverage.

Zubrow was not merely offering his opinion. JPMorgan and Bank of New York were the bankers to Wall Street (they were known as tri-party bankers because each of their trades involved a client and a broker as well as a bank). As such, they controlled the flow of money that washed in and out of investment banks each day. Wall Street brokers in large part financed their trading and investment activities through intraday borrowings from agent banks such as Morgan—to whom they pledged securities as collateral. At 6 or 7 P.M. each night, when the day's trading was done, each broker and its bank squared up. But the bank was at risk if the value of the collateral declined during the day.

Morgan had been increasingly worried about the quality of collateral. Once, only Treasury bills had been acceptable, but during the boom, trades were funded with all sorts of lesser-quality paper. Zubrow's message was that Morgan would lend more warily and only against higher-grade collateral. This was like squeezing the artery through which Wall Street's lifeblood flowed. Perhaps a whiff of the danger seeped into markets; on Monday, Lehman's stock fell seven points.

Paulson briefed President Bush on the crisis that day and divulged the plan to use Fannie and Freddie to buy more mortgage securities as a means of helping hard-pressed banks. He stressed that the agencies would raise capital later. "Can they?" the president asked. "We're hoping so," Paulson replied.[18] Two days later, the deal was announced: OFHEO would let the twins stretch their capital by investing $200 billion more in housing; at some undefined date in the future, the companies would try to sell stock.

This was a fantastic scheme, which Paulson must have realized. Fannie and Freddie were close to insolvent; to use them as agents for curing the market's illness risked infecting the twins even more. Rodriguez, the investor, considered it a desperate measure that could lead to a taxpayer bailout. "They were not in a position to address this mortgage crisis, for which they had originally been created, because their balance sheets had become impaired by unsound profit motivated activities," he noted. If the latest plan failed, Washington would be forced to socialize Fannie's and Freddie's losses.[19]

The regulators were widely criticized for their two interventions, especially in the case of Bear. To critics, the Bear rescue seemed to promise a helping hand to the next financial firm, no matter how reckless, that came running for help. Bernanke insisted that Bear was a special case, not a blueprint for subsequent crises.[20] Yet the Fed had broken new ground, and the landscape would not be easily restored. The government had all but forced two private parties to merge, even dictated the price. Moreover, the Fed had blurred a time-honored distinction between depository institutions (banks) and investment firms. Though the Fed had an interest in every part of the economy, its legal domain extended only to banks. By charter and by long-standing practice, the Fed was a banker to banks—not to investment houses or to railroads or automobile manufacturers. This is why Chrysler, in 1980, had been forced to go to Congress for a bailout, and why teetering investment firms (such as Drexel Burnham Lambert) had often failed.

Paulson, Bernanke, and Geithner worried that modern finance was too interconnected to preserve the distinction. Every financial firm, and even many industrial companies, were linked via derivatives. The specter of a chain reaction—one firm's failure to honor its commitments swiftly begetting another's—preyed on the regulators' darkest fears. In lending to Bear, Bernanke invoked an obscure clause from the Federal Reserve Act of 1932 that authorized the Fed to lend to nonbanks in "unusual and exigent circumstances." That he relied on a

Depression-era statute was more than symbolic. The regulators worried that if Bear and then the rest of Wall Street failed, Main Street could suffer a devastating recession. The Fed dispatched a pair of regulators to each of the other investment banks, where they were stationed on a permanent basis. This was something new—a soggy blanket draped over the uninhibited revelry of Wall Street.

Minutes after the Bear rescue, the Fed announced another precedent-shattering step. It would open the discount window—where, since 1913, only banks had been welcome—to overnight borrowings by investment banks and other Wall Street firms. Just as stunningly, the central bank said it would accept less-than-triple-A securities—even mortgage securities—as collateral. Since profit-motivated bankers were unwilling to lend against deflating collateral, the Fed was doing so itself.[21] Not only had the Fed become the bank to Wall Street, it was willing to take the Street's paper. To further buoy markets, the Fed cut interest rates.

These actions did not, as some argued, entice firms to fail, but they did sustain their ability to take the sort of risks that might lead to failure. In particular, they encouraged lenders to keep lending. The press focused on whether the price paid for Bear's stock imposed a sufficient penalty on shareholders,* but the real moral hazard was that people who had *lent* to Bear suffered no pain at all. In fact, they were rewarded. Prior to the acquisition, Bear's credits traded at a discount. (Its IOU was worth much less than face value, or "par.") Once its debts became the obligation of JPMorgan, they returned to par. Robert Barbera, a prominent Wall Street economist, naturally counseled clients that they could count on the United States to back up Wall Street credits.[22] Thanks to the Fed, the lending could go forth; thus was the illusion of solvency sustained.

The rate cuts, the provision of loans to investment banks, and the prodding of Fannie and Freddie to be more active in the market—all these addressed liquidity, while the heart of the problem was insuffi-

---

* Later in March, to ward off a possible no-vote by shareholders, the price was raised to $10 a share.

cient capital.[23] Liquifying markets might help, but it would not restore ailing banks to health. And in its manifold efforts, the government had crossed a serious line. Without public consideration (or even discussion), and with flimsy legal basis, the Fed and the Treasury had effectively nationalized responsibility for private obligations.[24] While Paulson, like Bernanke, insisted that the government's role was transitory, both the secretary and the Fed chief had revealed an interventionist streak belying their Republican affiliations. They had begun a process that, once under way, would be difficult to abort. As Rodriguez put it, "It is inconceivable that the Fed can place its balance sheet at greater risk" without, eventually, attaching more controls on how Wall Street behaves, or further deepening its involvement. "We have crossed the Rubicon into a new financial era."

The first reaction among traders was one of relief. Solvency is a pleasant condition, and the notion that the government would provide a backstop to everyone who needed it was a welcome tonic. A hedge fund manager was heard to tell his partner, "I think we've hit bottom"—a hunch echoed from San Francisco to New York to Greenwich. John Mack, the CEO of Morgan Stanley, stated publicly that the crisis was in the eighth or ninth inning. Goldman chief executive Lloyd Blankfein reckoned that the misery was closer to its end than its beginning.[25] Markets rallied from the Bear rescue well into May. The Dow climbed from 11,700 back to 13,000; more importantly, bond prices, including prices of higher-rated mortgage bonds, rebounded.

But nothing had changed fundamentally, that is, in the underlying economy. The subprime delinquency rate crept up to 16 percent. Wachovia, whose recently acquired Golden West portfolio was turning sour, became the latest superbank to report a massive loss. Citigroup reported more write-downs. Home prices kept falling. What's more, Main Street businesses were showing stress. Month by month, the Bureau of Labor Statistics counted fewer jobs—a disquieting turn for an economy judged by the central bank to be in forward gear. But markets, as they are wont to do, interpreted these data more kindly. Wall Street had a window in which to raise capital, and several banks did.[26]

Trading revived; buyers materialized as well as sellers, though still at deeply depressed prices.

Bankers felt, if not victorious, more hopeful than in months. They regained a bit of their swagger. Michael Perry, chairman of IndyMac Bank, a California mortgage lender founded by Angelo Mozilo, charged that his company had suffered unjustly due to the plunge in mortgage securities. "In my opinion," he told investors, "these [prices] in no way represent the economic value." Perry assured his listeners that IndyMac was well capitalized.[27] Kerry Killinger, the WaMu chief who had engineered adjustable loans for mass retail, displayed similar hubris. Though the bank was engulfed in losses, Killinger told restive shareholders at the annual meeting to calm down, "have a little faith," because "terrific days" lay ahead.[28] He sniffed at a takeover bid from Dimon at JPMorgan, finding its offer of $8 a share unworthy. John Thain, also optimistic, solicited bids but was reluctant to trim Merrill's CDO portfolio.[29] Selling meant realizing a loss and having to replenish capital. Not selling meant he thought prices would be higher later. Thain could not be budged. In the spring, he even hired two of his former Goldman cronies, guaranteeing them each tens of millions of dollars—evidence anew of the compensation disconnect at a bank losing billions every quarter.[30]

The regulators that spring were more worried than the bankers. They were torn between their desire for expanded powers and the wish not to seem either overly meddling or insensitive to moral hazard. Geithner insisted in testimony to the Senate that the Fed only lent to "sound institutions," though that hardly described Bear Stearns.[31] But he, like Paulson and Bernanke, were concerned that their scope was *too* limited. The system should not be so fragile as to depend on ad hoc, extralegal improvisation.

The Treasury and Fed were still worried about the remaining investment banks, in particular Lehman. Treasury's David Nason hosted working sessions with Fed and SEC officials, scrutinizing Lehman's balance sheet and studying its assets with the zeal of Talmudic scholars. Undersecretary Steel, thinking like the Goldman banker he had once been, tried to orchestrate a prophylactic merger. Calling Robert Diamond, the head of Barclays Capital (a unit of the British bank) Steel said heartily, "I have no official authority—I am brainstorming— but if markets take another lurch down and Lehman is exposed, is there a price at which you would buy it, and if so how can I help?" Despite themselves, the free-marketers in Washington were becoming central planners.

Fuld wasn't selling. In fact, he had suspended his annual practice of selling personal Lehman stock, of which he owned about ten million shares, apparently feeling its price was too low. He even margined (borrowed against) the value of two million shares, a bravura doubling down of his bet.[32]

Fuld was, however, deeply concerned with his standing in Washington. He and Paulson dined in April; this was just after Lehman had raised $4 billion in preferred stock, which Paulson naturally applauded. Fuld returned from dinner and, like a boy enthusing over praise from his teacher, e-mailed Tom Russo, Lehman's vice chairman, "1—we have huge brand with treasury. 2—loved our capital raise."[33]

At once cocky and insecure, Fuld reflexively understood the need to suppress any outward sign of lack of confidence. Before the sale of preferred, Lehman had solicited an investment from Warren Buffett, thinking that the endorsement of the famous stock picker would bolster public confidence. Buffett had been willing, but on cut-rate terms. Lehman's bankers worried that the deal would seem like an act of desperation and turned it down. The tension between confidence and gnawing anxiety permeated the firm. At a senior management meeting in April, Scott Freidheim, Fuld's cochief administrative officer, turned to the group and declared, "Bear's gone. What's obvious to everyone now is we're the smallest." Paolo Tonucci, Lehman's young treasurer, felt that Lehman was a bigger and better firm than Bear, more likely to survive. Its credit remained investment grade, and, like few of its rivals, in the first quarter of 2008 it had operated in the black. Yet its leverage, more than 30 to 1, was simply too much. Since Bear, Lehman had been busily trimming assets, but markets for the diciest mortgage securities remained in a state of permafrost. Signaling heightened concerns about Lehman, Moody's canceled its positive outlook on the firm.

Such anxieties extended up and down Wall Street. Lehman's Russo, in private correspondence in April, compared the Street to a bank suffering a massive run. He focused on the lack of credit, particularly for securitizing assets such as mortgages. The effect was highly constricting; as Russo noted, "banks will hoard capital unless and until they can borrow the money."

The surest sign of Wall Street's unease was the prickliness with which Fuld and Russo, along with executives at other banks, responded to the phenomenon of short-sellers—hedge funds and others who were betting against their stocks. Short-selling is a legal and also a justifiable feature of markets, allowing traders to register negative as well as positive convictions. Indeed, Wall Street firms had been active promoters of short-selling, so long as the stocks being shorted were not their own. Now those same CEOs were haranguing the SEC, demanding a crackdown.

In the CEOs' defense, they had just seen Bear all but die, and the shorts' campaigns against the other Wall Street firms—especially Lehman—had the same predatory edge. There were frequent charges of "naked shorting," an abusive tactic with greater potential for manipulating prices.* Short-sellers publicized biting critiques of their targets, often involving complex accounting issues, the truth of which was difficult to determine. Shorts claimed that Lehman had not properly marked down its real estate values—a charge to which markets were hypersensitive—that its management was in turmoil, that Fuld was on his way out. The press reported both sides, but the mere mention of an accounting issue was enough to do damage.

---

* When a client shorts a stock he doesn't own, his broker is required to "locate" shares that may be borrowed and eventually delivered to close out the trade. One way of evading the intent of the rule was for multiple short-sellers to locate the same shares, meaning that more stock would be shorted than was available for delivery. This regrettable complexity was pithily summarized in a ditty attributed to the nineteenth-century robber baron Daniel Drew: "He who sells what isn't his'n, must buy it back or go to prison."

In an open society, criticism of a stock is unavoidable* and the effects of unwarranted criticisms are generally temporary. But financial stocks, as we have seen, are particularly susceptible to fire-in-the-theater type panics, and the banks' high degree of leverage left them uniquely vulnerable. They could not risk even a passing disparagement, because they might not survive to see the record set straight. If the banks' high leverage left them vulnerable, that was, of course, their own fault. After Bear, the noose tightened perceptibly. The price of borrowing short term, in commercial paper markets, soared along with lenders' appreciation of the risk. And the banks were suddenly aware of a dangerous mismatch in their funding. Though the banks' assets were long-dated, their liabilities shortened. Some three-quarters of a trillion dollars of Wall Street's paper was due to mature within fifteen months. Who would refinance it?[34] The Wall Street houses, so long the masters of the country's finances, had left themselves few options. As the maturities on their debts approached, two-year notes became one-year notes; paper maturing in eighteen months now was due in six, and so forth. Creditors were less willing to go home at night with monies owed from Merrill or Lehman; the Street, perforce, survived on a diet of short-term paper. No wonder Fuld was on edge.

---

* A proper limitation on free speech in the context of securities markets prohibits deliberate falsehoods for the purpose of manipulating prices. In practice, manipulation is difficult to spot and harder to prove.

10
TOTTERING

*How can you live in a black swan world?**

—TOM RUSSO

LEHMAN BEGAN TO TOTTER in the second week of June. Toting up its second quarter, Lehman was staring at its first loss as a public company, a bloodletting of nearly $3 billion. Its execs, who had most of their net worth tied up in Lehman's sinking stock—down by half since the start of the year—quickly became alarmed. Skip McGee, the head of investment banking, heard murmuring from the troops, faint hints of rebellion. Over the weekend of June 7, he went to Fuld's office and implored him to change course—presumably, by firing some of those responsible. On Monday, McGee kept up the pressure, forwarding to Fuld what he called a "representative e-mail" from a Lehman banker in Europe: "The mood has become truly awfull [*sic*] in the last few days and for the first time I am really worried that all the hard work we have put in over the last 6/7 years could unravel very quickly."[1]

At an executive committee meeting later in the week, Fuld blurted out: "If you all think it's so horrible, what should we do?" He called on McGee first. Stretching out his Texas drawl, McGee said someone had to be held accountable. Lehman needed to make a change in its senior

---

* In *The Black Swan*, Nassim Nicholas Taleb discussed the impact of highly improbable unforeseen events.

management. After McGee was done, Fuld called on the others. None of them dared to touch the issue of leadership. That night, McGee told his wife, "I'm dead; I'll be gone by the end of the week." But in private, several other bankers went to Fuld and said they agreed with McGee. Joe Gregory, the president, realized that the budding rebellion was aimed his way; both he and Erin Callan, the chief financial officer, abruptly resigned. Bart McDade, the firm's quiet and thoughtful head of equities, replaced Gregory. He immediately convened an inquiry that posed in writing the accusatory question, "How did we let ourselves get so exposed?" The firm had seen "warning signs," the write-up answered bluntly, but it had failed to promptly respond.[2]

Outsiders still saw Lehman as a survivor. Even in the midst of the management turmoil, it raised $6 billion in a private stock offering. Although the shares were discounted, the offering proved that Fuld and his firm still commanded great respect. One of the bedazzled investors commented on Lehman's "great franchise." This was a poor choice of words. If Lehman had a franchise at all, it was in a sector of Wall Street (mortgage finance) that had ceased to exist.

Moving quickly, McDade rehired Michael Gelband, the banker who had been pushed aside for urging that Lehman cut its risk. Gelband started in June and right away began coaxing traders to unload mortgages and reduce the firm's leverage. Amazingly, they were reluctant to sell. Prices, they felt, were simply too low. (Nothing so irritates a banker as when the market refuses to conform to his opinion.) Russo, the vice-chairman, thought mortgage securities were so out of line, he bought a big slug of mortgage-backed bonds for his kids. To Russo, to capitulate to such prices was to live in a "black swan" world, in which risk-taking was totally proscribed for fear of an unlikely but catastrophic event. That was exactly how the Street did *not* do business. Every little bet, every accumulation of bets, was based on the faith that a devastating crash remained but a theoretical possibility, a topic only for drawing room debate.

Fuld, relegated to the role of ambassador while McDade took charge of operations, was in continuous contact with regulators, investors, and a coterie of Wall Street advisers. He called Paulson incessantly.[3] Everyone was telling him the same thing: raise capital and get rid of real estate assets—or better yet, sell the firm. Laurence Fink, the head of BlackRock, an investment management firm, practically screamed at him to sell.*

Paulson did the same, exhorting Fuld to cash out while he could. At Paulson's and Steel's urging, Fuld grudgingly reached out to Barclays about a possible merger. The British bank had been hungering to expand into Wall Street, but it wanted Lehman only at a steep discount to the share price. Having seen Jamie Dimon snatch Bear Stearns for a song, no one else on the Street wanted to pay retail. While Fuld waited, the shares steadily lost ground. During the month of June the stock fell from 37 to 20.

Even if Fuld wasn't interested in a Barclays deal, he had no choice but to keep deleveraging. Lehman had three sets of problem assets: bad corporate loans, bad mortgages, and bad commercial real estate. The corporate loans were still saleable, albeit at a discount, and residential mortgages, essentially a generic product, were saleable at very steep losses. Worst by far were the commercial real estate assets, of which, by June, a staggering $40 billion remained.[4] These included a bewildering array of two thousand properties: apartments from the Archstone deal, office buildings, land from California, a mortgage on a Ritz-Carlton. The market mistrusted any values that Lehman put on them. Fearing that write-downs of such assets were inevitable, the rating agencies were sending a clear message that Lehman had to rid itself of commercial properties, but selling them was a laborious, loan-by-loan affair, with the buyers holding every advantage.

After briefly easing in May, credit markets froze again; the opportunity for selling assets narrowed. This had serious implications. JPMorgan, which had been nervous in its role as tri-party banker ever since the collapse of Bear, was eager to limit its risk in financing the Lehmans of

---

* It was a testimony to Fuld's powers of persuasion that Fink nonetheless participated (on behalf of BlackRock) in Lehman's private stock offering. Advisers may have been telling Fuld to get out, but to some extent, they shared his faith in Lehman's powers of resurrection.

the world. The precise degree of Morgan's exposure to Lehman was a matter of debate, as was the value of the Lehman securities that Morgan was holding as collateral. What was certain was that in June, Morgan asked for $5 billion in higher-grade collateral. Though the parties could, and did, negotiate terms, the relationship was one of unequals. If Lehman wanted to stay in business, ultimately it had to satisfy Morgan. This meant Lehman had to borrow less or support each loan with more (or better-quality) securities. In short, it had to shrink.

By the late spring of '08, the entire of Wall Street was caught in this vicious circle. Prices of mortgage securities resumed their sickening slide, and as they did, capital eroded. The more banks sold, or tried to sell, the less mortgage securities fetched. By June, an index of mortgage bonds was down two-thirds for the year, melting formerly solid balance sheets as if in some financial version of global warming. Reverberations from the mortgage market shook the Dow Jones average, which suffered brisk, triple-digit plunges. Subprime delinquencies soared to a new high—utterly unforeseen in the rating agency models—of 18 percent.[5] Institutions touched by subprime could not escape collateral damage. At Wachovia, Ken Thompson, the chief executive, had predicted two years earlier that his acquisition of Golden West could get him fired. In June, it did.

As subprime plummeted, AIG was forced to park a growing stash of funds with trading partners—a ransom against the possibility that it might not make good on its credit default swaps. By June, the ransom had swelled to $14 billion. These huge margin payments were imperiling AIG's credit rating, and were it to lose its rating, its access to capital would disappear. Luckily, AIG had sold stock in May, before the market's most recent slide. But the company had lost $13 billion in the previous two quarters, wiping out the capital raised.[6] And the offering had not gone smoothly; AIG's banker, JPMorgan, had strenuously disputed AIG's disclosures relating to its derivative deals.[7]

AIG's board was, now, more than wary of the chief executive. Sullivan, they felt, was not moving decisively. In mid-June, they called for his head—the fifth sacking of a marquee CEO in less than a year.

Wall Street had never seen such rapid turnover at the top. As a reward for his botched reign, Sullivan got $47 million—equal to what the average American would earn in a thousand years. And Sullivan had *failed.**

The board elected a fellow director, Robert Willumstad, a Sandy Weill protégé who many thought should have gotten the nod at Citigroup ahead of Prince. The genial, sixty-two-year-old executive had to be talked into running AIG, which seemed to promise nothing but headaches. Willumstad reckoned his first task was to figure out what AIG's default swaps were worth and what he should do with them. Presumably, he would wind down the derivatives unit and sell off other ancillary businesses. He gave himself a timetable of three months, or until just after Labor Day, to formulate a plan. Willumstad thought he had time. The habit of believing that the Street would muddle through, and eventually recover, was deeply ingrained. America had lived through many previous financial debacles—even if none, in recent memory, had lasted so long.

A S THE CRISIS ENTERED its second summer, Washington officials began to contemplate truly radical steps. Steeped in his Depression history, Ben Bernanke worried that the problems had become too big for ad hoc responses. He thought the time was ripe for a broader, legislative solution. As matters stood, the Fed was permitted to lend to institutions only in return for sound collateral; it was not authorized to gamble with the public purse. The Treasury, on the other hand, could finance anything—banks, railroads, food stamps—but only with Congress's approval. This dichotomy of powers has a logical basis. The Treasury, part of the executive branch, is subject to political control from Congress. Since the Fed is independent of any checks, and yet cannot be allowed to bankrupt the republic, banks within the Reserve system are forbidden from risking loss.

---

* Sullivan got $19 million in severance and "bonus." He also was allowed to keep $28 million in long-term awards.

That summer, the need for a quicker method of responding to a crisis weighed heavily on both Bernanke and Paulson. Each was preoccupied with a sense of looming danger. Though Bernanke took time out, with an economist friend and their wives, to see *In the Heights*, a Broadway musical, it was one of his only diversions. Hank Paulson was working every moment, occasionally sleeping in his office, where an oil portrait of his earliest predecessor, Alexander Hamilton, stood sentry over a fireplace. In his waking hours, the secretary was impulsive and woefully unorganized—he would toss one scheme in the air, followed by another, barking commands as punctuation. This pattern broke only at day's end, when his office partner, Steel, habitually ventured to his office to reflect on the crisis's latest turn. One afternoon, late in June, the fifty-six-year-old Steel came in with unsettling news: he had been offered the top job at Wachovia. Paulson replied, thoughtfully, that he himself had found being a CEO stimulating beyond his expectations. He generously encouraged Steel—his one peer in the department—to take the job.[8]

With Steel gone, Paulson was lonelier, and frustrated by his inability to get ahead of events. Bernanke advised that he go to the Hill and seek greater powers, but the secretary worried relentlessly about moral hazard—the risk that he would encourage the next bout of speculation by providing too much morphine for this one. A lifelong banker, he loathed the thought that federal action would undermine private incentives. Yet the price of inaction often seemed worse. Paulson regularly spoke to the president; for a Treasury secretary, he had uncommon freedom to make policy. And he cultivated decent relations on Capitol Hill, oddly faring better with the Democrats, in particular Barney Frank, than with the rigid federalists in the GOP. Yet Congress proved a frustration. With the November campaign heating up, members of Congress (of both parties) were nervous about supporting either bankers or bailouts. The secretary's options were limited.

In June, Paulson convened a group of regulators to ask whether the government should seek emergency authority. Geithner, who was less worried about moral hazard, suggested legislation to let the president guarantee every debt in the banking system.[9] The idea sounded radical, almost unheard-of, and the group did not give it serious attention.

In fact, even Geithner was hesitant to act. He had serious concerns about Citigroup—which over the past year had written down an astonishing $40 billion of its assets.[10] Geithner prodded Citi to raise capital, but, perhaps influenced by his former mentor, Rubin, he did not think it prudent to preempt management or intervene. "*After* we get through this crisis," he vowed in a speech to the Economic Club of New York, "we will put in place more exacting expectations on capital, liquidity, and risk management for the largest institutions [emphasis added]."[11]

Paulson and Geithner were each torn between the desire to act boldly and the fear of inciting a deeper panic. Paulson aired his concerns in a speech in London on July 2, in which he called for legislative changes to permit federal takeovers of failed investment banks. Betraying his fear of another Bear Stearns, Paulson declared, "We need to create a resolution process that ensures the financial system can withstand the failure of a large complex financial firm." He stressed that he wanted to reduce the "perception" that the government considered some firms too big to fail. Yet he added, in somewhat contradictory fashion, that his first duty was ensuring market stability.[12]

The tension between stability and moral hazard had raged since Bear Stearns, and it was not going away. Investors in Fannie Mae and Freddie Mac were highly unsettled, and Fannie and Freddie—responsible for about half of America's mortgages—were as close to "too big to fail" as any corporations in existence. On June 30, two days prior to Paulson's speech, Fannie Mae's stock had plunged by 6 percent and Freddie Mac's by 8 percent. This was no small matter. Any lessening in confidence could imperil the twins' ability to refinance their debts—of which they had $5.3 trillion outstanding. Slightly more than a quarter of that debt was owned by foreigners, mostly government agencies and banks in China, Japan, the oil states, and Russia. For years, financial experts had worried that if overseas investors stopped lending to the United States, the economy might collapse. Now, as Fannie's and Freddie's stocks plummeted, international finance ministers and central bankers worriedly called the Treasury. "We thought they [the GSEs] were *guaranteed*," a perplexed Chinese official told his counterpart at Treasury. Since the guarantee was merely implicit, there was little the American could say. Paulson and his aides debated whether the U.S. should seek to nationalize the twins' debts, but feared having to go to Congress, whose Republican members regarded the twins with born-again hatred. The selling continued into the following week, and so did the calls.[13]

On July 7, the first trading day after the July 4 holiday, Fannie's stock fell to 15, merely a quarter of its level a year earlier. Paulson knew that the sinking stock would also pound the price of Fannie's bonds, a serious concern. "I've seen this before," he noted, alluding to his Wall Street years. "When the equity gets pounded it's going to bleed into the debt."[14] Foreign lenders to Fannie and Freddie were already shortening their maturities. Russia had sold some of its paper. The Chinese held more than $500 billion of GSE debt—presumably, more than they could sell—but this only heightened the pressure on Paulson to protect Fannie's and Freddie's credit.[15] If the agencies failed, a run on Treasuries (the government's paper) would follow.

As Fannie's and Freddie's stocks were being battered, trouble was flaring at IndyMac, the Pasadena bank spun off from Countrywide. IndyMac, which had specialized in Alt-A loans, had been left holding thousands of shaky mortgages when the securitization market shut down. From late June to early July, Indy was hit with a bank run. Depositors withdrew $1.3 billion, about $100 million a day. On July 11, two months after the bank's chairman, Michael Perry, had assured investors that his company was well capitalized, the Office of Thrift Supervision seized Indy—the second biggest bank to fail in U.S. history, trailing only Continental Illinois in 1984.

IndyMac's collapse socked the FDIC with an astronomical $10.7 billion in insurance costs, and enraged Sheila Bair, FDIC's chairwoman.[16] She resolved that regulators would move sooner, and more aggressively, against weak banks in the future. In a curious aftermath, depositors lined up at IndyMac's doors to reclaim their deposits, as if they did not quite trust that the FDIC would honor their claims. Some waited days. Symbolically, the next Great Depression had arrived.

Indy's failure greatly heightened concerns over WaMu and Wachovia, the most vulnerable big banks left. But the fear of banking distress was generalized. Over the boom years, banks had come to rely less on deposits and more on debt that had to be repaid every day—clearly, a less-secure source of funding.[17] On form, now, every bank was open to a run. Meanwhile, terms of funding were shrinking. By the time of the Indy collapse, the short-term debt for the ten largest banks and investment banks had reached an astronomical $2.6 trillion.[18] This evidenced a deep sickness in the credit system—an unwillingness to harbor risk over any medium term. Banks were borrowing from the discount window—the Fed—which meant they were not lending to each other.[19]

This was the worrisome context in which Paulson considered the run against Fannie's and Freddie's stocks. On Thursday, July 10, the twins' regulator insisted (for the umpteenth time) that the agencies were adequately capitalized.[20] On Friday, the same day that Indy was seized, Fannie closed at 10, Freddie at 7¾, and the Dow traded below 11,000 for the first time in two years. Freddie was due to sell bonds on Monday. Paulson could not afford a failure, nor could he afford another run. Finally, he pulled the trigger.

At 6 P.M. on Sunday, July 13, as black clouds darkened the horizon, he quickly read an announcement from the steps of the Treasury. Paulson was asking Congress for authority to invest public money in the twins and—should the need arise—to make them full wards of the government. His words were followed by a thunderclap and a massive downpour. Fearing a fight with Congress, Paulson asked Bernanke to help sell the plan, an unusually political role for a Fed chief. Then, Paulson called Dan Jester, a former Goldman colleague, and persuaded him to join the Treasury as a high-level problem solver. In a battle, the secretary turned to his natural allies, neither Democrats nor Republicans but Goldman alums.

Paulson regarded his bombshell proposal as the last best shot at preserving the status quo.* He reckoned that the government's readiness to invest in the twins might obviate the need for it; as he said to the Senate, "If you have a bazooka in your pocket and people know it, you probably won't have to use it."[21] In the opinion of his staffers, savvier in the ways of Washington, Paulson did not quite realize the enormity of what he was asking—a federal safety net for the world's biggest mortgage market. It had never been done.

While Paulson was moving to stabilize the GSEs, Bair, the strong-willed FDIC chief, was urging the White House to prod mortgage lenders into modifying loan terms—with the deficit to be made up by public funds.[22] Bair was a Republican but, as she emphasized, a "Kansas Republican," more attuned to the plight of individual homeowners than the Wall Street–centric bankers at other agencies.[23] She temporarily suspended foreclosures at the seized IndyMac—a gesture of forbearance that she hoped would serve as a template for more general relief. The administration balked. Paulson, always worried about moral hazard, feared that if the government gave delinquent mortgagors a break, homeowners who were quite capable of making payments would default.

In truth, there was no sure way of preventing such abuse. Nor was every foreclosed borrower, some of whom had lied on their loan applications, morally entitled to assistance. (In a capitalist system, even mortgage owners who had been forthright were not *entitled* to assistance.) The more complicated question was whether to help a large class of homeowners, of differing individual merits and circumstances, in order to buffer a large-scale economic crisis. Arguably, the government had answered this very question in the affirmative with respect to the rescued creditors of Bear Stearns.

In social terms, homeowners had at least as valid a claim to public aid as did Wall Street investors. Bernanke was sympathetic to the no-

---

* Purists on his staff, and at the Fed, were disappointed that Paulson did not seek to have the twins seized as insolvent. But Paulson never opted for a draconian solution when a more moderate one was at hand. Since Steel had finally gotten the Senate to consider a Fannie and Freddie reform bill, Paulson simply attached his measure to the bill already on the floor.

tion of doing *something* to limit foreclosures, but Paulson felt that granting relief carte blanche smacked of welfare. And selecting which households to help would be difficult at best. Moreover, banks that had experimented with modifying loan terms were experiencing bracingly high rates of re-default.[24] Many families who had their payment schedules eased had fallen into arrears only a few months later. Mortgage balances were so bloated, relative to falling home values, that no mere tweaking of loan terms could ensure that homeowners would stay current.

Another roadblock sprang from the byzantine structure of mortgage finance. Since mortgages had been sliced and diced into so many disparate pieces, no one party could authorize a loan modification. The mortgages were owned by varied investors at different levels of the payment waterfall—often with conflicting interests.[25] Congress approved only a modest measure of relief—intended more to address appearances than to actually keep people in their homes. Foreclosures, meanwhile, reached a post-Depression high. By summer, Americans were handing their keys to their bankers at a rate of 280,000 a month, up from a mere 74,000 in 2005. Relief seemed impossible as long as housing continued its downward spiral, and with prices falling for the ninth consecutive quarter and five million homes on the market unsold—two million of them vacant—no bottom was in sight.[26]

The merciless pressure on mortgages steadily eroded bank assets and also bank shares. On July 15, the lead headline in the *New York Times*, "Confidence Ebbs for Bank Sector and Stocks Fall," had faintly Depression overtones. (One almost imagined the subheadline: "Hoover Urges Calm.") For Wall Street, though, this was no joke.

Merrill Lynch, choking on the CDO portfolio it acquired only two years earlier, had written down a staggering $46 billion in assets. When the firm's chief financial officer divulged a loss of nearly $5 billion for the second quarter, the usually self-possessed John Thain lost his temper and slammed a door. Thain had been resisting asset sales; now he capitulated. Here, in microcosm, was the story of the mortgage bust. At the tail end of the boom, Merrill had acquired a set of CDOs with a face value of $30.6 billion. Prudently, or so it supposed, Merrill bought policies on the CDOs from a trio of insurers. When the insurance failed to protect it from the mortgage tsunami, Merrill negotiated settlements.[27] By mid-2008, Merrill had written the CDOs all the way down to $11.1 billion. In July, it sold them to Lone Star Funds, a private equity firm, for a paltry $6.7 billion—a mere twenty-two cents for each dollar of original face value. The fire sale to Lone Star sent an unmistakable message to the Street. It meant that in Merrill's expert judgment, mortgage securities were not coming back. It also gouged a hole in Merrill's balance sheet, forcing it to sell stock at severely depressed levels.

And it wasn't just Merrill. Low stock prices were inhibiting every bank from raising capital—an issue that Fuld, along with other CEOs, repeatedly complained about to Washington. Fuld suspected hedge fund short-sellers of spreading rumors to drive down his stock.[28] He compiled a dossier of sorts to try to document his charges, now little short of an obsession, and even called the CEOs at rival Wall Street firms, beseeching them to rein in their traders. In mid-July, the SEC, responding to such alarms, as well as pressure from Paulson and Geithner, imposed a temporary restriction on short-selling for nineteen financial stocks.[*]

Meanwhile, Geithner returned his attention to the four remaining big investment banks—Goldman, Morgan Stanley, Merrill, and Lehman—which were increasingly, if informally, under his jurisdiction. The SEC, their statutory regulator, went through a laborious process of familiarizing the four with the central bank. Officials of each investment house, including their CEOs, trooped over to the New York Fed to meet with Geithner and his staff and with SEC officials.

Geithner focused in particular on Lehman. The bank's treasurer, Paolo Tonucci, was called while on holiday with his wife and kids on Lake Garda, in northern Italy, to explain Lehman's stress scenarios to

---

[*] Rather than just locate a share to be borrowed, the SEC required that short-sellers actually borrow the stock.

Fed examiners over the phone. The grilling lasted three hours. When the questions continued, Lehman told Tonucci to come home.

By now, Lehman had its balance sheet down to $650 billion or so—nearly a one-fifth reduction, thanks to its steady pruning of assets. Belatedly, it shuttered what remained of its mortgage origination business. Fuld, meanwhile, was avidly trying to seduce investors. One plainly interested party was the Korea Development Bank, whose CEO, Min Euoo-sung, was a former Lehman executive. However, the negotiations were complicated because the bank was controlled by the Korean government. Fuld also met with Bank of America, whose chief executive, Ken Lewis, having failed to acquire Merrill Lynch, was still pining for an investment bank. Others, such as General Electric, HSBC, and a smattering of private equity funds, quickly said no.[29] Most suitors simply wanted no part of Lehman's unfathomable commercial real estate.

Skip McGee, Lehman's investment banking chief, devised a possible solution: spin the commercial loans into a separate corporation (dubbed "Spinco" by the bankers) with its own stock. The troublesome assets would be segregated, in effect frozen until values recovered. Left in Lehman would be a smaller bank, and one that was freed of the troubling commercial portfolio. Tom Russo, the general counsel, pitched the idea to the SEC in July, which assured him the agency would not object. The bankers put Spinco in motion; however, the spinoff couldn't be executed until the first quarter of 2009. Lehman needed to buy a little time.

Russo had another card up his sleeve, a proposal to convert Lehman into a bank holding company, or to use a tiny Utah subsidiary (a so-called industrial loan corporation) for the same purposes. The point of being a bank was to be able to collect deposits, a more reliable source of funding than selling bonds. Moreover, it was dawning on Lehman that institutions regulated by the New York Fed were more likely to weather the storm than those under the jurisdiction of the SEC.

The Fed, though, was cool to the idea. Geithner feared it would make Lehman look desperate. The FDIC was resolutely opposed; its mission was to insure customer funds, and it was in no mood to add

Lehman's sizable and ailing commercial portfolio to the list of troubled assets underlying bank deposits. The regulators did not see Lehman's plight as urgent, and it remained outside the Fed's protective skirts.[30]

A smattering of hedge funds, as a precautionary measure, began to lighten their accounts at Lehman—a dark echo of the liquidity pressures that had befallen Bear Stearns.[31] One investment manager who called Tonucci sensed that the treasurer was "going call to call," assuring each party of Lehman's putative soundness.

Nothing so worried regulators as a shaky investment bank, but nothing they did to boost its confidence worked. Not rate cuts and increased lending at the Fed, not restrictions on short sales, not the assisted merger of Bear and the help for Fannie and Freddie—none of this effectively shored up confidence, or did so for very long. Regulators were trying to corral a gale that would not be quieted until the real estate market stabilized. That would require home prices falling to defensible levels. The math was simply terrible. Pomboy, the consultant and scribe, pointed out that if an institution leveraged 10 to 1 lost a single dollar, it had to sell $10 in mortgage securities or other assets just to keep its leverage stable. If the bank lost $1 billion—these days, not at all uncommon—it had to sell $10 billion in assets. Each loss resulted in an exponential accretion of selling. And even after a year of brutal losses, banks' exposure to real estate was still equivalent to more than half their assets. The deleveraging seemed far from over.[32]

Deleveraging is the process of borrowing less. Banks with less liquidity necessarily cut lending as well. And that is what banks were doing. Credit creation was falling. Consumers were pulling back. Bank loans and related commitments were slipping at an annualized rate of 9 percent—the fastest decline in more than thirty years. The commercial paper market was shrinking. On form, the credit system was shriveling away.[33]

Still, most forecasters that summer did not predict a recession. The administration had passed a stimulus package, under which qualifying taxpayers were receiving $300 checks, and economists put inordinate faith in this relatively modest program, and in the economy's demonstrated resiliency. Despite six straight months of shrinking job totals, the Fed's Open Market Committee, led by Bernanke, stuck to its rosy outlook. As the Federal Reserve Board put it in July 2008: "The economy is expected to expand slowly over the rest of this year. FOMC participants anticipate a gradual strengthening of economic growth over coming quarters."[34]

Forecasting is the most hazardous of scientific endeavors. Like meteorologists, modern economists employ computers to project trends from the visible present into a future yet obscure. The reliance on standard (and backward-glancing) models is their great weakness. Any knave can project a continuation of a trend. To call a *turn* requires judgment—the capacity and courage to read the data and analyze the factors likely to cause a reversal. Very few individuals can do it with any reliability. It is less likely that a group, which naturally strives for safe-seeming consensus, will ever do it. On the margin, Bernanke trusted the models more than his own ability to override them. Contrariwise, Pomboy anticipated a psychological shift from a general mood of relief that policymakers were on the case to one of "frantic concern" that the problems were, perhaps, beyond their capacity to repair. One of the words she used was "panic." It was illogical, she wrote, to think that mainstream businesses that were dependent on credit would survive a contraction in credit unscathed. "Where the financial sector goes, the broader economy and market invariably follow."[35]

On July 30, the president signed the Housing and Economic Recovery Act of 2008, giving Paulson the "bazooka" he did not expect to use. The law also created a strengthened regulator—a long-sought triumph for the secretary—with the power, if need be, to take over the twins' operations or even liquidate them. Rodriguez, who had sold his GSE bonds two years earlier, rushed out a letter that day. Since the government's sponsorship of the twins was the root of the problem, he did not see a potential full bailout as a solution. Nor did he take comfort in the birth of a new regulator. "Excuse us for being skeptical, but our existing regulatory agencies failed to control the excessive leverage building up within." Bear Stearns, Rodriguez admonished, supposedly was to have been the last of such rescues. Now it had been followed by Fannie and Freddie. "We feel disgusted and betrayed that the socialization of risk continues." Worse, the investor wailed, "We believe our financial and social systems are traveling down a road that will eventually leave our children and future generations financially impoverished."[36] Nothing but new capital would help.

The criticisms were widespread. Senator Jim Bunning, a Republican from Kentucky, proclaimed that he thought he had woken up in France (France being, in the post-Soviet era, the economic nationalist's epithet of choice). "But no, it turned out it was socialism here in the United States of America." The *Economist,* less moralizing, observed that the twins had recently been counted on to buoy the housing market. "Now the rescuers have needed rescuing."[37]

Paulson emphasized that he had no intention of bailing out Fannie's and Freddie's stockholders. But in the campaign to forestall moral hazard, he had given ground. His greatest concern now was that the twins recover without the Treasury's having to invest. He uttered some brave words to the effect that he supported the companies in their current form.

The trouble was, as Rodriguez and Paulson himself had been saying, the twins needed heaps of capital. Losses continued to be astronomical and seemed far from over. By August, the twins owned or had guaranteed an estimated $1 trillion in junk mortgages, one of the great speculative excesses of the age.[38]

Ominously, Paulson's possession of a bazooka had yet to ease the market's fears. In the two weeks after the bill's enactment, Fannie's stock sickeningly slid from 12 to 8. The potential for federal action had created a dangerous vortex. Knowing that the Treasury stood ready to invest, private investors withdrew (lest they be diluted by oceans of government capital). Was it possible that, having loaded his gun, Paulson would be *compelled* to use it?

With their stocks falling and their losses mounting, Paulson felt the GSEs were in an untenable position. He was certain to leave office after the November election (regardless of who won) and he did not want to leave the problem dangling for his successor.[39] But Treasury could not, on its own, figure out what to do with them. So Paulson hired Morgan Stanley to advise on a solution. Laying out the assignment to Ruth Porat and Bob Scully, who led the Morgan Stanley team, Paulson enthused, "This will be the most grueling, and the most rewarding, thing you've done in your career." He set forth three goals. The bankers might have wondered how they were supposed to square the first two, "market stability" and "mortgage availability," which would presumably cost money, with the last, "taxpayer protection." Paulson ended the meeting abruptly, saying, "I'm going to the Olympics," meaning Beijing. "When I come back I want a lot of progress."[40]

As Porat and Scully quickly realized, the challenge was daunting. Fannie had just reported another quarterly loss and—belatedly—suspended purchases of Alt-A mortgages, the category that had done it the most harm. (Alt-A accounted for approximately a tenth of Fannie's assets and fully half its losses.[41]) Since the previous fall, Fannie had raised its estimate of expected losses from $7 billion to $25 billion. Freddie Mac, in worse shape, had simply ceased making forecasts.

Porat and Scully put forty people on the job. They analyzed the twins' assets, liquidity, accounting. The Morgan Stanley data center in Mumbai ran an analysis, mortgage by mortgage, of every GSE loan. In the end, the team would work five weeks for a total fee of $95,000—barely lunch money for bankers.

Before leaving for China, Paulson hired yet another Goldman alum, Kendrick Wilson, a classmate from Dartmouth (and a Harvard Business School classmate of President Bush), to be his adviser and emissary to Wall Street. The Goldman nucleus at Treasury was beginning to grate on rivals, who routinely suspected Goldman bankers of the darkest conspiracies. Now the fear that Treasury harbored a Goldman cabal, or at least, a receptivity to Goldman's interests, could not be so easily dismissed.

Wilson was a shrewd choice; he had once worked with Lew Ranieri at Salomon, the cradle of securitized mortgages. Paulson suggested that he start by checking in with AIG. The insurer had just reported a big loss, and Willumstad, the new CEO, was frightened. Out of the blue, he had received a call from a senior vice president at his home, around 9 P.M. one night. "We have a potential liquidity mess," the employee warned. Willumstad hired the investment manager BlackRock to figure out what AIG's swaps were worth. "Just tell me," he pleaded, "what they will cost me." Meanwhile, he was begging the rating agencies not to downgrade AIG before he developed his promised plan. Wilson, the Paulson adviser, didn't think it looked promising. AIG was scurrying for investors, entertaining a parade of financial entities that included some of the firms trying to raise money for Lehman, and even Lehman itself.[42] But mortgage assets kept falling, and AIG's CDO positions kept sinking.

Moreover, Wilson learned, AIG was grappling with another mess, emblematic of Wall Street's blatant disregard for the perils of leverage. The insurer had been holding cash for third parties as collateral for having lent out other securities. That much was routine; the difference was that AIG wasn't in fact holding the cash, but had invested it in mortgage-backed bonds. The third parties would want their cash in twenty or thirty days, but the bonds AIG was holding had an average life of ten to twelve *years*, and their market value, of course, had tanked. AIG had billions of dollars in such obligations. Once again, the oldest lesson on Wall Street, not to borrow short and lend long, had been violated with abandon. Wilson reported to Paulson, "This looks like a freight train coming down."

Wilson began to dig into the underbelly of the credit system. He was aghast at the massive debt accumulating in American banking. Everywhere he looked he saw leverage upon leverage—a dangerous pyramid of obligations. For instance, commercial paper, the lifeblood of corporate finance, was supported with backup credit lines that Wilson doubted could ever be drawn. He reckoned the Asian central bankers who were pestering the Treasury about Fannie and Freddie were right to be nervous about American credits. Worried himself and still new at the office, Wilson asked an official what the Treasury's plan was in case another Bear Stearns developed. The reply came quickly: "Ken, we don't have a fucking plan."

11

FANNIE'S TURN

*I'll lay my marker down right now, Mr. Chairman. I
think Fannie and Freddie need some changes, but I
don't think they need dramatic restructuring in terms
of their mission, in terms of their role in the secondary
mortgage market, et cetera.*

—CHUCK SCHUMER TO THE SENATE BANKING
COMMITTEE, APRIL 6, 2005[1]

In early August, Fannie's and Freddie's stocks fell for six straight days.
On the seventh day, August 14, the stocks staged a rally. Then, four
more down days. On Wednesday, August 20, Fannie plunged to 4½,
down 94 percent in a year. Jim Cramer, the television stock jock, called
for a halt in trading. The bazooka did not seem to be working.

Daniel Mudd and Richard Syron, Fannie's and Freddie's respective
CEOs, were pleading with the Treasury, and with their new regulator, the Federal Housing Finance Agency, for more time. They were
desperate to avoid the ignominy of a government takeover, and ardently
wanted to raise capital privately—though with the government providing a backstop if they failed. The Morgan Stanley bankers saw
problems with this approach. If the twins, thought to be facing steep
losses, tried to raise capital and failed, the market reaction could be
devastating.

The GSEs' distress preoccupied central bankers at their late-August retreat in Jackson Hole, Wyoming. Fed officials, slipping away from the symposiums to analyze the mortgage pair, agreed that the twins' current arrangement was untenable.[2] Despite the tranquil setting in the valley of the Grand Tetons, Bernanke seemed out of sorts. Though usually game for intellectual exchanges, he was laboring under a tremendous strain, and irritated at being the brunt of criticism. He sloughed off barbs from journalists but was offended by some from his academic peers, who enjoyed the luxury of the professorial life that Bernanke no longer had. Given the risks to the financial system, he felt, attacks on the Fed for saving Bear Stearns were naïve, bordering on personal.* The most trenchant note at Jackson Hole was struck by a former Japanese central banker, who recalled his country's severe slump in the 1990s—a precedent much on Bernanke's mind. Japan's experience, he said, argued for an "early and large-scale recapitalization of the financial system."[3]

In Washington, Mudd lobbied Paulson for time, and pointed out that Fannie, unlike Freddie, had raised capital the previous spring, and was in relatively better shape. But the practical significance of its superiority was slight, because foreign investors had come to treat the companies as, indeed, twins. Both were losing the confidence of the market.

Paulson, moreover, was wearying of the endless melodrama over the GSEs, which had occupied his entire tenure. He was laying the groundwork to overhaul their managements and, possibly, make more extensive changes, and asked Ken Wilson to look for potential new CEOs. The search had to be performed with absolute secrecy; any leak would rock the market.

Paulson was eager to move fast. Lehman was due to report earnings early in September, and he wanted Fannie and Freddie out of the way before Lehman disclosed yet more losses, which would possibly unhinge markets again.[4] In a bold step, he conferred with the House

---

* Allan Meltzer, a noted economist and historian of the Fed, pointedly praised the independence of Paul Volcker and Greenspan (Bernanke's immediate predecessors) before jibing, "The current Federal Reserve seems spineless." The *Wall Street Journal* called Bernanke a "Pavlovian" slave to the market.

Speaker, Nancy Pelosi, and with the Senate majority leader, Harry Reid, about seeking expanded powers to deal with Lehman. Neither thought they had the votes.[5]

Dick Fuld had had little luck finding a buyer, despite peddling a chunk of Lehman to a laundry list of global banks. The Koreans were interested, but the negotiations were torturous. Fuld also rang Bob Diamond, the CEO of Barclays, in the guise of a social call, craftily adding, "Should we be talking?"

Morale at Lehman remained surprisingly high, thanks to its new president, Bart McDade, who fostered an inclusive, open spirit. Though hardly a backslapper, he was quick to tell underlings they were doing a good job. But he had no quick fix. "Spinco" (the envisioned spinoff of Lehman's most problematic assets) was progressing slowly. Also, in mid-August, the SEC let the restriction on short-selling expire, exposing Lehman to the shorts once more. Russo was apoplectic, but Lehman's stock, now down to the midteens, held its own through August.

Equally distressing to the banks, Wall Street had constructed an alternative way of speculating against troubled corporations, via derivatives, and this wholly unregulated market doubled back on its Wall Street creators with a vengeance. Credit default swaps had been invented by financial engineers at Bankers Trust as a form of insurance on corporate defaults.[*] The initial purpose was supposedly as a hedging vehicle. A bank that had lent money to General Motors could hedge its risk by purchasing a credit default swap from another party who believed that the loan would be repaid. Thus, if GM defaulted on the loan, the bank would recoup its investment via the swap. Unfortunately, such hedges dulled the bank's incentive to perform the one function for which society depended on it: thoughtfully rationing credit to worthy borrowers.

A larger problem was that anyone—not just a lender with a stake

---

[*] A credit default swap is not as forbidding as its name sounds. It refers to a trade in which one party exchanges—or "swaps"—a cash premium in return for protection against a corporate failure—literally, a "credit default."

in the corporation's well-being—could purchase a swap. In the world of traditional insurance, there are long-standing rules that prohibit disinterested parties from taking a flier (you cannot, for instance, buy a life insurance policy on your neighbor). But speculators, short-sellers, or anyone else could buy credit default swaps. The market evolved into a casino in which market sentiment determined the supposed odds of default.

In time, lenders, even rating agencies, conferred on this market a presumption of authority that affected actual credit decisions. By way of illustration, imagine that you go to insure your car and the agent says, "I'd love to write you a policy, but the market thinks you are a bad risk." "But I haven't had an *accident*," you stammer. "No," the agent sighs. "But someone has been placing bets with the neighborhood bookie that you will, and I'm worried he knows something. Perhaps next month."

The default swap market became a kind of hall of mirrors in which Wall Street's credit was reflected or distorted at the market's will. By late August, the casino was running wild. The price of insuring $10 million worth of AIG's senior debt had climbed from $70,000 at the start of the year to $375,000. Lehman registered a similar increase, and insurance on other banks (troubled or not) rose as well. Premiums for Goldman, a perfectly solvent firm, surged from a negligible sum to $150,000.[6] Some of this was rational; the risk had increased. But credit was effectively being rationed by rank speculators. Worse, some of those purchasing "insurance" were short-sellers with an interest in seeing insurance prices soar.

Because rising prices in the swap market were contagious, they contributed to fears of systemic weakness. They were not unlike the bank runs that fed the gloom of the 1930s. A junior Lehman executive, reflecting on rising swap rates, the pressure from short-sellers, and tightening credit conditions in general, sensed "the world falling apart." The deepening woes of Fannie and Freddie further darkened the mood at Lehman—as did the nonstop articles speculating on the firm's demise, which felt to AIG's Willumstad like a tourniquet suffocating his company, too. In normal times, corporations were judged individually, but in times of stress the distinctions were buried by a sense of shared risks. Traders who wanted no part of one investment bank wanted no part of any. This credit turmoil roiled AIG. Interest rates on its debt were rising. Ominously, lenders who had purchased commercial paper for forty-day terms now refused to go beyond fifteen days.[7] As the price of insuring AIG's credit on the swaps market soared, the rating agencies were more and more nervous. And counterparties, in particular Goldman Sachs, were howling at its door for more cash.[*]

AIG worriedly summoned JPMorgan, its banker-adviser, and Morgan dispensed the unwelcome opinion that a credit downgrade was likely.[8] AIG did not agree; its relations with Morgan had been difficult since the spring, and this struck AIG as another example of Morgan's diffidence. But Willumstad did not have other options.

During the last week of August, Willumstad went over see Jamie Dimon, his former colleague at Citigroup, and Steve Black, Morgan's de facto number two. Willumstad said he was anxious about the possible downgrade and needed to secure funding to get through the quarter; after September 30, he hoped to raise capital. Looking Dimon in the eye, Willumstad said, "I'm going to need your balance sheet. Will you make it available?" Dimon replied, "Absolutely."[†]

T HE NEW YORK FINANCIAL community departed for the Labor Day weekend in a state of unease reminiscent of the August ten years before, when Russia's bond default had roiled markets. Then, as now, money was flowing from riskier assets into T-bills, and stock market volatility was spiking. Then, however, the trouble had originated overseas, and had no effect on average Americans. This time, it was a homegrown crisis, with brutal repercussions on Main Street. Foreclosures in

---

* Goldman's interest in AIG did not stop it from pursuing an assignment as AIG's adviser. Willumstad pointed out to Lloyd Blankfein, Goldman's CEO, over an otherwise pleasant lunch, "You're conflicted."
†Willumstad heard this as an expression of intent, not a binding commitment.

August reached 300,000; fully 20 percent of subprime holders were seriously delinquent, an unprecedented credit disaster.[9] Also, in 1998, the most prominent U.S. casualty was LTCM, a hedge fund. This time, Wall Street banks—the heart of the financial system—were wobbling. Dick Fuld was desperately trying to secure a deal with the elusive Koreans. He also put out a feeler to the ever-acquisitive Ken Lewis at Bank of America.[10] Paulson and Bernanke, hoping to resolve the crisis over the GSEs before the Lehman situation worsened, spent the final Saturday and Sunday of August in Washington.

Labor Day weekend, the Treasury was buzzing with officials, investment bankers, and lawyers. The Treasury building dates to 1842, and is preceded among federal buildings only by the White House (immediately to the northwest) and the Capitol. It was built in the Greek Revival style, with thirty-six-foot granite columns on the eastern façade beckoning to a spacious interior and spiral stairs.

Early Saturday, Porat and Scully, the Morgan Stanley bankers who had been assigned to figuring out the GSE mess, decamped in the comfortable conference room across from Paulson. They were joined by Ed Herlihy, a partner at Wachtell, Lipton, Rosen & Katz who was advising Paulson and various officials including, at times, Paulson, Bernanke, and the Fed's Kevin Warsh.

Porat and Scully's report put forth three options: (1) let the GSEs raise money on their own, which would essentially preserve the status quo; (2) "conservatorship," under which the twins would operate under federal stewardship; and (3) "receivership," close to a controlled liquidation. Though each of the choices posed problems, neither Paulson nor the Fed had any doubt that they had to act. Foreign central bankers, ever more nervous about their bonds, were calling the Treasury relentlessly. Paulson could not bear the thought of the Chinese rejecting U.S. paper; he had to stabilize the market.

With the twins facing large but undetermined losses, no one knew how much capital they would need. The fear was that almost *any* amount would be regarded as too little. What about $500 billion? Bernanke said that was too big; it would frighten people.[11]

Just as crucial was the vexing issue of how, if the government intervened, it should treat Fannie's and Freddie's investors. For reasons of moral hazard, Paulson did not want to protect common stockholders. On the other hand, to reassure the bond market, creditors had to be saved. That left a middle tier, people who had invested in the GSEs' *preferred* stock. Almost any decision would amount to an interference in the markets. Treasury officials even wondered whether they could be sued.

Mudd and Syron, the company heads, continued to lobby against a takeover. Mudd recognized that with his stock so cheap, Fannie could not raise capital immediately, but he prodded Paulson to give him time—a "breathing space," as Mudd's lawyer put it. Paulson didn't really respond.[12] With the public still in the dark, the stocks edged up. On Friday September 5, Fannie closed just over 7, Freddie at 5.

The night before, Paulson had called Herbert Allison, a sixty-five-year-old retired Wall Street executive. In 1998, as the number two man at Merrill Lynch, Allison had played a key role in the rescue of LTCM. Now Paulson reached him at Caneel Bay, a resort in the Virgin Islands, where he and his wife and their two boys were enjoying a long-promised vacation. Paulson said the situation with the GSEs was serious. "Can you come up and run one of these things?"

Allison said, "I'll do whatever you want. I need to go back home and get some suits." Paulson, who wanted Allison to run Fannie Mae, said, "No, come here tomorrow." Allison countered that all he had were khakis and boat shoes. "Come as you are," Paulson said.

On Friday, James Lockhart, the GSEs' regulator, called Mudd and told him to appear at his office at 4 P.M. Mudd asked what the meeting was about; Lockhart was mum. Mudd went over with his lawyer, Rodgin Cohen. It was a steamy afternoon, with the temperature in Washington hitting ninety degrees and Tropical Storm Hanna nearing the city. Mudd was delayed getting past security, and in the lobby, he spied Bernanke and his Secret Service agent headed for the same meeting. Then, Mudd saw a reporter from the *Wall Street Journal* furiously talking on his cell phone. Clearly, big doings were afoot. Upstairs,

Mudd and Cohen were led to one side of a conference table; the three officials, Lockhart, Paulson, and Bernanke faced them on the other. Lockhart and Paulson did the talking. Bernanke looked plainly uncomfortable, betraying the Fed's long-standing displeasure over every aspect of the GSEs' arrangement. The Fed chief said almost nothing, other than a scripted-sounding, "We are supportive."[13]

The regulators told Mudd the government was putting Fannie into a conservatorship. Mudd played for time—perhaps there was some middle ground between this and Fannie's plan, he suggested—but Richard Alexander, an attorney hired by the government, cut him off. "Your regulator, the secretary of the Treasury, and the chairman of the Federal Reserve, have called you here," Alexander noted drily. "They did not come for a dialogue." The government people told Mudd he had until Sunday morning to get agreement from his board. Otherwise, Lockhart would declare the company undercapitalized and seize it— along with Freddie Mac, which had been summoned to a similar meeting—unilaterally.

Saturday, as Hanna pelted the city with violent winds and more than an inch of rain per hour, Fannie's and Freddie's board heard the gruesome details. The government would invest up to $100 billion in a new issue of preferred stock in each company, supplying the capital as they needed it to pay their creditors and stay in business. In return for its support, the government expropriated four-fifths of the common stock, all but wiping out the shareholders.* Cohen, the lawyer, raised the delicate issue of whether the preferred stock would be saved. Dan Jester, the Treasury official, said they had to draw the line somewhere—the preferred was gone too. The executives were stunned. Then came the clincher: the CEOs were summarily dismissed from their posts.

The bailout of the twins was unfortunate but probably unavoidable. The U.S. government had encouraged investors around the world to

---

* The government received 100 percent of the voting rights, as well as warrants representing a 79.9 percent stake in the common stock of each GSE. Their stock prices fell to under $1.

think that Fannie and Freddie had its backing. Though the policy had been woefully misguided, Paulson was bound to honor it.

In the weeks and months to come, departing officials of the twins faulted the preemptive nature of the bailout, noting that the GSEs were not at imminent risk of failure. Also, they alleged, what crisis did exist was manufactured by Paulson, whose surprise legislation had aggravated the market's loss of confidence.[14]

There are kernels of truth to these criticisms, but the market would never have had such confidence in the GSEs to begin with had it not been for their unusual alliance with the Treasury. The alliance created inextricable conflicts between the public and the private interests. Paulson rightly concluded that the arrangement no longer worked—perhaps never had. Intervening before an actual crisis developed was merely prudent.*

One other postmortem analysis centered on the Alt-A loans that had done the twins so much damage. Alt-A mortgages were not specifically targeted toward the poor, and did not help meet HUD's goals for lower-income housing. In other words, the twins had invested in them not for social good but for profit. This suggested to some that corporate overreaching—not social engineering by Congress—caused the twins' failure.[15] The truth is more nuanced. The reason Congress and its regulator permitted Fannie and Freddie such largesse (both in the pursuit of shareholder profit, and to assist low-income housing) was to allow them to pursue their social mission. Had the GSEs been purely economic animals, presumably no guarantee would have existed, and markets would not have permitted them such leverage. This does not mean (as many on the right argued) that Fannie's and Freddie's friends in Congress were entirely to blame, but to ignore the influence of those friends is to be blind to how the twins could so casually borrow that $5 trillion.

---

* After the takeover, Alan Greenspan called Paulson and asked, "Why didn't you just nationalize them?" Paulson shot back: "Why didn't you?" Greenspan replied that he wouldn't have been able to get it through Congress.

The Monday after the bailout, September 8, the stock market rallied, and Treasury officials congratulated themselves on a well-executed coup. The only down note was struck by Lehman; its shares disturbingly slumped 13 percent to a mere 14, spoiling Paulson's short-lived feeling of relief. Worse, Fuld had received worrisome indications that the bid from the South Koreans, his most likely savior, was falling through. Over the weekend, he visited John Mack, the Morgan Stanley chief executive, at his home to discuss a merger, but nothing came of it. Interest in Lehman was greater at Barclays, but Diamond, the chief executive, was waiting for the Fed to invite him into the bidding. As a representative of a foreign bank, he could not be seen as poaching. Moreover, Barclays was still demanding a federally assisted deal. The Bear Stearns rescue had poisoned the waters; everyone expected the government to help with Lehman, too.

Paulson feverishly tried to dash such hopes. He spread the word to Wall Street that Treasury had no money for Lehman, and no authority to provide any.[16] This was useful as a bargaining tactic, and reflected his disgust at the thought of another bailout. It was also a measure of his political acuity; after Fannie and Freddie, the public had had enough of bailouts, which it regarded as handouts to wealthy bankers.*

O N TUESDAY, the stock market, worried by Lehman, reversed course and tumbled 2 percent. Credit markets fared even worse. Eschewing risk, lenders were pulling funds from private borrowers and parking them with the government for safety. After a day's reflection, traders were unsettled by the loss of Fannie's and Freddie's preferred stock, and by the larger truth that removing the twins from danger had not resolved the banking crisis. In a telltale reminder that the country's subprime problems were far from over, WaMu's board sacked its CEO, Kerry Killinger, the banker who once had presumed that mortgages

---

* The *Wall Street Journal* sharply opined, "The Treasury Secretary has set a terrible precedent, leaving subordinate debt holders at other large financial institutions to calculate that they too will receive a government bailout if they stumble."

were just like retail. These assorted blows, striking on a single day as if from the fury of an angry god, weighed deeply on other troubled institutions, especially AIG. Its stock dropped under 20, and it was being forced to refinance billions of its debt under difficult conditions. JPMorgan, AIG's banker and presumptive savior, was moving slowly in devising a remedy. As AIG's credit weakened, the cost of insuring its bonds in the credit default swap market was rising precipitously. At the end of August its swaps had traded at $375,000; on Wednesday, September 10, they touched $520,000.

Willumstad, the AIG chief, went to see Geithner, realizing that supervision by the New York Fed, which had long been considered a straitjacket, now might be his life jacket. Willumstad proposed that the Fed reclassify AIG so the insurer could borrow at the Fed's discount window—and, not incidentally, be subject to the Fed's powers. Tight-lipped and seemingly distracted, Geithner promised to "look into the mechanics." The AIG chief stammered that matters were urgent, but Geithner was busy on the phone. Willumstad gathered he was talking to Fuld. Plainly, his focus was on Lehman.

For good reason: As word leaked out Tuesday that Lehman's deal with the South Korean bank was off, its stock traded four hundred million shares—almost the entire company changing hands in a day. The share price plunged 45 percent, falling below 10, and the market value fell to a paltry $6 billion, down from $37 billion at the start of the year. Seeing its shares in single digits, Skip McGee, Lehman's head of investment banking, had a sickening premonition. The Lehman executive suite had the feeling of a war room, as bankers surviving on rations of M&M's and Diet Cokes desperately mapped out thrusts and counterthrusts. Fuld, seeing the stock plummet, cried aloud, "Here we go again, perception trumping reality once more."[17] Short-sellers had pounced on the stock. Fuld felt like hunted prey.

In Washington, it dawned on Paulson that he could be facing a second Bear Stearns, only this time without an obvious savior. Only a couple of days had passed since the Fannie and Freddie bailout, and Paulson was facing a new crisis, now over Lehman. Treasury officials called top executives at Barclays as well as Ken Lewis at Bank of America and urged them to enter the bidding. Of the two, the British bank was clearly more interested. However, both suitors said they would need government help; Paulson insisted it would not be forthcoming.[18]

Wall Street was nonetheless focused on Washington. Steve Black, the JPMorgan executive, visited with Paulson Tuesday morning and was scheduled to see the House Republican leadership after lunch. However, as shares of Lehman—a major Morgan client—tumbled, Black had second thoughts. He decided to skip the House Republicans and put in a call to Lehman.

Decamping in Morgan's Pennsylvania Avenue office, Black reached Fuld Tuesday afternoon. He told him bluntly that Morgan was worried. "I understand your issues," Black added, trying to sound reasonable, "but we're very concerned about our intraday exposure." Morgan already had a request pending for additional collateral; now Black demanded $5 billion more, which he promised not to hold longer than Morgan deemed necessary.

Fuld said, "How about $3 billion?" Black agreed.

With that unpleasant business out of the way, Black inquired what Morgan could do for Lehman. He suggested that Fuld call Geithner and ask him to "herd the cats"—that is, use the Fed to round up banks that might contribute capital. The New York Fed had performed precisely that mission ten years earlier, for LTCM.

But Fuld, who had drawn much reassurance from his previous escapes, refused. He said it would be seen as an act of desperation that would devastate the stock. Black recalled his gut conviction that Fuld would never sell Lehman when he could—only when he had to. "Dick," he said bluntly, "You are in dire straits. The best people to herd those cats are the Fed." Fuld was unmoved. He had joined Lehman in 1969 and in the ensuing thirty-nine years (a quarter of the firm's existence) had survived many crises. He had seen his personal fortune grow to $900 million, a once-unthinkable sum, and then shrink in recent days to approximately $75 million.

Fuld merely asked Black to send some bankers by that evening, to see if Morgan could help, perhaps with a plan for raising capital. Citigroup would attend as well. The meeting was at Simpson Thacher & Bartlett, one of the law firms representing Lehman. Lehman was planning to stage an earnings "call" with investors Wednesday morning to preview its third-quarter earnings. The purpose of an earnings call, one of the Street's time-honored rituals, is to reinforce the Street's natural tendency toward optimism. Lehman would also present "Spinco"—the plan to divide its assets between a "good bank" and a "bad bank" and which, according to Lehman's bankers, would save the firm.

At the meeting at Simpson Thacher, John Hogan, the head of risk for Morgan's investment bank, listened with disbelief. The Lehman team was vague on when or how they would raise the necessary capital. Hogan said the market would sniff out the plan's weakness; any plan that could not be executed until 2009 was unlikely to calm investors. He advised Lehman not to go ahead with the call.

Back at headquarters, a glass skyscraper on Seventh Avenue, Lehman's bankers furiously debated Morgan's advice. To open the field to unanswerable questions might, as Morgan believed, alienate investors at a critical juncture, yet to say nothing at all might raise suspicions, too. The argument lengthened into the evening until, the executives wearying and the lights of Times Square coming into full glow, the bankers decided they would go ahead.

On the earnings call, Fuld was his vintage salesman self. He chortled, "We have a long track record of pulling together when times are tough."[19] Lehman's report was not all bad; its efforts to sell assets had lowered its leverage. However, its quarterly loss was the worst in the firm's history, magnified by a stupefying $8 billion markdown in the value of its mortgages. What would happen, investors wondered, if more write-downs followed? Lehman had only $20 billion of common equity left.[20]

Most troubling to its already nervous audience was that Lehman still had $50 billion in real estate assets remaining—of which a third were residential and the rest commercial. Investors saw the former as the stuff that had brought down Fannie and Freddie, the latter as toxic and, indeed, untouchable.

Lehman made much of its plan to split itself in two, but a single phrase in its press release—"Expected to be completed in first quarter of fiscal 2009"—drained it of promise. The earnings call developed into a tug-of-war between executives furiously spinning their situation and investors doubting the sufficiency of Lehman's capital and the adequacy of its write-downs. For a financial firm, to engage in such a battle is to lose it.

After the call, Goldman, Merrill Lynch, and Morgan Stanley gamely announced they would continue to do business with Lehman. But the credit-rating agencies perceptibly pulled back. Deservingly or not, the rating agencies were still the gatekeeper of Wall Street. The same investors who had sheepishly followed them into mortgage securities would just as slavishly heed their call on Lehman. Pronouncing as if from on high, Moody's ordered Lehman to find a well-heeled acquirer, failing which it would lower Lehman's credit rating three notches and possibly more. Thinking of the rapid unwind of Bear Stearns, Moody's gave Lehman to understand that its deadline was Monday.[21] Lehman received similar warnings from Standard & Poor's. These were deadly serious threats, and not only for their effect on the crowd. Under the terms of various borrowings, Lehman would immediately have to post more collateral if its rating was reduced. Thus, the agencies held the key to Lehman's fate.

The existence of a deadline crystallized the Street's sense of urgency. The CDS market erupted. Premiums soared to $580,000 to insure $10 million of Lehman bonds, up from $320,000 the previous week.[22] The mortgage market froze; potential buyers stopped bidding. Lehman creditors became palpably anxious. John Hogan, the JPMorgan risk manager who had urged Lehman not to go ahead with its earnings call, was impressed with Lehman's pluck. But he doubted whether it could stem the tide. JPMorgan abandoned any thought that it could raise capital for Lehman. It was now more worried about itself.

After conferring with Steve Black, Hogan produced an inventory of

Morgan's exposure to Lehman, some 75,000 trades, and grouped them by asset type and risk level. The inventory was meant to determine what would happen if, as Hogan demurely phrased it, Lehman "went away." Morgan's exposure was considerable. Hogan put Lehman on preapproval status, meaning no one at Morgan could trade with Lehman without his or his deputy's OK. As far as the most powerful bank on Wall Street was concerned, Lehman had been reduced to conditional status, a limbo for firms that had lost its trust.

Hedge funds backed away from Lehman as if from a victim of plague. Funds and other counterparties who had outstanding trades with Lehman wanted to be rid of any connection; they were begging stronger banks to step into Lehman's shoes and assume its obligations. It had finally dawned on the market that Lehman's capitalization was weak. In its earnings report, Lehman had boasted of its liquidity; investors needed to see equity. The upheaval of 2008 was proving the oldest maxim of banking: in a crisis, only capital will ensure an institution's survival.

Paulson spent Wednesday fielding calls from politicians hostile to even the suggestion of a bailout: the presidential contenders, Barack Obama and John McCain; Nancy Pelosi; Chuck Schumer; Republicans; Democrats. Sentiment against helping Lehman had coalesced in a form rarely seen on Capitol Hill: fervent and fully bipartisan.[23] Paulson, of course, shared those feelings. He reiterated the no-bailout policy to reporters and underscored it to the Fed. Neither Bernanke nor Warsh thought this wise, as it reduced their options. But Paulson was determined, like a man who, after months of waiting, will enter a long-expected battle in the morning. Lehman had not sneaked up on him unnoticed, as had Bear Stearns. The various agencies of the federal government knew Lehman's assets, knew its liabilities. They were, they supposed, ready.

Most of the bankers inside Lehman thought the firm would survive—that a deal would get done. Russo, the executive closest to Fuld, felt sure of it. As Russo was aware, senior executives from Barclays in London would soon be en route to New York. Bank of America was already on the ground. With two—perhaps more—sharks in the water, one of them would bite. As Fuld had said, Lehman had a history of surviving tough times.

All the same, a call went out from Lehman late Wednesday afternoon to Harvey R. Miller, a partner in the New York City law firm of Weil, Gotshal & Manges, asking if he could start gathering preliminary data on Lehman. Miller was the foremost legal expert in business reorganization. His specialty was bankruptcy.

12

SLEEPLESS

*I wake up every single night thinking what I could
have done differently.*

—RICHARD FULD, HEARING OF HOUSE
COMMITTEE ON OVERSIGHT AND GOVERNMENT
REFORM, OCTOBER 6, 2008

HARVEY MILLER was on business in Delaware when the call came
from Lehman. On Thursday, September 11, his office advised that
he come home early. Preparatory work on Lehman was moving ahead,
and Miller, a tall, nattily attired lawyer who had worked on the bankruptcies of Texaco, United Airlines, Macy's, and, most recently, IndyMac,
would be indispensable if Lehman were to file. Russo, Lehman's ranking
in-house attorney, admonished Miller not to mention the assignment to
a soul. In the next breath, Russo implored him to sequester the associates
working on the case in a sealed conference room. The effort was assigned
a code name, "Project Equinox." Russo assured Miller that the bankruptcy preparations were purely precautionary. "This is not going to happen," Russo said. "We have things in the fire that will work out."

Bank of America, a potential acquirer, was poring through Lehman's
books at Sullivan and Cromwell's midtown conference center, while
Barclays was involved in a parallel exercise at Simpson Thacher.
Radiating from these legal hubs, a fair swath of Manhattan had plunged
into the urgent issue of Lehman's survival. At the Fed, officials were

exploring whether Lehman's demise, if it came to that, would capsize derivative markets.[1] Unable to break for long enough to go home, the Fed officials checked in to the Millennium Hotel, overlooking Ground Zero, site of the terrorist disaster exactly eight years earlier. At Lehman, Fuld was furiously calling officials and Wall Street friends, waving off the rumor (published, painfully, in the *Times*) that he could be sacked.[2] As if to give Fuld a shot in the arm, John Macomber, a Lehman director, strode into the war room, where a dozen bankers were clustered, and proclaimed buoyantly, "This is bad luck; you have all done a great job." Few of the bankers believed him.

Further uptown, John Thain, the Merrill chief, was attending an off-site meeting at the swank Regency Hotel, periodically excused himself to answer urgent cell phone calls. Lehman's crisis had thrown a shadow over every investment bank, Merrill in particular. To ordinary Americans, Merrill's iconic bull was the very symbol of the stock market. But it suffered from the same disease as Lehman—too much leverage, too much reliance on short-term funding, and assets, especially real estate, of dubious value.

Thain believed that Merrill was secure, but Greg Fleming, its forty-four-year-old president, was not so sure. The son of teachers from Hopewell Junction, New York, Fleming was a graduate of Yale Law School and had already clocked sixteen years at Merrill, to which he had developed a soldierly loyalty. What scared him was the fast-traveling news that Lehman was talking to Bank of America, which previously had seemed so eager to acquire Merrill. All Fleming could think was, "If Bank of America saves Lehman, who will save us?"

Fleming called Ed Herlihy, the Wachtell lawyer, who had a close relationship with Ken Lewis, and begged him to get Thain and Lewis talking about a Bank of America–Merrill merger before it was too late. "You must have Lewis call Thain," Fleming pleaded. He sounded panicky. Herlihy responded that Thain had to get the ball rolling; Lewis would not respond to a feeler from anyone else. Merrill's stock was weak that Thursday; Lehman's plunged to an anemic 4¼.

AIG was oddly off the public's radar. However, in financial terms, its troubles were larger than Lehman's. The giant insurer had lost the daunting sum of $18.5 billion over the past three quarters, and it was staring at $78 billion in exposure to subprime CDOs, with even more in other varieties of CDOs. As its swaps contracts had swooned, AIG had been forced to post $22 billion in collateral; if its credit was down-graded, as the almighty rating agencies were threatening, it would be liable for an additional $18 billion, perhaps as much as $30 billion.[3]

Unlike Lehman, which had been fervently attempting to reduce its exposure for months, AIG had been moving deliberately and slowly. Worse, it had been quarreling with JPMorgan, its presumptive ally. Willumstad did not care for Tim Main, the Morgan banker assigned to AIG, who appeared self-satisfied and arrogant. Morgan, for its part, was convinced that AIG's figures were wrong. Neither firm trusted the other; neither was entirely blameless. However, AIG did not have the luxury of indulging wounded feelings, even if provoked by the swagger-ing Morgan; it had to raise liquidity. Hank Greenberg, AIG's deposed chieftain and its largest stockholder, called Willumstad Thursday and bellowed, "What the hell are you people waiting for?"[4]

Willumstad and Morgan's Jamie Dimon made an effort to restore good relations. That same Thursday, Dimon sent his top investment banker, Douglas Braunstein, to work through AIG's books, and Braunstein made considerable progress. Nonetheless, tension between the firms persisted. Later in the day, Brian Schreiber, AIG's young head of planning, got a call from Tim Main, pestering him for a signed engagement letter. Schreiber screamed back, "Where's my repo line?" (Wall Street lingo for an over-night loan.) Main retorted, "Are you crazy? You think I'm going to lend to you when you need $30 billion?" Presently, Schreiber heard from Steve Black, Morgan's uninhibited effective number two. "Every bit of info we get from you is wrong," Black thundered. "You're so screwed!"

These theatrics did not particularly surprise Willumstad. As a banker, he knew that banks did not lend tens of billions of dollars on an unsecured basis. AIG did have assets to pledge—but mostly, they were held in its regulated insurance subsidiaries. AIG needed cash available at the parent company level. Its best—perhaps its only—hope was to find investors. The most likely source of large investment on such short notice would be a private equity firm.

Willumstad unleashed a furious volley of calls. Schreiber, his executive, called the investment manager BlackRock and beseeched a senior executive to find a buyer by the weekend. Given AIG's complexity, the request seemed faintly absurd.* Next, Willumstad called Chris Flowers, the private equity banker who had bid for Bear Stearns. He asked Willumstad what was up.

"We're going to run out of cash on Wednesday," Willumstad said bluntly. Flowers blinked. AIG had $1 trillion in assets, 130,000 employees. It was the world's largest insurer. Flowers was already working on one potential shotgun merger, advising Bank of America on its Lehman Brothers bid.[5] The thought of simultaneously rescuing both Lehman and AIG would, at any other time, have seemed preposterous. But Wall Street, and its way of doing business, hung on the outcome. If AIG toppled, others would go with it, and where it would end?

Flowers glanced at his firm's managing director, John Oros, who had just arrived from Kennedy Airport, where he had gotten off a twenty-two-hour flight from Australia. They agreed to divide resources, and Oros and some of their staff went downtown, arriving at AIG in the evening, New York time. There, Oros made a specific request—for the consolidated balance sheet. He was not interested in the individual claims of AIG's multitudinous subsidiaries; rather, he wanted to know how much cash the company—the *whole* company—had right now. No one seemed to know. An employee departed and returned with what resembled a wheelbarrow laden with ledgers and file folders. The calculation of AIG's cash resources was apparently more complex than it had appeared. As Oros would recall, with numeric imprecision but a fine grasp of the larger truth:

---

* A graphic depiction of AIG's corporate structure resembled a financial Rubik's Cube, with names of subsidiaries stretching thirteen columns across and extending twenty-five rows down.

Think of AIG with these fabulous insurance companies—individual subsidiaries [that] are great companies. The parent company went out and issued credit default swaps in the hundreds of billions of dollars where they get [paid] a quarter percent or three-eighths of a percent. While you are triple-A, you have to put up no collateral. Turns out if you are downgraded to a double-A, you have to come up with $5 billion, and if you get downgraded to an A, you have to come up with $50 billion, and if you get downgraded below that you have to come up with $180 billion. What kind of a decision is it that you say, as you reach financial problems, you compound geometrically your cash negatives?[6]

While AIG remained largely out of view, Lehman's drama had attained the aspect of public theater. Reporters staked out its headquarters, television pundits opined on the odds of its survival, and worried investors called to check their holdings. (The Reserve Primary Fund, which owned Lehman's debt, assured its clients that Lehman paper was safe.)[7] Hedge funds were trying to move securities from Lehman to other brokers. All the while, Lehman executives, believing a deal would be reached, seemed preternaturally calm. Tonucci, the treasurer, spirited data to Lehman's two suitors, Barclays and Bank of America. Each had serious questions about the quality of Lehman's assets, especially its troublesome commercial loans. The more urgent issue was whether Wall Street would continue to fund the embattled company until a deal was hatched.

Thursday night, Tonucci was at Sullivan & Cromwell, helping Bank of America conduct due diligence. He was yanked out of the room to take a call from Jane Buyers Russo, the head of JPMorgan's broker-dealer unit. Buyers Russo and Tonucci spoke almost daily, and were on collegial terms. This time, her news was grave, her tone almost apologetic. Morgan had yet to receive $5 billion in collateral; it needed the money Friday morning. She added that if anyone at Lehman wanted to discuss it, it would have to be with "Jamie."[8]

Tonucci immediately called his superiors. A short while later, Rodgin Cohen, the soft-spoken Sullivan & Cromwell attorney, whose influence in such matters was peerless, called the New York Fed to see if it might urge Morgan to grant Lehman a reprieve. Geithner's office icily replied that Morgan's demand was "appropriate." Although, as a banking matter, Morgan was clearly within its rights, Cohen was shocked by the unsympathetic tone of the Fed's response.

Geithner and Paulson certainly wanted Lehman to survive, but they viewed JPMorgan, one of the strongest banks extant, as the cornerstone of a solution, not as an obstacle. Late that evening, the officials conferred. They agreed the time had come to spring into action and settled on a plan. It was to be kept secret until markets closed on Friday.

FRIDAY MORNING, Paulson briefed President Bush, emphasizing that Lehman Brothers might not survive the weekend. Bush, naturally, asked why Lehman was different from Bear Stearns. Paulson replied that, thus far, no buyer had appeared. And Paulson, now, was fully invested in the cause of preventing moral hazard. The president agreed that bankruptcy was a natural and proper outcome for failing firms. Moreover, Paulson's concern with regard to Lehman was somewhat eased by reports that AIG would be rescued by private means. The prospect that the fate of both firms would be resolved in the marketplace, and that AIG, at least, would be saved, stanching Wall Street's wounds, satisfied Paulson's fierce and conflicting agendas—to refrain from unnaturally tipping the scales, and to preserve the market's equilibrium.[9]

AIG, however, was nowhere near as resolved as Paulson believed. S&P issued a downgrade threat that day, and frightened lenders continued to back away, especially from AIG's commercial paper. By Friday morning, the insurer's cash deficit was judged to be $10 billion, and the more Morgan looked, the wider the deficit grew. Meanwhile, AIG's stock was plunging. It closed Friday at 12, down 30 percent.

Trying to sound calm, Willumstad called Kohlberg Kravis Roberts & Co., a leading private equity firm (and no stranger to leverage itself) and asked if *it* could organize a buyout. By now, AIG's hole was estimated at $20 billion. Credit default swaps on its paper soared to $900,000 per $10 million of bonds, a sign of intense credit market jitters.[10] In desperation, late that afternoon, AIG called Eric Dinallo, the state insurance superintendent; the company reached him Friday evening at his weekend home upstate. Realizing the gravity of the situation, Dinallo canceled his weekend plans and decided to return to New York.[11] Meanwhile, the attorney for AIG's board notified the directors to be on call.

While the state superintendent was dealing with AIG, federal banking regulators were focused that Friday on WaMu, still the country's largest thrift. Its stock had tumbled to under 3, its credit downgraded to junk bond status—on a par with that of the subprime borrowers whom, in the heyday of the credit bubble, it had been so eager to lend to. Finance is often harsh but, of a fashion, poetically just. WaMu was in need of credit, but the fad for lending to poor mouths had abated; WaMu was now in a position not dissimilar to that of the millions of subprime borrowers facing foreclosure. Though WaMu insisted it was liquid, rumors swirled that it would be seized.

Paulson, Bernanke, and Geithner were preoccupied with the more urgent issue of what they could do for Lehman. Neither of the two Fed officials shared Paulson's preoccupation with moral hazard—or at least, neither thought it outweighed the need to keep the crisis from getting out of hand. But they were subject to legal restraints. By law, the Fed was permitted to lend to private individuals and corporations only so long as their credit was "secured to the satisfaction of the Federal Reserve bank."[12]

This language is not exactly airtight, and the Fed governors knew they had bent the rule (if not broken it) in the case of Bear Stearns. However, Lehman and Bear were not entirely analogous. Lehman's assets, especially its commercial loans and private equity, were considered riskier than Bear's. And Paulson had preempted the issue with his fiat against government assistance, in effect prevailing over Bernanke because of his more forceful and impulsive personality. When Bernanke won a round, it was usually when he had time to reflect and muster his resolve.

CNBC broke the news that the Treasury would not be assisting Lehman, which further unnerved the firm's creditors. As Lehman scrambled to fulfill JPMorgan's demand for collateral, it failed to execute on several hundred million dollars of trades. In a panic, customers clamored to withdraw funds, Lehman's cash management system could not keep up, and its London subsidiary went home Friday short of funds and essentially broke.[13] The stock closed under 4.

By now, Lehman was strictly playing for a deal. The due-diligence processes, by which Bank of America and Barclays were to judge the value of Lehman's assets and therefore what the firm was worth, were murderously one-sided. Each of the suitors marked down every commercial and private equity asset by ruinous proportions. Lehman, of course, was free to reject their bids; it was also free to file for bankruptcy. It was not a question of the correctness of the valuations; the law of the jungle prevailed. At one point, the Bank of America negotiators told the Lehman executives Skip McGee and Bart McDade, "We know you marked this [asset] down but just to be conservative we'll take it down more." The evidence suggests that the Bank purposefully attached low marks, so that Lewis could demonstrate to Paulson that Lehman was too sickly to be acquired without assistance. Barclays was more hopeful of a positive outcome, though it, too, attached very low marks to Lehman's assets. The good news, from Lehman's perspective, was that both negotiations were progressing.

With anxiety over Lehman mounting all day Friday, Merrill called an emergency telephone meeting of its board. One director queried Thain whether he, too, would seek a buyer. Thain, still sounding cocky, replied, "We're not Lehman." Merrill, however, had received a call from Barry Zubrow, the Morgan risk officer, demanding an immediate $5 billion in collateral. Evidently, Merrill was viewed in the same class of risk as Lehman. Greg Fleming, Merrill's second-in-command, left the board meeting feeling exposed. It gnawed at him that Bank of America,

Merrill's intended, might acquire Lehman. In desperation, Fleming again called Ed Herlihy, the Wachtell lawyer, and begged him to call Lewis to get merger talks rolling. Herlihy said, "Greg, we've been through this. *Thain* needs to call Lewis."

Whiffs of these discussions sifted into the market—not enough to inform, merely to agitate. Traders reacted by pulling money away from any organization suspected of bearing risk and redeploying it with the only one judged to be risk-free: the U.S. government. Thus, as barrelfuls of cash were offered to Uncle Sam, the government was able to borrow more cheaply. The rate on thirty-day Treasury bills fell Friday from 1.53 percent to 1.31 percent, an advance that, however innocent it appeared to the novice, spoke volumes to the cognoscenti. Wall Street, after a year of steadily backpedaling from risk, now was in headlong retreat from it.

Late Friday John Thain was in midtown, trying to make a quick exit through sluggish traffic, which was slowed by a summer shower, when he got a call to appear at the New York Federal Reserve at 6 P.M. This was the secret Paulson plan. Steve Black, who was making a golf date for the weekend, heard the news from Jamie Dimon. "You're not going to believe this," Dimon said. "We've been invited with our closest friends to a cocktail reception at the Fed with Geithner and Paulson." Sensing an historic moment, Black thought he should save the next day's newspaper, and the ones after that.[14] The regulators, along with Chris Cox, the SEC chairman, assembled with top representatives of ten financial institutions, mostly CEOs and some of their number twos—the elite of American finance—in a solid, stone conference room on the main floor, adjacent to the more expansive Liberty Room, which was fronted by wrought iron–grated windows where, in the Fed's early years, customers with bills would queue up to do their business.

Paulson began by announcing that the group should find a way to save Lehman over the weekend; he quickly added that no government money was available. "We're here to facilitate," Geithner elaborated. "You guys need to come up with a solution." Both emphasized that their concern was not for Lehman specifically but for the good of the system. Regulators had delivered precisely the same message ten years before, when the Fed had marshaled fourteen banks at the same site to rescue Long-Term Capital Management. Some of those banks, such as Chase and Bankers Trust, had since been merged out of existence. Bear Stearns, which had refused to participate in the LTCM bailout, had failed—an irony lost on none of those present now. Only one CEO—Richard Fuld—remained from that era, and he had not been invited to this cocktail hour.* Still, the memory of the LTCM affair hung in the air.

Paulson told his former colleagues they had a "responsibility" to the marketplace.[15] Among the CEOs, Vikram Pandit of Citigroup spoke first, obscurely suggesting, "We have a bigger problem to solve than Lehman." An uncustomary awkwardness lingered over his words. Pandit meant that if Lehman failed, a run against other credits would follow. The banks were all leveraged to the hilt; it was a question of which was the next weakest. John Mack, the Morgan Stanley chief, and Dimon began to discuss whether they would need to save Merrill Lynch. An executive remembered the presence of Thain and weakly apologized to the Merrill chief.

Black, sitting two places away from Geithner, murmured that, as long as they were here, they should also tackle AIG. Geithner hushed him: "That is totally inappropriate for this discussion." But Pandit, whose bank, like JPMorgan, was advising AIG, delivered a firm rebuke. "I heard you," he told his regulator. "AIG is absolutely appropriate."

The CEOs divided their weekend labor into three groups: one would assess Lehman's most problematic assets; another, steered by Thain, would devise a structure for acquiring Lehman (or parts of it); and a third, a "doomsday" unit, would explore how to minimize the damage to the payment system and other banking functions if a rescue failed. Around 8:30 P.M., the CEOs left, scattering to restaurants and homes.

---

* Dimon, like Thain, had been involved in LTCM, but they were not yet CEOs.

John Mack picked up a takeout Italian dinner and headed back to Morgan Stanley, where he briefed his lieutenants.[16] Dimon phoned Hogan, his associate, on his way uptown, advising him to order JPMorgan hands to report early Saturday morning. Black drove on to Greenwich, where he and his wife had a reservation at Rebecca's, an exclusive French restaurant. No sooner were the Blacks seated than Thain and his wife and another couple eased past them to a far table.

Paulson returned to his suite at the Waldorf-Astoria; late that evening he heard from the two CEOs negotiating with Lehman. Each had concluded that Lehman suffered from a "hole"—a deficit in its net worth—running into the tens of billions of dollars. Each, therefore, insisted their company would need help to make the purchase. However, their pleas differed in a crucial respect. Ken Lewis, the more reluctant suitor, wanted the government to take over some $65 billion of Lehman's most problematic assets—a suggestion he knew Paulson would reject. Barclays's Bob Diamond, however, proposed that the private banks that had assembled at the Fed play the savior, as they had with LTCM. Barclays would buy the "good" Lehman assets if Citi, Goldman, JPMorgan et al. would form a consortium to buy the rest.* All Paulson had to do was give them a nudge.

Meanwhile, the Barclays bankers, who had yet to sleep or even leave the Simpson Thacher office since arriving from London, worked through the night. The Bank of America team, similarly, picked over Lehman until daybreak. Bart McDade, promoted to president of Lehman just months earlier, shuttled between the two law firms. Fuld nervously hung back at Lehman, like a general who didn't know which of his officers would report next with news from the front.

Lehman's executives considered a merger with Bank of America the most likely outcome. This prospect, of course, horrified Fleming, the Merrill president. If Bank of America bought Lehman, who would

---

* Diamond likened this to a "reverse Spinco." Instead of spinning off Lehman's bad assets, as the Lehman bankers had proposed, Barclays would acquire the good assets, leaving a rump collection of toxic loans for the banks.

save his firm? Returning Friday night to his home in Bedford, New York, he again called Herlihy, the lawyer who was close to Lewis; Herlihy wouldn't budge. Fleming had trouble sleeping that night. He admitted to his wife he feared that Merrill was in jeopardy. Knowing of Thain's opposition to a merger, Fleming felt the burden of initiative fall on him. Merrill was a ninety-four-year-old firm—the best-known brokerage in America. Fleming had decided to sell it.

He called Herlihy at six-thirty in the morning Saturday, as Herlihy was leaving his apartment for a cab to go to the Fed. Riding with him were Greg Curl, Bank of America's top deal maker, and Joe Price, its chief financial officer—the stroke of luck Fleming had been hoping for. And the Bank of America operatives knew more than Fleming suspected. Herlihy had been keeping Lewis informed of Fleming's calls, stoking Lewis's ardor. Curl had been privy to their minuet. In the cab, Herlihy handed the phone to Curl, who repeated that it was up to Thain to initiate merger talks. But Fleming, now, had direct evidence that Bank of America was interested—and, apparently, that it hadn't struck a deal with Lehman yet.

In the financial district, bankers were reporting for Saturday duty. Thain was in his black Escalade, en route to the Fed. Harvey Miller, the Lehman bankruptcy attorney, was e-mailing Weil Gotshal colleagues, explaining that he had an urgent need for partners to pitch in on Lehman. Dick Fuld, who had risen early and donned a crisp blue suit, was already at the office, where he had been since 7 A.M.[17]

Shortly after eight, Paulson and Geithner greeted the same group of CEOs from the night before, who had returned with their various lieutenants to the Fed's ground-floor conference room. "You guys are going to bail out Lehman," Paulson said, echoing his message from the previous night with a more urgent tone. "I'll come back to hear your plan." He and Geithner departed to the thirteenth floor, where Geithner's office was, and where Paulson and Cox and their staffs were keeping temporary quarters. Pete Kelly, the Merrill lawyer, rolled his eyes. Something about Paulson's manner—his brusqueness—made

Kelly doubt the entire project. He said to Thain, "This is not going to happen." "No," said Thain. "It's not."

Curl and Price, the Bank of America negotiators, were escorted to the executive floor, to brief the trio of Paulson, Geithner, and Warsh. The bankers said the hole at Lehman was worse than supposed—a conclusion they had themselves made inevitable by aggressively marking down Lehman's assets. No bid would be possible without federal assistance, they said. Paulson told them to keep working.

By now, scores of investment bankers and lawyers were descending on the Fed in the hopes of crafting a solution to a problem that, though it bore Lehman's name, felt increasingly a collective burden. Sandwiches, pastries, and drinks were laid out in the Liberty Room, a vast area on the main floor divided by stone columns, reminiscent of a cathedral, where bankers could gather informally at small tables. The building, completed in 1924, was modeled after a Renaissance palace, with fortress-like stone to project an aura of financial security. Five floors below ground level, the Fed stored its bullion: 540,000 bars of gold worth $250 billion. Owing to security concerns, guests were restricted to the first floor. Guards led bankers to the upper floors, where various work groups convened. Meanwhile, Geithner and Paulson conducted a running stream of private interviews. A leitmotif of these sessions was that Lehman's fever had to be contained, lest it contaminate the system. In practical terms, that meant saving Merrill. The regulators told Thain he definitely should do a deal with *someone*.

Fleming worked up the nerve to talk to Thain and give him the same message. He pleaded with his boss to call Ken Lewis.

THE CHIEF FUNCTION of the CEOs at the Fed was to consider whether to contribute several billion dollars each to buy Lehman's bad assets. (In contrast, the total rescue package for LTCM was under $4 billion.) The foreign banks, such as Deutsche Bank and UBS, said they could not help Lehman without consulting their boards. By virtue of

JPMorgan's strength and prestige, Jamie Dimon naturally assumed a leadership role. Worried about a generalized disaster, he exhorted his colleagues to pull together. This grated on Pete Kelly, of Merrill, whose firm was, at the moment, being squeezed by Morgan.

Though some of its rivals had a cynical view of Morgan's intentions, Dimon was in fact gravely worried about the potential for a chain reaction. He called his risk manager, John Hogan, at Morgan headquarters early Saturday and told him the bank should be prepared for the failure of Lehman Brothers, Merrill Lynch, Morgan Stanley, *and* Goldman Sachs. Hogan set up a command center, assembling a staff that would reach two hundred. They parsed JPMorgan's exposure to each of the investment banks. Most frightening of all was its vulnerability to AIG, with whom Morgan had 120,000 open trades.[18]

Lehman was represented at the Fed by Bart McDade, its president, and a team of mortgage experts. Among these was a banker named Alex Kirk, who had left Lehman in January '08 and returned after the management shakeup in June. Since then, he had been focusing on Lehman's commercial property loans. McDade and Kirk were interrogated by the CEOs in the corner of the first-floor dining area. Thain, Mack, and Pandit demanded to know how Lehman financed every line on its balance sheet, which McDade and Kirk patiently walked them through. Pandit did most of the questioning, as though he were leading a seminar. An executive from Credit Suisse sauntered over, squared off in front of Kirk, and said, "Are you the guys from *Lehman?*" as if they were specimens in a zoo. Mack, the Morgan Stanley CEO, graciously piped up, "I'm so sorry for you guys; it could have been us rather than you." Thain silently nibbled at a muffin, as if his thoughts were elsewhere. Then, the Merrill chief said he had to make a phone call and bolted.[19] The Lehman bankers were led to a series of meetings on the upper floors, eventually settling in a room across from Barclays. They did not see anyone from Bank of America.

Fuld, meanwhile, had been frantically trying to reach Lewis at his home in Charlotte. "I can't believe the son of a bitch won't return my calls," he fumed. Fuld's exclusion from his own drama infuriated him.

He kept trying to call Paulson, too, with no better luck.[20] Still refusing to give in, he assured a friend, "We'll get through this."

Lehman's office was eerily quiet, as if the executives were waiting for an honored guest who had failed to show. It dawned on one banker, then another, that Bank of America was not returning their calls. McGee had a sudden epiphany; he guessed they were talking to Merrill.

He was right: Thain had given in to Fleming's entreaties. At 10:30 A.M., after his sudden exit, he called Lewis. Getting quickly to the point, Thain said Merrill needed a partner, and would be willing to sell Bank of America a minority stake. Lewis, who had coveted Merrill for so long, replied it would have to be all or nothing. He ventured that he could be in New York by two. Without resolving the difference in their agendas, the chief executives agreed to meet that afternoon. The Bank of America acquisition team, its work on Lehman finished, was already en route back to Charlotte. When they landed, a new set of instructions was waiting: don't go home, don't unpack, just return straight to New York.

S ATURDAY MORNING, as the CEOs were deliberating, Bob Willumstad, the chairman of AIG, and Braunstein, his JPMorgan banker, strolled over to see Paulson and Geithner at the Fed. The visit turned out to be brief. Preoccupied with Lehman, the regulators emphasized that AIG should pursue whatever private remedies were at hand.[21]

Willumstad returned to the AIG tower, with its sweeping views of New York, where would-be rescuers seemed to have arrived from every corner of the city. Four crews of private equity bankers were swarming over the sixteenth floor, intent on gleaning any fact about AIG that might be relevant to an investment. Schreiber, the strategic planning chief, managed the auction process—more nearly a bazaar—in which bankers darted from room to room, hearing various presentations and toting up sums. Mercifully for Willumstad, the Kohlberg Kravis Roberts team was led by Sir Deryck Maughan, a former colleague of Willumstad's at Citigroup. Maughan told Willumstad he was there to help; Willumstad seemed grateful. KKR's assignment, shared with Goldman and TPG Capital Parters, a private equity firm, was to raise $20 billion by Monday.* AIG was hoping for $20 billion more from banks. Flowers, the private equity banker, intentionally aloof, was sequestered in a windowless room working on a separate bid. The London unit that had engineered AIG's parlous derivative bets was patched in via video conference, but gave a muddled presentation.

Willumstad was juggling countless propositions. While the various equity bankers collected data at his headquarters, he sounded out Travelers, the insurance giant, on buying AIG's flagship property and casualty business. Such a deal could hardly be fashioned overnight, though. As a stopgap, he leaned on Dinallo, the state insurance superintendent, to let the holding company access $20 billion in liquidity that was buried within the corporation at the subsidiary level.† Dinallo arrived with a crew of twelve—the only government officials in the building among what Dinallo guessed to be more than a hundred bankers. Transferring assets from a regulated insurer is a serious business. Dinallo called David Paterson, the governor, emphasizing that the transfer would be an *exchange* of assets that would not weaken AIG's ability to make good on the claims of ordinary policyholders. Various pieces of AIG's rescue seemed to be moving ahead, but the apparent size of the capital hole was in continuous flux, a serious impediment to the fundraising. Equity investors did not want to invest without assurance that the money would be enough. The whispered hope was that the billionaire investor Warren Buffett, who in the past had shown a flair for acting boldly during a crisis, would jump into the ring. Executives placed calls to Omaha, Buffett's home. Meanwhile, AIG waited.

Ken Lewis read about Project Alpha—Bank of America's code name for a Merrill Lynch deal—on the corporate jet en route to New York.[22] While he knew, of course, of Merrill's mortgage troubles, he was im-

---

* A joke began to make the rounds of bankers: they only worked Saturdays and Sundays.
†The plan was for the holding company to exchange its stock in life insurance subsidiaries, which were illiquid, in return for liquid securities held by the regulated property casualty units.

pressed that it had unloaded so many of its CDOs. He fancied that a prime investment bank, shorn of most of its problematic assets and discounted due to a generalized crisis, could soon be his, and visions of Merrill's 17,000 stockbrokers—the so-called "thundering herd"— stirred his hunger. He settled in at the Bank's apartment at the Time Warner Center, the angled glass towers at the foot of Central Park, to wait.

Thain came alone, arriving around two thirty that Saturday. Lewis proposed a merger. Thain, who had run Merrill for all of nine months and did not fancy giving up the reins so soon, replied, "I am not here to sell Merrill Lynch."[23] He offered, instead, to sell Bank of America a 9.9 percent stake. Still moving along parallel tracks, they agreed to send negotiating teams to Wachtell Lipton, seven blocks south, under the supervision of Herlihy. After some hours, as the talks moved along, Lewis joined them.

Thain, however, returned to the Fed. He had to dodge reporters, who were beginning to hear whispers; moreover, he felt uncomfortable about the deal that was forging ahead in his absence. John Mack, the Morgan Stanley chief, spied him; sensing Thain's ambivalent mood, he blurted out, "Shouldn't we be talking?" Bankers' propositions had become as casual as those of college students.

Saturday evening, Thain met Mack and his two copresidents at the Upper East Side apartment of one of the Morgan Stanley execs. Along with Thain were Peter Kraus and Thomas Montag, both (like Thain) formerly of Goldman Sachs, and both very new to Merrill. It occurred to the Morgan Stanley trio that the Merrill team was rather a Goldman party in drag. The Goldman lineage, a branding that could never be removed, helped to explain the elitist tastes of Thain. The thought of selling to the middlebrow Bank of America was vaguely repellent.

The soiree with Morgan Stanley got off to a promising start. Mack was interested in a combination and said he would air the idea with his board, which was to meet on Tuesday; meanwhile, they could start due diligence. Thain, however, needed to move faster. With a Lehman collapse looming, he wanted to announce a deal, or at least an agreement in principle—anything to appease traders—before the markets opened in Asia, which would be Sunday night in New York. For Mack, such a hurried timetable was out of the question. Thus, the talks ended.

Thain still had options. Goldman, too, had inquired about the possibility of making an investment in Merrill. This would preserve Merrill as an independent company and, what's more, reconnect Thain to his roots, which he must have found irresistible. And so, he turned toward home.

Lehman, having no recent contact with Bank of America, shifted its energies toward Barclays. A deal was taking shape in which Barclays would acquire Lehman sans its most toxic assets. The leftover "rump" portion—a set of commercial properties and investments in troubled corporations such as Chrysler—would be sold to the Wall Street banks, which would put up at least $3 billion apiece. (The banks' motive was simply to avert a generalized calamity.) To complete the due diligence, Lehman bankers had to divulge their risk positions loan by loan, a demoralizing labor. Mark Walsh, the maestro of Lehman's fallen commercial portfolio, was subjected to a merciless grilling.[24] The picture he revealed was less than lovely. A couple of the banks, including Goldman, were sullen over the prospect of acquiring these assets, as if it were better to let Lehman go. But Paulson and Geithner put intense pressure on the bankers, arguing that a Lehman failure would cost them more. Bankruptcy would lead to asset fire sales, pulling down the prices of their own positions. The spiral would intensify. Barclays optimistically assembled a term sheet. The deal was getting close.

But the deficits attached to the rump Lehman assets—of which there were more than two thousand individual pieces—kept growing. Warsh and Geithner worked furiously to figure out a way to apportion the risk. The terse Geithner was laboring under a terrible strain; the tension knotted him. Though not one of the bankers, like Warsh he understood them. And he and Warsh were generally the most eager of the regulators to intervene. Periodically, the two ventured downstairs, increasingly sensing that the private offers for Lehman would be insuf-

ficient. This implied a government role, Paulson's fiat notwithstanding;
Warsh felt they had no choice.

There was a pending snag, which seemed so minor as to be almost
a technicality, in the Barclays deal. Someone would have to guarantee
Lehman's trading positions in the interim between the signing of the
merger and its closing. Otherwise, traders would fear that the acquisition might not happen, the bank run against Lehman would go on, and
the firm would fail all the same. According to the listing rules of the
UK Financial Services Authority (equivalent to America's SEC) Barclays
could not guarantee Lehman's positions without a shareholder vote,
since a guarantee would in effect consummate the merger. And a shareholder vote would require time. Barclays began to kick around solutions. Jerry del Missier, the wiry, midfortyish president of Barclays
Capital, thought a third party, such as a large insurer, could issue a
guarantee. It was the sort of problem for which he might have called
AIG—but AIG was no longer in a position to help. The next logical call
was to Warren Buffett, who presided over huge insurance operations.
Del Missier reached him in Edmonton, where the oracle was attending
a charity dinner and considering whether to put $5 billion into AIG.
Since the risk involved was incalculable, Buffett did not want to guarantee Lehman's trades. He declined to be Lehman's savior.[25]

Bob Diamond, the Barclays Capital CEO, thought there was only
one party that could do it: the Federal Reserve. Paulson insisted that
since the rule at issue was a UK rule, it was up to the Brits to waive it.
Diamond knew that that was unlikely. The FSA (the UK regulator) did
not have the power to waive its rule, and to ask the Bank of England to
guarantee the trades of an American investment bank sounded mad. But
the Fed could do it. All Lehman needed was an *interim* guarantee.

With such complications unresolved, Weil Gotshal continued to as-
semble data for a possible bankruptcy. Corporations cannot just proclaim
insolvency; they must provide the court with lists of their assets and
liabilities, the states they operate in, information about their employees,
their payroll, insurance, and much more. As Lehman had been preoc-

cupied, the process had dragged. Saturday night, with time running short, a Weil partner named Lori Fife, and several colleagues, trooped over to Lehman. The mood was chaotic but not dispirited. McDade, the Lehman president, had returned from the Fed. Russo, the vice-chairman, was working his contacts. Fuld was holding court. McGee, the investment banker, was upbeat on the progress with Barclays. Hope still flickered for a Bank of America deal as well. Employees who had no role in the events remained at the office to look on, as if at the bedside of an ailing relative who is given fighting odds.

However, the mood at AIG was darkening. By Saturday night, the size of the estimated "hole" had grown to more than $40 billion. Willumstad believed that he could count on private equity bankers for $10 billion in investment, and that Dinallo, the insurance regulator, would free up $20 billion, but he still faced a sizable gap.[26] Striding over to the Fed for the second time that day, Willumstad shared his doleful news with Paulson and Geithner. Clearly more pessimistic than he had been that morning, he showed them daily cash projections, according to which AIG would run out of money by the end of the week. Paulson was angry at being confronted with this second calamity. He asked how AIG marked its books. Willumstad said, "Aggressively." Paulson growled, "What does that mean?" "The opposite of conservatively," Willumstad snapped. This elliptical exchange irritated both sides, and Willumstad departed under a cloud.

Jim Wilkinson, Paulson's chief of staff, wondered aloud what would happen if AIG were allowed to fail. Paulson said it would sink every construction project, and every organization, in the country that was insured by AIG.[27] Although the company's rogue derivatives unit was little more than a hedge fund, alongside it there was a valuable, and vital, insurance operation. No one could imagine its failing.

Before turning in, Paulson called England to push for a waiver of the listing rule for Barclays. The response was not encouraging. Meanwhile, lawyers and bankers at the Fed were grinding away at myriad details. Donald Bernstein, a lawyer with Davis Polk & Wardwell, was preparing documents for the tens of billions of dollars of "bad"

Lehman assets that would be left for the banks should Barclays gobble the rest. Even after so much haggling, no one seemed to have a clear idea which assets would go and which would stay. Bernstein began to sketch a plan on his laptop, but the deadline was frightfully close. For Lehman to survive, it needed a deal before "daylight exposure"—that is, the opening of markets in Tokyo. Bernstein kept at it until after 2 A.M. on Sunday. The Barclays team worked through the night, its third in succession.

Willumstad returned to AIG in an unsettled mood, and he and Maughan, the KKR banker, played with private equity options until midnight. As Maughan walked out onto the darkened streets, he wondered how a company that had earned $20 billion in the two years prior could now be on the verge of failure. In midtown, the Bank of America and Merrill teams were still talking. At 3 A.M., they broke for pizza.[28] Then, the negotiations resumed. Greg Fleming, the Merrill president, did not get to his nearby hotel room until 4:30 A.M. Even then, he was far too excited to sleep.

13

THE FORCES OF EVIL

*Words cannot express the sadness in the franchise that
has been destroyed.*

—Lehman executive, e-mail to clients,
September 14, 2008[1]

At seven Sunday morning, September 14, Peter Kraus, one of
Merrill's new, high-level bankers, and Pete Kelly, its lawyer and
senior vice president, trooped over to meet the top executives of
Goldman Sachs. Goldman had entered the Merrill sweepstakes. It was
interested in buying only a 9.9 percent stake, though, and Kelly doubted
that would be enough to salvage Merrill. Moreover, though he understood the negotiating value of securing an additional bid, Kelly had a
strong aversion to showing confidential material to the opportunistic
Goldman. "Emotionally, this is hard for me," he candidly told his colleague. Kelly could scarcely forget that Kraus had been with Merrill
precisely a week, prior to which he had been at Goldman, or that Thain
had sprung from the same crucible. For Kelly, Goldman seemed to be
everywhere.

After an hour, they wound up the meeting, with the idea of regroup-
ing at Merrill so Goldman could see the books. However, the Merrill
people who could guide them were now at Wachtell Lipton, conducting the very same exercise with Bank of America. And the Merrill–Bank
of America merger talks were moving ahead. Thain and Lewis had met

over breakfast, and their negotiators—Greg Fleming and Greg Curl—were trying to hammer out an agreement.

Thain knew he could secure a deal; he just didn't know if he wanted it. Hearing that Goldman was itching to have a look at Merrill, Thain told Fleming to send some of his folks downtown to nurture the Goldman option. Fleming politely told his boss to butt out. He was not about to tell Bank of America, "The people talking to you have to take a break so they can talk to Goldman Sachs." Moreover, to lose the Bank of America deal was to risk losing all. With JPMorgan and Citigroup threatening to cut credit lines, Merrill did not have many friends. They could not afford to lose Ken Lewis.

Thain, now, commanded Fleming to part with some of his troops. Kraus, who had secured a fabulous pay package upon signing with Merrill,* was similarly smitten with the prospect of dealing with his former firm; he also told Fleming to divide his resources. Backing down only slightly, Fleming agreed to send a single banker.

By now, Fleming was close to snatching the main prize. Closeted with Curl of Bank of America, he argued that Merrill stock had been temporarily depressed by the Lehman news and deserved a premium over the current share price. Curl conceded the point, perhaps because he had been made aware by Thain that Merrill had other options. The price they agreed to, 29 per share, was 70 percent higher than Friday's close. Though it was a pittance of what Bank of America would have paid a year earlier, when Stan O'Neal's board blocked him from doing the same deal, it was nonetheless a coup for Merrill now. Thain returned to the Fed, slipping past a pack of reporters. He had yet to approve the merger; however, Paulson had gotten wind of the tentative deal from Lewis. The secretary walked Thain away from the crowd of bankers and said, "John, Ken tells me you have a deal. You will do this deal!"[2]

The main agenda at the Fed, where some ten-score lawyers, bankers, and officials, disturbing their normal Sunday rhythms, had again

---

* Kraus was hired in May '08, but did not start at Merrill until September. He resigned that December and received a reported $29 million after three months' work.

converged in the conference room, was the Lehman-Barclays deal. Bernstein, the Davis Polk lawyer who had worked until the wee hours the previous night, reviewed the terms with nearly a dozen CEOs in the dining area. Collectively, the banks would have to finance some $50 billion of Lehman's least desirable assets.[3]

Lloyd Blankfein said he doubted that Lehman posed a systemic risk—but if the group opted to rescue Lehman, Goldman would go along. Dimon, Pandit, and Mack thought they had no choice. The consensus was not so much that Armageddon loomed as that prudence required them to act. While details of the package still had to be thrashed out, the Treasury's Steve Shafran confidently told Bart McDade, Lehman's president, "We may have the outlines of a deal."[4]

McDade sent word to a colleague, Michael Gelband, and the news that Lehman had yet again escaped disaster spread through its headquarters. Lehman employees, who had been keeping vigil on little or no sleep, felt a surge of relief that nearly quieted their flutters of remaining doubt. Fuld told his directors to be at Lehman by noon, by which hour he hoped they could vote on the sale. He heard confirmation from Barclays—pending, the British bank added, agreement by the Fed that it would back Lehman's trades until its shareholders voted to approve the merger.

The Fed had provided such a conduit for JPMorgan, when it acquired Bear. Lehman's financial staff anticipated it would do the same on their behalf. Tonucci was making a list of unencumbered assets (that is, those it had not borrowed against); these assets, it was hoped, would give the Fed security to extend a guarantee.

The Fed did not ask to see Tonucci's list, nor did it give much thought that morning to providing a guarantee. Bernanke was in Washington, and he remained in a passive role, receiving reports from the front. Paulson, the official most in charge of policy, was engaged in difficult discussions with his UK counterpart, Chancellor of the Exchequer Alistair Darling. Paulson instructed Geithner and Cox to call their UK counterparts as well.[5] Paulson's aim in these myriad transatlantic calls was to persuade the FSA to waive its listing rule, thus letting Barclays proceed without having to gain its shareholders' consent.

The bilateral aspect of these talks seriously slowed them down. Though corporations had learned to operate across borders, governments were still bound by their territories. Paulson's request was, in any case, highly dubious, as waiving the rule would have permitted Barclays to disenfranchise its own shareholders. But the evidence is that the British didn't *want* to waive the rule. The UK was deeply worried about its own problem banks, such as Halifax Bank of Scotland and the Royal Bank of Scotland, which were also stuffed with unholy mortgages. The Brits saw Wall Street trembling; they had no interest in importing America's contagion. Certainly, neither Darling nor the prime minister, Gordon Brown, with whom he conferred, had any desire to be the lender of last resort to an American investment bank stocked with mortgages. Darling bluntly informed Paulson that the British would not make an exception to help out Lehman.

By Sunday morning, the technical dispute regarding the guarantee had become a deal-breaker. Diamond, the Barclays CEO, blamed an inexcusable lack of coordination between the United States and the UK. But the U.S. could have acted alone. As Diamond had suggested, the Fed itself could have provided a guarantee. Paulson's resolve against moral hazard was simply too great, and the Fed never challenged him.

At 10 A.M., Sunday, Paulson summoned Bart McDade and abruptly told him, "The FSA has turned it down." McDade called Fuld to break the bad news.

At Lehman headquarters, word filtered out that the deal was off and that, indeed, a bankruptcy filing loomed. Once again, the mood darkened. The directors' meeting was put on hold. Fuld, though, kept fighting. He called Paulson, then Geithner and Cox, pleading for a stay. Gelband dialed George Herbert Walker IV, a second cousin of President Bush who was head of Lehman's asset management business, and told him Lehman's collapse would create a catastrophe. He begged him to call the president.

Preparing for the worst, the Fed tried to ensure an orderly wind-down, hoping that trades would settle, and that derivative markets would not implode. Officials again reviewed Lehman's positions, trying to size up the effect of a bankruptcy, in particular, on swaps and repo markets.[6] Bernstein, the Davis Polk lawyer, rounded up signatures from the CEOs to create another pool of assets to stabilize other broker-dealers in the aftermath of a Lehman filing—a last-ditch effort to head off a meltdown.

This scurrying about sustained the illusion that regulators were in control, or at least could minimize the damage—what Geithner liked to call "spreading foam on the runway." Regardless, his underling, William Dudley, who oversaw the bank's trading, feared that markets would suffer a serious shock. Remembering Bear, people had been expecting Lehman to be saved. The market wasn't ready for this.[7]

Warsh pushed the other senior regulators—Paulson, Bernanke, and Geithner—to consider their options. The four discussed an outright nationalization of Lehman. Bernanke floated the idea of simply lending Lehman $100 billion. Geithner shrugged, "We'd be lending into a run. Banks would call their loans." These halfhearted sallies went nowhere. Overseas, Lehman operations were shutting down, their assets being frozen. Already, the UK subsidiary of Lehman was under the control of its auditor. Events were rushing, the officials sensed, toward a point of no return.

Maddeningly, Paulson and Geithner were diverted to the brewing crisis at AIG. Bob Willumstad dropped by the Fed Sunday morning with seemingly good news. He thought he could get his hands on $20 billion from KKR, the private equity firm, and $10 billion in liquidity from the banks. The hitch was that the investors did not want to be the "last dollars in"; they needed the comfort of more money behind them. Therefore, Willumstad wanted a very large loan from the Fed, which he would repay by selling assets. This was, in theory, a bankable idea: AIG had valuable insurance units, which were unaffected by the turmoil (an executive of Warren Buffett's Berkshire Hathaway was at AIG that very moment, investigating which of its assets he might bid for).[8] But asset sales take time.

The regulators, in any case, were not really paying attention to AIG. It is arguable that no Treasury secretary, no Fed official, ever had to deal with so many crises in a single hour. Even during the Depression, events moved more slowly. The officials met with Willumstad barely ten minutes, and mechanically repeated that no government money was available.

The government was hoping for an assist from Chris Flowers, the self-important private equity banker, who was buzzing through AIG's headquarters and preparing a bid. The offer, presented that afternoon, turned out to be highly complicated, rather a lowball effort and— thought Willumstad—utterly impractical. Willumstad's patience finally deserted him, and he ordered Flowers to leave the building.

Sunday afternoon, Fed officials turned up the heat on Lehman. They were anxious for Lehman to file, and when Harvey Miller, the Weil Gotshal bankruptcy attorney, said the firm was not yet ready, the discussions became unpleasant. Officials at the New York Fed, accompanied by their lawyers, got on the phone with a roomful of Lehman bankers and began fairly screaming, their voices variable, often unidentifiable and rather accusatory. Fuld felt sick.[9]

McDade and Kirk realized they had better return to the Fed. Miller and a group from Weil Gotshal went as well. Their cab ride was agonizing, inching through torturous traffic in Greenwich Village. En route, they heard from another partner who was starting bankruptcy preparations on AIG. There were not enough lawyers to go around.

The Weil Gotshal partners, along with McDade and Kirk, were ushered into a room with dozens of regulators and *their* lawyers sitting or standing three-deep on one side of the conference table. Although the private lawyers were in Saturday slacks, the government people, underscoring the gravity of their agenda, were dressed in starchy suits.

McDade and Kirk argued that Lehman had enough collateral to continue operations for a day or two or even longer. The regulators countered that the parent company of Lehman should file for bankruptcy immediately. Then, they intimated, its broker-dealer subsidiary would be permitted to borrow from the Fed, repay its repo lenders and keep operating. In other words, the route to an orderly transition was to file. The lawyers, never having seen such bullying by the Feds, were shocked. Miller pointed out that no one in the room was authorized to file for bankruptcy without the approval of the board. Stephen Dannhauser, Miller's partner, argued that there was no cause for a panic filing. He thought it would be catastrophic.

The regulators insisted that Lehman should summon its board—which, in fact, had been on call, and some of whom had been cooling their heels at Lehman. Though Thomas Baxter Jr., the New York Fed's general counsel, seemed to be in charge, on either side of him sundry and mysterious bureaucrats, who did not trouble to identify themselves, hurled inquiries and demands at the Lehman people, who groped as if in a Kafkaesque cloud to identify their pursuers.[10]

The regulators took a break to privately confer. When they returned, after 5 P.M., Baxter said, "We considered all your arguments, but we have a rollout of all the things that have to get done. We need you to file tonight." Lehman's UK subsidiary was expected to file shortly. Moreover, Paulson had gotten word that a parallel drama was nearing its climax: Thain had recommended the Bank of America offer to his board, meaning the Merrill merger was a certainty. In the government's mind, this had ramifications for Lehman. The officials at the Fed, doing the Treasury secretary's bidding, wanted Lehman's news and Merrill's to go out at the same time. Paulson's gambit was that markets would digest the bad news with the good—perhaps even open Monday on the upside. Lehman could serve as a catharsis, its bankruptcy a purifying fire or, in Paulson's clumsy but revealing phrase, a "cleanup play."

Kirk argued, to the contrary, that if Lehman filed, messiness and panic would ensue. Baxter blandly said the Fed was prepared. Then, Kirk asked for some Fed people to accompany him back to Lehman, to help prevent a chaotic free fall. Baxter rebuffed him. A palpable hostility seemed to animate the regulators—as if, now that they had decided to let Lehman die, its presence evoked a guilty embarrassment.

Back at Lehman, a dozen bankers crowded into Russo's office and tried to reach Geithner. He didn't come to the phone. Finally, the Fed produced Christine Cummings, Geithner's number two. Michael Gelband, the banker who had been dismissed from Lehman as its risk careened out of control, and who had returned to try to save it, got on the phone and said the bankruptcy wouldn't be orderly, as the Fed believed; people at Lehman wouldn't come to work, there would be chaos. Cummings was unmoved. Gelband said, "You're unleashing the forces of evil."

The Lehman board convened a little past 7 P.M. The directors were vociferous, especially Henry Kaufman, a Wall Street sage known in the 1980s as Dr. Doom for his warnings of impending disaster, who now maintained that the tragedy had been foreseeable—although, evidently, neither he nor the other directors had foreseen it. As the directors spoke, a secretary entered the boardroom and whispered in Fuld's ear: the SEC chairman, Christopher Cox, wanted to talk to the board. They put him on the speaker, and Cox, marshaling an air of gravitas, said market conditions were serious; it was very, very important that Lehman do the right thing.

A director bluntly queried: "Are you directing us to file a bankruptcy case?"[11] The question was highly awkward for Cox. The SEC chairman was acting as a messenger for Paulson—whom Cox, ignored for most of the weekend, thought had been far too unyielding. Cox put the call on mute. A moment later, he came back on the line and, as if reading a script, carefully pronounced, "That is your decision."

Then, the board debated. John Akers, a director and a retired chairman of IBM, rhetorically asked, "What will we gain by not filing?" To a person, the directors believed the government had told them to file, which was also what McDade had reported from the Fed. In all likelihood, markets would have forced them to file, probably on Monday. Fuld was quiet, letting the independent directors discuss. He was stunned that Paulson, once his fellow CEO, had failed to come to his aid. Leaning back, his jacket slung over his chair, he stammered, "I guess this is time to say goodbye." He looked defeated and incredibly sad.[12]

Hoping to soften the impact of Lehman's crash, the Fed announced it would widen its definition of acceptable collateral. Henceforth, investment banks could trade an expanded group of securities for cash. Such lending, though, would not be available until *after* Lehman filed. Russo, the Lehman lawyer, was furious—it was as if his firm had been singled out for failure.

The other banks focused on self-preservation. Some of the CEOs thought they should lobby for renewed controls on short-selling; Blankfein, the ever-confident Goldman chief, said it wasn't necessary. Zubrow, of JPMorgan, called Merrill again, demanding collateral. Merrill was hours from signing an agreement with Bank of America and ignored him.

AIG had no such luxury. Lehman's pending bankruptcy would surely weigh on markets, and the hole in AIG's securities lending would deepen. By Sunday evening, Willumstad had revised his funding needs to $60 billion or more. Overwhelmed, the private equity bankers gave up. Maughan, the KKR banker who had seemed the brightest hope, reluctantly admitted, "This is bigger than we can solve."

Willumstad called Geithner, at about the time the Lehman board was meeting, and said simply, "I got nothing." The $30 billion seemingly in his pocket that morning had melted away.[13] For the first time, Geithner seemed to give Willumstad his full attention. He summoned JPMorgan and Goldman and told them they should get busy arranging a lending facility for AIG.[14] Government money for AIG was still off-limits, which meant AIG would face the market Monday with nothing to show for its efforts, unless one counted its hiring of bankruptcy counsel. Paulson, who was set to return to Washington, said, "Tim, get your hands around this." He told his staff to get busy, as well, on new legislation, as if the failure were not of businessmen and bureaucrats but of laws.[15]

The Lehman board finished its labors shortly after 9 P.M. The Weil Gotshal partners went room to room at Lehman, telling the bankers what to expect. Scores of employees streamed into the office to collect personal items, some rolling suitcases to cart away files. Bankers who prided themselves on pin-striped decorum were hugging and teary-eyed. Employees bearing boxes onto the street were glimpsed, a couple of blocks south, by a late-working Morgan Stanley exec, who felt a flicker of relief it wasn't him. No bankruptcy judge was available at that hour, but modern civilization permits the electronic filing of a Chapter 11 petition, and a first-day affidavit, online. Fed officials kept calling Miller to see if they had a corpse; they were adamant that Lehman file before midnight. But the papers weren't quite ready. The Weil Gotshal lawyers soldiered on. The Lehman workers departed, with groups of them gathering in bars and toasting the firm that, at 1:45 A.M., having been so long denied in its search for protection, found it at last in the oaky chambers of the court.[16]

14

AFTERSHOCKS

If we have learned anything throughout this year, we
have learned that this financial crisis is unpredictable
and difficult to counteract.

—HANK PAULSON, NOVEMBER 18 OP-ED,
New York Times

LEHMAN'S BANKRUPTCY, the biggest in U.S. history, overwhelmed markets. The direct hit to creditors, from whom Lehman had borrowed $600 billion, reverberated around the world. Investors as diverse as Norway's state pension fund and the State of New Jersey were suddenly staring at worthless paper. The disruption was immediate. By Monday morning, investors were calling the New York Fed in a panic, reporting that no one at Lehman was picking up the phone.[1]

The psychological blow of seeing a major bank disintegrate was profound. The comforting precedent set by Bear Stearns and reinforced by Fannie and Freddie—that creditors would be protected—was demolished in a stroke. If Paulson had wanted to demonstrate that investors bore a hazard, he succeeded beyond his wildest dreams. Credits of banks—all banks—now were judged at risk. As lenders bolted, borrowing costs for banks soared. And as rates rose, industrial companies drew down bank loans to be assured of funds, reducing what was left of banks' already dwindling liquidity.

Yields on T-bills collapsed as well, as money was rechanneled toward the government, seen as the only safe haven. The Friday before the Lehman filing, the interest rate on thirty-day bills had been a paltry 1.3 percent; on Monday, it crashed to 0.22 percent. Investors were not "investing" in bills; they were using the government as a store of safe-keeping; even a microscopic return was judged to be better than the risk of loss that tainted every private investment. Wall Street for so long had been characterized by boldness; now extreme caution was the watchword. Lehman's collapse had lowered the curtain not just on a historic, scrappy firm but on an era. Fuld, like an exiled autocrat, sent a forlorn note to the staff: "I know that this has been very painful for you, both personally and financially. For this, I feel horrible."[2]

The Fed immediately took the place of Lehman's "repo" lenders, in hopes of letting the bankrupt firm wind down in orderly fashion. Its loans over the next few days totaled $46 billion, all backed by collateral.[3] At the same time, Barclays continued to negotiate with Lehman's estate in the hopes of purchasing the carcass out of bankruptcy.

However, while the U.S. subsidiary was temporarily shielded by the Fed, Lehman ceased to exist as an integrated firm, and this wreaked unexpected havoc. Money flows between its subsidiaries were sus-pended, and Lehman's London branch, occupied by scores of accoun-tants and lawyers, was virtually shut down. UK bankruptcy practices did not, reliably, segregate corporate from customer accounts; as a result, monies of hedge fund clients from the United States and elsewhere were frozen by British law. This triggered a ruinous stampede. Some seven hundred hedge funds awoke on Monday and learned that a por-tion of their assets were trapped.*[4] They panicked, and others with them; the effect was as if a sloth of bears went marauding through a helpless village.

The hedge fund industry, whose capitalization was $2 trillion, re-taliated by purchasing credit default swaps, in particular on Morgan Stanley and Goldman—the only investment banks that remained in

---

* Hedge fund groups with money frozen in Lehman included Amber Capital, Autonomy Capital Research, Bay Harbour Management, D. E. Shaw, GLG Partners, Harbinger Capital Partners, and Och-Ziff Capital Management.

independent form. Some were acting defensively, merely purchasing insurance; others were making outright (and hostile) speculations. No matter, the effect was the same. Premiums soared, unnerving the two firms long considered the class of Wall Street.

Rising CDS rates triggered huge losses for firms that had sold insurance. They were hit with demands for margin money, estimated for Monday alone at well over $100 billion.[5] The viral effects were incalculable. Stocks plunged, the Dow losing 504 points, its worst fall since 9/11. As with the various parts of Lehman, the larger financial community began to disintegrate. Investors trimmed portfolios, traders withdrew, especially from credit markets, and financial flows quieted, as if a gurgling brook had turned deathly still.

Lehman had a million and a half derivative contracts, with thousands of different counterparties, and the prospect of unwinding them horrified the Fed. As formidable as the derivatives seemed, they proved less troublesome than a single investment that, in the chaos of the previous weekend, the government had overlooked.

Aside from Treasury securities and government-insured bank deposits, money market mutual funds have long been considered the safest haven on Wall Street. They were the brainchild of a single creator, Bruce Bent, who in 1972 opened a fund to invest in a diversified group of short-term credit instruments. He offered investors a higher return than on savings accounts with seeming safety and instant liquidity. Indeed, the attraction of the money market industry was its reputation for *total* preservation of capital, pegged at $1 a share. Reserve Management, Bent's firm, swore an oath to maintaining net asset value, boasting in its literature, "The Reserve is committed to a $1.00 NAV."[6]

Bent was something of a prophet, warning the industry, as it grew, against the dangers of reaching for higher yield by stooping to inferior credits. In particular, he denounced commercial paper as overly risky. After the rash of near-failures in 2007, when money funds were infected by SIVs, Bent held forth on the particular risks of mortgage-backed securities, and on the foolhardiness of those who traded in them. But he did not live up to his rules. Reserve's Primary Fund, its flagship, had since then been stocking up on commercial paper—including $785 million issued by Lehman Brothers. All the while, Bent continued making high-minded pronouncements, commenting in July: "Wall Street—they don't have any brains—all they do is market."[7]

Monday morning, investors in the Primary Fund awoke to the fact that 1.2 percent of their assets were invested in Lehman (a fact that had been posted on the fund's Web site). Some of its investors were individuals but most were institutions, including Fortune 500 corporations such as Time Warner and public entities such as school districts, who parked their cash with Primary to earn a slightly higher yield, under the premise that it remained risk-free.

Sensing that the first to redeem would be the most likely to get out whole, these investors ran for the doors; soon, the rest of Wall Street followed. At 7:51 A.M., Reserve received a redemption order for $56 million. One minute later, another, larger, redemption arrived. By 8:30 A.M., twenty-two investors, mostly institutional, had redeemed $5 billion of their money—or at least, they had submitted orders for same. The rout was on.[8]

The fund trustees hastily conferred (Bent, who had flown to Italy the previous day to celebrate his fiftieth wedding anniversary, participated by phone) and decided to value Lehman's paper at eighty cents on the dollar, maintaining the hope that losses on Lehman would be modest. Sales personnel were instructed to tell callers that even this twenty-cent loss was inconsequential, only temporary, as Lehman's paper would eventually be redeemed at par. Callers were told, further, that if any loss *was* sustained, the Reserve company would cover the difference. As the tide of redemptions swelled, State Street, the independent custodian that oversaw the fund, halted payments. Fund employees assured investors that it was not suffering liquidity issues, merely processing delays, and urged investors not to redeem. Meanwhile, Reserve frantically sought help from the Fed.[9]

Though Lehman was a big issuer of commercial paper, in all of the regulators' preparations no one had considered its likely impact on money market funds. This is less a criticism of the regulators than of the conceit that officials can ever foresee every significant aftershock. Market earthquakes, like those in nature, produce unexpected fissures and seemingly random jolts. From the Greenspan era on, official policy had been predicated on Washington's ability to manufacture soft landings when market excesses led to busts. But mortgage speculation had been so extreme, it is doubtful that any virtuosos in the Treasury and the Fed could have avoided a crash landing.

Paulson doggedly defended his actions—or rather, nonactions—on Lehman. Briefing reporters at the White House on Monday, he all but boasted, "I don't ever take lightly putting the taxpayer on the line to support an institution." This sentiment was praiseworthy, but it was in conflict with what Paulson uttered at the same gathering, that "nothing is more important right now than the stability of our capital markets."*

As for AIG, Paulson insisted to reporters that the deliberations still going on in New York were a private sector effort—"nothing to do with any bridge loan from the government." Given the example of Lehman, markets had every reason to believe him.

But Paulson was far more involved in AIG than his laconism suggested. By that Monday, he and Geithner were quietly staging a replay of the Lehman weekend—only this time, with the object of saving AIG. JPMorgan and Goldman were charged to form a lending syndicate of private banks. Goldman deployed Lloyd Blankfein, its chief executive, as well as two of his most senior associates. Morgan sent Braunstein, its head of investment banking, and Jimmy Lee, the dean of high-yield bankers, whose clients ranged from Rupert Murdoch to DreamWorks, and who was said to have lent, over his career, a total of a trillion dollars.[10] Monday morning, attorneys from prestige New

---

* Paulson's press conference comment, "I never once considered that it was appropriate to put taxpayer money on the line in resolving Lehman Brothers," has the mark of an off-the-cuff declaration rather than the literal truth. When asked why Lehman had not received help, as had Bear, he said the situation and facts were "very different"; he did not specify the differences. Bernanke gave a fuller explanation the following week, when he declared in Congress, "In the case of Lehman Brothers . . . we judged that investors and counterparties had had time to take precautionary measures." Neither official alluded to the explanation subsequently, and vehemently, offered, that Lehman's collateral was insufficient to support a loan. This became the standard response only *after* the crisis deepened.

York law firms, Treasury officials, advisers from BlackRock, as well as Porat and Scully, the Morgan Stanley pair that had worked on Fannie and Freddie, descended on the New York Fed.

Geithner, as if reading from the Lehman playbook mechanically told the group, "There is no federal money for AIG." The bankers, accustomed to the drill, quickly split into work groups. One looked at how long AIG might last, and concluded Wednesday or Thursday was the most they could hope for. Another evaluated its underlying businesses—Japanese credit cards, life insurance in Taiwan, consumer finance, railcar finance, and many more. A third developed a financing plan.[11]

Goldman's conspicuous presence in the talks fueled persistent intrigue. Goldman was not just a potential syndicate lender, but an AIG counterparty with a direct interest in its survival. It did not escape the attention of JPMorgan, among others, that the government's point person on AIG was Dan Jester, a former Goldman strategist who, they feared, would be especially accessible to his former partners. Even the joking, lighthearted manner of the Goldman bankers inspired suspicion among their wary competitors.

Willumstad, the AIG chief, was preoccupied with downgrade threats from the rating agencies. He had an ace up his sleeve—Eric Dinallo, the state insurance superintendent. Though awed by the presence of so many financial celebrities at the Fed, Dinallo contributed more than all the bankers combined. The peripatetic regulator lobbied the governor, David Paterson, who appeared at a hastily called press conference that morning. Warning of the loss of jobs should AIG collapse, the governor endorsed Dinallo's plan to free up $20 billion from AIG's subsidiaries.

With the State of New York in his pocket, Willumstad, accompanied by Dinallo and by the poker-faced Jester, called the rating agencies. Willumstad begged them to hold off on a downgrade, arguing that New York's cooperative stance had improved AIG's outlook. The agencies were unimpressed. If the State was going to such an exreme, they reckoned darkly, AIG must *really* be in trouble. Also, the agencies were motivated by a herd instinct; having missed the credit bubble, none wanted to be caught out again. They even threatened to downgrade the operating units of AIG, active insurance units unaffected by its derivative bets.[12] In a rerun of Lehman, firms began to back away from trading with the once fearsome insurer, slowly cutting off its air.

Jimmy Lee of JPMorgan concluded that AIG would need at least $75 billion—a figure he soon raised to $85 billion—and suggested the lenders could get stock warrants (in case its shares recovered) worth 80 percent of the company. In effect, they were proposing an out-of-court bankruptcy, under which AIG would be taken over by its lenders. But $85 billion was a massive sum—far more than the annual budget of New York City—and neither Morgan nor Goldman knew if they could raise it. Credit default swap premiums on AIG were going through the roof, an indication that lenders considered it unbankable. Generally, a premium above $500,000 on a $10 million bond is a danger signal; AIG's soared to $1.9 million. Late in the day, Moody's, Fitch, and S&P all delivered on their downgrade threats. That meant AIG would have to fork over another $18 billion to counterparties, including Goldman.[13] This was simply beyond its means.

Around 6 P.M., Willumstad, despairing of getting a private loan, alerted Geithner that AIG could file for bankruptcy as early as Wednesday. "Tim," Willumstad added, underscoring his urgency, "we will have to call our backup lines." Backup lines are emergency credit lines, meant to be used when commercial paper is unavailable. Generally, when firms resort to backup lines, they are as good as dead. Geithner protested that such a move would signal distress, but Willumstad was running out of options.

Paulson and Geithner embarked on a conference call with various AIG operatives; it started at 8 P.M. and went on until well past midnight. JPMorgan and Goldman Sachs had solicited their peers and come up empty. The banks preferred to risk the consequences of a bankruptcy than lend to the hopelessly overcommitted insurer. As if to telegraph their feeling that AIG was not worth saving, Morgan's bankers departed AIG's headquarters at 70 Pine Street having left used pizza boxes strewn about—one more irritant in the bank's and AIG's strained relations. With bankruptcy seemingly the only option, Simpson Thacher, retained by AIG's board, advised the directors to prepare for a filing.

Porat and Scully, having completed their work on Fannie and Freddie, now were helping the Treasury to unravel the AIG riddle; they recommended to Geithner that the government develop a fallback plan. This was at 2:30 A.M., and Geithner was haggard from serial all-nighters. He had consistently opposed giving AIG help, but now he nodded to indicate he would consider it.

Tuesday morning, the Goldman and JPMorgan bankers returned to the Fed to try to puzzle out a solution. Geithner was expected in Washington for a meeting of the Federal Open Market Committee, so Dan Jester, the gaunt Treasury official, who faintly resembled Ichabod Crane, presided, accompanied by a covey of lawyers, the Morgan Stanley duo, and the ubiquitous Dinallo. The JPMorgan and Goldman bankers looked unusually dour; fingering their BlackBerrys, they saw that credit markets overseas had turned ugly. Jon Winkelried of Goldman and Scully of Morgan Stanley thought an AIG collapse would be catastrophic; Braunstein of JPMorgan was more sanguine. As the group, perhaps thirty financiers and others, pondered alternatives, Geithner burst into the conference room. "Turn off your cell phones," he commanded with a theatrical flourish. "I don't want anyone communicating this, but if we were to do something, how big would it need to be, what would the terms be, how would you do it?"[14]

The JPMorgan and Goldman bankers began to pencil out terms. They relayed a proposal to Geithner; then, the bankers sat back to wait while nibbling on a luncheon of tired wraps, courtesy of the Federal Reserve.

AIG, meanwhile, was being pushed closer to the edge. Counterparties were refusing to clear its foreign exchange trades, depriving it of billions in cash. The State of Texas was threatening to seize assets to protect policyholders within its jurisdiction. Willumstad kept trying to get through to Geithner and to the JPMorgan bankers, but without success. In desperation, he called his banks for backup lines. But where was Geithner? Three of the insurance exec's consiglieri—Jamie Gamble and Michael Wiseman of, respectively, the law firms Simpson Thacher and Sullivan Cromwell, and Larry Nath of the Blackstone Group—trooped over to the Fed.[15]

Calling a contact at the Fed, Wiseman got them past security. In the big room downstairs, they saw, scattered in various corners, a Goldman group, a Morgan group, and others. Some sort of plot was brewing. Gamble didn't think it was a private deal; the bankers looked too calm. The lawyers found Dinallo, the superintendent, and asked him to help with Texas. Eager to keep AIG from filing, yet fearful of violating Geithner's gag order, Dinallo urged AIG not to do anything "precipitous." Gamble shot a withering look at the Goldman table and deadpanned, "Talk to *them*; they're the ones pulling money away from us."

A little before noon, Willumstad finally reached Geithner. "Tim," he said, "We're effectively bankrupt at the end of the day. We have no cash. We're going to default on all of our agreements." Geithner again urged him not to call his backup lines.

"It's too late," Willumstad noted.

Relenting slightly, Geithner admitted, "We're working on a solution. Don't tell anybody."

A short while later, Jester returned to the bankers' room and drily announced, "The federal government has decided AIG is too important, systemically, to fail. We're getting approval from the board of governors." The plan was for an $85 billion loan at a hefty interest rate; in exchange, AIG would give warrants to the government for 79.9 percent of the stock. Essentially, this was the scheme proposed on Monday by JPMorgan, which private banks had been unwilling to implement. The important point, Jester said weightily, was that the AIG shareholders would be punished.

Gamble, one of the AIG lawyers, bristled over the terms, and asked

Jester if the government could tweak them so that AIG would still have an incentive—some value left for the shareholders if it ever emerged from the ruins. Jester didn't budge.

The bankers and officials at the Fed were extremely tense; outside the bank's stone walls the country's financial problems were spreading, and in unforeseen directions. The one-month Libor (London Interbank Offered Rate)—a measure of what banks pay for thirty-day loans—surged a quarter of a point, suggesting that banks were having difficulty getting funding. The overnight Libor rate surged three percentage points, a record and altogether bizarre advance. Depositors began to pull assets from weaker banks, particularly WaMu. The board of another mortgage-era darling, Wachovia, opted to either raise capital or, failing that, look for a partner or even a buyer.[16] Even funding for industrial companies weakened.

Most troublesome were the rumors of distress swirling around Morgan Stanley. Its stock was plunging throughout the day on Tuesday and credit default swap premiums soared, reaching $755,000 per $10 million of Morgan Stanley bonds, implying serious credit market concern. Then, it was hit with a collateral call from its clearing bank, Bank of New York Mellon—exactly what had happened to Lehman in its last days.[17] Goldman's stock was hit hard, too, even though the bank had reported positive earnings that morning.

The dreaded chain reaction was becoming real. Hedge funds that had monies trapped in Lehman were yanking accounts from the two survivors, especially Morgan Stanley. Their clients were withdrawing at a breathtaking pace; on Tuesday, Millennium Partners, a fast-trading New York hedge fund, pulled $800 million in assets. Piling injury upon injury, Millennium shorted Morgan Stanley's stock. Millennium's manager, Israel Englander, offered a self-justifying explanation, telling a Morgan Stanley executive, "We have to protect our assets. This is not a personal thing."[18]

Unlike Merrill and Lehman, Morgan Stanley remained a profitable corporation, and viewed through the prism of its sterling reputation, as well as its earning power, the 23 percent plunge in its stock over a mere two days was inexplicable. But having begun the year leveraged 33 to 1 (a figure since reduced), it was vulnerable to a panic whether warranted or not. This is the peril that haunts even the savviest financiers. Leverage raises the bar for survival. It requires that one is ever able to access credit.

John Mack, the Morgan Stanley CEO, tried to stem the panic. Thinking it would calm markets, he decided to announce the firm's earnings after the market closed, a day ahead of schedule. Its numbers were good, with profits down only slightly from 2007. In the earnings call to the Street, Colm Kelleher, the chief financial officer, urged investors to return to sanity, and denounced the rumors that it was in trouble.[19] But markets are rarely talked into calm.

Even as Kelleher was talking, a problem was flaring in credit markets. In only twenty-four hours, the Primary Fund, the besieged money market fund, had been swamped by a deluge of redemption orders, most of which it had not paid. By the morning, the orders totaled $25 billion. Worse, the trustees decided to revalue the fund's Lehman paper, not at eighty cents as initially indicated but, instead, at zero. The loss in value meant the fund had "broken the buck," or fallen through the hallowed $1 a share value, the first such loss in fourteen years. This spelled serious trouble for the money market industry, considered a bedrock of stability. The crisis, once deemed the "subprime" crisis, and more recently the mortgage crisis, was spreading to regions far afield of Fannie Mae or Angelo Mozilo. No one knew who would be the next Lehman creditor to stumble; no one knew where it would end. As Fleming, the Merrill president, would say, "None of us anticipated the magnitude of the ripple effects."

At the Fed, lawyers were puzzling over when, exactly, AIG would run out of cash. Gamble, the Simpson lawyer, asked the Fed to keep its wire open late, so the loan money could be transmitted that evening. But before it could wire a dime, the Fed needed collateral. Kathy Shannon, AIG's corporate secretary, dug into a safe and fetched the stock certificates that the parent company held in its subsidiaries—a stack of paper worth tens of billions of dollars.* Accompanied by a security guard, she walked them over to the Fed.

Among the lawyers advising AIG's board was Simpson Thacher's Richard Beattie, famed for counseling corporate directors in difficult situations. Realizing how hard it was for Willumstad to give up control of his company to the Fed, Beattie chuckled and said, "Bob, you always wanted to work for the government."

Willumstad barely had time to respond when he was diverted by a call from Paulson. After a terse conversation, Willumstad, forcing a smile, turned back to Beattie and said, "The good news is, I don't have to work for the government." Paulson had fired him, and coaxed him into renouncing his $22 million severance—a bitter pill, given that Willumstad, a newcomer to management and a diligent exec, was hardly responsible for AIG's troubles. Perhaps Paulson, having gone back on his no-bailout pledge, wanted to underline that the government was not dispensing favors. His treatment of Willumstad was uncharacteristically harsh.

AIG's board met at 5 P.M. It had only two choices: accept the Fed's offer or file for bankruptcy. Geithner said he needed a decision before markets opened in Asia, which left only two hours. Beattie, already miffed at the rough treatment of Willumstad, resisted. "Tim, you can't do that," he protested. "The board has to consider this." The directors felt painted into a corner, forced by the government to violate their fiduciary oath.

Beattie advised them to do whatever was best for the shareholders, implying bankruptcy was an option. One of the directors argued strongly for filing Chapter 11.[20] However, the lawyer Rodgin Cohen, who was also advising the board, dampened these rebellious stirrings, observing that the directors also had a duty to AIG's creditors.

---

* The final loan papers would not be prepared until later in the week. As a stopgap, the Fed was planning to wire cash in return for a demand note, for which it needed AIG's stock certificates as security.

Moreover, financial-company bankruptcies are difficult to recover from. In AIG's case, the insurance units would likely be seized to protect the policyholders. Also, the company feared a run in Asia, where AIG owned a bank in Hong Kong, credit card companies, and vast insurance interests. Blackstone, AIG's adviser, said a filing would be disastrous.

The board voted ten to one to accept the Fed's proposal, and at 9:30 P.M., the first tranche of the $85 billion was wired. AIG was now a ward of the U.S. Federal Reserve, which had committed to its defense a sum orders of magnitude larger than any offered before in its history. Paulson, following a plot he had sketched out between three and four o'clock the previous morning, installed Edward Liddy, a former chief executive of Allstate, as AIG's new chairman.

The choice was astonishingly obtuse. Liddy was a Goldman Sachs director (a post he immediately quit), and Paulson was already relying on far too many former cronies, violating at least the appearance of impartiality. The Treasury was infiltrated with Goldman bankers who presumably harbored at least a passing loyalty to their former firm. Also, Paulson in this period spoke frequently to Blankfein, the self-effacing former gold trader who had succeeded him at Goldman.[21] Blankfein, the son of a New York City postal worker, had been groomed by Paulson for his present post.[22] The connection was close, and it was whispered (and later asserted in press accounts) that Paulson had engineered the AIG bailout to spare Goldman from further harm.

This charge does not hold up. Paulson necessarily consulted with the firms (JPMorgan as well as Goldman) involved with AIG; Paulson had also called Blankfein during previous crises that bore no relation to Goldman.[23] He would have been wise to call Blankfein less, but Paulson did not think of the AIG bailout as critical to Goldman *in particular*, because, in fact, Goldman's exposure to AIG was less than life-threatening. Thanks to its zealous collection efforts prior to the rescue, Goldman was already holding $7.5 billion of collateral from AIG. After the bailout, Goldman collected an additional $7.3 billion; however, it was at risk of losing only about a third of that sum. In short, a forfeiture by AIG would not have been crippling to a firm with $40 billion in net tangible assets.*

A more plausible explanation for the decision to bail out AIG is that officials as well as bankers feared the indirect but systemic effects—a Lehman-style tidal wave that would swamp what was left of Wall Street. Goldman would have been affected, but so would a host of others; indeed, Morgan Stanley, which had little exposure to AIG, also supported the effort. It is noteworthy that the day after the rescue, the Fed asked Paulson to join in a call that specifically dealt with the investment banks, including Goldman. On that occasion, Paulson recognized the conflict of interest and requested an ethics waiver. That he did not do so on Tuesday reaffirms that Paulson thought of AIG as a threat to the system, but not specifically to Goldman Sachs.

Why then AIG and not Lehman? The Fed advanced the notion that AIG's underlying businesses were more enduring than Lehman's and its collateral was more secure; thus it was a better credit risk. This was more a rationalization than a reason. The regulators were mostly confident going into Lehman; by the time of AIG's crisis they were scared. The Lehman failure, or its fallout, was already considerably worse than they had predicted. The prospect of a second disorganized bankruptcy—this time, of a company with a trillion dollars in assets (half again as much as Lehman), and when markets were considerably more fragile—seemed too much.

Geithner had never been comfortable with the laissez-faire approach. And Bernanke had begun to push back against Paulson's rigid antibailout stance. The Fed chairman, who made the final decision,

---

* The press (e.g., Gretchen Morgenson and Don Van Natta Jr. in the August 9, 2009, *New York Times*) widely reported that Goldman received $13 billion of the bailout money. This was misleading for the purposes of analyzing the rescue, because $5.6 billion of that sum was conveyed only after a second AIG bailout in November, and after further price declines—which Paulson could not have anticipated. As a result of the initial, $85 billion loan, Goldman was paid $2.5 billion as collateral on underwater swaps—money it stood to lose absent a bailout. It also received $4.8 billion as a counterparty on AIG's troubled securities lending program. However, Goldman (like other counterparties) held collateral on these loans, and would not have suffered a total loss on them even without the Fed's assistance. A November 2009 report by the special inspector general for the TARP confirmed that Goldman had protection, but noted it would have been exposed to market losses after September. (Source: AIG filings, Goldman, special inspector general report.)

was truly frightened of a 1930s-style financial panic. He told his colleagues, "There are no ideologues in financial crises."[24] His comment fit Paulson as well as himself. Now that the crisis was spreading, the secretary quickly embraced intervention and left his qualms about moral hazard for another day. Willumstad surmised that had AIG come first, *it* would have been allowed to perish and Lehman saved. That may be as close as there exists to an explanation: AIG came second.*

Lehman, the precipitate cause of so much misery, enjoyed a life after death. The assets of its U.S. broker-dealer were sold in bankruptcy to Barclays—largely thanks to the lawyers Miller and, in particular, Lori Fife, who, without so much as a change of clothes, worked through from the Sunday night filing to the agreement of sale on Tuesday. Fife didn't step outside; she ate her meals in the Lehman kitchen. Some ten thousand Lehman employees, on an emotional roller coaster, came streaming back to work, now gratefully in the service of Barclays. The price was a paltry $1.75 billion (most of it for Lehman's headquarters; its going-concern value, decimated by the bankruptcy, was judged to be trifling). Loans from the Fed (amply collateralized) kept Lehman functioning for seventy-two hours more, or until the Barclays deal could close—rather ironic, as this was similar to the assistance sought by Barclays before the filing for Chapter 11. Other Lehman subsidiaries were also auctioned. Dick Fuld asked to remain at what he called "the firm"—now Barclays—in the hopes of rebuilding his personal wealth. He was told there wasn't a place for him.

Ben Bernanke was oddly relaxed when he convened the Federal Open Market Committee, which met that Tuesday, September 16. He declined to lower interest rates any further. Forced to abandon its earlier prediction that the economy would strengthen in the latter part of 2008, the FOMC clung to its forecast for an improvement early in 2009. Even

---

* Bernanke's later testimony was consistent with this theory. He told the Congress that the Federal Reserve rescued AIG because "it judged that, *in light of the prevailing market conditions* [emphasis added] and the size and composition of AIG's obligations, a disorderly failure of AIG would have severely threatened global financial stability and, consequently, the performance of the U.S. economy." Lehman, of course, had hugely aggravated those "market conditions."

after eight straight months of declining job totals and skyrocketing foreclosure rates, the Fed did not see an economic slowdown as the paramount risk. (The FOMC statement declared, "The downside risks to growth and the upside risks to inflation are both of significant concern.") Many economists persisted in thinking of the financial crisis mainly as a problem for Wall Street. John McCain, the Republican candidate for President, declared on the stump, in Jacksonville, Florida, "The fundamentals of the economy are strong." This Hooverish comment was pounced on by his challenger, Barack Obama, as seeming evidence that McCain was out of touch. The crisis was now major campaign news, displacing the war in Iraq, the issue on which the soldierly McCain was best prepared, and tilting the election toward the Democrats.

Wall Street finished Tuesday on an up note. Stocks rose, buoyed by the Morgan Stanley and Goldman earnings, and bankers, not for the first time, dared to hope that the crisis had bottomed out. With AIG no longer a worry, the thinking went, finance could slowly return to normal. David Viniar, the Goldman executive, even told his wife, who was in California on what was supposed to be their vacation, that he would be able to join her for the weekend.

The next morning, he called to take it back. Stocks were plunging for the second time in three days. Morgan Stanley was under virtual assault from hedge funds. Money market funds were being stormed with redemptions. The redemptions were causing funds to cancel their normal purchases of commercial paper—a key source of funding for everyday businesses. In spite of the Fed's rescue, the financial system was unraveling.

15

THE HEDGE FUND WAR

We have become concerned about the sudden and
unexplained declines in the prices of securities.

—CHRISTOPHER COX, SEC CHAIRMAN,
SEPTEMBER 18, 2008

WITH LEHMAN AND MERRILL out of the way, the focus of Wall Street's agita turned to Morgan Stanley. John Mack, its CEO, was, rather like Dick Fuld, a pronounced risk-taker who exuded loyalty to his firm. Raised in Mooresville, North Carolina, where his father, a Lebanese immigrant, ran a grocery store, Mack attended Duke University and was hired as a bond salesman at Morgan Stanley, then a close-knit, private firm, in 1972. He was a fearsome boss. He once laid into a trader for keeping a pizza deliveryman waiting half an hour, which offended his sense of how a Morgan Stanley professional should behave. For all his devotion, he risked the firm's top-drawer franchise by orchestrating a merger, in the late '90s, with Dean Witter, Discover, a commonish mutual fund and credit card concern. The merger played to the vogue for financial "supermarkets," and destroyed what was left of Morgan Stanley's partnership ethos. In 2001, Mack was edged aside. He ran a rival bank for several years but, in 2005, when Morgan Stanley was flailing, he returned to run it. Again following the fashion, he raised the firm's risk level and aggressively expanded in mortgages. Both moves would cost him.[1]

On September 17, the Wednesday after Lehman's failure, hundreds of his hedge fund clients pulled their accounts. Many of the same funds were shorting Morgan Stanley's stock, which fell an agonizing 24 percent on that one day. Rumors spread that the investment bank was going out of business, and premiums on its debt surged to $1 million, a level implying that Morgan Stanley would soon be the next Lehman.[2] Some forty million of its shares were shorted, an avalanche moved by unfounded rumor as well as honest fear.[3] Whether driven by virtue or vice, markets will always exploit a weakness.

One hedge fund manager got a call from his contact at Morgan Stanley thanking him for *not* pulling assets. This so alarmed the fund manager, he called the rival JPMorgan to switch his account. But JPMorgan was deluged; there was a waiting period to get in. The sophisticated hedge fund manager experienced what any depositor running to the bank has ever felt: acute fear. CNBC fanned the fire by flashing the headline: "Is Morgan Stanley Next?"

The firm was hemorrhaging in a business that customarily minted tidy profits. Servicing hedge funds, known as "prime brokerage," had been enormously lucrative for Morgan Stanley, and for others. This was in part because hedge funds had parked their securities with the banks, which they in turn used to generate excess liquidity. (Put differently, Wall Street helped finance itself with the surplus reserves of its clients.) Now, with every fund wanting out, Morgan Stanley was being drained of this liquidity. And since funds naturally tended to pull their *most* liquid securities, such as Treasuries, Morgan Stanley was left to finance a greater proportion of dicier credits. Unable to keep up with the funds' demand for cash, it was forced to slow payments to clients— which speeded the rush to the door.

JPMorgan coolly exploited its rival's weakness by courting its accounts. The two Morgans glowered at each other from opposite sides of the boundary between commercial and investment banks—Wall

Street's equivalent of the Mason-Dixon line.* In the recent past, gilded investment bankers had held the upper hand, whereas commercial bankers were seen as slow-footed and dull. In a sudden inversion, commercial banks now were prized for their greater capital, and for the aura of security ascribed to firms under the umbrella of the Fed.

Mack, meanwhile, was fighting on three fronts. He scoured the globe for capital, he vigorously lobbied Washington for help, and he retaliated against well-armed competitors. He protested to Jamie Dimon that JPMorgan was stealing his hedge fund clients; he made similar calls to swaps dealers. On the same Wednesday, he called Chris Cox at the SEC, as well as the two New York senators, Hillary Clinton and Charles Schumer, to demand that the SEC intervene against short-selling. He rang Lloyd Blankfein, who had maintained only a few days earlier that curbs on short-selling weren't needed. Now, with Goldman's stock plunging 14 percent on Wednesday, and his firm also suffering a degree of asset flight, Blankfein joined the lobbying campaign. Both banks also raised with Geithner the idea of converting to a commercial bank—another strategy once floated by Lehman.

Officials were noticeably more receptive to Mack and Blankfein than they had been to Dick Fuld. They could live with Lehman failing, but not all of Wall Street. Also, the temperature of the complaints was rising. Larry Fink, the BlackRock CEO, screamed at Paulson's adviser Kendrick Wilson, "The shit is hitting the fan; you guys have to *do* something." Wilson also heard that day from money fund custodians who

---

* Though wholly separate today, Morgan Stanley and JPMorgan Chase are each descendants of J.P. Morgan & Co. In the late nineteenth and early twentieth centuries, the latter was the kingpin of Wall Street—architect of railroad and steel consortiums, preeminent banker to the rich, and a leading underwriter. However, during the Depression, the involvement of banks in Wall Street promotions was cited as a cause of the Crash. In 1933, Congress enacted the Glass-Steagall Act, which forced commercial banks and investment banks to separate. Morgan Stanley was spun off as an independent firm. While J.P. Morgan continued to be a depository institution regulated by the Fed, Morgan Stanley was financed via short-term borrowings—a crucial distinction that persisted into the twenty-first century. Despite its merger with Dean Witter in the '90s, Morgan Stanley retained its character as a top-tier underwriter and mergers and acquisitions adviser. For many years, J.P. Morgan remained a prestigious, if rather stodgy, commercial bank. In the '90s, as Glass-Steagall strictures were gradually repealed, it moved into trading. Weakened by several missteps, it was acquired by Chase in 2000 (it retained the Morgan name). The bank's troubles continued, and in 2004, it struck a deal with Bank One, bringing Jamie Dimon into the fold. Thereafter, JPMorgan Chase's performance improved.

warned of mass redemptions. Pondering the way credit traveled from firm to firm, Wilson began to fear that the shadow banking system was collapsing. He relayed his fears to Paulson, and late Wednesday morning, Paulson, Bernanke, and Geithner agreed that they had to devise a plan to salvage money markets.[4]

The central bank hosted another call in the afternoon, this one to consider the soundness of the investment banks.[5] Financial firms were abstaining from trading even with the erstwhile lions of finance; key sources of Wall Street's liquidity, such as Fidelity, PIMCO, and BlackRock, were pulling commercial paper and repo loans. This pushed the credit crisis in a startling new direction. The notion that firms wouldn't lend, even against collateral, upset every principle of banking. The Fed had never anticipated such a turn. From credit markets to banking to money funds, the Street was coming undone, its components like runaway eggs loosed from their snug cardboard moorings tumbling precariously down Wall Street.

Paulson, hoping to get a view from the battlefield, spent much of the day talking to Mack and other CEOs he trusted—Blankfein of Goldman, Jeffrey Immelt of General Electric, Fred Smith of FedEx, and Jamie Dimon. "What are you seeing?" he barked at each. Lesser officials darted in and out or hovered in a corner of Paulson's office. Fed officials called continuously. To one participant, the day, and the recent days, felt like a single long conference call, an anguished blur. Every call was a crisis; every brick in the mortar of finance was loose. Despite the supposed salve of the AIG rescue, the stock market fell 450 points, a 4 percent plunge.

Wilson's warning on money markets proved prescient. That Wednesday, investors withdrew tens of billions of dollars. Money funds and banks play a similar role, pooling individual savings and lending them to industry. Their fragility was an ominous sign, reminiscent of the bank runs of the '30s.

Investors who abandoned money funds (and other types of loans) en masse shifted their savings into government securities.[6] Rates on three-month Treasuries fell to two one-hundredths of a percent—

effectively zero. Investors were so frightened they were willing to accept, in return for safety, a null return. Moreover, America's crisis had spread. England had been forced to broker an emergency sale of its biggest mortgage lender, HBOS. China and Russia were rushing to enact their own bank bailouts. Bernanke, acting in concert with central bankers in Europe, England, and Japan, responded on an unprecedented scale, adding hundreds of billions to the supply of dollars available for loans overseas. Still, the international panic rolled on. In the early '30s, an international contagion had helped to aggravate, and prolong, the Great Depression. Bernanke, attuned to the historical echoes, decided he had seen enough.[7]

Late Wednesday, the Fed chairman called Paulson. Bernanke felt, profoundly, that they could no longer get by on improvised responses; they had to formulate a policy. "Listen, we cannot do this anymore," he said as if to a furtive partner, while Kevin Warsh nodded encouragement. "Hank," Bernanke insisted, leaning into the phone and affixing to his mild and reasonable tone with all the urgency it would bear, "You've got to go to the Hill." On the other end, Paulson was quiet.

To Bernanke, the most laudable quality of the New Deal technocrats was their willingness to experiment—to try an antidote for the poison in the system and, if it failed, try another. Many did fail, but the patient revived.[*] This was the tactical creativity he was urging on Paulson. Thursday morning, September 18, the chairman asked again, "Will you go to Congress with me?" Paulson, his concurrence burbling up like boiling lava, suddenly exclaimed, "I agree—we're going!"[8] They resolved to go to Congress that day. Both men recognized they would be launching the country on a new, and heretofore unimaginable, course.

Paulson's aides had long ago prepared an emergency plan—which

---

* The early New Deal medicine—jobs programs, agricultural and mortgage relief, and budgetary pump-priming—worked. From 1933 to 1937, unemployment fell from a cataclysmic 25 percent to an appreciably lower (though still-alarming) 14 percent. GDP rose by more than half. However, tightening by the Fed, as well as government austerity measures, sent the U.S. into a renewed and sharp tailspin in 1938.

they had not expected to implement—under which the Treasury would purchase mortgages from ailing banks.[9] The idea was to free the banks of their crippling deadweight, permitting them to recommence normal lending. In time, markets would recover and the Treasury could transfer its portfolio back to the private sector. However, such a solution did not address the banks' lack of capital (a point that Rodriguez, the investor, had been harping on). As long as banks were undercapitalized, they were forced to sell loans instead of issuing new ones. The selling drove down prices, and home prices had already deflated by more than a fifth.[10] The regulators, of course, knew that injecting capital in the banks was an option—but since it amounted to a partial nationalization, it was a frighteningly radical step.

Thursday morning, as Treasury officials began to draft legislation, Nancy Pelosi, the House Speaker, worriedly realized she hadn't heard from Paulson lately and called to see how he was faring. The reply: "Not very well." Pelosi asked if he would come by the next day to brief the Democratic leadership. Paulson, as if flirting with the apocalypse, said, "By tomorrow, it may be over." They agreed to meet that evening. Then, Paulson called the White House.

The money market rout was continuing—by Thursday, investors had withdrawn $200 billion, and Putnam Prime, another brand-name fund that had been overwhelmed by redemptions, was forced to close.[11] This moved the credit crunch from Wall Street to Main Street. As investors fled, funds had to disgorge themselves of assets, and bread-and-butter corporations lost a prime source of credit. Rates on commercial paper soared, and many companies couldn't borrow at any price. Blue-chip AT&T, which normally funded itself with thirty-day paper, was reduced to living on the shoestring of overnight credit.

Corporate America's dependence on short-term IOUs had its roots in the intellectual revolution sparked by financial deregulation in the late 1970s and early 1980s. In the emerging Age of Markets, academics posited a theory of perfect (or, as they phrased it, "efficient") markets, in which risk management practically took care of itself. Gurus of efficient-market theory, notably Michael Jensen of the Harvard

Business School, preached the gospel of maximizing every asset at every instant, with the corollary that it was a waste of shareholder resources to maintain a rainy-day fund—some extra cash—in the till. According to this doctrinaire theory, liquidity would always flow to where it was most needed, therefore even bankruptcy, should it occur, was not to be feared, as it would merely occasion an arithmetic reshuffling of assets, creditors replacing shareholders, under the market's knowing eye. Surely this was a theory that never encountered a real business! Jensen and his supporters saw networks of cold calculation; they did not envision carnivals of panicky or predatory short-sellers. The notion that insolvencies could destabilize corporations and trigger other insolvencies, that messy, imperfect solutions would be hammered out during the dead of night by sleep-deprived officials, was not a part of their calculus.* Corporate treasurers, though, took it as gospel; accepting the market's perfection, they placed themselves at its mercy. When the market froze, they were desperate for cash.

Compounding the crisis, companies that had relied on investment banks had to look elsewhere for funds. Ford Motor, for instance, could no longer borrow from Lehman Brothers. Such clients called their banks to draw down credit lines. The banks, though, were not prepared to satisfy all their customers at once. This was a wholesale version of a bank run. Morgan Stanley clients drew down facilities they didn't need, just to have the cash in hand—further straining the bank's dwindling liquidity.[12]

THURSDAY MORNING, John Mack took his war against hedge funds public. In a Morgan Stanley town hall meeting, he lashed out at short-sellers, asserting, "We are in a market today where rumor and innuendo are much more powerful than real results." Trying to buck

---

* Harvey Miller, the bankruptcy lawyer, daringly rebutted Jensen in a 1983 talk at the Harvard Business School Club of New York, arguing that companies that were prone to cyclical downturns, such as the Big Three automakers, should always hold funds for a rainy day. The pro-Jensen audience responded with the Harvard version of a Bronx cheer.

up the troops, he added, "It pains me to go on the floor and see how you guys look."[13] He took questions from the crowd, and Stephen Roach, the firm's well-respected economist, asked Mack the final question: "Many of these short-sellers are our clients. What would you say if you were in a room with them?" Mack said his response would be unprintable.

Roach was right, though; they *were* Morgan Stanley's clients. The war with hedge funds was Wall Street's war with itself, a revolt against a financing stratagem that the banks had conceived and long exploited. After the meeting, Roach made a scheduled presentation to Julian Robertson, the legendary founder of Tiger Management. Robertson was livid over Mack's drive to curtail short-selling. The courtly North Carolinian (born in Salisbury, a half-hour's drive from what was to be Mack's hometown) fumed at Roach: "Do you know a man named John Mack? Well you tell him his campaign against short-selling is going to cost him the goose that laid the golden egg. The hedge fund industry produced the revenues that drove Morgan Stanley's prime brokerage business."

Roach coolly replied, "Correct me if I'm wrong, but in the stock market crash of 1987, a lot of hedge funds, including Tiger, had liquidity problems. We were there for you."

Robertson returned a stream of expletives. "You just tell Mr. Mack our money is gone."

Mack was unrepentant. Morgan Stanley had analyses of trading records that strongly suggested many of the funds shorting its stock were also driving up the price of its credit default swaps. The combination was lethal and presumably intentional. During trading on Thursday the stock plummeted to less than 12 (down from 40 at the start of the month), though later in the day it rebounded. Meanwhile, the hedge funds were draining the firm of $100 billion of liquidity.[14]

Even JPMorgan eased off, either out of deference to Mack or because the game was getting out of hand. Steve Black and Bill Winters, the coheads of Morgan's investment bank, issued a memo warning employees not to capitalize "on the irrational behavior in the market toward some of the U.S. broker-dealers." Referring by name to Goldman and Morgan Stanley, Black and Winters admonished, "We do not want anyone approaching their clients or employees in a predatory way." Jamie Dimon conceded that the drop in his rival's stock was simply irrational.[15]

Mack's best defense was to raise capital. The previous December, during Wall Street's bout of equity sales, Morgan Stanley had sold a stake to China Investment Corporation (an arm of the Chinese government), and Mack now invited its vice-chairman to come to New York—that weekend.

He also heard from Robert Steel, the former Paulson aide who was running Wachovia, who called with a curious message: the *government* wanted their firms to explore a merger. The Fed's Kevin Warsh (a former Morgan Stanley executive) fancifully imagined that, like the proverbial sidewalk drunks, the two imperiled banks could prop each other up. The pairing had an intuitive logic. Morgan Stanley had a first-class investment bank but shaky funding; Wachovia had a huge deposit base. But Mack was cautious. Given that Wachovia had approximately $120 billion of option ARM mortgages (the now-bitter fruit of its acquisition of Golden West), he needed an estimate of its losses before moving forward.

Thursday afternoon, a Wachovia team laden with data arrived at Morgan Stanley's midtown headquarters. To avoid news cameras they were spirited through a side entrance. That night, Morgan Stanley cracked open 400,000 Wachovia mortgages and calculated an estimated loss ratio of 30 percent, rather than the 12 percent Wachovia had suggested. Morgan Stanley could not afford to take on losses of that scale without government help. However, if it couldn't find a partner, the run against its own stock would presumably continue. Frightened almost beyond words, Mack rang his lawyer, the well-connected Ed Herlihy. His firm's business was sound, Mack contended, but it had only two or so days of liquidity. "You tell your friends at Treasury this is serious," he blurted out. "We could go out of business Tuesday!"[16]

On Thursday, Goldman Sachs also made a fund-raising call, to

Warren Buffett. Although Goldman was in better shape than its rival, if Morgan did fail, it was no secret that Goldman could be the next target. Its liquidity was draining more slowly but was draining nonetheless; some firms had stopped dealing with it while others, either out of loyalty or out of fear that Goldman's demise would create a generalized disaster, pledged support. Its stock closed Thursday at 108—down 72 points from a month earlier. With swap premiums on Goldman's debt reaching $500,000, the market was treating Goldman as only borderline financeable. In such a weakened state, the firm could survive for a matter of weeks but probably not more. For the first time, the partners were worried.[17]

Lloyd Blankfein, the CEO, revived an idea that Morgan Stanley had also floated—of becoming a bank holding company. During Paulson's reign as Goldman's CEO, the firm had periodically considered merging with a big commercial bank. But the nimble Goldman, with its smaller balance sheet, earned higher returns than goliaths such as Citibank.[*] The latter seemed sluggish and overcapitalized, and Goldman had preferred to retain its identity as a sleeker, smarter investment bank. In the era dawning now, however, "too much capital" was oxymoronic. Poorly capitalized firms were dying.

And the damage was not contained to investment banks; traditional commercial banks were undergoing a crisis as well. (In simplified terms, the former had too many mortgage securities, the latter too many mortgages.) WaMu, the country's largest thrift, was suffering a loss of liquidity as depositors withdrew funds, and Wachovia was experiencing similar duress. With every aspect of the system quaking, there was no doubt the Treasury would propose a broad bill to rescue the U.S. banking system.

One idea, of course, was to seek authorization to invest in stricken banks directly. Paulson was more comfortable with the less extreme remedy of buying the banks' underwater mortgages. Direct investment

---

[*] Goldman already owned depository banks in the United States and Europe—both tiny relative to the overall firm.

smacked of state control. Paulson feared it would frighten investors, further depress bank stocks, and arouse political opposition. America, particularly between the coasts, has a long tradition of viewing government involvement in banking with suspicion.

Thursday afternoon, Paulson and Bernanke scurried to the White House. They met the president in the Roosevelt Room, named for both Theodore and Franklin, both champions of financial reform. Bernanke stressed that the banking panic, if allowed to run unchecked, could trigger a general economic slowdown, with severe repercussions for ordinary Americans. Paulson asked for broad authority, though he was focused on using it to purchase assets, not to buy stock.

The president inquired, "Are you sure you don't have the power to do this? Because if you have to go to Congress, they are going to make you say there is a crisis."[18] Bush had been detached from the mortgage crisis in its early rounds, but now he sensed that the meltdown on Wall Street, rather than the endless war in Iraq, could determine the mood of the country when he exited the Oval Office, and help to shape his legacy. When the meeting ended, Bush lingered with the officials. Putting a hand on the shoulder of Paulson's press aide, he drawled reassuringly, "We're going to get this. You guys do what you need to; we'll take care of the Hill."

That night, Paulson and Bernanke briefed the congressional leadership (the scheduled meeting with Pelosi had turned into a bipartisan session). Putting the full force of the central bank behind Paulson's proposal, Bernanke warned the assembled lawmakers of disaster if the legislation wasn't approved. However, Congress had its own concerns. The legislators, mindful of the approaching elections, were unenthusiastic about putting their stamp on a plan to bail out bankers, and seemed dubious that working Americans had much at stake in this bill.

Determined to mount a coordinated assault, the government simultaneously proposed four new rescue measures. The SEC issued an emergency order temporarily prohibiting short sales of financial firms, and another beefing up disclosure by hedge funds. (Earlier in the day, the

UK had banned short-selling of financial stocks.)* Bernanke also introduced a new lending facility, under which the Fed would buy high-quality commercial paper from banks. This was yet another measure to increase liquidity—the ability of banks to borrow. The bailout plan itself, which envisioned a government channel for purchasing loans, was similarly contrived to bolster liquidity. None of the measures addressed the banks' capital.

The fourth edict concerned money market funds. The Treasury labored overnight Thursday on a plan to temporarily guarantee their investors—an unprecedented intervention in private markets. Fund executives tried to discourage the Treasury from promulgating the guarantee, which they feared would make the industry look weak. An official, David Nason, noted, "I'm not asking permission. You have to tell me how to make this work." He still hadn't worked out the details Friday morning, but Treasury, hoping to stem the panic, announced the guarantee anyway. Presently, Nason heard from Paulson, who was highly agitated over a call from Sheila Bair, the chairman of the FDIC. Bair rightly pointed out that if the government protected money funds, depositors would pull assets away from *banks*. Strengthening one shoe weakened the other. So Nason retooled the plan: only existing money fund deposits would be protected; new investors would not be. Thus, there would be no incentive to transfer.

Treasury financed the guarantee by stretching the letter of its authority and dipping into a pool of reserves intended for foreign-currency purchases. It selected this pool on the basis of a simple criterion: it was the only $50 billion available. Now reborn as an interventionist, Paulson was not to be deterred by legal or regulatory fine points.

---

* Hedge funds argued that short-sellers were merely messengers of distress—not its agent. The argument is long-standing, and given the inherent difficulty in deconstructing stock market moves, it is probably irresolvable. The SEC, in any case, hardly had time to indulge an epistemological inquiry into cause and effect. In the midst of a market panic, prudence required that it take preventive action, and halting short sales of vulnerable stocks was a plausible means of throwing "sand in the gears" of an overheated market. Indisputably, though, the agency went too far. Its protected list started with 799 stocks and grew to more than 1,000, including companies far afield of finance.

Paulson outlined the measures at a Rose Garden briefing Friday, September 19. Energized in battle, Paulson was at his best, cogently dissecting the "lax lending practices" that led to "irresponsible lending and irresponsible borrowing" earlier in the decade. He aptly summarized the credit bubble: "This simply put too many families into mortgages they could not afford." As a result, he said, banks were burdened with "illiquid mortgage assets that have lost value as the housing correction has proceeded . . . choking off the flow of credit to our economy."

Reckoning with the scale of the problem—five million homes delinquent or in foreclosure—Paulson suggested that Wall Street could not be allowed to return to its former ways. Bold interventions rarely restore the world *ante bellum,* and Paulson signaled that change was in order. He concluded, "When we get through this crisis—which we will—the next step must be to improve the regulatory structure so that these crises do not recur."

Treasury lawyers hastily wrote a three-page draft that authorized $500 billion for mortgage purchases. Just before sending it to Congress, Paulson and his legislative aide bumped it to $700 billion—a sum, they imagined, that would overwhelm any conceivable need. In his eagerness, Paulson made a bid for powers worthy of a MacArthur; the draft specified that "Decisions by the secretary pursuant to the authority of this act are nonreviewable . . . by any court of law or any administrative agency."

The rescue plan lifted the market Friday, leaving the government to focus on Morgan Stanley and Goldman. Geithner pushed both firms to start the process of converting to bank holding companies. Normally it would take weeks, but the Fed was signaling it would greatly expedite matters. Conversion would give Morgan Stanley and Goldman full access to the central bank, and insulate them from danger, as if the Fed would not let one of its children perish. Geithner also pressured the two to raise capital.

While Goldman again called Buffett, Mack dialed investors in Asia, banks in America, and others. All Wall Street was mulling either raising capital or investing it. In such a dynamic climate, bankers sensed extraordinary opportunities, and CEOs indulged in a sort of hypothetical dating game. Vikram Pandit, the Citigroup CEO, made repeated calls to Wachovia. Bob Steel, Wachovia's CEO, was evaluating these and other entreaties. It had occurred to Steel that if Wachovia could sell its bad mortgages to the Treasury (under the program to be presented to Congress) Wachovia might not *need* to merge. Government policy was becoming a major element in banking tactics—an unforeseen consequence of intervention.

The government, for its part, did not think Morgan Stanley could survive the week without new capital. Two possibilities seemed alive: China Investment Corp. and Wachovia. However, Friday night, a third investor surfaced. Colm Kelleher, Morgan Stanley's chief financial officer, was dining at a Japanese restaurant across the street from work. Spearing a piece of sushi, he got a call from Tokyo: Mitsubishi UFJ, Japan's biggest bank, was interested in acquiring a chunk of Morgan Stanley.[19] In a vivid illustration of the global nature of markets, the Asian capital that once had bankrolled American mortgages now was coming to the rescue of American banks overloaded on mortgage securities. Morgan Stanley now had a weekend to fish out capital from one of three sources.

Its board decided Saturday that no matter what occurred with potential investors, it would push ahead on the bank holding company option. (It suspected that Goldman was on a parallel track.) Mack also enlisted JPMorgan to look at its unencumbered assets to see if they would serve as collateral for a loan. Over the weekend, a team of JPMorgan bankers hightailed it to a secondary Morgan Stanley location—avoiding the reporters keeping watch at headquarters—to pore over the books. Meanwhile, Mack was in touch with the brass, Jamie Dimon and Steve Black. Black thought Mack was a consummate pro—maintaining his cool under enormous pressure, without trying to mask his distress. "Whatever you guys can do," Mack conceded, "we would really appreciate some help."[20]

By Saturday evening, Morgan Stanley thought it was beginning to see daylight. It completed an application for bank holding company status in record time; its talks with Mitsubishi were progressing. However, both the Fed and Treasury were worried that these efforts would fall short and the market would renew its attack. Paulson was worried about Morgan Stanley *and* Goldman. He had dropped all pretense of noninvolvement and was hell-bent on saving what was left of Wall Street. Geithner and Bernanke shared his alarm. The Fed and Treasury were tracking Morgan Stanley's capital-raising discussions by the hour and desperately wanted a backup plan. The unspoken consensus was that the government could not let the remaining big investment banks fail. They would not permit another Lehman.

Fear drove the regulators to unprecedented meddling. Saturday afternoon, Kevin Warsh of the Fed called Steel, the Wachovia CEO, and urged him to sell his bank to Goldman Sachs. Warsh had a notion of killing two birds with a single stone: Wachovia would be in stronger hands, and Goldman would become a bank.[21]

David Carroll, a Wachovia senior executive, was attending the University of North Carolina football game in Chapel Hill when his BlackBerry started buzzing. He had a message that Hank Paulson was looking for him. Carroll went behind the stands to try to reach someone at Treasury and learned that a different agency, the FDIC, wanted Wachovia to talk to Goldman. The various agencies had distinct agendas: the Fed and Treasury were fixated on saving the investment banks; the FDIC, guardian of the nation's deposits, was eager to strengthen Wachovia. As Carroll and his wife drove home through the back roads of North Carolina, Steel called and said, "You won't believe this. I've been directed to go back to New York. Lloyd Blankfein is going to pick me up." Steel, who had been an undersecretary just three months ago, was forbidden from petitioning the Treasury Department for a year; this prevented him from dealing directly with his former boss. But the government was clearly concerned that Goldman find a match. The firm seemed to have a merciful angel watching over it from the office of the secretary.

Blankfein personally made the trip to Westchester County Airport to pick up Steel and escort him back to Goldman. That evening the former partners evaluated a deal that neither, previously, had remotely considered. On Sunday, the banks began to negotiate a shotgun merger.[22] A confidentiality agreement was signed, giving Goldman the right to examine Wachovia's loan portfolio. Like Morgan Stanley, Goldman was unsettled by Wachovia's potential losses. It did not want to do the deal unless the government chipped in capital. But until the bill that was now before Congress passed, there was no practical way for the U.S. government to invest in a private bank.[23]

That morning, Paulson appeared on the Sunday talk shows, insisting that Congress act "this week" on his legislation. But the bill was already becoming mired in politics. Banks were fiercely lobbying for relief on mark-to-market accounting;[*] auto-finance and student-loan companies were clamoring for a share of the gravy, and much of Congress seemed less intent on helping banks than on clamping down on bankers' pay.

Morgan Stanley, meanwhile, was moving ahead with its Chinese and Japanese suitors, Mitsubishi in particular. But the government remained extremely worried—*panicked* is not too strong a word.[†] The Mitsubishi deal could still fall through. Even if it were signed, it would not be binding until a definitive agreement was reached, which could take a week. Morgan Stanley did not have a week. The regulators—Paulson, Bernanke, Geithner, and Warsh—expected the market to test Morgan Stanley on Monday. As for converting to a bank, no one knew if that would calm the market. It was mostly about image—what Bernanke liked to call "optics."

Sunday afternoon, Geithner, with Paulson joining in, called Mack and directed him to sell his company to either JPMorgan or Citigroup.

---

[*] Mark-to-market accounting requires financial firms to write down (or up) the value of mortgage and other assets in accordance with market fluctuations. During the crash, it resulted in more immediate recognition of losses.

[†]Paulson, later, disputed this characterization. "Panicked," he argued, applies only to *irrational* fear.

Mack felt his stock was too cheap, but Geithner insisted, "Sell it for a buck if you have to!" The U.S. government was now trying to orchestrate the sale of *both* remaining investment banks.

Mack protested, "I've had discussions with Vikram, I've had discussions with Jamie. They don't want to do it."

Geithner, like a newly crowned czar, replied, "You have to. We'll tell them you have to."

Mack insisted that the government was overreacting. "I'm not going to destroy my franchise and sell it to Jamie Dimon!" he snapped. Mack was a superb battlefield leader: quick, decisive, bold. In the emerging era in which Washington held the power to anoint survivors, Mack had dared say no to the government.

Ultimately, he was forced to call Dimon—an awkward call that ended quickly, as Dimon had no interest. JPMorgan was still digesting Bear Stearns and had no stomach for acquiring another investment bank.[24] Moreover, JPMorgan concluded it could not justify even a loan to Morgan Stanley. A group of its senior bankers—Dimon, Black, Jimmy Lee, and John Hogan—retired to Lee's office to see whether Morgan Stanley would succeed at raising capital, and to plan a strategy in the event it did not. As they waited, they nervously flipped channels between the Giants football game and the Ryder Cup.

Toward late afternoon, the Fed announced it had approved the expedited applications of Morgan Stanley and Goldman to convert to banks. In a practical sense, this did not greatly enhance their borrowing capabilities; from the time of the Bear Stearns rescue the Fed had gradually liberalized the borrowing options for Wall Street. Significantly, that Sunday, it permitted investment banks to use the same collateral as banks. Psychologically, though, converting was huge. To a Goldman executive, it was as if the Fed had drawn a circle and proclaimed that everyone inside it would live.

Sunday night, Mitsubishi agreed to a "letter of intent"—still far short of an ironclad deal—to buy a 20 percent stake in Morgan Stanley. Mack went home to await approval from Mitsubishi's board, which was meeting in Tokyo. At 5 A.M., he was awakened with good news.

16

THE TARP

If it doesn't pass, then heaven help us all.

—HANK PAULSON, IN A PRIVATE MEETING
WITH LAWMAKERS.[1]

On Monday, September 22, the *New York Times* ran a story about Paulson's legislation; cheekily, the piece was situated next to a photograph of the Venezuelan president Hugo Chávez, as if to suggest that the secretary's reach for unreviewable authority was worthy of a Latin strongman.[2] This was not the only connection. Chávez, a socialist hostile to free-market institutions, had been exploiting America's crisis to score propaganda points on the spiritual poverty of *Yanqui* capitalism. Such critiques now touched a sensitive nerve. America's market system had failed. Its banks had failed. Its investors had failed abysmally. Also, the model of international markets—the idea that investors would regulate world economies, appropriately apportioning capital and limiting risk—had failed. The United States had been lustily pushing this model on the world since the fall of the Berlin Wall. It had been deregulating at home since the 1980s. The disaster raised an unavoidable question: If America had taken a wrong turn, how far back should the clock be set?

International opinion was already shifting, sharply, toward the view that free markets had been too free. Angela Merkel, the German chancellor, a onetime advocate of American-style capitalism, was espousing government protection of essential industry. Broadly, Europe was backing away from the Milton Friedmanesque theology praised in political salons since the era of Ronald Reagan. The ideological reexamination was also under way at home. Chris Cox, the SEC chairman, once an extreme proponent of deregulation, told a Senate hearing the United States needed new oversight of exotic derivatives; he then admitted that the SEC's regime of voluntary supervision of investment banks had proved to be woefully inadequate. Striking a more activist tone, Cox was already shaking up hedge funds by demanding to see their trading records.[3]

While structural reforms, Paulson noted, would have to wait until the crisis passed, case by case the government was reversing America's bias toward laissez-faire. The Fed and the Treasury were now at the center of American finance, wielding the equivalent of wartime powers. The Treasury was anointing winners and, perforce, losers. The Fed, through special facilities as well as its normal market operations, was lending tens of billions of dollars to banks and also investment banks.[*] It was propping up money markets and buying debt securities issued by Fannie and Freddie (an effort to maintain a pulse in the housing market). With private channels blocked, the Fed had become the sole credit supplier of consequence.

The daunting challenge for Paulson was that saving the system implied saving the banks, for whom the public had zero sympathy. Trying to marshal support, the secretary said gamely that bank failures threatened the well-being of American families. Realizing he had a fight on his hands, Paulson redrafted the Troubled Asset Relief Program—TARP—in a more detailed form that eliminated the strongman language. The new version of the bill also included authority to invest in banks directly—an idea that continued to percolate, particularly at the Fed. However Treasury aides hastened to assure Congress that this authority would not be used, and Paulson still regarded government

---

[*] As an example of the Fed's ballooning balance sheet, prior to the failure of Lehman the Fed had no loans outstanding to so-called primary dealers (investment banks). By September 17, the day after the AIG bailout, such loans totaled $60 billion. A week later, its credit to Wall Street had swelled to $106 billion.

investment as undesirable and, in a political sense, suicidal. Testifying on Tuesday, September 23, four days after the TARP was proposed, the secretary asserted that granting the government "equity stakes . . . would render [TARP] ineffective" because it might dissuade banks from participating. More rhetorically, Paulson added, "Putting capital in institutions is about failure. This is about success."[4]

The underpinning of Paulson's plan was the pervasive belief in liquidity—the belief that the value of any asset (in this case, mortgages) would recover provided there was a market for it. This notion was a close cousin to the germ that begat the original bubble, namely, the willingness of investors to buy mortgage securities, regardless of underlying merit, as long as the securities were liquid.

Rodriguez learned of the TARP while vacationing with his wife, along with his brother and sister-in-law, in Italy, where he had been attempting to avoid the dismal market news. In Positano, on the Amalfi coast, he had rounded a corner one morning and found himself staring at a glaring headline in the *International Herald Tribune*: "Conservatorship." Thus he learned of the seizure of Fannie and Freddie. The group continued their travels, but for Rodriguez the fun was all but over. Touring the sites of ancient Rome, it occurred to Rodriguez that most of the currencies over the course of history no longer existed, the price of fiscal imprudence. At the Uffizi Gallery in Florence, he became too preoccupied with monitoring the news on Bloomberg to take in the art. Nights he spent in the bathroom (so as not to disturb his wife) hunched over his BlackBerry, an older model with a broken track wheel that rendered scrolling more than ordinarily painstaking. In Venice, after touring the Doge's Palace, he penned an office e-mail critiquing the first, power-accreting version of the TARP (Rodriguez called it "Emperor Paulson"), pointing out that the only cure for the disease of undercapitalization was to invest capital in banks. The best of all medicine, Rodriguez believed, was to let the market function. Bank stock prices would fall, ultimately to a level at which investors would return.

As for Paulson's plan to use the TARP to buy mortgages, Rodriguez was dubious. "The U.S. Treasury–proposed plan," he noted, "only provides liquidity, not the necessary hundreds of billions of new capital that will have to be replaced."[5] Repurchasing assets from banks would add to their capital only if the Treasury overpaid for them, which would amount to "a gift" from the U.S. taxpayer. This criticism pointed to a central flaw in the asset repurchase scheme. If the assets were purchased at the current depressed market price, it would not help banks. If the government paid a premium, the taxpayers would be fleeced. Ultimately, someone had to absorb the losses on fallen mortgages. If it wasn't the banks, it would have to be the government.

Bernanke was emphatic about preserving both options—repurchasing mortgages and injecting capital—and Bernanke was the TARP's most effective advocate.[6] Perhaps because he had underestimated the crisis's severity for so long, his warnings now carried special alarm. Transformed into a prophet of doom, in the days after the TARP proposal the Fed chief repeatedly warned lawmakers of frozen credit markets, of bank losses spreading from mortgages to car loans and other assets and, worst, of credit being denied to consumers and to ordinary businesses.

Congress, though, was preoccupied with venting scorn on wealthy bankers. Having been eager to please the banking industry all through the bubble, legislators now discovered that Wall Street was, in fact, shot through with greed. Senator Sherrod Brown of Ohio inquired of Bernanke whether Wall Street owed America an apology. The Fed chief replied, "Wall Street itself is an abstraction. There are many people who made big mistakes."[7] That was a calculated dodge. Outrage at bankers who had reeled in eight-figure paychecks while failing to protect their institutions was fully justified. But it was not especially useful in coining legislation. Congress insisted on linking TARP assistance to caps on executive pay, which deserved its own, more thought-out bill, and was irrelevant to the immediate issue. The restrictions on bonuses addressed only banks and only during the period of federal assistance. They were, in short, mostly sizzle and little steak.

As Congress deliberated, Wall Street tried to salvage itself. On Tuesday, September 23, Goldman Sachs raised $5 billion from Warren Buffett (Goldman bankers, at least, needed no convincing on the value of capital). Though Goldman agreed to generous terms, Buffett's endorsement helped solidify its image as the cream of Wall Street—and, indeed, helped it raise another $5 billion in a public stock sale the next day.* Morgan Stanley, still waiting for regulatory approval for its agreement with Mitsubishi, was in a more tenuous state. Its hedge fund accounts were for the moment stable but, ominously, premiums on its swaps began to rise again, reflecting fears that the Mitsubishi deal might yet collapse.

More imperiled yet was WaMu, the savings and loan that had blanketed America with retail outlets and that, as a result of so much negative mortgage news, was now suffering a true run on the bank. Management, desperately looking for a buyer, was talking to a handful of banks and private equity firms. During the third week of September, the week of the TARP debate, all went silent. WaMu could not figure out why its calls to suitors were going unanswered. The reason was that federal regulators had preempted the auction. The FDIC was aghast at the thought that WaMu could turn out to be another IndyMac, which had cost it $11 billion. Regulators decided they could not let WaMu's problems fester.

On Thursday, September 25, WaMu was seized, making it the ninth bank failure since July and the biggest by far in U.S. history. The agency awarded the carcass of the bank—2,200 branches and relationships with twelve million account holders—to Jamie Dimon's JPMorgan, which had coveted WaMu, and which instantly gained a sizable presence in California and in Florida. Dimon's coup demonstrated that for wounded subprime lenders, waiting out the storm was not a viable strategy. The previous March, Morgan had offered WaMu $8 a share; Kerry Killinger, the then-CEO, had rejected it. This time, the shareholders got nothing.

In the two weeks prior to the seizure, beginning roughly at the time of the Lehman failure, WaMu had lost 10 percent of its deposits,

---

* Berkshire Hathaway, Buffett's holding company, received a 10 percent dividend as well as the right to buy Goldman stock at a discount. These rich terms underscored Buffett's singular value as an endorser.

about $17 billion. The acquisition stopped the run, as Morgan now stood behind the depositors. However, Morgan did *not* underwrite WaMu's bond obligations, nor did the banking authorities. Bondholders suffered immense losses. The zigzag nature of federal responses (Fannie and Freddie debt holders protected; Lehman's not; AIG's honored and, now, WaMu's not) sorely troubled both Bernanke and Geithner, who faulted Paulson for lurching through the various crises. In a telling example of the pain caused by the inconsistency, community banks that had bought Fannie's and Freddie's preferred stock, which the government had decided not to bail out, suffered staggering losses.* The fault was not all Paulson's, but bondholders were horrified at the lack of predictability. Debts of financial firms were now uniformly seen as risky. When WaMu failed, insurance premiums on Morgan Stanley bonds soared to $1 million.[8]

The WaMu failure darkened the outlook, in particular, for Wachovia, the country's fourth-biggest commercial bank and one with greater implications for the banking system. Bob Steel, the Wachovia CEO and recent Treasury official, had spent the previous week dangling his company before Morgan Stanley and Goldman Sachs. Those flirtations had ended quickly. As WaMu was tottering, he began to explore a union with the only banks left that could plausibly acquire a bank of its size: Wells Fargo and Citigroup. Steel was also preparing to sell stock, but his stock price was being pounded.

By the Wednesday before WaMu's seizure, premiums to insure $10 million of Wachovia's debt had climbed to $700,000, well above the danger level. On Friday—the day after WaMu failed—they soared to $1.6 million.[9] This was the sort of rate that might be offered to a homeowner downwind of a levee in advance of a category 5 hurricane. Meanwhile,

---

* State of Franklin Bancshares, a community bank in Johnson City, Tennessee, was forced to sell itself to an out-of-town rival due to losses on Fannie's and Freddie's preferred stock—which government officials had stressed was a sound investment. "Our bank has excellent earnings and a very clean loan portfolio," Franklin's chairman told the *Wall Street Journal.* "The only mistake we made was in owning U.S. government agencies."

depositors yanked out billions.* The stock fell to 10, down 27 percent for the day and 70 percent for the year, killing any chance of an equity sale. Going into the weekend, rating agencies were preparing to downgrade Wachovia's bonds. Counterparties were backing away from trading, canceling commitments and (as with Morgan Stanley the previous week) draining the bank of liquidity. The class 5 storm had struck.

Steel was well aware of the downward momentum that could chase a financial firm out of existence. At precisely 4:27 A.M. on Friday, he and Vikram Pandit, the Citigroup CEO, exchanged e-mails about a possible merger. (Like lonely hearts trolling for mates, deal-chasing bankers never stopped.) He also accelerated talks with Wells Fargo, the San Francisco–based bank, which had shrewdly avoided the worst of the mortgage bubble and was now in a strong position. Later on Friday, Steel concluded that Wachovia would have difficulty funding "normal banking activities" come Monday. He alerted his board that absent a merger agreement over the weekend, he expected the FDIC to place Wachovia in receivership.[10]

For the fourth successive weekend, Wall Street teetered on the cliff-edge of failure. Each apparent rescue had yielded a bigger crisis (Wachovia was more than twice the size of WaMu) and each seeming salvation turned out to be a mirage. The problem was not just with particular institutions; the entire system was shot through with overvalued, and impossible-to-value, loans, leveraged to an intolerable degree. Lacking confidence, the market resembled a vacuum that drew into it every fearful impulse. The fear simply migrated from one vulnerable institution to the next.

Underlying the panic, credit markets were collapsing. The commercial paper market was shrinking so fast, at the current rate of decline there would be no such paper by the following June.[11] Industrial companies such as automakers were squeezed for cash. Corporations that

---

* Wachovia suffered a net loss of $17 billion in deposits over ten weeks, about half over the final two weeks.

borrowed in the junk bond market were having to pay 15 percent interest, close to loan shark rates. A widely watched indicator, the Treasury Eurodollar spread—the so-called TED—had tripled, from 1 percent to 3 percent. The TED measured the gap between borrowing costs for the government and those for banks. Such a surge was without precedent.

And the distress was plainly spreading to Main Street. Companies were cutting deeply into payrolls; job losses in September would top 300,000—the worst monthly loss since the 2001 recession. As people lost jobs, credit card delinquencies were rising sharply, a telltale sign of a downturn. General Electric, a bellwether of the economy whose assets stretched from finance to manufacturing, abruptly lowered its earnings forecast. The worst harm was in residential real estate, where the storm had begun. Among Americans with mortgages, nearly one in five owed more money than their homes were worth. For them, the dream of home ownership had turned into a nightmare. Fully 20 percent of subprime borrowers were seriously delinquent—an extraordinary credit market bust. Even 5 percent of conventional mortgagors were delinquent, evidence that the disease of overleverage had penetrated the middle class.[12]

Despite these doleful augurs, the administration was still having trouble persuading the public that it had a stake in the banking crisis. The crisis was still widely seen as a Wall Street problem, and mail on the TARP was running solidly against. Senator Jon Kyl, Republican of Arizona, quipped that his mail was split: 50 percent "No" and 50 percent "Hell, no."[13] Trying to rally votes, President Bush gave a prime-time address on the economy—his first in eight years. He warned that without the legislation the United States could face "a long and painful recession." Shorn of his usual satisfied grin, the president seemed humbled. He admitted that the bailout violated his conservative instincts.

Pressing ahead on the TARP legislation, the White House was able to work through its differences with the Democrats. The administration's difficulties were with its own party. House Republicans, who represented, essentially, the antigovernment wing of the GOP, were in open rebellion against Paulson, whom they saw as a dupe for Wall Street. Mistrust of high finance struck a chord with Middle America, one that had reverberated since the eras of Jefferson and Jackson. In contemporary times, rage against bankers fused with antiestablishment suspicions, as though the TARP would trample on frontier freedoms. Of course, the party's foot soldiers harbored a visceral dislike of usurping the free market. Added to that, the bill, now 120 pages, was difficult and dense. The mechanics of purchasing assets (which assets? from which banks? at what price?) were frightfully messy. Opponents had no trouble presenting their case in simplistic terms. Representative Deborah Pryce of Ohio rhetorically demanded of Paulson, "Why this, and why now? Explain how this is not a bailout of Wall Street executives and their golden parachutes." The anti–Wall Street wing imagined banks could fail and their constituents at home would simply go on.

The lawmaking was complicated by the intrusion of presidential politics. On Wednesday, September 24, John McCain announced he was suspending his campaign and backing out of the first debate, scheduled for Friday, because he was needed in Washington to help forge an agreement on the TARP. Barack Obama shrugged off this bizarre tactic. Neither senator had much expertise in economics, but Obama had a much surer grasp of the politics.

On Thursday, McCain jetted into the capital under Secret Service escort and met with House Republicans, who voiced their objections to using taxpayer funds for banks. Then he headed to a White House parlay with congressional leaders, including Obama. An agreement had seemed within reach, but McCain's presence prompted the House Republicans to renew their protests. With Bush scoring dismally low approval ratings in polls, McCain felt pressured to distance himself from the White House, and therefore from the TARP. Asked whether he sided with the GOP dissenters, the candidate hedged, and the meeting dissolved into shouting. By Friday, opposition to the TARP had acquired the trappings of a populist crusade. Minority leader John A.

Boehner, from Ohio (a state with one of the highest foreclosure rates in the country), denounced the proposal before his fellow House Republicans and received a standing ovation.[14]

Paulson, desperately trying to save the bill, frantically worked the phones. All his urgencies of the past months were condensed into the single urgency of passing the TARP. His natural bent led away from such massive government interventions, but he had the raw experience of having attempted many lesser measures. None had worked. Now he lobbied for the TARP incessantly. He spared no effort to rally the members. He barely slept. On the edge of a physical breakdown, he went to his private restroom and puked.

On Friday the 26th, while the administration counted bailout votes, banking regulators were closely monitoring Wachovia, whose execs were holed up at the midtown adjunct of Sullivan & Cromwell. David Carroll, Wachovia's senior executive, feared that if such a colossal bank, with its three-quarters of a trillion in assets, collapsed, it could trigger a generalized meltdown. He told Rodgin Cohen, the Sullivan partner, "You're looking at 1929." Carroll, Cohen, and Bob Steel, the CEO, were in continuous dialogue with the FDIC and with their most eager suitor, Citigroup, whose headquarters were one block north, also on Park Avenue. Teams of Citigroup executives trekked over to Sullivan & Cromwell; however, in a now familiar pattern, they concluded that Citi could not afford to acquire Wachovia and its portfolio of adjustable mortgages without government help. Sheila Bair, the FDIC head, did not want to provide this help.

Bair was expecting that another suitor, Wells Fargo, would make an unassisted bid. Richard Kovacevich, the Wells CEO, had displayed an uncanny knack for assessing risk. (Recruited out of high school to pitch for the Yankees, he judged he could do better by enrolling at Stanford.) He began his banking career at Citi, where, in the 1980s, he directed an aggressive mortgage operation, an experience that disabused him of the more naïve fantasies that later flowered in the mortgage industry. As head of Norwest Bank and, since 1998, Wells Fargo, Kovacevich shunned subprime lending and steered a wide berth around credit derivatives. Nor was Kovacevich, like so many bankers, always looking for the next deal. But he did want Wachovia. Wells did not have a presence on the East Coast, and Wachovia would make it a potent force there. Plus, its stock was cheap.

Over breakfast Sunday morning, Kovacevich told Steel that Wells would unveil a stock-for-stock offer as soon as it finished due diligence. Once again, the inquiry did not go smoothly. Like others who had seen Wachovia's books, the Wells examiners were troubled by its soaring delinquencies. The Golden West mortgages, acquired at the peak of the bubble, were defaulting at astronomical rates. Default rates in parts of inland California were projected to reach 80 percent. At the very least, Wells Fargo would need more time to evaluate a bid.[15]

Realizing that an unassisted bid wasn't in the offing for now, Bernanke began to push Bair to make FDIC assistance available. The agency is authorized to offer help in cases that present a "systemic risk," but in its seventy-six-year history it had never done so. The primary function of the FDIC is to pay off depositors of banks that fail, and this is the mission for which Bair was guarding her resources. Bernanke, though, was convinced that the United States was indeed facing a systemic banking panic. Bair was worried about her agency; Bernanke was worried about a second Depression.[16]

Sunday night, Bair broke. Realizing that Wachovia could not find a partner before Monday, and under relentless pressure from Bernanke (who refused to go home until the bank was saved), she agreed to implement Section 13 of the Federal Deposit Insurance Act to effect an "assisted transaction" with an institution that the agency would select. The bidding started that night, with the FDIC naturally intending to award the prize to the suitor that requested the least assistance. Holed up at the law firm, Steel had a sudden epiphany. "Why shouldn't we put in our own bid?" he wondered. If the FDIC was going to support a potential buyer by taking a share of Wachovia's losses, it could provide the same help to Wachovia without a merger, letting the bank remain independent. Shortly after midnight, Wachovia submitted its own bid. Kenneth Phelan, Wachovia's risk officer, cleverly lobbied the

FDIC not to force Wachovia into the arms of Citi. "We're a *Main* Street bank," he argued. "Don't push us into the hands of Wall Street."[17]

But at 4 A.M., Bair, after conferring with Bernanke, informed Steel that Citigroup would indeed acquire Wachovia's banking assets, pending negotiation of a binding agreement. Citi's refusal to purchase the entire corporation (just its banking assets) unsettled Steel, who was not sure whether the rump Wachovia business that remained, mostly a brokerage operation, would be viable. Also, the price was a pittance, only $2 billion. But it was a good deal for Citi, which would claim the bank and FDIC protection on a $312 billion pool of loans, which Citigroup could select.[18] This was a staggering amount—far larger than the total of Wachovia's identified problem. Whose assets, then, was the government protecting?

Wachovia executives were dumbfounded that the government would assume so much taxpayer risk. Bair told them it was the best deal for *both* banks.[19] On form, the government was worried about Citi, too. Though it was widely thought to have taken its licks (by writing off tens of billions of bad loans) Citi's portfolio remained rife with problem assets, including mortgages and credit card and auto loans. Steel and others in Wachovia's upper ranks suspected that the government was hoping to administer a salve to Citigroup without drawing public attention to its woes. Thus, by providing Citi with an FDIC guarantee, the government could backstop loans in Citi's *existing* portfolio as well as the loans it would acquire from Wachovia.[20]

Bair rushed to get the deal confirmed before markets opened. She put enormous pressure on Jane Sherburne, Wachovia's general counsel, to sign the agreement in principle—even before Sherburne read it. The agreement gave Citi the exclusive right to negotiate a binding commitment and finalize a merger. Sherburne wanted to insert a stipulation that the parties would negotiate in good faith—giving Wachovia a smidgeon of leeway. Citi refused.[21] At 6:30 A.M. on Monday, Wachovia's board reluctantly approved the transaction, still in its preliminary form. Steel donned a suit, strode across 53rd Street and shook hands with Vikram Pandit.

Despite the cordial gesture, the match remained a forced marriage—forced on Wachovia, Steel suspected, to bolster Citigroup, which was far and away the country's largest troubled bank. A disturbing side effect of the government effort to merge big banks was that banking power was becoming consolidated among fewer firms: big, protected institutions were swallowing everyone else.

Hank Paulson was detached from the Wachovia talks for the simple reason that he spent the weekend trying to forge an eleventh-hour deal on the TARP. As time grew short, Representative Rahm Emanuel of Illinois and Senator Kent Conrad of North Dakota hand-carried pages between Speaker Pelosi, Paulson, and the Republicans camped in the office of the House minority leader.[22] Paulson, agreeing to compromises on bonuses, foreclosure relief, and oversight, announced a tentative deal with the legislative leaders early Sunday. He went into Monday feeling optimistic. President Bush issued a plea to Congress and personally called Republican holdouts. McCain, the party's standard-bearer, also—if belatedly—encouraged members to vote in favor. There still was the question of whether conservatives could stomach a $700 billion spending authorization. Boehner, the House minority leader, refused to risk the ire of the rank and file by flatly supporting the bill. Instead, he tepidly urged "every member whose conscience will allow them" to vote in favor.[23]

Wall Street, smelling trouble, pushed stock prices down on Monday. At 1:28 P.M., as the roll call began in Congress, the sell-off gathered steam. Two-thirds of Republicans voted nay. Anger on the left (four in ten Democrats also voted no) sealed the measure's fate. At 1:43 P.M., the gavel fell, and the Dow plunged 400 points in the next five minutes. Traders stared at their screens in disbelief. The TARP was dead, and by the afternoon close, the Dow was off 778 points. The broader S&P 500 was down almost 9 percent, its worst day in twenty-two years. Financial stocks, the hardest hit, suffered double-digit losses.

The vote left banks no quarter. Paulson had long been reluctant to go to Congress because he feared it would limit rather than expand his options. Now his fears had been confirmed. He was devastated by the defeat. Representative Barney Frank consoled the secretary—noting that, like a group of unruly children, Congress might still come to its senses. "Sometimes," Frank offered, "the kids have to run away before they get hungry and come back to the dinner table."

Tuesday, September 30, was the first day of Rosh Hashanah, the Jewish New Year. With Congress closed to formal business, Senate leaders started backroom talks to revive the TARP. Meanwhile, the permafrost in credit hardened. The ninety-day Libor rate—an inverse measure of banking liquidity—crept above 4 percent for the first time since January. As Bernanke predicted, the banking freeze was leading to more serious fissures in the workaday economy. Interest rates on auto loans were bucking 10 percent, casting a gloom over Detroit. Demand for steel had sagged and construction spending had tanked. Negative economic news was weighing on stocks, which were now off 21 percent for the year.

America's troubles had been the source of smug valedictories in Europe, where the Anglo-American model of capitalism was viewed as the crisis's main culprit. Europe had thought itself shielded from the worst, largely because, under the opposing German model of capitalism, banks had remained under the thumb of the state, less driven by the desire to raise their share price, less voraciously in search of profit, and more attuned to social mores and government restrictions. Peer Steinbrück, Germany's finance minister, crowed that the crisis marked the end of the era of America's dominance in finance.[24] This overstated Europe's relative immunity, as Herr Steinbrück was soon to discover.

Europe's banking culture had also liberalized, in particular by entering the U.S. mortgage market as well as swap markets. Financiers on the Continent, though still more conservative than a Countrywide loan officer, were no longer the prudent gnomes of Swiss legend. Also, a fact beyond their control, markets were sufficiently interconnected ("global," in the favored idiom) that immunity on a grand scale was something of a myth.

In late September, as the TARP was going down to defeat in Washington, Europe's banking system became seriously drained of liquidity, as everyone from small depositors to banks refused to lend. Governments from Dublin to Berlin were forced to rescue, or nationalize, major lenders, including a German bank with significant commercial property loans in the United States.[25] The scale of the bailouts was huge; in Germany the rescue cost $40 billion. Ireland, which also suffered a stock market crash, took the extraordinary step of guaranteeing every deposit in its six biggest banks—a guarantee equal to two times the country's gross domestic product. The ripples from the United States, more like a tidal wave as it washed over Rotterdam and Dieppe, raised the fear of a serious European slowdown and put paid to the dream of a Continent-only recovery.

Regulators on both sides of the Atlantic feared a "hoarding mentality," the instinct that, in preindustrial times, had caused peasants to withhold grain from cities, leading to starvation and riots. In 2008, nervous bankers were hoarding capital. With money markets frozen around the world, central banks were pressed into service as lenders of last resort. Europe's Central Bank loaned banks on the Continent $150 billion. America's Fed, reaffirming the still-central role of the dollar, added an eye-popping $330 billion in facilities for lending greenbacks overseas.

At home, the Fed expanded lending facilities available to U.S. banks, making available another $300 billion. It also was steadily ratcheting up its loans to Wall Street, whose borrowings from the Fed soared from zero to $150 billion in a matter of a few weeks.[26] These efforts were unprecedented and, given their scale, nothing short of heroic. Still, they addressed only liquidity, not capital, for no amount of loans will increase a bank's net worth, just as providing credit to consumers cannot make them "richer." (Assets go up, but so do liabilities.) Bernanke was creating liquidity as the Fed had never done before, but the dismal truth, the *New York Times* noted, was that "those attempts have done little or nothing to bolster confidence in the financial markets."[27]

STEEL'S TURN

Anyone who doubts that the U.S. is heading for
recession is living in denial.

—NIALL FERGUSON, *Time*, OCTOBER 2, 2008[1]

THREE TIMES IN THE past forty years, Citigroup had made the same bet. Equally brazen and naïve, it gambled that its size and diversity of holdings would offset the risks of perilous loans. In the 1970s, it confidently led the way in recycling petrodollars to third-world states. As a truly international bank, Citi was virtually an adjunct of the Fed in managing global capital flows, and its legendary chairman, Walter Wriston, was confirmed in the belief that nation-states did not go bankrupt, and certainly not all at once. In the early 1980s, though, countries from Argentina to Poland defaulted on or simply renounced their debts, leading to horrendous losses for Citi.

Wriston retired in 1984 and passed control to a younger executive, John Reed, who glimpsed the power of the ATM and built up the bank's consumer franchise. Citi refocused its lending on commercial real estate, financing urban office towers and suburban shopping malls, which in the mid-'80s underwent a boom. Reed believed that Citi's portfolio was secure by virtue of its geographic dispersion, as well as by the sheer number of its assets—the premise being, again, that not all projects would default at once, especially not projects in distinct regions. Alas, in the early 1990s, it became clear that developers had vastly overbuilt and a great many projects did default. But for a friendly injection of capital from Saudi Arabia, Citibank would have likely failed.

The twice-taught lesson—that a multiplicity of bad loans does not make them good—went unlearned. During the 'oos, Citigroup jumped into subprime and, what's more, into a full panoply of risky assets.* Its supposed strength was its diversity—Citi's portfolio was stuffed not just with mortgages but with CDOs, consumer and business loans, private equity, derivatives, the full gamut. As late as October 2007 (the month before Chuck Prince was sacked), it remained the country's most highly valued financial company. However, its strategy of secreting assets off the balance sheet in SIVs collapsed, following which it suffered crushing mortgage losses. Even after Prince was replaced by Vikram Pandit, Citi continued to rack up numbing quarterly losses. Its strength began to look like a weakness. If the United States succumbed to a recession, Citi would have to contend with faltering consumer and business loans along with sunken mortgages.

Its international portfolio was similarly vulnerable. Citi had little margin for error on these assets because the bank was perennially undercapitalized. Investors began to wonder how many hits it could sustain at once. The stock, 35 when Pandit had taken the helm, had plummeted to 20 in less than a year. By September of '08, Pandit knew, even if Wall Street didn't, that Citi was staring into the abyss.

Pandit's grandest scheme for engineering a recovery was to buy Wachovia, and it was a plan that regulators, in particular Tim Geithner, Citigroup's closest supervisor, eagerly embraced. In simplified fashion, Citi envisioned running its retail business out of Wachovia's superior retail franchise, which would come gift-wrapped in a government guarantee, and would also provide cover for Citigroup's loans. By cherry-picking Wachovia's banking business, rather than buying the whole corporation, Citi could leave behind its brokerage as well as myriad

---

* Citigroup acquired Associates First Capital, a major subprime lender, in 2000. It also bought Argent Mortgage, a troubled lender, and AMC Mortgage Services, a servicer, in September 2007, as the bubble was popping.

other assets and liabilities it didn't want, such as Wachovia's golden parachutes. This was the deal on which Steel and Pandit shook the morning of September 29.

Wachovia executives repeatedly urged Citi to reconsider its approach and simply acquire Wachovia outright. Splitting up a company with hundreds of distinct legal entities was simply too complex, especially since Citi needed a definitive agreement within four days, or by Friday, October 3, so it could raise capital to support the purchase. The FDIC wanted an expedited deal as well. It could not risk another broken bank. Steel's lieutenants, though, could not make headway in the negotiations.[2]

Citigroup kept trying to foist more liabilities onto the rump Wachovia that was to be left behind. Having won from the government a massive guarantee, Citi was hungrily, even greedily, attempting to extract from its partner every morsel of its remaining worth. Perhaps Pandit judged that he could dictate terms because, as he knew, the government was so invested in the agreement. Citigroup was seen as truly too big to fail, and any upset to it horrified the Fed.

For the better part of the week, Pandit's negotiators ploddingly pressed their case. On Thursday, the two CEOs met in New York again. With the deadline only twenty-four hours away, the rival teams were laboring under tremendous pressure, two of the execs frantically scribbling terms on a napkin. Citigroup was still seeking an edge. Jane Sherburne, Wachovia's general counsel, had worked at Citi and knew the players, but was unable to persuade her former colleagues to soften their demands. When Steel departed for New Jersey's Teterboro Airport, where his jet was parked, significant issues remained.[3]

Wachovia was counting on a "solvency clause," which would permit it to abandon the deal if a third party could not affirm, at the closing, that it would remain viable. Early that evening, as Sherburne continued to negotiate, an associate pulled her aside and informed her that Citigroup was backing out of the solvency clause. The prospect of closing a deal that could render her company defunct alarmed Sherburne. She immediately got hold of Andrew Felner, Citi's deputy general counsel and her former colleague. "Andy, let's get a grip here," Sherburne began.

Then, her cell phone rang. Sheila Bair was on the line. The FDIC chief had dramatic news: Wells Fargo was reentering the bidding.

The San Francisco bank, which had given up hope of winning Wachovia, had rethought its options in light of Citigroup's dallying. Bair had relayed this news to Steel (it had come to seem normal for government officials to serve as intermediaries in banking deals). Steel, who was on the tarmac, readying to take off for Charlotte, was stunned. He told Bair to call Sherburne and rang off. Then he sat back and smiled in wonderment at this latest twist as he watched the Jersey landscape fade into a blur.[4]

Bair informed Sherburne (who hastily exited from her meeting with the Citigroup lawyer) that Wells's offer did not require federal assistance, did not entail cleaving Wachovia into parts and, at $7 a share, was worth far more to the shareholders than Citigroup's bid. In short, it was superior in every respect. Sherburne instantly recognized that Citi would litigate if Wachovia so much as curtsied in Wells's direction. However, it would probably be sued by its own shareholders if it balked at such an attractive offer. And the U.S. government was urging her to pursue it. Thinking fast, Sherburne replied that she would need to see a merger agreement signed by Wells and approved by its board before Wachovia would consider it.

KOVACEVICH, THE WELLS CEO, reached Steel as he was landing, at 9 P.M. He promised that an approved agreement was forthcoming. Knowing that it would add to the pressure, Kovacevich mentioned that Wells would make its offer public the next morning. At 9:04 P.M. Steel received, via e-mail, the board-approved merger agreement. In approximately four minutes, Wells Fargo had accomplished what Citigroup had failed to achieve in a week.

As Steel hurried home, Rodgin Cohen, the Sullivan lawyer, read the document from Wells and advised Steel that it passed muster. Steel convened his directors via telephone around midnight. The board, recognizing that the Wells offer was financially superior—more lucrative, issued from a sounder bank, and, unlike Citi's, unconditional—heartily gave their approval. As Steel signed the agreement, one thought troubled him, a disquieting shadow. He said to Bair, "I think we have to call Vikram."[5]

Steel, Sherburne, and Bair together placed a call to Pandit sometime after 2 A.M. Steel had known Pandit for years, since their days as young investment bankers. He said, "Vik, I have to talk to you about important things."

Pandit was instantly awake, and instantly furious. In desperation, he said, "Sheila, you know this isn't just about Wachovia. There are other issues at stake"—a reference to Citigroup's exposure.[6] But Bair, who was thrilled that a buyer was willing to acquire Wachovia without her agency's support, refused to intervene. The Wells deal was announced that morning, sending Citigroup's stock plummeting and Wachovia's soaring.*

The pretense that Citigroup had needed help just to handle Wachovia's portfolio was now exposed, and Citi promptly asked the government for loan protection for itself.[7] The regulators knew that Citi's issues would have to be addressed. But their first priority was curing the banking system and enacting the TARP.

Strangely, the stock market had latched on to the TARP as though it were the last hope for redemption. Traders normally repelled by a hint of government meddling now were clamoring for the biggest banking rescue in history, without which stocks were continuing to founder. Warren Buffett, the country's wealthiest investor, appeared on the *Charlie Rose Show* and declared that the United States faced an economic Pearl Harbor that required action by Congress. A Depression baby, Buffett instinctively rallied to the government in times of crisis, and he knew that Paulson needed his support. He also endorsed the

---

* Citigroup sued but failed to derail the merger, which closed as planned on December 31, 2008.

STEEL'S TURN · 255

market, after a fashion, by buying a slice of General Electric, on terms similar to his Goldman deal.

Buffett's example failed to rally the public. On Thursday, October 2, the Dow fell 350 points. Convening in an atmosphere of siege, the Senate approved the TARP (which had been modified only slightly since the House rejection, with the addition of a provision to increase the ceiling on deposit insurance from $100,000 per account to $250,000). When the House received the bill, on Friday, it was essentially the same legislation as a week earlier—except that, over that week, stocks had lost 9 percent of their worth, a crushing blow to every American with a retirement account, a mutual fund, or the like. Wall Street may be said to have enacted the legislation, for the representatives switched their votes not because their hearts had softened, or because the modest amendments had swayed their intelligence, but because they did not want the blame for a continued Wall Street crash. Bush signed the TARP with the stock market at its lowest ebb in four years.

Credit markets, more vital to the economy, were in even worse shape. There was simply no credit to be had. One-month Treasury bills yielded a mere tenth of a percentage point, three-month bills only half a point—continued evidence that investors were balking at lending to anyone aside from Uncle Sam. What credit did exist was tilted toward the ultrashort term (for instance, loans expiring within four days).[8] Investors were retreating en masse from securities backed by student loans or consumer debts—the sort of asset-backed paper that, for a generation, had stitched the economy together. The unexamined (and remarkable) premise of capital markets—that traders would lend to counterparties they had never met or spoken to, weaving a continuous strand of credit—had ceased to hold. Hardest-pressed were banks, which are simply entities that borrow from some organizations and people and lend to others. The TED spread, an inverse measure of credit flows to banks, hit an all-time high.

The effect of diminished bank liquidity was similar to that of a tourniquet on a body's circulation. Starved for credit, corporations were faced with having to buy goods with cash. Michael Jackson, the CEO of AutoNation, the United States' biggest auto dealership, complained to CNBC that banks were looking for any excuse to say no, "and they are saying no to good customers." Jackson warned that without credit, three thousand showrooms could go out of business.

Even blue-chip corporations were feeling the pinch. The market for commercial paper had plunged by $95 billion in a week, to $1.6 trillion, down precipitously from $2.2 trillion before the credit crisis began. Without these short-term loans, business began to grind to a halt. An example of the pervasive nature of the crunch, and one particularly worrisome to Paulson, was General Electric, which was suddenly crimped for cash. It raised funds on onerous terms, and premiums on GE's bonds spiked to $600,000, up four times since August. A failure by GE, a company as familiar as the lightbulb and one whose credit was rated triple A, would be devastating to public confidence. Jeffrey Immelt, the CEO, pleaded with Paulson that any government programs to resuscitate bank liquidity also provide for GE.[9]

As the damage spread, bond investors shunned municipal borrowers, squeezing state and local governments, who faced the prospect of declining tax receipts combined with long-ignored pension bills. The day the TARP passed, California's governor, Arnold Schwarzenegger, said the state could run out of cash in weeks. Washington, D.C., citing a lack of buyers, killed a bond offering for airport expansion; Billings, Montana, was struggling to finance a new emergency room for the local hospital; Maine could not raise funds for highway repairs.[10]

On the same Friday, October 3, AIG divulged that, as it had been unable to sell any assets, it had already drawn $60 billion of the $85 billion loan from the Fed—news that shocked the rating agencies, which had expected the drawdown to occur more gradually. Moody's promptly issued a downgrade. Even bailouts did not seem to be working. Bernanke immediately approved an additional AIG loan of nearly $40 billion. The loan fell into a disturbing pattern: yet another huge agency commitment effected utterly without democratic process or review.

The root of the crisis was that every bank in the Western world had orders to reduce leverage, perforce to sell loans. The great hope of Paulson, that the financial system could deleverage gradually and relatively painlessly, lay in ashes. The number and size of bad loans was simply too great. As an indication of the scale, by September 30 Moody's had, since the beginning of the crisis, downgraded 4,221 tranches of CDOs worth a total of $450 billion. More than 80 percent (by dollar value) had originally been rated Aaa, and half had not only been downgraded but had filed notices of default. Those downgraded and defaulted bonds were on the books of banks, and others, and there was no painless way to unload them.[11]

In a perceptive essay published in *Time*, the British historian Niall Ferguson calculated that bank losses during the crisis amounted to $100 billion more than the total of new capital raised, implying (since each dollar of capital supported $10 or more on the balance sheet) that banks would have to reduce their assets by at least a trillion dollars.[12] This guaranteed further price plunges, further bank losses.

The devastation of banks implied an ever-stronger case for using the TARP for a capital injection. A group of professors with whom Bernanke periodically consulted were at the Fed that Friday, and strongly recommended capital investment, noting that it had worked in Sweden during its banking crisis in the 1990s. Bernanke surely mentioned this to Paulson, as the secretary told his staff he wanted them to work on a "capital program."[13] Then, Paulson took his family to an island off the coast of Georgia for a weekend of fishing and a respite from stress. The Monday he returned, stock markets around the world crashed.

18

RELUCTANT SOCIALIST

*The holders of the cash reserve [the central bank]
must be ready not only to keep it for their own
liabilities, but to advance it most freely for the
liabilities of others. They must lend to merchants, to
minor bankers, to "this man and that man" whenever
the security is good.*

—WALTER BAGEHOT, EDITOR,

THE *Economist*, 1873[1]

O N MONDAY, OCTOBER 6, the world experienced a global panic. Foreigners who had breezily invested in American mortgages on the offhand assumption that America was immune to financial collapse woke up to the sobering realization that global markets were just as connected on the downside of the cycle. China's stock market fell 5 percent in a day, Japan's and Korea's more than 3 percent, Russia's a devastating 19 percent. Germany's government, acting to arrest the contagion as though it were a westward-swirling plague, guaranteed every deposit in the banking system. The panic rolled on: France fell 9 percent, Britain 8 percent. In America, the Dow closed under 10,000 for the first time since 2004. Jim Cramer, broadcasting's jittery market oracle, told listeners to "sell everything now."

Bernanke was focused less on the stock market than on the slumping economy. After many months of minimizing the threat, the Fed was faced with unmistakable evidence that America was entering a recession, if it wasn't in one already. Bad credit card debts were mounting, retail sales were plunging, manufacturing was falling, and home prices were down for the ninth consecutive quarter. Job totals had slid for nine straight months. Increasingly seizing the initiative, Bernanke tripled the amount of loans, to $900 billion, that the Fed would auction to banks via the Term Auction Facility, one of a welter of lending mechanisms it had created over the past year. Like other Fed prescriptions, this one addressed the liquidity of banks but not their capital. "Liquidity is being thrown at the system," a blogger posted dubiously, "but it's just making things worse."[2]

More fairly, the Fed's action was a bold step but not a sufficient one. On Tuesday, October 7, Bernanke went one better, announcing that the Fed would create a facility to buy commercial paper. This was as revolutionary as paper money or aluminum bats. The Fed had always been a banker to *banks*. If it wanted to stimulate auto sales or manufacturing, it lent money to financial intermediaries, confident that the added liquidity would flow toward the rest of the economy. But the banks were moribund—useless. Bernanke was saying that the Fed would lend directly to department stores, computer makers, and airlines by buying their commercial paper. It would be the banker to, if need be, every firm in America.*

Markets crashed anyway—again. The Dow lost 500 points that Tuesday. Financial stocks were torched. Bank of America, which cut its dividend and reported growing credit troubles, concluded a dismal equity sale as its shares fell 26 percent. Morgan Stanley, which had inked a definitive agreement but was still scurrying to close its investment from Mitsubishi, plummeted 25 percent. The stock closed below 20 for the first time in a decade, as rumors swelled that Mitsubishi

---

* There was a distant precedent. During the Depression, the Fed lent to diverse industrial firms, often in modest amounts: a St. Paul lumber firm borrowed $100,000; a Wisconsin manufacturer, $40,000; and a merchant in North Dakota, $3,000. Such loans were known as "Section 13(b) lending," after a section added to the Federal Reserve Act in 1934 to deal with "exceptional circumstances." It was invoked again in 2008.

might renege. The market was also pummeling stocks well removed from finance. Ford Motor, highly sensitive to recession worries, fell to under 3, its lowest level since the mid-1980s. Even Google, the Internet king, fell to half its all-time high. Over the past year, U.S.-listed stocks had lost $7 trillion in market value.

Wall Street was entering the territory of theoretical extremes, the territory plumbed by Bernanke soon after his appointment to the Fed, in 2002, when he had outlined how the Fed might respond to a severe economic crisis—dropping cash from a helicopter, as he whimsically put it. Speaking hypothetically, he had observed:

> [T]he U.S. government has a technology, called a printing press (or, today, its electronic equivalent), that allows it to produce as many U.S. dollars as it wishes at essentially no cost. By increasing the number of U.S. dollars in circulation, or even by credibly threatening to do so, the U.S. government can also reduce the value of a dollar in terms of goods and services, which is equivalent to raising the prices in dollars of those goods and services. We conclude that, under a paper-money system, a determined government can always generate higher spending and hence positive inflation.

The specific problem Bernanke was considering in 2002 was deflation, as distinct from recession, but they are similar phenomena or at least strongly coincident. And the cure for one (stronger demand, leading to higher prices) is also medicine for the other. Typically, to revive a moribund economy the Fed injects money into the system by purchasing Treasury securities or the debt of federal agencies. The more it purchases, the greater the money supply and hence the more that interest rates will fall. But what if rates drop to zero and the economy still fails to revive? Bernanke stressed that all would not be lost. "To stimulate aggregate spending when short-term interest rates have reached zero, the Fed must expand the scale of its asset purchases or, possibly, expand the menu of assets that it buys." Bernanke was extraordinarily prescient:

> The Fed does have broad powers to lend to the private sector indirectly via banks, through the discount window. Therefore a second policy option, complementary to operating in the markets for Treasury and agency debt, would be for the Fed to offer fixed-term loans to banks at low or zero interest, *with a wide range of private assets (including, among others, corporate bonds, commercial paper, bank loans, and mortgages)* deemed eligible as collateral [italics added].[3]

In 2002, Bernanke had imagined first lowering rates to zero and then, if necessary, broadening the menu of assets that the Fed might buy or lend against. In the credit storm of 2008, Bernanke reversed the order. As a JPMorgan economist observed in October, "Much of the activity in which the Fed has been engaged over the past year has involved creating new tools that alter the composition of assets on its balance sheet."[4]

The remaining tool, clearly, was to lower rates. As Bernanke had observed, there was no theoretical limit on how much money the Fed could pump into the system. In the past month, the Fed's balance sheet had ballooned by 60 percent. Fed watchers were already worried that the Fed was debasing the dollar by printing money willy-nilly. The Federal Funds rate was down to 2 percent, within range of the theoretical lower bound: zero. A zero rate is equivalent to free money, which tends to induce aberrant and highly speculative behavior. Indeed, the last time rates had been so low, after the 2001 recession, cheap money had ignited the mortgage bubble. This was not a precedent that the central bank was eager to revisit. Since April, even as the mortgage economy and then Wall Street had collapsed, the Fed had not dared to cut rates further.[5]

But the economic data emerging in early October was simply awful.

Unemployment hit 6.2 percent, its highest level in five years. Mortgage lending in the quarter fell to an eight-year low. Retail sales at JCPenney, a fixture of Middle America, plunged 12 percent, and upscale Neiman Marcus fell even more. With consumer credit (a number that almost invariably expands) falling for the first time in eleven years, indicating that families were reining in their debts, the pall in consumer activity was sure to continue. As for Detroit, auto sales in the quarter plunged by a third, a drop bespeaking a Depression-like level of distress. With car loans on hold and potential buyers out of credit, GM was burning through more than $1 billion a month. Its solvency was at risk—another reminder that the financial crisis was destroying the industrial heartland. To Bernanke, the threat was sufficient to risk the lower bound. However, he did not think the United States should act alone.

One of the bitter lessons of the 1930s was that unilateral economic policies were almost as destructive to the world as unilateral military acts. In the 1930s, countries raised tariffs thinking they would protect their home markets. Since other nations were compelled to follow suit, the result was a collective (and crushing) loss of trade. Countries also tried to gain a competitive advantage by cheapening their currency, leading, similarly, to a vicious cycle of "beggar-thy-neighbor" devaluations.

Whatever their flaws, central bankers in the twenty-first century were under no illusions that they could engineer recoveries in isolation. The economies of England, France, and Germany were contracting and presumably in recession. Iceland, a former boom state where entrepreneurs had once brandished $10,000 watches, was essentially insolvent—its banks and the national government alike. A global recession had always been Bernanke's deepest worry, because it carried the germ of a viral contagion in which one country infected another. Acting to blunt this threat, on Wednesday, October 8, Bernanke and five other central banks (those of Europe, England, Canada, Switzerland, and Sweden) announced a coordinated rate cut—the first ever. The Fed funds rate was cut to a paper-thin 1.5 percent.

National budgets remained the province of individual states (taxpayers in the UK were not about to bail out American banks, as Lehman had discovered). However, governments were eyeing each other. On Wednesday, October 8, as central bankers were preparing their joint rate cut, Alistair Darling, the British chancellor of the exchequer, dropped a bombshell. Darling, who in his youth had been a Marxist, declared his intent to inject £50 billion into British banks—the first major Western power to take a step toward nationalization. Simultaneously, Darling lobbed a second shell across the pond, guaranteeing £250 billion of British bank debt. Ireland had already announced a debt guarantee, and the other European states were hotly considering same.

These ministerial interventions failed to halt the panic in America, where, on Wednesday, markets fell another 2 percent. However, the timing of the British actions was providential. The G7 finance ministers (representing the economic powers of the West plus Japan) were due to arrive in Washington on Friday, October 10, followed the next day by a broader group, the G20, as well as the International Monetary Fund. In a stroke, Darling had supplied the agenda.

With markets unraveling, the scheduled summits obtained the aura of an emergency world cabinet. In America, rescue proposals were flying through cyberspace, with politicians and pundits variously calling for more liquidity measures, a second New Deal and, at the opposite end of the spectrum, an end to bailouts. The effect of the British move was to refocus Washington on the long-simmering idea of acquiring equity ownership in banks.

The initial concept of using the TARP to purchase mortgages had gotten off to a slow start. No one at Treasury knew which mortgages to buy or how much to pay for them. With the British precedent looming large, Bernanke and Geithner urged Paulson to inject capital into the banks directly. Paulson was hearing similar advice from his own lieutenants. Treasury officials sounded out Wall Street on the possibility of a joint government and private investment, but bankers warned against it. The market was dead. It had to be a government infusion.[6]

Rodriguez was so buoyed by the rumors of a capital plan that he resumed buying stocks. He subsequently wrote: "The Federal Reserve and the U.S. Treasury were finally beginning to understand that the core issue of this crisis is CAPITAL deficiency and not LIQUIDITY."[7]

The charge that the government mishandled the crisis should be seen in context. The tools available to the Fed—adjusting rates, providing loans—all deal with liquidity. Absent an act of Congress, Treasury had no tools. Bernanke, in retrospect, said he always understood the need for capital but lacked the means to provide it, and certainly, he pushed for what would become the TARP earlier than Paulson. However, Bernanke was also late to recognize that the banking system was weak. In one crucial respect, his Depression training may have misled him. The bank failures of the 1930s were *liquidity* events—bank runs. Thus, in 1930, when the panics started in earnest, banks were not as a group undercapitalized (though many later became so).[8] They were simply unable to satisfy their depositors' immediate demands for cash. This year was different; while runs were a feature of the crisis, the banks were stuffed with exotic assets whose value had plummeted or that the market was unwilling to put any value on. Their weakness was *inherent*. Once he recognized that, Bernanke emphatically concluded that the United States could not let sick banks linger in a vulnerable state. By early October, he was telling an audience in Washington, "We have learned from historical experience with severe financial crises that if government intervention comes only at a point at which many or most financial institutions are insolvent or nearly so, the costs of restoring the system are greatly increased."

Thursday, October 9, the one-year anniversary of the stock market's all-time high, the market crashed again. The Dow plunged 679 points. Traders were numb—stocks had entered a distorted Wonderland governed by unrecognizable forces. Ordinary investors were panicking—some were said to scream at mutual fund operators, "Just get me out!" Since the year-ago peak, the market was down 42 percent. It had fallen 26 percent in a *month* and 22 percent in the seven trading days of October. Retirement savings built up over lifetimes were being vaporized in days.

Investors in financial stocks, like manics coming off a high, were selling indiscriminately. Michael Cerenzie, a film producer, dumped a large bank-stock portfolio, matter-of-factly explaining to the the *New York Times*: "This [the market] isn't going to come back."[9] Investors at market troughs, no less than those at market tops, perceive the trend to be unending, as if the cyclical forces that govern valuations have simply been repealed.

Savvy pros were as stricken as ordinary investors. Ralph Schlosstein, a cofounder of BlackRock, felt as though the world were ending. A normally canny hedge fund manager was too overwhelmed by gyrating stock prices to invest in any of them. Pundits breezily spoke of Armageddon, stoking the panic. Jim Rogers, an expatriate investor in Singapore, confided to Bloomberg News, "People are selling everything no matter what the fundamentals. It's a forced liquidation." A poll of economists forecast the longest recession in more than half a century. Wall Street feared that whatever the Treasury did to resuscitate banks would dilute the value of private bank shares. As a result, bank stocks were wantonly slaughtered.

The market mayhem ratcheted up Morgan Stanley's anxiety with respect to its slowly progressing deal with Mitsubishi. With approval from regulators finally in hand, the firms had to suffer through a five-day waiting period to close. As it happened, the waiting period coincided with the expiration of the ban on short-selling. The hedge funds, still furious at John Mack, took aim again. That Thursday, October 9, Morgan Stanley plunged 26 percent, to 12½, down more than half since the deal had been announced.

Mitsubishi reiterated its intent to go ahead with the investment; in any case, it was contractually bound. But falling stock prices create their own rules. Having seen the shares of Fannie, Freddie, and AIG drop to a dollar or two, Mitsubishi was petrified that a Treasury bailout of banks would dilute its investment. Bankers were learning a disquieting truth. The market interprets private capital as a vote of confidence; it interprets public capital as almost the reverse: a sign that private capital is unwilling. The TARP rumors were like a gravitational force pulling bank share prices ceaselessly lower.

On Friday, Morgan Stanley was pummeled again. Its stock fell to $9.68—a twelve-year low and a drop of 60 percent for the week. At that price, the company was worth only a little more than what Mitsubishi was planning to invest. The contract was beginning to seem untenable. Though Morgan Stanley's liquidity had improved, rumors swirled that it was running out of cash, that Mitsubishi was pulling out.[10] Premiums on its bonds soared to $1.3 million—a level forecasting imminent bankruptcy. Moody's put its bonds on the watch list for a downgrade.

Paulson, who was terrified—again—that Morgan Stanley would unravel, met with Japan's minister of finance, as well as Japan's central bank governor, who were in Washington for the global financial meetings, and pleaded with them to keep Mitsubishi in the deal. Paulson promised not to use the TARP in a manner that would dilute Morgan Stanley's stock—an extraordinary offer to a foreign state. Paulson had *not* met Britain halfway when Barclays was attempting to acquire Lehman. But the proud belief that the free market could deal with any exigency lay in tatters. There was no talk of moral hazard now. Paulson followed up with a formal letter from the Treasury to the ministry, pledging America's intent to respect the interests of equity investors, including foreign banks.[11]

Foreign ministers and central bankers had now descended on Washington, with their retinues of aides wielding stacks of reports dense with doleful analyses and gloomy numbers. As the ministers' limos eased toward the Treasury Department, the financial crisis, as if on cue, reverberated around the globe. In Japan, an insurance firm failed and the stock market crashed 10 percent. Markets in Brazil and Russia virtually stopped trading. Iceland, now beset by IMF fact finders, lurched toward national bankruptcy.

Given the stress in Japan, its government was wary that Mitsubishi might import America's troubles. The Fed's Kevin Warsh, duplicating Paulson's efforts, tried to assuage the minister's fears. America had become a supplicant, pleading with Japan for capital. Tokyo responded via an unexpected channel: Rodgin Cohen, the securities lawyer, who was representing Mitsubishi. Cohen called Warsh and with little preamble, blurted out, "Kuroyanagi and I want to come down." Nobuo Kuroyanagi was CEO of Mitsubishi, the world's second-largest bank. He was in New York preparing for rounds of toasts with Morgan Stanley, but remained edgy regarding the Treasury's plans. Kuroyanagi traveled with an interpreter to Washington. They met with Fed officials in the library of the central bank, where they heard firsthand the government's pledge not to do investors harm.

Rob Kindler, a Morgan Stanley banker, had been nervously monitoring Mitsubishi, whose bankers were conducting due diligence at the American bank's headquarters. When markets closed on Friday, he breathed a sigh of relief. Apparently, Mitsubishi was still on board. On Saturday, Kindler flew to his summer house on Cape Cod. He played a round of golf. Then he heard from the office. Mitsubishi was demanding changes. Kindler flew home and spent the rest of the weekend revising the deal. With a $9 stock, Morgan Stanley needed Mitsubishi's capital before the market reopened. However, there was a problem. Monday was Columbus Day; although the market was open, banks were closed and Mitsubishi could not wire the money. Kindler suggested that it deliver a paper check—written on a napkin if need be—for the $9 billion.

WHILE PAULSON WAS distracted by Morgan Stanley and by the G7 meeting Friday, America's bond markets were deader than ever. Investors gave up trying to forecast which companies might stay solvent and stopped lending altogether. Interest rates on high-yield debt (what junk-rated corporations had to pay for loans) soared to 22 percent, a rate suggestive of a Mafia enforcer. Even investment-grade bonds soared to a high of 9½ percent. The fear of lending was contagious. A savvy bond investor in Tennessee espied what he thought were incredible bargains. GE Capital's one-year paper was yielding 10 percent. Morgan Stanley two-year paper was yielding 25 percent. If the firm merely remained solvent for twenty-four months, an investment would increase by more than half. The Tennessean looked hungrily at these and other deeply depressed bonds. Citigroup was yielding

40 percent, GM and Ford between 50 and 70 percent. But catching the contagion, he lost his nerve. What if GE shut down in six weeks? Or two? Rather than buy more bonds, he started selling them.[12]

The rate most watched by Paulson was surely Libor (the price of loans to banks), which surged to new highs. The TED spread, the gap between bank borrowing costs and the government's, hit 4.6 percent, a record. A month before, it had been 1 percent. In other words, the premium for lending to a private bank instead of to the government, if one were so foolish as to try, had more than quadrupled. As the surging TED implied, investors were throwing money at the government. The yield on thirty-day T-bills had plunged to a microscopic five one-hundredths of a point. But capital was abandoning private industry—which is, after all, the basis of the capitalist system. The decimation of bank credit added to the pressure on Paulson to reorient the TARP. Also, the convergence of international financiers created a groundswell for a unified policy. A sense of shared alarm hung over the ministerial meetings. Formal scripts, typically a feature of such dry conclaves, were dropped, as the ministers, like delegates arguing over a new constitution, tried to rough out the framework of a new financial order.

Many of the Europeans, including Jean-Claude Trichet, head of Europe's Central Bank, had to hustle home ahead of schedule to address the Continent's banking crisis. On Sunday, the fifteen euro-zone nations regrouped in Paris; all agreed to guarantee bank debts. Germany and France also prepared capital injections, joining Britain. The delegates didn't formally articulate a policy, but the policy was clear nonetheless. Europe was saving its banks. Paulson could wait no longer.

On Sunday, under a shroud of secrecy, Paulson, Bernanke, Geithner, and Sheila Bair hashed out the details of a recovery package that embraced both the main features of the European plans. The three senior regulators pressed Bair to guarantee bank debts; only the FDIC had such authority. As usual, Bair balked at exposing the FDIC to risk. Her counterparts, especially Geithner, were adamant that only with a guarantee would people resume lending to banks. Geithner thought the banks should get it for *free*—an enormous gift to an industry that a year earlier had virtually been coining profits at will.[13]

The strongest argument for the guarantee was that Europe's banks already had one, potentially putting America's banks at a competitive disadvantage. Bair eventually yielded—though to her credit, she insisted that the amount of debt eligible for the guarantee be capped, and that the banks pay a fee for it. The compromise they worked out meant that banks could replace a portion of their debt without fear of default—and therefore, at much-lower interest rates.[*]

In terms of its equity, the guarantee was among the most dubious of any of the Paulson-Bernanke-Geithner remedies. It would create a windfall for banks by reducing their borrowing costs. This was not only a gift from the taxpayers (though the United States would collect the fee), it was blatantly discriminatory against every nonbank that did not receive a guarantee and had to pay higher rates. The U.S. was in effect bestowing on the entire banking industry the privileged and protected status long enjoyed by Fannie Mae and Freddie Mac.

Capital injection was less controversial, and also more equitable: if the banks survived (and prospered), the taxpayers would reap a profit, as would any investor. The *amount* of profit would depend on the terms, and political considerations restrained the government from imposing harsh ones. Warren Buffett could extract a maximum price for his capital; Paulson, by contrast, did not want to extract too much of the banks' value, as this would amount to a transfer of wealth from the banks' already depleted owners to the government.

Treasury officials argued that the United States should receive common stock—probably the best value, given the bank stocks' depressed prices. However, Paulson was wary of taking any security that smacked

---

[*] The program enabled banks, thrifts, and bank holding companies to refinance 125 percent of senior unsecured debt that would expire by June 30, 2009, with new debt that would be federally guaranteed for a period of three years. The guarantee meant that banks could raise money at much lower cost, as lenders would not have to worry about default risk. Only debt issued by June 2009 qualified—a deadline later extended to October. To protect General Electric (which has a huge financial subsidiary) from suffering a competitive disadvantage, Paulson specifically designated GE as eligible.

of state ownership.[14] The British example cautioned as well as encouraged: Britain had offered to purchase (mostly) common stock from seven leading banks, in amounts that transferred control to the government, and only two very troubled banks had accepted.[*] Instinctively, Paulson felt that if the U.S. were to invest in banks, it should invest in healthy institutions as well as troubled ones. He did not want a stigma attached to participants. Finally, he was wary of diluting the existing stock (and had promised the Japanese he would not do so). The whole business of the government investing in banks, he told an aide, "is abhorrent to me and abhorrent to the country."[15] He was a reluctant socialist, and even allowed the banks to continue paying dividends, thus siphoning capital to stockholders that would better have been retained for issuing loans. Clearly, Paulson's primary goal was to revive the private banking industry, including the confidence of their stockholders. Earning a profit for the taxpayers was secondary.

On the afternoon of Sunday, October 13, Paulson personally called the CEOs of the leading banks and told them to be at the Treasury at 3 P.M. the next day. He didn't divulge his purpose, and the bankers didn't know it. Some were already in Washington, for the IMF meeting. John Mack had to fly home to receive the $9 billion check from Mitsubishi and then return to Washington. The CEOs—more humbled than the group that had gathered at the Fed precisely a month earlier—met in the conference room adjacent to the secretary's office, at a dark mahogany table set only with coffee, water, and Cokes. Paulson, flanked by Bernanke and Bair, was on one side: facing them were the CEOs of Bank of America (Ken Lewis), Bank of New York Mellon (Robert Kelly), Citigroup (Vikram Pandit), Goldman Sachs (Lloyd Blankfein), JPMorgan (Jamie Dimon), Merrill Lynch (John Thain), Morgan Stanley (John Mack), State Street (Ronald Logue), and Wells Fargo (Richard Kovacevich).[†] Paulson abruptly told them about the debt guarantee and, then, stunned them with news of the capital

---

[*] Britain invested £37 billion, good for a 58 percent stake of Royal Bank of Scotland and 44 percent of HBOS/Lloyds.

[†]The Bank of America/Merrill merger was still pending, thus the companies were invited separately.

program. The United States was seeking—more nearly, insisting—on purchasing a preferred stock that the banks were to issue according to the Treasury's conditions. The government would get a 5 percent dividend, plus warrants to purchase common stock, though it was Paulson's hope that, as the banks returned to health, they would buy back both the preferred and the warrants. Paulson stipulated $25 billion in the four biggest banks and lesser amounts in the rest, giving the government the rough equivalent of a 20 percent stake in each. There were restrictions attached on executive bonuses.[16]

Mack immediately said he would take the money. Kovacevich protested that Wells Fargo, which had sidestepped the subprime mischief, didn't need the capital and didn't want it. Most of the CEOs were too surprised to say anything.

Paulson said the group should think it over, call their boards if they wanted, and return later that afternoon with a decision. If they didn't accept the capital, Paulson added, the regulators would declare them undercapitalized and simply force them to take it. Still, he wanted the CEOs to sign voluntarily.

Ken Lewis urged his peers not to waste time arguing; it was obvious they were going to say yes. Kovacevich continued to grouse. He called Steel, disclosed the news, and told him he was deliberating. Steel said, "Dick, save yourself some time, you're going to sign it." Jamie Dimon presented the ultimatum to his board as one that would whittle away Morgan's advantage over less well capitalized banks, and could come with unwanted political strings. Still, Dimon recognized that for the stability of the system, they had to accept.[17]

By six thirty, all nine had done so, clearing the way for the U.S. Treasury to invest $125 billion in the country's biggest banks—a precursor, it was implied, to pumping money into smaller banks across the country. In other words, the United States was rescuing both Wall Street and the banking system.[*] It was the greatest intervention in the

---

[*] Once again, there was a Depression-era precedent. From 1932 to 1936, the Reconstruction Finance Corporation, created under Herbert Hoover, invested $1 billion in six thousand banks and loaned those and other banks an additional $2 billion.

financial system in seventy years, and perhaps ever, enacted under a conservative president, a Treasury secretary who hailed from Goldman Sachs, and a Fed chief reared on the virtues of financial models and the supposed perfectibility of the market.

The market, or the capitalists who plied it, were indeed smart, but they were not perfect. They had thought of clever ways to reengineer securities; they had stripped balance sheets of their assets and mortgage banks of their mortgages. They had invented derivatives that let banks flip risks like baseball cards; they had lent long and borrowed short. They had overleveraged and, while their profits rolled, they had paid themselves astronomical and often shameful sums. They had invented mortgage products designed to circumvent the banking wisdom of the ages, and they had peddled these mortgages with a willful disregard, bordering on fraud, for whether their customers could repay them. They had bullied the Congress and their regulators into ignoring all this, or into accepting their methods and their models. Clever as they were, the capitalists had forgotten one thing. Capitalism requires capital. No amount of leverage, not even record quantities of liquidity from the Federal Reserve, can obviate this need.

Rodriguez e-mailed colleagues the following day that the liquidity crisis was only a "symptom" of the disease of capital destruction. After years of deteriorating capital standards, followed by crushing losses, the TARP would begin to treat the disease. "It appears that the Fed and Secretary Paulson finally get it," Rodriguez wrote, and he sounded almost grateful. However, the aftermath of such a debacle would be painful—for Wall Street and its customers, for the greater economy and for the ordinary citizen. Rodriguez predicted that more government investment would be needed, and that the United States would have to issue record quantities of federal debt—he estimated $2 trillion over the next year—to pay for it. Notwithstanding the day's welcome news, he concluded on a somber note: "The harder part of the crisis still lies ahead."[18]

19

GREAT RECESSION

We must acknowledge that many in the financial community, including those at the Federal Reserve, failed to either detect or act upon the telltale signs of financial system excess.

RICHARD FISHER, PRESIDENT, FEDERAL RESERVE BANK OF DALLAS, FEBRUARY 2009

THE INJECTION OF TARP capital proved to be the nadir of the financial crisis. In the significant sense of halting the plunge in credit markets, the program had an immediate and salutary effect: for banks and many corporations, borrowing costs would never again return to the skyscraper levels of mid-October.[1] For the economy at large, however, the Treasury's intervention arrived too late. By the end of October 2008, the slowdown had mushroomed into what by many measures was the worst recession in seven decades.

Within days of Paulson's forced investment in banks, household-name businesses were firing hordes of workers. Citigroup let go 34,000; Bank of America, Goldman, Merrill, and Morgan Stanley thousands more. Nor was the slump confined to financial firms. The litany of Main Street corporations pruning payrolls soon included Merck, Chrysler, Pratt & Whitney, Yahoo, Xerox, Whirlpool, Alcoa, and Coca-Cola.

The recession was not only wide, it was deep. The mild downturn of 1990, like that of 2001, had seemed to verify Ben Bernanke's contention that economic cycles were moderating, but the present slump recalled the painful recessions of the smokestack America of the 1950s. Auto sales plunged 40 percent, a throwback to an era predating the abundance of credit, when only by scrimping and saving could Americans upgrade their automobiles. Home building plummeted to its lowest level in fifty years. Newer and greener industries, hallmarks of the modern, service economy, were devastated. Nortel, the telecom powerhouse, filed for Chapter 11. Pfizer sent 19,500 chemists and others packing. International trade collapsed; law firms, universities, and state agencies shrank their payrolls. In the dark winter of 2008–09, jobs were everywhere a scarce commodity. In Cambridge, Massachusetts, Harvard law grads had to struggle to find work. In Miami, when the city posted openings for thirty-five firefighters, it drew one thousand able-bodied applicants.

The Great Recession, as journalists dubbed it, rolled back the clock to an earlier, more vulnerable time. Pink slips from formerly recession-proof employers inflicted a psychological blow. Americans hooked on spending on credit reverted to the musty habit of their grandparents—saving. As they cut back on shopping, retail suffered a shock. Circuit City, the purveyor of electronics, filed for Chapter 11; so did General Growth Properties, the mall operator. As spending slumped, advertising crashed, and newspapers across the country shriveled, their reporters—media-savvy, educated, and urbane—laid off in droves. The prosperous upper middle of the country was unhinged from its breezy confidence, its expensive indulgences, and high-end tastes. Whole Foods, the organic retailer, hit the skids, its stock collapsing 80 percent. Starbucks saw its profits crash to less than a penny per drink and shuttered nine hundred stores.

Wall Street itself went into a terrible funk. Investment banks, already battered by the crash, fell idle. IPOs, derivatives, and private equity all stopped dead. Corporate America ceased doing deals. The stock market fell and kept falling (in this sense, October was far from the bottom). As confidence in business evaporated, investors shoveled their money at—and only at—the government until, in December, so much liquidity was offered to the Treasury that the yield on its T-bills touched zero. For a brief moment, American capitalism ventured into an illogical and absurd mathematical space; the yield on bills turned *negative*.

As the market crashed, the wealthy suffered with everyone else. The Yellowstone Club, a Montana ski resort offering lavish homes for the ultrarich (Bill Gates was a member) filed for bankruptcy. In New York, Christie's failed to auction works by Manet, Renoir, Cézanne, and de Kooning.[2] The embarrassed auctioneer explained that the desired prices, determined during the summer, "were from an earlier time," as if from another century.

Not having lived through such a slump before, people did not know if, or how long, it would endure. Confidence in private markets evaporated; government was again a protector. An era of widespread regulation was foreseen, a tide of legislative reform. Jeff Madrick, an economist, published a tome with the suddenly plausible title, *The Case for Big Government*. Its thesis proved truer than its author dreamed.

Once they decided to bail out Wall Street, Paulson and Bernanke agreed there was no going back. And their interventions proved much broader than initially conceived. Paulson aggressively utilized the TARP; 650 banks received injections of public capital. The Fed became the dominant provider of mortgages, car loans, short-term commercial credit, and loans to banks. The central bank became the financier to the government itself, purchasing Treasury securities by the billions. Like a patient on ever-increasing doses of morphine, the country subsisted on public funds.

The Fed could offset the scarcity of lenders, but it could do little about the lack of *borrowers*, a more serious malady. Credit can always be manufactured—not so the willingness to borrow, which rests on faith in the future. In its absence, economies stagnate. Japan's had idled for a decade in the 1990s, and the fear of a similar lull fairly traumatized Bernanke. Neither people nor businesses wanted to borrow; they were overleveraged from the bubble years and they were uncertain that the future was worth borrowing for. The total of mortgage loans outstanding had risen in every quarter since the Federal Reserve began tracking such data, in 1946; now it fell for six straight quarters.[3]

In December, three months after Lehman failed, Bernanke dared to emulate his mythical experiment of dropping cash from a helicopter in the sky. In a desperate effort to stimulate, the Fed lowered its target rate for overnight bank loans from a paltry 1 percent to a range of ¼ percent to *zero*—a record low and, indeed, abutting the theoretical extreme. The cut, however, was largely symbolic. Owing to a paucity of demand, the actual rate at which banks were borrowing had already fallen to a tenth of a percent. No one wanted the money.

The grim recession handed the Democrats a golden opportunity to retake the White House—and also, so the faithful hoped, roll back the credo of laissez-faire. On the campaign trail, Obama stirred hopes of a second FDR, or at least a second New Deal. He artfully blamed the financial crisis on eight years of extreme Republicanism. The truth was muddier. Given how boldly the administration had intervened to save the banks, Bush was no Herbert Hoover.* Nor were the Democrats free of blame for the crisis's origins. While Bush-style conservatives had loudly championed deregulation, Democrats such as Robert Rubin had deregulated in practice. The Democrats had done the most to insulate the mortgage twins, Fannie and Freddie, from demands that they reform and trim their balance sheets. On the other hand, blame for the

---

* In truth, not even Hoover was a Hoover. Through programs such as the aforementioned Reconstruction Finance Corporation, which propped up thousands of banks, he was far more active in fighting the Depression than history recalls. His reputation for heartlessness stems mostly from his deep-freeze personality. Dour and remote, he failed to inspire and seemed not to empathize with the millions of his countrymen out of work. It was said by a contemporary that a rose would wilt at Hoover's touch—words never uttered about the outgoing and congenial Bush. But the two shared an ideological preference for aiding institutions (banks) rather than people. Thus, Hoover scorned welfare and Bush sidetracked foreclosure relief. However, the thirty-first president would have been horrified at Bush's blithe spending and reckless deficits. The son of a Quaker blacksmith, orphaned at ten, Hoover was a self-made striver famous for his efficiency campaigns and his rigid morals—the polar opposite of the happy-go-lucky White House heir.

ineffective or tardy response to the crisis rested with the Bush administration and with the GOP naysayers in the House. Obama hung his
candidacy on the slogan of "Change," and by November 4, change was
what the electorate wanted.

After the election, Obama's financial policy was more moderate than
many expected; indeed, it was largely a continuation of the Paulson-
Bernanke-Geithner regime. The president-elect ensured a smooth transition by elevating Geithner from the New York Fed to Treasury secretary.
This was a clear signal that any "change" would be incremental. Paulson,
comforted that his two principal partners would remain on the job,
continued to intervene in the economy up to his last days in office.

The government's response to the financial crisis consisted of three
main policies. The first was bailing out tottering banks and other companies. The second consisted of numerous Fed facilities to maintain a
minimum level of liquidity in the banking system and in the economy.
These two policies began, of course, well before the transition of
power, and they continued seamlessly under Obama. The third was a
massive government stimulus, which the Democratic Congress enacted during Obama's first thirty days.*

Taking these in order, the bailout reflex was especially hard to un-
learn. A seminal moment occurred in November, weeks after the election, when Citigroup began to tremble. A stream of deposits left the
bank as customers began to jump ship and, as in the previous death
spirals, the stock cratered. In the third week of November, Citi's shares
lost 60 percent, finishing on Friday, November 21, at under 4, its lowest
level in sixteen years. Pandit, the CEO, lashed out in an employee conference call at "fearmongering." To avoid demoralizing the troops, the
company stopped displaying its stock price at headquarters. Meanwhile,
Robert Rubin, chairman of the executive committee, called Paulson,
his former Goldman colleague, and pleaded for government help. Five

---

* Obama's policy also had a fourth element—financial reform. This is discussed in the concluding
chapter.

U.S. agencies were involved in the talks. Citi insisted that *it* wasn't the problem so much as the banking system—although Citi itself had written off $49 billion in charges over the previous four quarters, and its balance sheet was freighted with $2 trillion of assets that the market couldn't value or that (to judge from its plummeting stock) it refused to value.

The independent-minded Sheila Bair, head of the FDIC, dared to suggest that Citigroup be allowed to fail. Let the government protect the bank and its depositors, she argued, and allow the umbrella corporation, which had misused its capital by plowing it into CDOs, to suffer the market's justice. Paulson could not believe his ears. "I'm having an out-of-body experience here, Sheila," the secretary replied. "I can't believe we're having this discussion. You're talking about *Citigroup* going through receivership." Deliberations, in the usual pattern, continued through the weekend; Citi did not get a term sheet until nearly 10 P.M. on Sunday. The United States granted it roughly $250 billion in loss protection and invested $20 billion (in addition to the TARP money invested in October). In February, the Obama administration provided Citi with yet a third rescue.[4] The government was compensated for its largesse with a one-third ownership in Citi, but the November bailout—struck after the financial panic had passed its worst—protected the bank's managers and directors from the full effects of years of horrendous decisions. What the government failed to do was to send a message that here was a bank too poorly managed *not* to fail.

A similar dynamic ensued when Paulson and Bernanke forced a deeply reluctant Ken Lewis to complete the acquisition of Merrill Lynch. (This was the same Bank of America chief who had ardently coveted Merrill as recently as September. In the waning days of 2008, as Merrill posted new and staggering losses, he tried to wriggle out.) As *his* stock tumbled, Lewis demanded government protection against potential losses. This time, it was Kevin Warsh of the Fed who questioned whether a bank shouldn't be left to take its lumps. Once again, the government ran to the rescue.

Nor did the bailouts end there. The government upped its investment in AIG—chipping in additional capital in November of '08 and still more in March of 2009—a point by which, the panic well past, AIG's Wall Street creditors might have been expected to share the pain. The United States provided tens of billions in capital and loans for Fannie and Freddie. It also widened the safety net to insure the credit subsidiary of John Deere, as well as GE Capital. It converted American Express and also GMAC, the auto finance company, to banks, and supplied both with capital from TARP.

And there was more. In the fall, auto executives had driven, in hybrid cars carefully selected for their political appeal,* to the nation's capital to plead for aid. On the advice of Secretary Paulson, General Motors and Chrysler were rescued by President Bush, one of his last presidential acts.[5] Detroit did not present the same systemic risk as banking; the bailout was an old-fashioned subsidy (of the unions as well as the carmakers) disguised as financial necessity. The shrunken manufacturers closed two thousand dealerships, and Rick Wagoner, GM's chief executive, resigned at the government's behest. It was not enough. Months later, GM and Chrysler were forced to file for bankruptcy. GM's filing was the fourth largest in American history (behind Lehman, Washington Mutual, and WorldCom).

The bailout policy—perhaps a necessary evil when the financial system was in extremis—was thus continued well beyond the banking emergency. It is hard to escape the conclusion that, having been widely criticized for allowing Lehman to fail,† regulators were afraid to let *any* large institution go under, even as the most acute phase of the crisis receded. Far from restoring confidence, the bailouts reaffirmed in the public's mind a dispiriting truth: private markets were helpless. Confidence would only return when private investors manifested cour-

---

* Earlier, the executives had been widely criticized for flying to Washington on corporate jets.
† A Treasury official remarked, "People felt burned by Lehman; we didn't want another."

age. For that to occur, assets had to sink to a price at which private buyers would venture back.

While the bailouts were aimed at specific institutions, the Fed's actions to provide liquidity were aimed at salvaging the overall economy. Bernanke's Fed was easily the most energetic in history. The Fed singlehandedly propped up the real estate market, pumping an average of $20 billion into mortgage securities every *week*. It lent to small businesses, car buyers, consumers. It partially offset the collapse in corporate liquidity by purchasing $350 billion of commercial paper. It stocked up on Treasury bonds in a deliberate attempt to hold down interest rates, lest the government's borrowing drive rates higher. The Fed's own assets ballooned two and a half times, as it scooped up mortgages and government bonds and financed investments in asset-backed securities such as student loans, credit card debts, mortgages—all of the unwanted detritus of the bubble years.[6]

Still the economy kept shrinking. From October of '08 to the following March, GDP fell at an astounding annualized rate of 6 percent, the worst six-month stretch in fifty years. Fed governors, as well as private economists, were stunned by the sharpness of the downturn. Credit had been in ample supply for so long, it was forgotten that business couldn't function without it. A third of the country's manufacturing capacity was idled. General Electric, a mainstay of American industry, slashed its dividend for the first time since 1938. Companies that had operated profitably for decades saw their markets suddenly implode. Fastenal, a Winona, Michigan–based screw manufacturer with a stable business and a loyal customer base—the sort of bedrock company that had powered the economy through thick and thin—was an apt example. Fastenal had steadily increased sales for forty-two years. It did not take foolish risks or waste money on extravagances (executives traveling cross-country drove corporate cars and shared rooms in inexpensive hotels). Even in the spring of 2008, as the mortgage market was imploding, Fastenal was still reporting double-digit sales gains. Then, its business began to tail off. In the fall, it experienced a mild downturn. In the spring of 2009, Fastenal's sales plunged 25 percent. The stock fell by half and the workforce was pared by 11 percent. Such a brutal contraction defied every forecast.

The economic freeze sent the stock market into a tailspin that hit its worst in the two days after Obama's election, when the Dow plummeted one thousand points. By the end of 2008, the S&P 500 was down 38 percent, making it the worst year for stocks since 1937. The price of oil, a barometer of economic strength, plunged during the year from $96 a barrel to $46; junk bond portfolios were cut by a third. These were figures worthy of a Depression.

Stocks fell a further 11 percent between New Year's Day and Obama's inauguration, on January 20. From then to the second week of March, they fell 16 percent more. On the low of March 9, the Dow stood at 6,547, its lowest level since April 1997.[7] Ford and Citi traded at $1 and Bank of America at 3, a plunge of 90 percent from when it had agreed to acquire Merrill, a mere six months earlier. Peak to trough, banking stocks dropped 88 percent and the broader market fell 57 percent—the worst slide since the Hoover market of 1929–32, when the market plunged 86 percent. Market pros who had lived through Black Monday and other information-age crashes that were over in days or hours found them themselves in new, more frightening terrain—a relentless slump, inexorable, seemingly endless. What everyone wanted to know, what no one could answer, was: Would the selling stop?

This was the atmosphere in which Obama took office—as frightening an economic landscape as had greeted any new president since FDR in 1933. In January, as Obama moved in to the White House, the economy shed 740,000 jobs, a record high. The following month, the value of the median home fell to $165,000, erasing a full six years' worth of gains.

The administration immediately proposed a stimulus. Congress exerted control over the specifics of the bill, resulting in a balkanized package ranging from funds for new technologies to highway repairs. Broadly, it allocated $787 billion for three purposes: aid to the states, which were in desperate shape because of falling tax receipts; cuts in federal taxes; and a potpourri of investments in industries such as high-speed rail and alternative energy.*

It took time for the money to be spent and, arguably, long-range investment was ill-suited to the short-term agenda of reigniting the economy. In the meantime, the economy kept sinking. Office buildings lost tenants and their rents plunged. Commercial loans were foreclosed on in droves, imperiling lenders. Throughout 2009, banks failed at a rate of nearly three per week.[8] Incredibly, the performance of home mortgages deteriorated even from the abysmal standard of '08. By the spring of '09, 26.5 percent of subprime mortgage-holders were seriously delinquent and four in ten were either behind on their loans or in the process of foreclosure. About one in eight people with a mortgage of *any* kind—not just subprime—were in similar straits, and fully fifteen million families owed more than their homes were worth.[9]

In the spring of 2009, the orgy of federal spending began to show effect. The economy kept shrinking, but at a slower rate. The stock market rebounded off its lows, and in the second quarter, housing prices, after falling for three straight years, eked out a gain. Finally, in the third quarter, the economy began to limp forward. By then, the GDP had contracted 3.8 percent, the greatest drop in national output since the demobilization after World War II. Save for that, the present slump was the worst recession since the 1930s. It was also the longest. The National Bureau of Economic Research determined that the Great Recession had begun in December 2007—nine months before the fall of Lehman. It lasted until approximately the middle of 2009. And then, the longest recession in living memory was over.

---

* The government effort to rescue the economy cost easily more, even in adjusted dollars, than the Louisiana Purchase, the *Apollo* moon shot, or the Korean War. The U.S.'s $170 billion investment in AIG alone cost more than the Marshall Plan to rebuild Europe—such is the penalty for speculative excess. In total, the United States committed more than $12 trillion to various forms of relief, but most of that (such as funds set aside for potential losses) will likely never be spent. Actual expenditures will likely fall in the range of $3.5 trillion to $4 trillion, fifteen times the cost of the S&L bailout of the late 1980s. Much of the money spent, such as for asset purchases or loans, will likely be recouped. The U.S. should earn a profit on the TARP investments in banks. However, the stimulus was a sheer expense, and recoveries from General Motors, in which the country invested $70 billion, as well as the approximately $225 billion handed to Fannie and Freddie, appear problematic.

While a recovery commenced, the losses were far from expunged. Stocks remained a third off their highs and beneath their levels of a decade back.[10] Home prices, having fallen 32 percent, remained severely depressed. Although Obama, unlike Bush, made an effort to stem the tide of foreclosures, his policies were only marginally effective. Lenders were inundated with repossession proceedings; judges who wanted to work out accommodations between borrowers and banks found that the latter did not return their calls. Foreclosures rose throughout the first half of 2009, peaking only in July, when a record 360,000 families were stripped of their deeds. Thereafter foreclosures continued at abnormally high rates.[11] (One foreclosed dwelling was the ranch house on East Jefferson Street in Dillon, South Carolina, that had been the childhood home of Ben Bernanke.) Commercial real estate remained in a severe downturn. Commercial paper outstanding did not hit bottom until late July. In August, the economy was still so weak that the Fed grimly extended its facility for purchasing asset-backed securities. Bank lending and consumer credit were declining well into the autumn of 2009.[12]

Even after the crisis had ended, the federal government remained deeply involved in the ordinary business of American households and firms. As late as a year after the Lehman failure, government spending accounted for 26 percent of the U.S. economy—its biggest share since the Truman administration—and Washington continued to provide the financing for nine out of ten new home loans.[13] As an indicator of its far-flung reach, the government was actively overseeing General Motors, AIG, Citigroup, Fannie Mae, and Freddie Mac—respectively the country's biggest car company, biggest insurer, former biggest bank, and the bulwarks of the mortgage industry.* And the Fed, as of September 30, remained swollen with $2.144 trillion in assets, including roughly $700 billion in the mortgage-backed securities that private investors no longer wanted.

---

* The United States owned 34 percent of Citigroup, 80 percent of AIG and 60 percent of General Motors.

The financial industry had not begun to recoup its losses. According to the IMF, U.S. banks wrote down a total of $610 billion in loans and securities through the second quarter of 2009, a goodly portion of which was suffered by Wall Street banks, the rest by their mortgage-banking comrades. The loss in market value of the biggest banks alone, even after stocks staged an impressive rally, was roughly a trillion dollars.[14] Of course, three major investment banks failed or were acquired and more than one hundred depository institutions were seized.

The cost of the crash to ordinary citizens was astronomical. The total wealth of Americans plunged from $64 trillion to $51 trillion.[15] Another cost—to be borne by future generations—was the huge growth in the federal deficit incurred to pay for the rescue.

The most punishing blow was the devastation in jobs, and for ordinary workers the pain continued long after the worst was over on Wall Street. In October 2009, unemployment hit double digits—10.2 percent. In California, cradle of the subprime loan, 12½ percent of the population was out of work; in Michigan, devastated by the collapse in auto sales, 15 percent. As a measure of how disproportionate was the Wall Street scourge, Wall Street itself, presumably one of the prime agents of the bust, shed 30,000 jobs; the entire United States lost a total of eight million. Never, since the end of World War II, had so many jobs disappeared so fast, and never had the power of finance to inflict damage on the society it serves been so painfully clear. By the recession's end, the economy had lost all the jobs that had been added during the boom years and more. Even with a population that was 20 million larger, the job market was smaller.[16] In sum, the U.S. spent nearly a decade losing ground—a decade that, according to the country's highest sages, was to have ushered in an era of nearly uniformly advancing prosperity. The subprime binge that Bernanke had supposed was a contained problem turned out to be a symptom of a full credit mania. Ultimately, it destroyed the American workplace. Such was the bitter fruit of Wall Street's folly.

THE END OF
WALL STREET

Those of us who have looked to the self-interest of
lending institutions to protect shareholders' equity,
myself included, are in a state of shocked disbelief.

—ALAN GREENSPAN, TESTIMONY BEFORE THE
HOUSE COMMITTEE ON OVERSIGHT AND
GOVERNMENT REFORM, OCTOBER 23, 2008

THE CRASH PUT PAID to the intellectual model that inspired, and to a large degree facilitated, the bubble. It spelled the end of the immodest faith in Wall Street's ability to forecast. No better testimony exists than the extraordinary recanting of Alan Greenspan, the public official most associated with the thesis that markets are ever to be trusted. Ten days after the first round of TARP investments, Greenspan appeared in the House of Representatives to, effectively, repeal the credo by which he had managed the nation's economy for seventeen years:

> In recent decades, a vast risk management and pricing system
> has evolved, combining the best insights of mathematicians
> and finance experts supported by major advances in computer
> and communications technology. A Nobel Prize was awarded for

the discovery of the pricing model that underpins much of the advance in derivative markets. This modern risk management paradigm held sway for decades. The whole intellectual edifice, however, collapsed in the summer of last year because the data inputted into the risk management models generally covered only the past two decades, a period of euphoria. Had instead the models been fitted more appropriately to historic periods of stress, capital requirements would have been much higher and the financial world would be in far better shape today, in my judgment.[1]

This remarkable proclamation, close to a confession, was the intellectual counterpart to the red ink flowing on Wall Street. Just as Fannie, Freddie, and Merrill Lynch had undone the labors of a generation—had lost, that is, all the profits and more that they had earned during the previous decade—Greenspan undermined its ideological footing.[2] And even if he partly retracted his apologia (in the palliative that it wasn't the models per se that failed, but the humans that applied them), he was understood to say that the new finance had failed. The boom had not just ended; it had been unmasked.

Why did it end so badly? Greenspan's faith in the new finance was itself a culprit. The late economist Hyman Minsky observed that "success breeds a disregard of the possibility of failure.[3] The Fed both embraced and promoted such a disregard. Greenspan's persistent efforts to rescue the system lulled the country into believing that serious failure was behind it. His successor, Bernanke, was too quick to believe that Greenspan had succeeded—that central bankers had truly muted the economic cycle. Each put inordinate faith in the market, and disregarded its oft-shown potential for speculative excess. Excessive optimism naturally led to excessive risk.

The Fed greatly abetted speculation in mortgages by keeping interest rates too low. Also, the various banking regulators (including the Fed) failed to prohibit inordinately risky mortgages. The latter was by far the more damaging offense. The willingness of government to abide teaser mortgages, "liar loans," and home mortgages with zero down payments, amounted to a staggering case of regulatory neglect.

The government's backstopping of Fannie and Freddie, along with the federal agenda of promoting home ownership, was yet another cause of the bust. Yet for all of Washington's miscues, the direct agents of the bubble were private ones. It was the market that financed unsound mortgages and CDOs; the Fed permitted, but the market acted. The banks that failed were private; the investors who financed them were doing the glorious work of Adam Smith.

Rampant speculation (and abuse) in mortgages was surely the primary cause of the bubble, which was greatly inflated by leverage in the banking system, in particular on Wall Street. High leverage and risk-taking in general was fueled by the Street's indulgent compensation practices.

The system of securitizing mortgages lay at the heart of Wall Street's unholy alliance with Main Street, and several links in the chain made the process especially risky. Mortgage issuers, the parties most able to scrutinize borrowers, had no continuing stake in the outcome; the ultimate investors, dispersed around the globe, were too remote to be of any use in evaluating loans; these investors (as well as various government agencies) relied on the credit agencies to serve as a watchdog, and the agencies, being cozy with Wall Street, were abysmally lax. Wall Street's penchant for complexity was itself a risk. Abstruse securities were more difficult to value, and multitiered pyramids of debts were far more susceptible to ruinous collapse.

Such individual malfunctions were indicative of a larger failure: the market system itself came undone. What truly failed was the postindustrial model of capitalism. The market's tools for measuring risk simply did not work. And the most sophisticated minds on Wall Street proved no wiser than country loan officers. All in, the big Wall Street banks were stuck with an estimated 30 percent of subprime losses.[4]

The banks' stock prices offered unsettling evidence of how thoroughly the market failed to appraise the possibility of loss. By 2007, the banks had all disclosed massive holdings of mortgage securities, and mortgage defaults were soaring. And yet, as late as that October, Citigroup was trading near its all-time high. That investors could be so blind refuted the strange ideology that markets were somehow perfect ("strange" because the boast of perfection is never alleged with respect to other human institutions). By analogy to the political arena, American society respects the will of the voters, as well as the institution of democracy, but it limits the power of legislatures nonetheless. Market referendums are no less needful of checks and balances.

Counter to the view of its apostles, the market system of the late twentieth and early twenty-first century did not evolve in a state of nature. It evolved with its own peculiar prejudices and rites. The institution of government was nearly absent. In its place had arisen a system of market-driven models, steeped in the mathematics of the new finance. The rating agency models were typical, and they were blessed by the SEC. The new finance was flawed because its conception of risk was flawed. The banks modeled future default rates (and everything else) as though history could provide the odds with scientific certainty—as precisely as the odds in dice or cards. But markets, as was observed, are different from games of chance. The cards in history's deck keep changing. Prior to 2007 and '08, the odds of a nationwide mortgage collapse would have been seen as very low, because during the previous seventy years it had never happened.

What the bust proved, or reaffirmed, was that Wall Street is (at unpredictable moments) irregular; it is subject to *uncertainty*. Greenspan faulted the modelers for inputting the wrong slice of history. But the future being uncertain, there *is* no perfect slice, or none so reliable as to warrant the suave assurance of banks that leveraged 30 to 1.

In particular, the notion that derivatives (in the hands of AIG and such) eradicated risk, or attained a kind of ideal in apportioning risk to appropriate parties, was sorrowfully exposed. It should be recalled that when mortgage securities were introduced, they were applauded because they enabled lenders to issue loans without retaining risk. And this they did. They also created new vulnerabilities. The ability of Countrywide and WaMu to parcel loans to Wall Street incentivized them to issue more and riskier loans than had no securitization channel existed. The perception of decreased risk to the *individual* firm thus increased risk for society at large.

Paulson gave voice (on the day that Lehman failed) to the need for reform, and President Obama, as well as Congress, avidly pursued it. In general, there was greater agreement that reform was necessary than over what it should entail. Legislative attention focused on four areas:

1. Protecting consumers of financial products such as mortgages and credit cards
2. Regulating complex instruments such as derivatives
3. Obviating the need for future government bailouts, either by (a) keeping banks from becoming too big to fail or (b) ensuring that big banks did not assume too much risk
4. Limiting Wall Street bonuses

The public embraced only the last of these. Early in 2009, after revelations of continued outsized bonus payments at AIG and Merrill Lynch, an uproar ensued. Astonishingly, Merrill had paid million-dollar bonuses to approximately seven hundred employees in 2008, a year in which the firm lost $27 billion and in which both it and its acquirer were rescued with federal TARP monies. And Merrill was far from alone. Goldman's bonus machine barely paused for breath.[5]

Popular outrage was manifest; briefly, a vigilante spirit obtained. A bus tour organized by the Connecticut Working Families Party carried tourists through local suburbs to see the homes of bonus-recipients, as if in hopes of dragging them to the guillotine. A few of those judged complicit were actually sacked. John Thain, the Merrill chief, was denied in his quest for a $30 million bonus; his mere asking sealed his end. Ken Lewis, the Bank of America CEO with whom Thain had previously struck a match, fired him. When it emerged later that the bonuses paid by Merrill had been approved by Bank of America, Lewis resigned as well.

The problem of executive pay did not admit to an easy fix. On Wall Street, the habit of extravagance is deeply ingrained (indeed, excessive indulgence is not even recognized as such). Well into the crisis period, when banks such as Citigroup were operating on federal investment and when Citi's stock was in single digits, Vikram Pandit, the CEO, was observed with a lunch guest at Le Bernardin, the top-rated restaurant in New York. Pandit looked discerningly at the wine list, saw nothing by the glass that appealed and ordered a $350 bottle so that, as he explained, he could savor "a glass of wine worth drinking." Pandit drank just one glass; his friend had none. The rest was presumably poured down a gilded drain.

Bankers vigorously sought to defend their pay, and their perks. Setting wages is a function of labor markets; the best reform would have aimed at making the market work better. (For instance, forcing companies to seek shareholder approval of their executive pay arrangements would have restored proper control over wages and countered the executives' sense of entitlement.[6]) The government chose instead to supervise compensation, in various but limited ways. Congress banned cash bonuses for TARP recipients, and a "pay czar," appointed by Geithner, restricted executive salaries at government-controlled firms such as GM and Citi.

More intriguingly, the Federal Reserve set to proscribing bank practices that fostered too much risk, such as paying up-front bonuses for deals that could incur losses later. The government's hope was that federal suasion would move the banks to reform themselves. To some extent, this occurred. Several banks modified their pay systems along the lines of the Fed's scheme.[7] Such policies, along with federal scrutiny, exerted at best a modest check on total pay.

The Obama administration proposed a sweeping legislative package to deal with other aspects of reform, including derivatives, mortgage-backed securities, and systemic risk. The complexity of these issues, as well as the eagerness of Congress to weigh in, frustrated the desire for a neat solution. In the 1930s, the New Deal cured many of the ills of Wall Street by requiring corporations to disclose their finances, and creating a new agency (the SEC) to supervise them. No single bullet presented itself this time. Banks lobbied extensively and, partly as a result, reforms in the bill were incremental, not draconian.[8]

Obama proposed to move trading of some derivatives (not all) to an exchange where, presumably, they would be subject to more controls. However the White House measure did not set minimums on collateral, which was the root problem in 2008. Another proposal would make mortgage issuers at least modestly sensitive to loan quality by requiring that they retain a small portion of their loans. Another section, on credit agencies, left them as conflicted and as powerful as ever.

Passage was delayed by vigorous division in Congress, particularly over the question of which agency, post-crash, would head supervision of banks. The issue of "too big to fail," which Ben Bernanke had called "a top priority" for reform, hung over Washington like a dark cloud.[9] The crisis had bequeathed precisely the moral hazard that Paulson had feared. Post-crash, markets presumed that the government would, if necessary, bail out important banks. This meant that big banks could borrow on favorable terms (since the government would not let them fail). Being among the circle of protected was considered such a boon that both the administration and Representative Barney Frank, who managed the bill in the House, initially proposed keeping the list of "too big to fail" institutions secret. Experts consulted by the Congress sensibly advised an opposite tack—that the government discourage banks from becoming (or being) too big by making it *undesirable*.[10] They proposed that stricter capital requirements and hefty insurance premiums be imposed as a price for bigness. Greenspan reckoned that regardless of official policy, the market would conclude that every big bank enjoyed a federal safety net. Therefore, the surest way to prevent moral hazard was to break up Big Banking à la Big Oil.[11] But pending final passage of the legislation, Wall Street institutions emerged from the crisis more protected than ever.

Whether this was entirely to their advantage was debatable. Denial of the right to fail inexorably limits the right to succeed. Even though the legislative proposals were modest, the regulatory climate was noticeably stricter. Banks' leeway over setting various fees was restricted. Extremely speculative mortgages of the type that flowered during the boom were proscribed. The proposed consumer financial protection agency, if it comes to pass, would be a major headache for banks.

The Fed also elevated the role of regulation. At the Greenspan Fed, only monetary policy mattered. After the crash, the agency returned to the job of assessing bank loans and balance sheets, and with a more skeptical eye toward risk models. Daniel Tarullo, the first Fed governor appointed by Obama, tartly informed a Senate panel in October '09, "Things [for banks] are going to change. That means business models. That means the way of assessing risk. That means how you run your institution."

The central bank emerged from the crash sorely humbled. Bernanke admitted publicly that the crisis had caught him off guard.[12] Going forward, the Fed has a huge stake in ensuring that it is not embarrassed by a bubble again. Presumably, after the economy does recover, the Fed is unlikely to flirt with ultralow interest rates as it did in the '00s.

International regulators have also promised to crack down on banks' use of capital. The G20 delegates vowed to raise capital requirements on banks when the world recession eases. If they carry through, it will put a brake on the general level of risk. Compared with the pre-crash era, leverage on Wall Street was already down sharply.[13] Less leverage means fewer assets, fewer trades, and less profit. Indeed, in a world with tougher capital rules, the bubble of the 2000s could not have occurred.[*]

Finance was reborn when the panic subsided, but in many respects it was a changed industry—more sheltered, more regulated, more concentrated, and less competitive. The scrappier, smaller firms that previously challenged Goldman Sachs were licking their wounds or had disappeared altogether. Goldman's only true rival was JPMorgan, now the king of Wall Street. (Goldman and Morgan were among the

---

[*] The effectiveness of capital requirements will partly depend on whether regulators prevent firms from dodging the intent of the rules, as they did in the past, with shadow banking conducted off the balance sheet.

first to repay their TARP monies.) Commercial banking was exceptionally concentrated, with the four biggest banks claiming almost 40 percent of deposits and two-thirds of credit cards.[14] Effectively, the Wild West model was supplanted with a more European-seeming arrangement, in which a few elite players thrived within the government's embrace. During 2009, Secretary Geithner conferred with the head of either JPMorgan, Goldman, or Citi an average of once every two days.[15] Goldman still took big risks, but now with the backing (if needed) of the taxpayers. The banks were like Fannie and Freddie before the crash: for-profit institutions with a presumptive lifeline to the Treasury.

In the '90s and '00s, Wall Street financed consumer borrowings by selling securities into a global market. Post-crash, this dynamic would be under stress. Households had heavy debts to work through, a process expected to take years. Americans relied more on income, less on Wall Street financings. For regulatory and also cultural reasons (such as high unemployment) expectations downshifted. Wall Street's impression on American culture seemed to have eroded, its glossy optimism worn to a thrifty nub. Higher saving was itself a rejection of the Wall Street credo; it signaled Americans' unease about the future. For almost their entire adulthood, baby boomers had assumed that even small accounts (or their homes) would build into appreciable savings and provide for retirements. Now they were mere squirrels, storing acorns for winter.

The drop in spending revived an essential puzzle, prevalent in the Depression years and also in Japan in the '90s: how to create sufficient demand for goods and labor? As compared with Wall Street's golden age, government seemed destined to supply more of the answer, bankers less. After all, the recovery had been purchased with massive public-sector spending and loans, and the federal pipeline showed no sign of shutting down.

Everywhere one looked—credit markets, mortgages, the auto industry—the government was playing a conspicuous role in formerly private affairs. The administration was anointing preferred industries (energy, the environment) for investment, a throwback to the fad for industrial planning of the '70s. Unemployment was higher, the government's role as a social guarantor larger. Obama seemed close, finally, to enacting public health care, a goal pursued by liberals since the New Deal. Indeed, John Maynard Keynes, the twentieth-century British economist and statesman famous for his skepticism of the market, whose ideas had been shunned by a generation of neoconservatives, was reinstated to his previous perch in the canon. A trio of timely books argued that the way out of the recession was to heed Lord Keynes, who emphasized the uncertainty of economic life, and prescribed government fine-tuning as a permanent feature of industrial societies, necessary to balance the ups and downs of the economic cycle.[16] The stimulus itself was pure Keynesian economics, a standard tool of American policymakers through the 1970s that had been shelved during the bubble years.

Spending policies had a dark side—they shredded government finances. Among the G20 nations, deficits soared from an average of 1 percent of total GDP to 8 percent. The United States was among the worst offenders, with a deficit equal to 10 percent of GDP. In the year after Lehman, America's debt rose by $1.9 trillion (Rodriguez had predicted $2 trillion) to a staggering total of $11.91 trillion. "In our opinion," Rodriguez wrote, "this is a very dangerous road we have chosen."[17]

By 2009, each American (if accorded his or her share of the federal debt) owed $24,000—twice as much as a decade earlier. Moreover, unlike after World War II, when the government borrowed mostly from Americans—in effect, from itself—this time the country had borrowed from overseas; each American's share of the debt included $2,500 to China alone.

It is arguable that the U.S. government resolved the crisis simply by appropriating Wall Street's debts, transferring a private sector problem to the public. In any case, its "solution" further depreciated its international account. America borrowed from overseas to pay for the bubble; now it was borrowing for the bust. The British precedent comes to mind. Britain emerged from World War II in an indebted state; its currency was soon replaced as the international standard, and Britain acquiesced to American monetary leadership. The U.S. will be challenged to avoid a similar fate. (The dollar plunged 12 percent during Obama's first nine months in office.)

The failure of America's model stirred a geopolitical realignment. Europe no longer slobbered to imitate the U.S.; Asian economies were ascendant. Americans at the 2009 economic summit in Davos, accustomed to preaching the wonders of the market, were subjected to lectures by the potentates of command economies. Russia's prime minister, Vladimir Putin, gloated over the virtual death of investment banking. Premier Wen Jiabao of China aptly faulted "excessive expansion of financial institutions in blind pursuit of profit." Sounding as scolding as Western missionaries of yore, he excoriated Washington for promoting an "unsustainable model of development characterized by prolonged low savings and high consumption." Since China was the U.S. government's biggest creditor, his lecture could not be ignored. Indeed, Geithner promptly traveled to Beijing where, before an audience at Peking University, he pleaded, in the manner of a humbled plenipotentiary, that his government continue to be afforded credit.

The legacy of the bust—what Wall Streeters called the "new normal"[18]—entailed, prospectively, a weaker dollar, a greater government presence, more joblessness, and higher taxes. It was a world of pinched horizons. From roughly the 1980s on, no horizon had been deemed necessary. Ronald Reagan had decreed that government was the problem, not the cure. Markets were viewed as self-regulating ecosystems. The province of regulation shrank, the volume of market innovations commensurately expanded. By the 2000s, the market's innovations were no longer even questioned: Anything invented on Wall Street was perforce good. Complex creations such as securitized assets basked in the presumption of safety. Greenspan's 1998 testimony, recall, was that "regulation of derivatives transactions that are privately negotiated by professionals is unnecessary."[19] The notion that the Street should run a casino, taking bets on which companies will live and which will die, did not strike observers as even mildly objectionable. The belief that the market data composed a sort of sacred text, on which forecasters could reliably predict household default ratios and the like, was accepted on faith.

A generation invested a higher proportion in stocks, fed on the nostrum that risk was, essentially, outmoded. Just as the fall of the Iron Curtain supposedly ended history, Wall Street's smooth rise through most of the '90s and the '00s was to have ended market history. (No more earthquakes—just steady gains.) The crash of 2008 spelled the end of that end. The prejudices of a generation, the conviction, repeated so often it had become gospel, that stocks were ever and always a sound long-term investment, smoldered into ash. In the aftermath of the crash, not only was the return on stocks negative over ten years, it trailed the return on government bonds for the previous *twenty* years. Indeed, stocks were barely ahead over a thirty-year time frame.[20] The ramifications were profound. Portfolio allocations by individuals as well as by endowments, pension funds, and other institutions were rewritten. Society altered its view of an acceptable level of risk.

Previous to the crash, it was casually assumed that no statutes or rules were needed to prevent banks from making foolish loans; after all, the theory went, why would institutions ever jeopardize their own capital? This cornerstone of efficient market theory—the view of economic man as always *rationally* self-interested—was rather embarrassingly upended. Similarly, the faith that bankers know best, that they could be counted on to preserve their firms, was shattered.

The peculiar prominence of finance was now seen as dubious and, in all likelihood, temporary. Prior to the '90s, the profits of financial firms had averaged about 1.2 percent of the GDP, with little annual variation. But in the '90s and '00s they soared; in 2005 such profits totaled 3.3 percent.[21] There is no inherent reason why finance should have suddenly tripled its share of the national output, and in a world with less leverage, less risk, less appetite for exotic securities, and, off in the distance, higher interest rates—no reason why it should continue. The proper end of Wall Street is to oil the nation's business; it became, in the bubble era, a goal in itself, a machine wired to inhuman perfection.

It may be too much to expect that, in the future, economists take forecasting models with a grain of salt, or that executives refrain from relying on "liquidity" to bail them out of a jam. But the worst recession in sixty years—unsuspected by most economists even when it had been under way for more than six months—should inspire a modicum of humility. Speculation *will* return, of course, and so will bubbles. The question is whether Americans will treat them so lightly.

Overseas, the notion that central banks should restrain speculation is hardly controversial. In the United States, it was. Both Greenspan and Bernanke devoted many words to rebutting the notion that bubbles should be "pricked."* Instead, they endorsed a policy of cleaning the mess up afterward. This reflected their doubts that mere humans, even Fed governors, could detect whether an elevated market was irrational— whether *any* market was irrational. Even after the crash, Bernanke could barely bring himself to utter the word "bubble," preferring to speak of the mortgage "boom."²²

The formative lesson that Bernanke drew on in 2008 had been sketched prior to and during the Great Depression when, he believed, the Fed had erred in clamping down on credit formation, including the credit used to speculate in stocks. In other words, the Fed had been too restrictive. Future central bankers may draw an opposite lesson from 2008: the Fed let speculation go on far too long.

---

* Bubble pricking (and bubble spotting) would not require a new systemic risk monitor, as has been proposed. The Fed is already charged with raising interest rates to ward off excessive inflation. It could also raise rates to tamp inflation in the credit cycle—which is rather easy to recognize. Irrespective of the absolute level of interest rates, when the premium charged to risky borrowers narrows, it is a sign that credit standards are weakening. The economist Robert J. Barbera has proposed a simple formula for adjusting rates that would incorporate not only changes in the consumer price index but also credit spreads. If such a change were adopted, easy credit would constitute grounds for a presumptive, if not an automatic, tightening. This is not to say that a robot could run the central bank. Monetary policy is intuitive as well as mathematical. And banking regulation is inherently subjective. An effective Fed governor has to recognize that when banks across the country are issuing loans without asking the borrowers to document their income—to document their truthfulness, that is—something in the system is rotten.

. . .

The end of the era on Wall Street was also an end for Robert Rodriguez. The investor who anticipated the trouble earlier than most—who renounced the debt of Fannie and Freddie early in 2006, who scrubbed his bond portfolio clean of "suspicious" mortgage-backed securities, who warned of an "absence of fear" in mid-2007, and who saw that it would require capital, not just liquidity, to save the system—announced that he would leave his firm in 2010 for a one-year sabbatical. Coincidentally, 2009 marked his twenty-fifth year at the helm—a quarter century of investing in increasingly bubbly markets buoyed by ebullient bankers, optimistic investors, ever-tolerant officials, and, ultimately, a mortgage mania. Rodriguez had tried to avoid the speculation inherent in those bubbles so as, he thought, to lessen his exposure to the consequent busts. Through the end of September '09 his stock fund, FPA Capital, had recorded an annualized return during his stewardship of 14.77 percent, the best of any diversified mutual fund over 25 years. The S&P 500 returned only 10.36 percent over the same span.[23] Even in a market dominated by bubbles—perhaps especially through bubbles—careful investing still paid.

In October, already preparing his exit from Wall Street, the cautious investor entered an American Le Mans Series race in Monterey, California, sharing, with a codriver, the wheel of a Porsche GT3 Cup. The four-hour race was his first Le Mans. The field included thirty-three contestants, mostly professional racers, driving cars like his as well as Ferraris and Corvettes at speeds surpassing 150 miles per hour. The track was two and one quarter miles with eleven turns—one of which, known as the Corkscrew, was said to be equivalent to a three-story drop, or perhaps, in terms of the flow of adrenaline it occasioned, a bank run. "It gets your heart pumping," Rodriguez noted. Six cars were put out of action; two collided and one hit a wall at the finish. Rodriguez finished third in class. He survived to compete another day.

Afterword to the 2011 Edition

F INANCIAL STORMS OF LATE have been frequent but fleeting. Markets thunder, crowds panic, but by the morning after the terror is gone, a nightmare reduced to a wispy memory. The stock market crash of 1987, hyperbolically labeled "Black Monday," had almost no imprint on the larger society. Within little more than a year, the market had recouped its losses and the economy was chugging merrily along, its thirst for equities not even dented. So it was with the junk bond bust of 1990, after which speculation in credit continued apace. Perhaps the collapse of the hedge fund Long-Term Capital Management qualified as a partial exception. Having risen to such Olympian heights, LTCM, in its fall, proffered (or seemed to) some enduring lesson or cautionary morale. But the lesson failed to stick. No sooner was the firm of trader-academicians rescued, the players cleared from the stage, then, in the autumn of 1998, there ignited the bizarre frenzy for dot-com stocks, a speculative mania so unhinged from ordinary logic it seemed the product of some medieval sorcery—of a cloistered theology rather than modern math. Once again, the end was quick, the recession brief. The Internet gurus returned to gainful employ and, save for a deceleration in information services, the economy was restored to its customary rate of advance. After each such episode, normalcy was purchased by the Federal Reserve, at the price of ever-lower interest rates. With credit cheap and getting cheaper, Americans, in increasing numbers, did as the central bank had directed them—they borrowed. This eventually stimulated a decade-long expansion (dare we say bubble?) in housing and in mortgages.

In none of these prior episodes did the compass truly shift; a momentary wavering was the sole effect, after which finance continued on its relentless course of innovation, chiefly by means of products that disintermediated, or came between, users of capital (corporations, home buyers, and so forth) and suppliers of it (investors). The risks being less apparent as the complexity of such instruments grew, innovation occasioned a gradual increase in speculation. In the normal course of events, speculation would tend to heighten the general sense of alarm. However, as each of the above episodes proved so brief, the effect was to the contrary. A "Minsky effect" obtained: as banks, hedge funds and others survived each successive bubble with relatively little pain, they were emboldened to take ever greater risks in the ensuing cycle.

The thesis that the crash of 2008 was different was posited in the first edition of this book (and is implicit in its title). How do matters stand twelve months out? It should be said that the view of 2008 as a historic turning point—as the "end" of something—was not received with universal applause. Critics pointed to the rebounding stock market, as well as to the recovery in investment banking profits. Also, Wall Street executives seemed too much in the pink. Even if their bonuses were lower than in the salad days of no-doc mortgages and CDOs, the pain did not seem shared, or not equally shared. "Same old Wall Street," and variants of that cry, were heard on many lips, often with a cynical or fateful air.

The single greatest disappointment was that the government did not, at least immediately, deliver a tidy fix. Reality is messier than reformist dreams, and Congress was, for many months, preoccupied with health care reform, which was passed only in Obama's second spring. When lawmakers finally embraced financial reform, they conjured up a 2,000-page colossus of a proposal, ponderous in detail and devoid of the sort of bold strokes that would resonate with the public. The bill bore the moderating influence of the banking lobby and of Secretary Geithner himself. But for all its lawyerly detail, it did have teeth, and these were considerably sharpened en route to the bill's enactment.

Early in 2010, Congress was forced to reckon with a gathering political storm, loosely congealed around the Tea Party, populist in nature and hostile to Wall Street. The hostility was enlivened when the Securities and Exchange Commission, that spring, filed a landmark suit against Goldman Sachs, charging it with cheating its clients in the course of betting on the mortgage bubble's collapse. The Goldman suit crystallized the public anger, for here was a firm, recently the recipient of federal favors—in Goldman's hour of duress, the government had hastily approved its conversion to a bank—and seemingly devoid of the most basic standards of decency. Though the details were disputed (Goldman eventually settled), the damage to the firm's, and to the industry's, reputation, was significant, not least because the suit highlighted Wall Street's migration to casino-type activities with no conceivable social benefits. To make the distinction clear, Wall Street was once primarily engaged in raising capital for industry, advising on mergers, selling stocks to the public. Now, it was concentrated in high-stakes gambling. This evolution predated the mortgage bust; indeed, it was a feature in virtually all of the recent panics. But the stakes were raised, this time, by the string of government rescues. Just which of Wall Street's activities, precisely, were so essential that they merited federal protection? A prominent securities analyst seized on the crux of the matter, pointedly asking clients, "What part of Goldman Sachs is good for the country?"[1]

If Wall Street was not working in the public's interest, why had the government bailed it out? Outrage over this point changed the tone in Congress, as well as in the White House. Washington now hastened to establish its true reformist credentials. Paul Volcker, the eminent former Fed chief and Obama adviser, whose pleas for more stringent measures had been ignored, was suddenly the man of the hour. Hastily amended, the Dodd-Frank Wall Street Reform and Consumer Protection Act, signed into law in July 2010, embraced and codified the "Volcker Rule," which forbids banks from proprietary trading and from capitalizing hedge funds. Other provisions forced derivatives onto public exchanges, where they would be subject to more transparency and to capital soundness requirements. Abusive mortgage practices were barred, and a separate law cracked down on dubious credit card fees. Most significant, international regulators, meeting in Basel, tripled the minimum level of capital required for big, global banks.

Financial regulation is never completely effective (Wall Street is skilled at both adaption and avoidance). These recent measures may yet prove less effective than hoped. Dodd-Frank is an elaborate law, Joycean in its complexity and in its heft. Its usefulness will depend on the skill with which it is implemented, a process that will begin with scores of rules to be written by administrative agencies. Its framers hoped to instill in investors a proper fear of loss, and thus to prevent a future Lehman—and yet to provide an orderly shutdown mechanism should one occur. These policies are somewhat contradictory. Whether big institutions are indeed to be allowed to fail will not be known until the issue is tested in some future crisis.

As cloudy as that picture sounds, there is no disputing the law's epochal dimension. After several decades that saw a steady loosening in the constraints on Wall Street, the rules, at long last, were appreciably tightened. For the first time since Glass-Steagall was adopted in the 1930s, Congress proscribed specific activities to banks, various of which made fast to dismantle their proprietary trading units. The Basel proposal, with its requirement of greater capital, significantly reinforced the spirit of the original Glass-Steagall—that banks, being vital to economic stability, should operate within a healthy margin of safety. Society has an interest in restraining undue risk by large, complex institutions.

Post-reform, Wall Street will be safer and duller. The reforms will put a brake on banking, thus on the economy overall. Consumers will find it harder to get a mortgage or a credit card. Regulatory constraints will dampen the supply of loans; they will raise costs to banks and raise interest rates to borrowers. That growth may be trimmed to a more sustainable, and more realistic, rate, is small solace; it is a trimming none-theless. Such a downshift was discernible even before Congress acted. The recovery by the U.S. economy was one of the most tepid ever. Jobs remained scarce, unemployment high. Two years after Lehman, the total of banking assets continued to fall, as consumers were repaying old loans rather than seeking new ones. Loans are what bankers sell; bank-ing, in short, was an industry in decline. By definition, so was credit. Investors, having digested this news, withdrew money from equity mu-tual funds for the third year in a row. The generation reared to believe that stocks always go up had been supplanted by a newer, more fearful crowd, one scarred by too many panics and crashes.

With private enterprise chastened, the government remained a rather conspicuous presence. Washington was rewriting the rules for health care, restricting offshore drilling, spending at a rate well above its revenue. Federal agencies continued to provide virtually the only financing for the moribund housing industry. The administration's activ-ism (and the occasionally antibusiness rhetoric of Obama) led to a seri-ous rift with the business community. In a widely noted address to the Economic Club of Washington, Ivan Seidenberg, chairman of Verizon, declared in mid-2010, "By reaching into virtually every sector of eco-nomic life, government is injecting uncertainty into the marketplace and making it harder to raise capital and create new businesses."

Business is conditioned to complain about government (except when it is asking that government for a handout). The point is that the locus of power had shifted. Markets had steadily accreted power since the early '70s; now, the balance was shifting back. This shift was mir-rored internationally, as a weak banking sector and a near insolvency of the government in Greece, requiring an international rescue, and related afflictions elsewhere, highlighted the rising role of the state.

In September 2010, two years after Lehman's failure, the National Bureau of Economic Research ruled that the Great Recession had, in fact, drawn to a close the previous June. Officially eighteen months, the recession was thus the longest slump in postwar history. The very day that the bureau proclaimed its end, the price of gold soared to an all-time high, underscoring the continuing anxious state of markets. America's yawning deficits (both federal and local), a vulnerable dollar and festering high unemployment are among the recession's legacies; they seem likely to long outlive it. Though two years is hardly time to offer an historical view, it seems even surer today that the collapse of 2008 spelled the end of the age of unchecked faith on Wall Street, the beginning of an era of more modest horizons.

The character of this bubble was not so very different from those preceding, except perhaps in scale. But the very fact that it followed so many previous speculations made it impossible to ignore the systemic nature of the disease. The mortgage whizzes of the early 2000s built on those who preceded them, likewise the confidant bankers, the ratings experts, the indulgent corporate directors. The excesses at every stage were barely punished and never cured, and so the risks grew hopelessly out of whack. Markets will always push until they push too far. The speculative instruments brought low in 2008 didn't truly stand alone; they were the culmination of at least two decades of clever innovation, new derivatives and old securities sliced into new formulations, the rising risk betrayed by increasing volatility and intermittent panics. As in the case of the disputed Goldman trade, finance increasingly seemed to abandon its historic role as industry's servant—had become its master. Public markets, no longer a mere thermometer of the economy, assumed a terrifying life of their loan, subjecting individual savers and businesses alike to unpredictable and stomach-churning gyrations.

Markets have always been flighty, but through the early 1970s their domain was relatively restricted. Until then, it was near impossible for the average citizen (or even the average firm) to wager on Swiss francs or on the direction of mortgage rates. With deregulation, markets were in control. The decision of whether to issue a home mortgage was no longer up to an individual credit officer, but to investors scattered around the world; likewise, the decision of whether a public company should be bought or sold, and many more such decisions. Ordinary economic behavior thus became subject to market passions. As this model of unfettered markets spread, there were increasing fissures in the crust of the world's economies. Black Monday, the savings and loan crisis, LTCM, and similar if smaller quakes were ominous tremors that evidenced the underlying instability. The mortgage bubble produced a tectonic upheaval, similar in origins but greater in magnitude. Entire countries were upended—small wonder that the body politic revolted. It wasn't news but rather a confirmation. The model—the ideal of markets as self-regulating and safe—was deeply flawed: 2008 proved it.

Boston, September 30, 2010

ACKNOWLEDGMENTS

WRITING IS A SOLITARY BUSINESS. Why, then, do I feel surrounded by accomplices—pillars of support, faithful friends and colleagues, givers of such wise counsel? My father used to say that the journey matters as much, or more, than the destination, and those who helped with this book not only bettered the product, they enriched the trip more than words can say. I am extremely grateful, first, to the more than one hundred people who agreed to be interviewed about the events in this narrative. Some are sourced in plain view; some preferred to have their names out. Regardless, without them there would be no book. My access to these sources was greatly facilitated by various soldiers in public relations. It is the custom to leave such efforts unsung, but when professionals generously give of their time, and their understanding, it ought to be on record. Among others, a special thanks to PR pros Paul W. Critchlow, Michele Davis, Joseph Evangelisti, Kristin C. Lemkau, Jeanmarie McFadden, Calvin A. Mitchell III, George Sard, Michelle A. Smith, and Robert Stickler. Just as valued, various people read portions of individual chapters and offered criticisms that vastly improved the original draft. There were others, some of whom, again, prefer not to be mentioned, but my heartfelt thanks to Robert Glauber, Michael

Greenberg, Frank Partnoy, and Peter Wallison. As to the question of CDOs, and to the entire alphabet of mortgage-backed securities, I was lucky to be able to call on the expertise of my brother-in-law, Morris Pearl. While Morris was obviously successful on Wall Street, the precise nature of his job was for many years an utter mystery to his family. In all candor, it is a mystery still. But Morris was good enough to—in his straightforward, fact-focused, and earnest manner—enlighten me on the workings of mortgage securitizations. What's more, he read the entire book and shared his professional insights. Three dear friends, Neil Barsky, Mitch Rubin, and Jeffrey Tannenbaum, also read this book in process. At times they had comments; often not. Regardless, the gift of a friendly first audience was immensely appreciated. This book was researched and written on a timeline not unlike the year and more that it chronicles, which is to say, quickly. (Some wrote faster; hats off to them.) Particularly as I was pressed for time, I was fortunate, and probably spoiled forever, to have had Jeremy Kress as research assistant. Jeremy was diligent, meticulous, and uniquely skilled at gathering *relevant* information. During the final, hectic laps I took to sending him lists of points to be checked, facts to be verified, and the like; come the next morning, they would appear, sweetly enumerated and deftly resolved, in my in-box as if by the goodness of some electronic angel. Mere acknowledgment does not suffice.

I cannot imagine having gotten through this project, and this year, without the support of my family, too numerous to name. (But in particular, thank you, Matt, Zack, and Alli for being the wonders that you are; thanks to my steps for asking, with unfailing interest, how each step was proceeding; and thanks, Mom, for picking up the awesome slack so very well.) Finally—well, *almost* finally—my professional partners—my agent, Melanie Jackson, and editor, Ann Godoff—are of such long standing, such demonstrated loyalty, that writing this book would have been unthinkable without them. Melanie was immensely and, it seemed, reflexively supportive, especially when I needed it most. Ann, it may now be said, to my belated but no less grateful concurrence, persuaded, convinced, and, ultimately, all but dragooned me into tackling this book. Some editors would have left it at that, but Ann proceeded to—dare one say it in these budget-wary times?—edit, and edit well. What more could one ask? Well . . . My wife, Judy, with bottomless reserves of dedication and commitment, with her superior feeling for reading and for writing, teased out the hidden connections, assaulted the unclear linkages, insisted on clarity in the midst of authorial clouds, refused to be satisfied with the nearly good, the half-explained, or the almost right, and, generally, with the patience born, I trust and reciprocate, of love, helped to steer—verily to nurture—volumes of prose into something more nearly resembling a book. Words do not express.

NOTES

PROLOGUE

1. "Only a fifth": Mark Zandi, Economy.com, and Robert J. Samuelson, *The Great Inflation and Its Aftermath: The Past and Future of American Affluence* (2008), p. 218; "debt of financial firms": Martin Wolf, "Asia's Revenge," *Financial Times*, October 9, 2008.

2. Ben Bernanke and Mark Gertler, "Monetary Policy and Asset Price Volatility," *Economic Review*, Federal Reserve Bank of Kansas City, issue Q IV (1999), pp. 17–51; and Roger Lowenstein, "The Education of Ben Bernanke," *New York Times Magazine*, January 20, 2008.

3. Peter S. Goodman, "The Reckoning: Taking a Hard New Look at a Greenspan Legacy," *New York Times*, October 8, 2008.

4. Robert L. Rodriguez and Thomas H. Atteberry, "Buyer's Strike," FPA New Income Fund shareholder letter of June 16, 2003.

5. Rodriguez and Atteberry, FPA New Income semiannual reports for periods ending September 30, 2005 and September 30, 2006.

CHAPTER 1

1. Representative Barney Frank of Massachusetts, speaking during the hearing on HR 2575, *The Secondary Mortgage Market Enterprises Regulatory Improvement Act*, on September 25, 2003, to the House Financial Services Committee, 108th Cong., 1st sess. (online at financialservices.house.gov/media/pdf/108-54.pdf).

2. Edward Pinto. More precisely, principal, interest, taxes, and home insurance on prime conforming mortgages needed to be within 28 percent of total (pretax) income.

3. Bethany McLean, "Fannie Mae's Last Stand," *Vanity Fair*, February 2009.

4. Peter Wallison and Charles W. Calomiris, "The Last Trillion-Dollar Commitment: The Destruction of Fannie Mae and Freddie Mac," *Financial Service Outlook*, American Enterprise Institute for Public Policy Research, September 2008. When Wallison, a scholar at the American Enterprise Institute, wrote critically of the twins' privileged position, Fannie Mae cut off business with Mortgage Guarantee Insurance Corp., which insured mortgage pools for Fannie, and where Wallison served on the board. Wallison

resigned from the MGIC board to spare the company further trouble. He continued to write critically of the twins and once again suffered retaliation. This time, Freddie Mac threatened to suspend business with Gibson Dunn and Crutcher, a law firm where Wallison was "of counsel."

5. Paul Muolo and Mathew Padilla, "Angelo Rising," *Mortgage Strategy*, August 4, 2008.

6. "Political risk" and "arrangements": Wallison and Calomiris, "Trillion-Dollar Commitment"; "More than $1 million": McLean, "Fannie's Last Stand."

7. Wallison and Calomiris, "Trillion-Dollar Commitment," 3–4.

8. "Push products": "Trillion-Dollar Commitment"; "double shareholder earnings": "Fannie's Last Stand"; "from $100 billion": *Administrative Perspective on GSE Regulatory Reform*, hearing before the House Committee on Financial Services, 109th Cong., 1st sess., April 13, 2005, 61.

9. *Administrative Perspective on GSE Regulatory Reform*, 12.

10. Ibid., Snow: 12, 61; Greenspan, 23.

11. Ibid., 4.

12. "Single Family Guaranty Business: Facing Strategic Crossroads," Fannie Mae internal presentation, June 27, 2005 (hereafter, "Strategic Crossroads") disclosed by House Committee on Oversight and Government Reform as part of December 9, 2008, hearing, *The Role of Fannie Mae and Freddie Mac in the Financial Crisis*, 23, 25; Daniel Mudd, interview with the author.

13. David A. Andrukonis, e-mail to Mike May, September 7, 2004, and May, e-mail to Richard Syron and Gene McQuade, October 6, 2004, both released by the House Committee on Oversight and Government Reform as part of the December 9, 2008, hearing on Fannie and Freddie.

14. "Strategic Crossroads."

15. Charles Duhigg, "The Reckoning: Pressured to Take More Risk, Fannie Reached Tipping Point," *New York Times*, October 4, 2008.

16. Duhigg, "The Reckoning: Pressured to Take More Risk"

17. "Strategic Crossroads," 5.

Chapter 2

1. Matt Apuzzo, "Report: Banks Torpedoed Rules That Could Have Saved Them," Associated Press, December 1, 2008.

2. PRNewswire-FirstCall, February 4, 2003 (Source: Countrywide), http://www.prnewswire .com/cgi-bin/stories.pl?ACCT=104&STORY=/www/story/02-04-2003/0001885208&EDATE=.

3. David Andrukonis, e-mail, September 7, 2004.

4. Mortgage Bankers Association.

5. Meredith Whitney, Oppenheimer equity research report, December 11, 2008. Household growth was 2.5 percent.

6. Martin Wolf, "Asia's Revenge," *Financial Times*, October 9, 2008, and also Martin Wolf, "Seeds of Its Own Destruction," *Financial Times*, March 9, 2009.

7. Ben S. Bernanke, Sandridge Lecture, Virginia Association of Economics, Richmond, March 10, 2005.

8. Carmen M. Reinhart and Kenneth S. Rogoff, draft of "Is the 2007 U.S. Sub-Prime Financial Crisis So Different? An International Historical Comparison," February 5, 2008; subsequently published in *American Economic Review*, May 2009.

9. Fannie Mae found 932 articles in a Google search of "housing bubble" in the first four months of 2005, and 1,248 such articles in just the next two months—a sharp acceleration. See "Strategic Crossroads," 19.

10. Charles Mackay, *Extraordinary Popular Delusions and the Madness of Crowds* (New York: Farrar, Straus and Giroux, 1932), 89–97.

11. "Strategic Crossroads," 39. The figure on Boston is from David Leonhardt, "Do I Hear a Housing Rebound? Not Yet," *New York Times*, April 22, 2009. Similarly, Leonhardt documents, the ratio of median home prices to incomes in Los Angeles rose from 3.3 to 8.2 from the mid '90s to the mid '00s and in San Francisco from 4 to 8. Over an even shorter time frame (the late '90s to the mid '00s), the ratio in Las Vegas surged from 2 to 4, in New York, from 4 to 8, and in Miami, from 2.2 to 6.

12. Steve Dexter, *Real Estate Debt Can Make You Rich: What You Owe Today Is What You Will Be Worth Tomorrow* (New York: McGraw-Hill, 2006).

13. John Oros, webcast archive of speech, "The Current State of Financial Markets and the Federal Government Policy Response," September 29, 2008.

CHAPTER 3

1. John C. Dugan, address to the 13th Annual Economic Summit, Greenlining Institute, Los Angeles, April 20, 2006.

2. Background on Mozilo is largely drawn from Paul Muolo and Mathew Padilla, "Angelo Rising," *Mortgage Strategy*, August 4, 2008.

3. Consolidated Amended Complaint, *Pappas v. Countrywide Financial Corp. et al.*, no. 207CV05295, ¶ 94.

4. Quoted in *Pappas v. Countrywide*, ¶ 86.

5. *Pappas v. Countrywide*, individual citations as follows: Countrywide mortgage statistics: ¶ 107; "full financing": ¶ 106; Las Vegas and Hawaii: ¶ ¶ 109 and 251; sale force pitch (quoting Gretchen Morgenson, "Inside the Countrywide Lending Spree," *New York Times*, August 26, 2007): ¶ 247; food and clothing: ¶ 249; "failed to grasp": ¶ 109. Calculation of monthly mortgage payment on option ARMs ($125 to $876) is from "Strategic Crossroads," 35.

6. *Pappas v. Countrywide*, ¶ 120.

7. *Pappas v. Countrywide*, "bottom line": ¶ 128; "also relaxed": ¶ 131; "another loosening": ¶ 136.

8. *Pappas v. Countrywide*, "liar loans": ¶ 162; company manual: ¶ 168.

9. *Pappas v. Countrywide*, "paper the file": ¶ 160; "underwriter trainee": ¶ 187.

10. *Pappas v. Countrywide*, ¶ 199.

11. Press coverage was extensive. See in particular, Daniel Golden, "Countrywide's Many 'Friends,'" Portfolio.com, June 12, 2008, and Golden's "Angelo's Many 'Friends,'" *Portfolio*, August 2008; "Angelo's Angel," editorial, *Wall Street Journal*, June 19, 2008; James R. Hagerty and Glenn R. Simpson, "Countrywide CEO Helped Many Get Loans," *Wall Street Journal*, June 27, 2008.

12. *Pappas v. Countrywide*, ¶ 453.

13. Portrait of Killinger is drawn from Michael Dumiak, "Breakthrough for WaMu," *US Banker*, October 1, 2002.

14. Peter S. Goodman and Gretchen Morgenson, "Saying Yes to Anyone, WaMu Built Empire on Shaky Loans," *New York Times*, December 28, 2008.

15. Goodman and Morgenson, "Saying Yes," *New York Times*, December 28, 2008.

16. "Employees Were Grilled": Consolidated Class Action Complaint, *In Re Washington Mutual, Inc.*, securities litigation, no. 2:08-md-1919 MJP, ¶ 179. Rest of paragraph draws on Goodman & Morgenson, "Saying Yes."

17. Net income was $1.9 billion in 2000 and $3.43 billion in 2005.

18. *In Re Washington Mutual*, $70 billion: ¶ 74; Martinez: ¶ ¶ 114-115.

19. WaMu's appraisal procedures were covered extensively in *In Re Washington Mutual*. See esp. ¶ ¶ 202–205; 214; 228; 234–236; 244–.

20. John Dugan, interview with the author.

21. Meredith Whitney, Oppenheimer equity research, December 11, 2008, p. 5. Quoting Whitney, "Over $5 trillion in mortgages were funded through the securitization market from 2000 to 2007. . . . In comparison, banks grew their on–balance sheet mortgage exposure by under $1 trillion during the same period."

22. The happy phrase "infallible hand" was taken from Robert Barbera's *The Cost of Capitalism: Understanding Market Mayhem and Stabilizing Our Economic Future* (New York: McGraw-Hill, 2009), 8.

23. Background on the Sandlers and on Golden West drawn from Michael Moss and Geraldine Fabrikant, "The Reckoning: Once Trusted Mortgage Pioneers, Now Pariahs," *New York Times*, December 25, 2008.

24. Moss & Fabrikant, "The Reckoning: Once Trusted Pioneers."

25. Louis Lowenstein (the author's father), University Lecture, Columbia University, Spring 1989.

26. Pointed out by Mark Adelson and David Jacob in "The Sub-prime Problem: Causes and Lessons," report of Adelson & Jacob Consulting, January 8, 2008.

27. 69 percent: see the author's "Who Needs the Mortgage-Interest Deduction?" *New York Times Magazine*, March 5, 2006; "fully a third": Barbera, *Cost of Capitalism*, 34; "among subprime loans": Thomas A. Russo, "Credit Crunch: Where Do We Stand," report presented at Group of Thirty meeting, November 20, 2007, p. 5.

CHAPTER 4

1. Parts of this chapter are adapted from the author's "Triple-A Failure," *New York Times Magazine*, April 27, 2008.

2. E-mail from Yu-Tsung to Joanne Rose and Pat Jordan, May 25, 2004 (Rose was head of structured finance ratings). McDaniel's e-mail was written on October 21, 2007. Both were released by the House Committee on Oversight and Government Reform, October 22, 2008, as part of the hearing, "Credit Rating Agencies and the Financial Crisis."

3. There is no good housing price data before the late 1960s. On the basis of available information (generously supplied by Mark Zandi), however, it appears that housing prices fell, by less than 1 percent, in 1963, and by substantially more in 1941. Prices also fell very sharply during the Depression years 1929–33.

4. This discussion borrows from the author's "Long-Term Capital: It's a Short-Term Memory," *New York Times*, September 7, 2008.

5. "Federal regulators": Gerard Cassidy, interview with the author.

6. This figure was offered in June 2007. John Breit, interview with the author.

7. Mark Adelson and David Jacob, "The Sub-prime Problem: Causes and Lessons," report of Adelson & Jacob Consulting, January 8, 2008.

8. Frank Partnoy, "Overdependence on Credit Ratings Was a Primary Cause of the Crisis," presentation to the 11th Annual International Banking Conference, September 2008, sponsored by Federal Reserve Bank of Chicago & European Central Bank.

9. Mark Zandi, "In the Credit Sweet Spot," *Regional Financial Review*, May 2006.

CHAPTER 5

1. Gary Gorton, "The Panic of 2007," speech presented at Federal Reserve Bank of Kansas City, Jackson Hole Conference, August 2008.

2. Eric Dash and Julie Creswell, "The Reckoning: Citigroup Saw No Red Flags Even as It Made Bolder Bets," *New York Times*, November 23, 2008.

3. See Ron Chernow, "The Lost Tycoons," op-ed, *New York Times*, September 20, 2008.

4. According to company disclosures, trading and principal transactions accounted for less than half of revenue in the late '90s and 2000 and was over 50 percent (and sometimes 60 percent), in every year since, through 2007. Investment banking's share has been far less. Per the *New York Times* (Julie Creswell and Ben White, "Wall Street, R.I.P.: The End of an Era, Even at Goldman," September 28, 2008), that share plunged in 2007 to 16 percent.

5. "Strategic Crossroads," 25. Figures refer to 2004.

6. Thirty-seven layers: Vikas Bajaj, "Plan's Basic Mystery: What's All This Stuff Worth?" *New York Times*, September 25, 2008; rest of paragraph from "Strategic Crossroads," 25–26.

7. History of AIG and profile of Hank Greenberg drawn largely from James Bandler with Roddy Boyd and Doris Burke, "AIG's Risky Business," *Fortune*, October 13, 2008, as well as a previous *Fortune* article, Devin Leonard's "Greenberg & Sons," February 21, 2005, and Ron Shelp's *Fallen Giant: The Amazing Story of Hank Greenberg and the History of AIG* (Hoboken, N.J.: Wiley, 2006).

8. See, for instance, Management Discussion & Analysis of AIG's 2004 10-k. The crux of this section of the MD&A is that, spurred by New York attorney general and SEC investigations, AIG conducted an internal investigation that resulted in restatements that reduced 2003 and 2004 net income by $1.32 billion and $1.27 billion, respectively. In particular, see "Top Level Adjustments and Other Directed Entries."

9. Gretchen Morgenson, "Behind Insurer's Crisis, Blind Eye to a Web of Risk," *New York Times*, September 28, 2008.

10. Carrick Mollenkamp, Serena Ng, Liam Pleven, and Randall Smith, "Behind AIG's Fall, Risk Models Failed to Pass Real-World Test," *Wall Street Journal*, October 31, 2008.

11. Morgenson, "Behind Insurer's Crisis"; Robert O'Harrow Jr. and Brady Dennis, "Downgrades and Downfall," part 3 of a 3-part series, *Washington Post*, December 31, 2008.

12. Morgenson, in "Behind Insurer's Crisis," says Financial Products' compensation was 33 percent of revenues or more. Various published reports and company sources say Cassano earned more than $200 million over an eight-year period. The company has never disclosed his compensation. "Brooklyn College" and "degree": Dennis and O'Harrow "A Crack in the System," part 2 of series, *Washington Post,* December 30, 2008.

13. O'Harrow and Dennis, "A Beautiful Machine," part 1 of series, *Washington Post*, December 29, 2008.

14. O'Harrow and Dennis, "Downgrades and Downfall," and Bandler, "AIG's Risky Business."

15. "$80 billion": Mollenkamp, Ng, Pleven, and Smith, "Behind AIG's Fall." Company sources place the exact exposure at $78 billion. "20,000 individual securities": Robert B. Willumstad, interview with the author; "420 of the riskiest CDOs": Bandler, "AIG's Risky Business."

16. Rodriguez and Atteberry, FPA New Income semiannual report for period ending September 30, 2006.

17. "$225 billion": Mark Adelson & David Jacob, "The Sub-prime Problem: Causes and Lessons," January 8, 2008, 6. The figure applies only to CDOs backed by structured finance collateral, such as mortgage securities. Dealogic gives a figure of $388 billion in global CDOs (including those backed by corporate and emerging market debt) in 2006 (see Serena Ng and Carrick Mollenkamp, "Merrill Takes $8.4 billion Credit Hit—It Plunged into CDOs in '03, Hiring Pioneer of the Debt Securities," Wall Street Journal, October 25, 2007. "20 percent": Russo, "Credit Crunch," 4; also Robert Barbera, The Cost of Capitalism: Understanding Market Mayhem and Stabilizing Our Economic Future (New York: McGraw-Hill, 2009), 35.

18. Frank Partnoy, interview with the author.

19. Michael Lewis, "The End," Portfolio, December 2008.

20. Thomas Priore, interview with the author.

21. Quoted in Anthony Faiola, Ellen Nakashima, and Jill Drew, "The Crash: What Went Wrong," Washington Post, October 15, 2008.

22. This account is based on the author's interview with Michael Greenberger and supported by the excellent published account of Faiola, Nakashima, and Drew, "The Crash."

23. Roger Lowenstein, Origins of the Crash (New York: Penguin, 2004), 96.

24. Peter S. Goodman, "The Reckoning: Taking Hard New Look at a Greenspan Legacy," New York Times, October 8, 2008.

25. Quoted in Goodman, "The Reckoning: Taking Hard New Look at a Greenspan Legacy."

26. Roger Lowenstein, When Genius Failed: The Rise and Fall of Long-Term Capital Management (New York: Random House, 2000), 231.

27. Lowenstein, Origins of the Crash, 140–41.

28. Frank Partnoy, interview with the author.

29. Eric Dinallo, interview with the author.

30. See David A. Moss, "An Ounce of Prevention: Financial Regulation, Moral Hazard, and the End of 'Too Big to Fail,'" Harvard Magazine, September–October 2009.

31. See Lowenstein, When Genius Failed, 75–76.

Chapter 6

1. Case-Shiller Home Price Indices [hereafter Case-Shiller].

2. Eric Dash and Julie Creswell, "The Reckoning: Citigroup Saw No Red Flags Even as It Made Bolder Bets," New York Times, November 23, 2008.

3. See the author's "The Sandy Method," New York Times Magazine, August 27, 2000.

4. Carol Loomis, The Larger-Than-Life Life of Robert Rubin, Fortune, December 8, 2003.

5. Ken Brown and David Enrich, "Rubin, Under Fire, Defends His Role at Citi," Wall Street Journal, November, 29, 2008.

6. Dash and Creswell, "The Reckoning: Citigroup," and interviews with the author.

7. Jeff Gerth and Robert O'Harrow Jr., "As Crisis Loomed, Geithner Pressed But Fell Short," jointly published by ProPublica (http://www.propublica.org/feature/geithner-nyfed-tenure), April 2, 2009, and the Washington Post, April 3, 2009. See also Gerth's "How Citigroup Unraveled Under Geithner's Watch," jointly published by ProPublica (http://www.propublica.org/article/how-citigroup-unraveled-under-geithners-watch) and Politico (as "Geithner's Risky Oversight of Citigroup," http://www.politico.com/news/stories/0109/17437.html), January 14, 2009.

8. Stephanie Pomboy, *MacroMavens* newsletter, November 3, 2006, 4.

9. Case-Shiller.

10. Meredith Whitney, Oppenheimer equity research of December 11, 2008. See p. 5: "Liquidity in the mortgage market began to dry up in 2006."

11. "Worrisome dip": Michael Moss and Geraldine Fabrikant, "The Reckoning: Once Trusted Mortgage Pioneers, Now Pariahs," *New York Times*, December 25, 2008. "Non-mandatory 'guidance'": John Dugan, interview with the author.

12. History of Wachovia and of the merger with Golden West based on the author's interview with David Carroll. By 2001, the merging banks no longer had their historic names; by then they were known as Wachovia Corp. and First Union Corp.

13. Profile of O'Neal's youth based on John Cassidy, "Subprime Suspect," *New Yorker*, March 31, 2008.

14. Pete Kelly, interview with the author.

15. Profile of Ricciardi is based on Serena Ng and Carrick Mollenkamp's excellent "Merrill Takes $8.4 Billion Credit Hit—It Plunged into CDOs in '03, Hiring Pioneer of the Debt Securities," *Wall Street Journal*, October 25, 2007.

16. Ng and Mollenkamp, "Merrill Takes $8.4 Billion Credit Hit."

17. Ibid.

18. Goldman and Merrill compensation figures from Louise Story, "Wall St. Profits Were a Mirage, But Huge Bonuses Were Real," *New York Times*, December 18, 2008.

19. Company proxy reports.

20. Company reports, as of year-end 2006.

21. *MacroMavens*, April 7, 2006, 4–5.

22. *MacroMavens*, November 3, 2006, 6.

23. Shareholder Report on UBS's Write-downs, April 18, 2008; see especially p. 40 and also pp. 23, 32, 34, 41.

24. *MacroMavens*, April 7, 2006, 4, and Mark Zandi and Juan Manuel Licari, "Mortgage Market Fault Line," Moody's Economy.com, December 2006.

25. *S.E.C. v. Mozilo*; quotations that follow are from pp. 20, 26, 27, 29, 38.

26. 7¾ percent: Mortgage Bankers Association; 3 percent: *MacroMavens*, November 3, 2006, 3. According to Zandi and Licari, "Mortgage Market Fault Line," the delinquency rate for subprime mortgages issued in 2006 was 4 percent within five months of origination.

27. E-mail from Chris Meyer, December 15, 2006, released by House Committee on Oversight and Government Reform, October 22, 2008.

28. *MacroMavens*, November 3, 2006, 6.

29. Devin Leonard, "How Lehman Got Its Real Estate Fix," *New York Times*, May 3, 2008.

30. It was Saxon Capital.

31. Highlights from Cambridge Senior Management Group Offsite, attached to an e-mail written by Gary Friend, July 7, 2006, and e-mail from Enrico Dallavecchia to Daniel Mudd, October 29, 2006, each released by House Committee on Oversight and Government Reform, December 9, 2008.

32. Lowenstein, *When Genius Failed: The Rise and Fall of Long-Term Capital Management* (New York: Random House, 2000), 139.

33. David Viniar, interview with the author. Corporate junk-bond issuance: *MacroMavens*, December 15, 2006, 6.

34. Moss and Fabrikant, "The Reckoning: Once-Trusted Pioneers."

35. *MacroMavens*, December 1, 2006, 2, 5–6.

CHAPTER 7

1. JPMorgan Chase 2006 *Annual Report*, 10–11.

2. Citigroup 2006 *Annual Report*, 4–6.

3. Testimony available on Fed Web site. On February 14, Bernanke testified before the Senate Committee on Banking, Housing, and Urban Affairs that "household finances appear generally solid, and delinquency rates on most types of consumer loans and residential mortgages remain low." He referred to some classes of subprime loans as an "exception." His testimony from March 28 is quoted in the chapter epigraph.

4. Hank Paulson, interview with the author.

5. Profile of Bernanke largely drawn from Roger Lowenstein, "The Education of Ben Bernanke," *New York Times Magazine*, January 20, 2008, and also from John Cassidy, "Anatomy of a Meltdown," *New Yorker*, December 1, 2008.

6. Remarks by Governor Ben S. Bernanke, Conference to Honor Milton Friedman, University of Chicago, Chicago, Illinois, November 8, 2002.

7. See Lowenstein, "The Education of Bernanke."

8. Ben S. Bernanke, "Deflation: Making Sure 'It' Doesn't Happen Here," remarks before the National Economists Club, Washington, D.C., November 21, 2002.

9. Ben S. Bernanke, "Asset-Price 'Bubbles' and Monetary Policy," remarks before the New York Chapter of the National Association for Business Economics, New York, October 15, 2002. In the second paragraph, Bernanke asks: "Can the Federal Reserve (or any central bank) reliably identify 'bubbles' in the prices of some classes of assets, such as equities and real estate?" For more on Bernanke and bubbles, see "Monetary Policy and Asset Price Volatility," *Economic Review*, Federal Reserve Bank of Kansas City, issue Q IV (1999): 17–51, and also Lowenstein "The Education of Bernanke" and Cassidy, "Anatomy of a Meltdown."

10. Consolidated Amended Complaint, *Pappas v. Countrywide Financial Corp. et al.*, no. 207CV05295, 2008 WL 2195921 (C.D. Cal. Apr. 11), ¶ 208.

11. "Two dozen": Gregory Zuckerman, "How Street Hit Lender—'Subprime' King New Century Was Down But Not Quite Out; Then, Banks Shut Cash Spigot," *Wall Street Journal*, March 29, 2007; "a similar number": Rodriguez and Atteberry, FPA New Income semiannual report for period ending March 31, 2007. New Century filed for bankruptcy on April 2.

12. "White House analyst": Jo Becker, Sheryl Gay Stolberg, and Stephen Labaton, "The Reckoning: White House Philosophy Stoked Mortgage Bonfire," *New York Times*, December 20, 2008; delinquency rate: Mortgage Bankers Association. Figure is for first quarter 2007. Index of mortgage-backed securities: Markit Group.

13. Rodriguez and Atteberry, FPA New Income semiannual report for period ending March 31, 2007.

14. Ibid.

15. Roger Lowenstein, "Triple-A Failure," *New York Times Magazine*, April 27, 2008.

16. Ibid.

17. Ricciardi: Serena Ng and Carrick Mollenkamp, "Merrill Takes $8.4 billion Credit Hit—It Plunged into CDOs in '03, Hiring Pioneer of the Debt Securities," *Wall Street Journal*, October 25, 2007.

18. "$1.8 trillion": Kate Kelly, Serena Ng, and David Reilly, "Two Big Funds at Bear Stearns Face Shutdown—As Rescue Plan Falters Amid Subprime Woes, Merrill Asserts Claims," *Wall Street Journal*, June 20, 2007.

19. John Oros, tape of speech, "The Current State of Financial Markets and the Federal Government Policy Response," Wisconsin School of Business, September 29, 2008.
20. Merrill Lynch press release on departure of Dow Kim, May 16, 2007.
21. Devin Leonard, "How Lehman Got Its Real Estate Fix," *New York Times*, May 3, 2008.
22. Terry Pristin, "Risky Real Estate Deals Helped Doom Lehman," *New York Times*, September 16, 2008.
23. Delinquencies: Mortgage Bankers Association. Mortgage bonds: Markit Group.
24. Robert L. Rodriguez, text of speech to Chartered Financial Analysts of Chicago, June 28, 2007.
25. Bernanke: speech to Federal Reserve Bank of Chicago's 43rd Annual Conference on Bank Structure and Competition, May 17, 2007; Paulson: Reuters, April 20, 2007.
26. Mark Adelson and David Jacob, "The Sub-prime Problem: Causes and Lessons," January 8, 6. Their figure is for structured finance CDOs only. Global CDO production (of all types) was approximately $280 billion (Ng and Mollenkamp, "Merrill Takes $8.4 Billion Credit Hit"). Though both figures are for all of 2007, CDO production virtually shut down after July.
27. Markit Group.
28. Enrico Dallavecchia, e-mail to Daniel Mudd, July 16, 2007, released by House Committee on Oversight and Government Reform as part of December 9, 2008, hearing.
29. *Pappas v. Countrywide*, ¶¶ 10 and 253.
30. Lowenstein, "The Education of Bernanke."
31. The account of the crisis of August '07 largely relies on Cassidy, "Anatomy of a Meltdown," and Lowenstein, "Education of Bernanke."
32. Profile of Geithner based in part on Gary Weiss, "The Man Who Saved (or Got Suckered by) Wall Street," *Portfolio*, June 2008.
33. Cassidy, "Anatomy of a Meltdown."

CHAPTER 8

1. Devin Leonard, "How Lehman Got Its Real Estate Fix," *New York Times*, May 3, 2008.
2. Evan Thomas and Michael Hirsh, "Paulson's Complaint," *Newsweek*, May 25, 2009.
3. The official was Robert Steel.
4. Carrick Mollenkamp, Ian McDonald, and Deborah Solomon, "Big Banks Push $100 Billion Plan to Avert Crunch—Fund Seeks to Prevent Mortgage-Debt Selloff," *Wall Street Journal*, October 13, 2007.
5. JPMorgan Chase 2007 *Annual Report*, 10.
6. Eric Dash and Julie Creswell, "The Reckoning: Citigroup Pays for a Rush to Risk," *New York Times*, November 23, 2008.
7. "Mayo Mixes It Up with Citi's Prince," *Wall Street Journal*, October 16, 2007.
8. The speech was on October 15, 2007.
9. Citigroup's disclosure discussed by Rodriguez in the FPA New Income semiannual report for period ending September 30, 2007 (dated November 5, 2007); decline in mortgage securities: Markit Group.
10. Rodriguez, FPA New Income semiannual report for period ending September 30, 2007.
11. Meredith Whitney, "CIBC Equity Research: Citigroup," October 31, 2007.
12. James R. Hagerty, "Fannie Mae Hurries to Raise $7 Billion," *Wall Street Journal*, December 5, 2007.

13. Joseph W. St. Denis, letter to Rep. Henry A. Waxman, October 4, 2008, released in conjunction with hearings of House Committee on Oversight and Government Reform on AIG, October 7, 2008.

14. The episode is recounted in St. Denis's letter to Waxman, October 4, 2008.

15. October 7 hearings on AIG, p. 7; see also Liam Pleven and Amir Efrati, "Documents Show AIG Knew of Problems with Valuations," *Wall Street Journal*, October 11, 2008.

16. Pleven and Efrati, "Documents Show AIG Knew," and Carrick Mollenkamp, Serena Ng, Liam Pleven, and Randall Smith, "Behind AIG's Fall, Risk Models Failed to Pass Real-World Test," *Wall Street Journal*, October 31, 2008.

17. Delinquencies: Mortgage Bankers Association; home prices: Case-Shiller.

18. Fed bulletin, "Understanding the Recent Changes to Federal Reserve Liquidity Provision," May 2008, 3.

19. JPMorgan Chase 2007 *Annual Report*, 12.

20. Ibid., 10, 15, 16.

21. *Pappas v. Countrywide*, ¶ 253.

22. Robert L. Rodriguez, "Credit Crisis," FPA commentary, January 22, 2008.

23. Thomas A. Russo, "Credit Crunch: Where Do We Stand," presented at World Economic Forum, January 2008, pp. 5, 6, 15.

24. Lehman Brothers filings and Blaine Frantz, interview with the author. The figures are for February 2008 (end of Lehman's first quarter). The $49 billion in commercial real estate assets was down from $52 billion at the end of 2007. Leonard, "How Lehman Brothers Got Its Real Estate Fix," cites a smaller figure. He apparently uses a less inclusive definition of commercial assets.

25. Yalman Onaran and John Helyar, "Fuld Solicited Buffett Offer CEO Could Refuse as Lehman Fizzled," Bloomberg, November 10, 2008.

26. Russo, "Credit Crunch," 15–16.

27. Susanne Craig, "Lehman's Straight Shooter," *Wall Street Journal*, May 17, 2008.

28. Steve Black, interview with the author.

29. Ken Auletta, *Greed and Glory on Wall Street: The Fall of the House of Lehman* (New York: Random House, 1986), 209. According to Auletta, "Fuld believed no price justified selling something he considered family."

30. Susanne Craig, Jeffrey McCracken, Aaron Lucchetti, and Kate Kelly, "The Weekend That Wall Street Died," *Wall Street Journal*, December 29, 2008.

Chapter 9

1. 75 percent: Markit Group.

2. House Committee on Oversight and Government Reform hearings, October 7, 2008, p. 5.

3. Ibid., pp. 4, 5; Minutes of Meeting of Compensation and Management Resources Committee of AIG, March 11, 2008.

4. Charles Duhigg, "Doubts Raised on Big Backers of Mortgages," *New York Times*, May 6, 2008.

5. Ibid. Fannie's system of classifying subprime loans tended to undercount the total. Thus, the figure could well be greater.

6. With the mortgage twins, these calculations are inevitably complex. For Fannie, for instance, assets include the total book of business (that is, securities guaranteed as well as those owned outright), yielding a total exposure on March 31 of $2,969.8 billion—or almost $3 trillion. Common equity, including (for the sake of conservatism) equity raised

shortly after the quarter's end, was $27 billion. The exposure divided by the equity yields leverage of 110.

7. Interviews with Robert Steel and others, and Jo Becker, Sheryl Gay Stolberg, and Stephen Labaton, "The Reckoning: White House Philosophy Stoked Mortgage Bonfire," *New York Times*, December 20, 2008.

8. Ben S. Bernanke, speech to Independent Community Bankers of America, Orlando, Florida, March 4, 2008; Tim Geithner, speech to Council on Foreign Relations Corporate Conference, New York City, March 6, 2008.

9. "$120 billion": share price loss is from February 29, 2008, to March 10.

10. Kate Kelly, "Bear CEO's Handling of Crisis Raises Issues," *Wall Street Journal*, November 1, 2007.

11. This account draws on Bryan Burrough's excellent "Bringing Down Bear Stearns," *Vanity Fair*, August 1, 2008.

12. "Rodgin Cohen": Bob Steel, interview with the author; "$1 billion": John Oros, tape of speech "The Current State of Financial Markets and the Federal Government Policy Response," Wisconsin School of Business, September 29, 2008."

13. Burrough, "Bringing Down Bear Stearns."

14. Geithner's view: Bob Steel, interview with the author. Geithner and Rubin: Jeff Gerth and Robert O'Harrow Jr., "As Crisis Loomed, Geithner Pressed But Fell Short," jointly published by *ProPublica* and the *Washington Post*, April 2 and April 3, 2009, respectively.

15. Oros, "The Current State of Financial Markets."

16. Steve Black, interview with the author.

17. Douglas Braunstein, interview with the author.

18. Becker, Stolberg, and Labaton, "The Reckoning: White House Philosophy Stoked Mortgage Bonfire."

19. Robert L. Rodriguez, "Crossing the Rubicon," FPA commentary, March 30, 2008.

20. Cassidy, "Anatomy of a Meltdown," cites criticism from the *Wall Street Journal* and from Paul Volcker, and reports that Bernanke insisted that the rescue of Bear did not, as Cassidy put it, represent a new "template."

21. Sentence is quoted almost verbatim from *MacroMavens* newsletter, March 14, 2008, 3.

22. Robert Barbera, *The Cost of Capitalism: Understanding Market Mayhem and Stabilizing Our Economic Future* (New York: McGraw-Hill, 2009), 153–54.

23. Larry Summers, the former Treasury secretary, and the investor Rodriguez described the problem in strikingly similar terms. Summers told the *New York Times* in mid-March: "Emergency provision of loans is necessary but not sufficient. The financial system is short of capital and is under pressure to contract." Two weeks later, Rodriguez wrote, "The Fed proceeded under the assumption that this was a liquidity crisis, . . . However, with each lowering of the Fed Funds rate, there appeared to be very few positive responses. . . . Our capital markets were shutting down."

24. After the fact, and after the AIG and other dramatic episodes of failure, Bernanke seemed to acknowledge that the Bear Stearns rescue was not strictly grounded in either law or regulation. In a speech on December 1, 2008, the chairman remarked, "In the absence of an appropriate, comprehensive legal or regulatory framework, the Federal Reserve and the Treasury dealt with the cases of Bear Stearns and AIG using the tools available."

25. Susanne Craig, Jeffrey McCracken, Aaron Lucchetti, and Kate Kelly, "The Weekend That Wall Street Died," *Wall Street Journal,* December 29, 2008.

26. Among them were Lehman, Wachovia, and Fannie Mae. Freddie Mac opted to wait.

27. Quoted in a newsletter of Hayman Advisors, October 14, 2008, p. 3.

28. Drew DeSilver, "WaMu Shareholders Show Anger, CEO Killinger Asks for Patience," *Seattle Times*, April 16, 2008.

29. Pete Kelly, interview with the author.

30. Greg Farrell and Henry Sender, "The Shaming of John Thain," *Financial Times*, March 13, 2009.

31. Geithner's testimony is quoted in Gary Weiss, "The Man Who Saved (or Got Suckered by) Wall Street," *Portfolio*, June 2008.

32. Lehman 2008 proxy, pp. 18–19, and Susanne Craig and Kelly Crow, "Fallen Tycoon to Auction Prized Works," *Wall Street Journal*, September 26, 2008.

33. Released by the Committee on Oversight and Government Reform, hearings on "Causes and Effects of the Lehman Brothers Bankruptcy," October 6, 2008.

34. Ashish Shah, interview with the author.

CHAPTER 10

1. Hugh E. McGee III, e-mail to Dick Fuld, June 9, 2008, forwarding June 9 e-mail from Benoit D'Angelin, released in conjunction with the House Committee on Oversight and Government Reform hearings on "Causes and Effects of the Lehman Brothers Bankruptcy," October 6, 2008.

2. Released in conjunction with the October 6 hearings, "Causes and Effects of the Lehman Brothers Bankruptcy."

3. Steve Fishman, "Burning Down His House: Is Lehman CEO Dick Fuld the True Villain in the Collapse of Wall Street, or Is He Being Sacrificed for the Sins of His Peers?" *New York Magazine*, December 8, 2008, and author interviews.

4. Source: Lehman. Again, Leonard's otherwise useful "How Lehman Brothers Got Its Real Estate Fix," uses a less inclusive definition and gives a smaller total of commercial real estate assets.

5. "Two-thirds": Markit Group; 18 percent: Mortgage Bankers Association.

6. AIG raised just over $20 billion in May 2008, however, only $6.9 billion was debt; the remaining $13.35 billion consisted of equity and convertible securities.

7. Douglas Braunstein, interview with the author.

8. Bob Steel, interview with the author.

9. Jo Becker and Gretchen Morgenson, "Geithner, Member and Overseer of Finance Club," *New York Times*, April 26, 2009.

10. Refers to the period from June 30, 2007, to June 30, 2008.

11. Gerth and O'Harrow, "As Crisis Loomed, Geithner Pressed But Fell Short."

12. Remarks by U.S. Treasury Secretary Henry M. Paulson Jr., London, July 2, 2008.

13. David McCormick, interview with the author.

14. David Nason, interview with the author.

15. U.S. Treasury, as of July 1, 2008. The exact figure was $527 billion.

16. FDIC, estimated as of July 2009.

17. *MacroMavens*, July 25, 2008, 2.

18. The ten biggest banks refer (roughly) to the nine institutions that qualified for the first phase of the Troubled Asset Relief Program (TARP) enacted in October, plus Lehman, by then bankrupt. According to Pietro Veronesi and Luigi Zingales, "Paulson's Gift," November 5, 2008, p. 30 (draft), short-term debt of the original nine TARP banks, as of

June 30, 2008, was $2,151 billion. Lehman's short-term debt on May 31, 2008 was $485 billion, for a total of $2.636 trillion.

19. *MacroMavens*, July 31, 2008, 4.

20. "Disgusted and Betrayed," FPA commentary, July 30, 2008.

21. Testimony of Hank Paulson, July 15, 2008.

22. Charles Duhigg, "Fighting Foreclosures, F.D.I.C. Chief Draws Fire," *New York Times*, December 11, 2008.

23. Ryan Lizza, "The Contrarian," *New Yorker*, July 6, 2009.

24. John Dugan, interview with the author, and Duhigg, "Fighting Foreclosures." The reference to Bernanke is from Jim Wilkinson, interview with the author.

25. John Dugan, interview with the author.

26. Foreclosures: RealtyTrac; home prices: Case-Shiller; "five million . . . two million": *MacroMavens*, July 25, 2008, 3, and July 31, 2008, 4.

27. Pete Kelly, interview with the author.

28. See the internal Lehman e-mail of July 23, to Bart McDade among others, and forwarded to Fuld, relating that a banker who had recently left the firm had "stopped by" and commented, "it is very clear that GS [Goldman Sachs] is driving the bus with the hedge fund kabal [sic], & greatly influencing downside momentum [of] Leh[man] & others!" Released in conjunction with House hearings, "Causes and Effects of Lehman Bankruptcy."

29. Yalman Onaran and John Helyar, "Fuld Solicited Buffett Offer CEO Could Refuse as Lehman Fizzled," Bloomberg, November 10, 2008.

30. Rodgin Cohen and Paolo Tonucci, interviews with the author. Cohen characterized the Fed as "uncertain," rather than cool; either way, the plan wasn't acted on.

31. For example, the third quarter (2008) report of hedge fund Eton Park Capital Management states, "[W]e focused on our exposure to Lehman Brothers several months ago and sought to minimize it while maintaining our trading relationship" (p. 3).

32. *MacroMavens*, July 25, 2008, 2–5. "Banks' exposure" refers to that of commercial banks.

33. "9 percent": Vikas Bajaj, "At Midyear, the Economic Pain Persists," *New York Times*, July 1, 2008; "commercial paper": *MacroMavens*, July 31, 2008, 4.

34. Robert Barbera, *The Cost of Capitalism: Understanding Market Mayhem and Stabilizing Our Economic Future* (New York: McGraw-Hill, 2009), 67.

35. "Frantic concern": *MacroMavens*, July 31, 2008, 5–6; "Where the financial sector goes": *MacroMavens*, July 25, 2008, 4.

36. "Disgusted and Betrayed."

37. Bunning: Cassidy, "Anatomy of a Meltdown." See also "End of Illusions," *Economist*, July 17, 2008.

38. Peter Wallison and Charles W. Calomiris, "The Last Trillion-Dollar Commitment: The Destruction of Fannie Mae and Freddie Mac, "*Financial Service Outlook*, American Enterprise Institute for Public Policy Research, September 2008, 8.

39. Phil Swagel, interview with the author.

40. Ruth Porat and Robert Scully, interviews with the author.

41. "a tenth": Daniel Mudd, interview with the author, and Bethany McLean, "Fannie Mae's Last Stand," *Vanity Fair*, February 2009.

42. Author interviews with Robert Willumstad and others.

Chapter 11

1. Quoted in "What They Said About Fan and Fred," *Wall Street Journal*, October 2, 2008.
2. Deborah Solomon, Sudeep Reddy, and Susanne Craig, "Mounting Woes Left Officials with Little Room to Maneuver," *Wall Street Journal*, September 8, 2008.
3. "Irritated . . . criticism": Alan Blinder, interview with the author. The Meltzer quote is from "In Search of Maintaining Monetary Stability: Comment on Otmar Issing," delivered in a paper presented to the Bank for International Settlements 7th Annual Conference in Luzern on June 26, 2008—two months before the Jackson Hole gathering. His barb was well known to attendees in Wyoming. Japan's banker quoted in John Cassidy, "Anatomy of a Meltdown," *New Yorker*, December 1, 2008.
4. Hank Paulson, interview with the author.
5. Author interviews with Hank Paulson and others.
6. CMA (Credit Market Analysis). Price increases are from respective market bottoms, in early 2008 or earlier, to August 2008.
7. Robert Willumstad, interview with the author.
8. Douglas Braunstein, interview with the author.
9. Mortgage Bankers Association.
10. Rodgin Cohen, interview with the author. Cohen dates the talks from July.
11. Solomon, Reddy, and Craig, "Mounting Woes Left Officials with Little Room to Maneuver," and author interviews.
12. Rodgin Cohen and Daniel Mudd, interviews with the author.
13. Table arrangement: Solomon, Reddy, and Craig, "Mounting Woes Left Officials with Little Room to Maneuver"; "We are supportive": Rodgin Cohen, interview with the author.
14. McLean, "Fannie Mae's Last Stand," forcefully presents the case that the twins were preemptively, and unnecessarily, killed, as did Daniel Mudd, interview with the author.
15. See, for example, Daniel Gross, "Subprime Suspects," *Slate*, October 7, 2008. Both Morgan Stanley's Ruth Porat and Robert Scully, in an interview, and McLean's "Fannie Mae's Last Stand," affirm that the twins' Alt-A portfolio, which contributed to their distress, was accumulated for profit, not as a result of directives from HUD.
16. Jon Hilsenrath, Deborah Solomon, and Damian Paletta, "Paulson, Bernanke Strained for Consensus in Bailout," *Wall Street Journal*, November 10, 2008, and interviews with the author.
17. Volume in Lehman on September 9 was 384 million shares. Lehman had 689 million shares outstanding; however, once stock held by employees was deducted, roughly 450 million were held by the public. Thus, volume was about 85 percent of the "float." M&M's: Evan Thomas and Michael Hirsh, "Paulson's Complaint," *Newsweek*, May 16, 2009: "Here we go again": Onaran and Helyar, "Fuld Solicited Buffett Offer CEO Could Refuse as Lehman Fizzled."
18. Hank Paulson, interview with the author.
19. Onaran and Helyar, "Fuld Solicited Buffett Offer CEO Could Refuse as Lehman Fizzled."
20. Lehman third-quarter press release, September 9, 2008.
21. Blaine Frantz, Paolo Tonucci, interviews with the author.
22. CMA.
23. Michele Davis and other interviews with the author.

CHAPTER 12

1.   Theodore Lubke, interview with the author.
2.   Louise Story, "Tough Fight for Chief at Lehman," *New York Times*, September 10, 2008.
3.   Robert Willumstad and other interviews with the author. The $22 billion is as of September 15. AIG had posted $20 billion in collateral at the end of August and $33 billion by the end of September.
4.   James Bandler, with Roddy Boyd and Doris Burke, "Hank's Last Stand," *Fortune*, October 13, 2008.
5.   John Oros, "The Current State of Financial Markets and the Federal Government Policy Response," lecture at Wisconsin School of Business, September 29, 2008.
6.   Ibid.
7.   Steve Stecklow, "A Glimpse at Reserve's 'Buck' Race," *Wall Street Journal*, January 17, 2009.
8.   Sourced partly from Carrick Mollenkamp, Susanne Craig, Jeffrey McCracken, and Jon Hilsenrath, "The Two Faces of Lehman's Fall," *Wall Street Journal*, October 6, 2008.
9.   Hank Paulson, interview with the author.
10. CMA (Credit Market Analysis).
11. Eric Dinallo, interview with the author.
12. Federal Reserve Act, Section 13(3).
13. Mollenkamp, Craig, McCracken, and Hilsenrath, "The Two Faces of Lehman's Fall."
14. Steve Black, interview with the author.
15. John Helyar, Allison Fitzgerald, Mark Pittman, and Serena Saitto, "Ten Days Changed Wall Street as Bernanke Saw Massive Failures," Bloomberg, September 22, 2008.
16. Lisa Kassenaar and Christine Harper, "Mack Tells Wife He May Lose Firm Before Brokerage Bid," Bloomberg, January 26, 2009.
17. Miller's e-mail: Lori Fife, interview with the author. "Blue suit": Susanne Craig, Jeffrey McCracken, Aaron Lucchetti, and Kate Kelly, "The Weekend That Wall Street Died," *Wall Street Journal*, December 29, 2008.
18. Jamie Dimon and John Hogan, interviews with the author.
19. Harvey Miller, interview with the author.
20. "Son of a bitch": Craig, McCracken, Lucchetti and Kelly, "The Weekend That Wall Street Died"; Paulson: Thomas and Hirsh, "Paulson's Complaint."
21. Robert Willumstad, Eric Dinallo, and Douglas Braunstein, interviews with the author.
22. William D. Cohan, "Three Days That Shook the World," *Fortune*, December 15, 2008.
23. Craig, McCracken, Lucchetti and Kelly, "The Weekend That Wall Street Died."
24. Mollenkamp, Craig, McCracken, and Hilsenrath, "The Two Faces of Lehman's Fall."
25. Susan Pulliam, Kate Kelly, and Matthew Karnitschnig, "Buffett Drove Hard Bargain with Goldman," *Wall Street Journal,* September 25, 2008, and interviews with the author.
26. Douglas Braunstein and other interviews with the author.
27. Jim Wilkinson, interview with the author.
28. Craig, McCracken, Lucchetti, and Kelly, "The Weekend That Wall Street Died."

CHAPTER 13

1.   Carrick Mollenkamp, Susanne Craig, Jeffrey McCracken, and Jon Hilsenrath, "The Two Faces of Lehman's Fall," *Wall Street Journal*, October 6, 2008.
2.   Based on author's interviews with various former employees of Merrill Lynch.
3.   The number kept shifting and was never finalized. Fed officials said (after the fact) that

the total was $60 billion. Onaran and Helyar, in "Fuld Solicited Buffett Offer," reported $55 billion to $60 billion. Fishman, in "Burning Down His House," said the total could have been $70 billion.

4. William D. Cohan, "Three Days That Shook the World," *Fortune*, December 15, 2008.

5. Hank Paulson, interview with the author.

6. Carrick Mollenkamp, Mark Whitehouse, Jon Hilsenrath, and Ianthe Jeanne Dugan, "Lehman's Demise Triggered Cash Crunch Around Globe," *Wall Street Journal*, September 29, 2008.

7. William Dudley, interview with the author.

8. Eric Dinallo, interview with the author.

9. Steve Fishman, "Burning Down His House: Is Lehman CEO Dick Fuld the True Villain in the Collapse of Wall Street, or Is He Being Sacrificed for the Sins of His Peers?" *New York Magazine*, December 8, 2008.

10. Author interviews with Harvey Miller and other participants.

11. The director was John Macomber.

12. Akers and other details of board meeting: Harvey Miller, interview with the author; "What McDade had reported": Fishman, "Burning Down His House," and Cohan, "Three Days That Shook the World"; "Stunned": Onaran and Helyar, "Fuld Solicited Buffett Offer"; "Goodbye": Miller, interview with the author, and Craig, McCracken, Lucchetti, and Kelly, "The Weekend That Wall Street Died."

13. Robert Willumstad, interview with the author.

14. Robert Willumstad, interview with the author, and Susan Beck, "Chronicle of a Future Foretold," *American Lawyer,* November 2008.

15. Paulson quote from Paulson interview with author; "new legislation": Jon Hilsenrath, Deborah Solomon, and Damian Paletta, "Paulson, Bernanke Strained for Consensus in Bailout," *Wall Street Journal*, November 10, 2008.

16. Harvey Miller, interview with the author; Helyar, Fitzgerald, Pittman, and Saitto "Ten Days That Changed Wall Street"; Cohan, "Three Days That Shook the World," and, for Morgan Stanley exec, Kassenaar and Harper, "Mack Tells Wife He May Lose Firm."

CHAPTER 14

1. Norway: Carrick Mollenkamp, Mark Whitehouse, Jon Hilsenrath, and Ianthe Jeanne Dugan, "Lehman's Demise Triggered Cash Crunch Around Globe," *Wall Street Journal*, September 29, 2008; "calling the Fed": William Dudley, interview with the author.

2. Carrick Mollenkamp, Susanne Craig, Jeffrey McCracken, and Jon Hilsenrath, "The Two Faces of Lehman's Fall," *Wall Street Journal*, October 6, 2008.

3. Declaration of Shari D. Leventhal in the bankruptcy case *Securities Investors Protection Corp. v. Lehman Brothers*, U.S. Bankruptcy Court, Southern District of New York.

4. Seven hundred hedge funds: Saijel Kishan, "Amber Hedge Fund Gets Back Assets Frozen with Lehman," Bloomberg, July 24, 2009.

5. Mollenkamp, Whitehouse, Hilsenrath, and Dugan, "Lehman's Demise Triggered Cash Crunch."

6. Commonwealth of Massachusetts, "In the Matter of Reserve Management Co., Inc., Reserve Partners, Inc., Reserve Funds Trust, and Bruce Bent II," docket no. 2008-079, pp. 6–7.

7. The July interview was cited in John Helyar, Allison Fitzgerald, Mark Pittman, and Serena Saitto, "Ten Days Changed Wall Street as Bernanke Saw Massive Failures," Bloomberg,

September 22, 2008. Background on Bent is from Steve Stecklow and Diya Gullapalli, "A Money-Fund Manager's Fateful Shift," *Wall Street Journal*, December 8, 2008.

8. "In the Matter of Reserve Management Co.," 32, Exhibit L.
9. "In the Matter of Reserve Management Co.," 20, 26, 29, 33–47; see also Steve Stecklow, "A Glimpse at Reserve's 'Buck' Race," *Wall Street Journal*, January 17, 2009.
10. Dan Freed, "JPMorgan's Trillion-Dollar Man," *TheStreet.com*, July 1, 2009.
11. Douglas Braunstein, interview with the author.
12. Eric Dinallo, Robert Willumstad, interviews with the author.
13. Swap premiums: CMA (Credit Market Analysis); $18 billion: Carrick Mollenkamp, Serena Ng, Liam Pleven, and Randall Smith, "Behind AIG's Fall, Risk Models Failed to Pass Real-World Test," *Wall Street Journal*, October 31, 2008.
14. "Dour": Eric Dinallo, interview with the author; "Turn off your cell phones": Douglas Braunstein, interview with the author.
15. Robert Willumstad and other interviews with the author.
16. Wells Fargo S-4 SEC filing of October 31, 2008, see section entitled "Background of the Merger."
17. Swap premiums: CMA; Mellon: Susanne Craig, Jeffrey McCracken, Aaron Lucchetti, and Kate Kelly, "The Weekend That Wall Street Died," *Wall Street Journal*, December 29, 2008.
18. Susan Pulliam, Liz Rappaport, Aaron Lucchetti, Jenny Strasburg, and Tom McGinty, "Anatomy of the Morgan Stanley Panic," *Wall Street Journal*, November 24, 2008.
19. Ibid.
20. The director was Stephen Bollenbach, a retired hotel executive.
21. Gretchen Morgenson and Don Van Natta Jr., "Paulson's Calls to Goldman Tested Ethics During Crisis," *New York Times*, August 8, 2009.
22. James Doran, "Goldman Star Lives American Dream; Profile: Lloyd C. Blankfein," *Times* (London), June 3, 2006.
23. Morgenson and Van Natta Jr., "Paulson's Calls to Goldman Tested Ethics During Crisis."
24. Peter Baker, Stephen Labaton, and Eric Lipton, "A Professor and a Banker Bury Old Dogma on Markets," *New York Times*, September 20, 2008.

CHAPTER 15

1. Some biographical details from Emily Thornton, "Morgan Stanley's Mack Attack," *BusinessWeek*, June 21, 2006.
2. Premiums: CMA (Credit Market Analysis).
3. Many details of Morgan's Stanley's duress are from Susan Pulliam, Liz Rappaport, Aaron Lucchetti, Jenny Strasburg, and Tom McGinty, "Anatomy of the Morgan Stanley Panic," *Wall Street Journal*, November 24, 2008, and Lisa Kassenaar and Christine Harper, "Mack Tells Wife He May Lose Firm Before Brokerage Bid," Bloomberg, January 26, 2009.
4. Kendrick Wilson, interview with the author.
5. Gretchen Morgenson and Don Van Natta Jr., "Paulson's Calls to Goldman Tested Ethics During Crisis," *New York Times*, August 8, 2009.
6. Joe Nocera, "As Credit Crisis Spiraled, Alarm Led to Action," *New York Times*, October 2, 2008.
7. China announced that its sovereign wealth fund would invest $200 billion in shares of the country's three largest banks. Russia approved a $120 billion plan to rescue its financial system. Both moves were announced September 18. On Bernanke, the *New York Times* (Edmund L. Andrews, Carl Hulse, and David M. Herszenhorn, "Federal Reserve and

Treasury Offer Congress a Plan for a Vast Bailout," September 19, 2008) estimated that the Fed pumped almost $300 billion into "global credit markets" on a single day.

8. Interviews with the author; see also Joe Nocera and Edmund L. Andrews, "Struggling to Keep Up as the Crisis Raced On," *New York Times*, October 22, 2008.

9. Phillip Swagel, interview with the author.

10. Case-Shiller. The deflation is measured from the peak in 2006 to the third quarter of 2008.

11. Crane Data. Crane tracks assets at the 500 largest money market funds. Total assets were $3.116 trillion on September 12, the Friday before Lehman's failure, and $2.910 trillion the following Friday, a decline of $206 billion.

12. Douglas Braunstein, interview with the author. On Ford Motor, see Cynthia Koons, "Credit Tightens for Ford, GM," *Wall Street Journal*, September 23, 2008. See also Jeffrey McCracken and David Enrich, "U.S. Firms Gird for Hits and Draw on Credit Now," *Wall Street Journal*, September 25, 2008.

13. Kassenaar and Harper, "Mack Tells Wife He May Lose Firm."

14. Morgan Stanley. According to Pulliam, et al., "Anatomy of the Morgan Stanley Panic," of 1,100 hedge funds with accounts at Morgan Stanley, three-quarters sought to redeem at least a portion of their assets.

15. Jamie Dimon, interview with the author.

16. Interviews with the author; Kassenaar and Harper, "Mack Tells Wife He May Lose Firm"; Wells Fargo S-4.

17. CMA.

18. Hank Paulson, interview with the author.

19. Kassenaar and Harper, "Mack Tells Wife He May Lose Firm."

20. Steve Black, Douglas Braunstein, John Hogan, interviews with the author.

21. Wells Fargo S-4 and interviews with the author.

22. Wells Fargo S-4.

23. Wells Fargo S-4 and interviews with the author.

24. Hank Paulson and other interviews with the author.

CHAPTER 16

1. Deborah Solomon, Liz Rappaport, Damian Paletta, and Jon Hilsenrath, "Shock Forced Paulson's Hand," *Wall Street Journal*, September 20, 2008.

2. Andrew Ross Sorkin, "A Bailout Above the Law," *New York Times*, September 22, 2008.

3. Merkel: Jason Dean, Marcus Walker, and Evan Ramstad, "The Financial Crisis: Crisis Stirs Critics of Free Markets—Around the World, Calls to Reconsider U.S.-Style Policies," *Wall Street Journal*, September 25, 2008; Cox: testimony before Senate Banking Committee, September 23, 2008, and Stephen Labaton, "S.E.C. Concedes Oversight Flaws Fueled Collapse," *New York Times*, September 27, 2008.

4. Hank Paulson, testimony before Senate Banking Committee, September 23, 2008.

5. "The Elephant(s) in the Room," FPA commentary, September 23, 2008. Rodriguez, as noted in the text, was traveling in Italy and communicating with his partners via e-mail. The letter was signed "Steven Romick and the Partners at First Pacific Advisors." The language was probably Romick's, though consistent with what Rodriguez was now and had been saying for a year.

6. Jon Hilsenrath, Deborah Solomon, and Damian Paletta, "Paulson, Bernanke Strained for Consensus in Bailout," *Wall Street Journal*, November 10, 2008, and interviews with the author.

7. Ben Bernanke, testimony before Senate Banking Committee, September 23, 2008.

8. CMA (Credit Market Analysis).

9. CMA.

10. Wells Fargo S-4.

11. *MacroMavens*, October 3, 2008, 3.

12. Mortgage Bankers Association.

13. Sheryl Gay Stolberg, "Lawmakers' Constituents Make Their Bailout Views Loud and Clear," *New York Times*, September 25, 2008, and interviews with the author.

14. See, for instance, John D. McKinnon, Laura Meckler, and Christopher Cooper, "An Inside View of a Stormy White House Summit," *Wall Street Journal*, September 27–28, 2008, and Carl Hulse, "Conservatives Viewed Bailout Plan as Last Straw," *New York Times*, September 27, 2008.

15. Wells Fargo S-4; David Enrich and Matthew Karnitschnig, "Citi, U.S. Rescue Wachovia," *Wall Street Journal*, September 30, 2008, and interviews with the author.

16. Hilsenrath, Solomon, and Paletta, "Paulson, Bernanke Strained for Consensus in Bailout," and interviews with the author.

17. Wells Fargo S-4 and author interviews with Wachovia executives.

18. Wells Fargo S-4.

19. "Bair told them": Jane Sherburne, interview with the author.

20. Bob Steel and Jane Sherburne, interviews with the author; see also David Enrich, Carrick Mollenkamp, Matthias Rieker, Damian Paletta, and Jon Hilsenrath, "U.S. Agrees to Rescue Struggling Citigroup," *Wall Street Journal*, November 24, 2008. On Citigroup's continuing troubles, see Julie Creswell and Eric Dash, "Citigroup: Above the Fray," *New York Times*, September 21, 2008.

21. Wells Fargo S-4.

22. David M. Herszenhorn and Carl Hulse, "Congress Nears a Bailout in Intense Push," *New York Times*, September 28, 2008.

23. Greg Hitt and Damian Paletta, "The Financial Crisis: GOP Leaders Try to Secure Rank-and-File Vote," *Wall Street Journal*, September 29, 2008.

24. Carter Dougherty, "Authorities Aid Banks in Europe," *New York Times*, September 30, 2008.

25. In quick succession, European governments were forced to rescue, or nationalize, five major lenders: Glitnir (Iceland), Dexia (Belgium), Fortis (Belgium/Netherlands), Hypo Real Estate (Germany) and Bradford & Bingley (UK).

26. Federal Reserve Board. Figure on Wall Street (primary dealer) lending is rounded. The precise total was $146.6 billion as of October 1. For expansion of Fed facilities in Europe and in the U.S. see the Fed's press release of September 29, 2008,

27. Edmund L. Andrews and Mark Landler, "Treasury and Fed Looking at Options," *New York Times*, September 30, 2008.

CHAPTER 17

1. Niall Ferguson, "The End of Prosperity?" *Time*, October 2, 2008.

2. This account of the sale of Wachovia is based on author interviews with various Wachovia executives, as well as the Wells-Fargo S-4 filed October 31, 2008, which provides an in-depth factual framework.

3. Wells Fargo S-4.

4. Ibid.

5. Ibid.; see also Eric Dash and Ben White, "Wells Fargo Swoops In," *New York Times*, October 4, 2008.

6. Jane Sherburne, interview with the author. The *Wall Street Journal* (Dan Fitzpatrick, "On Crisis Stage, FDIC Plays the Tough," November 3, 2008) reported that Pandit asked Bair to consider "the effect of this development on systemic issues unrelated to Wachovia." That sounds dubiously formal for a conversation at 2:30 A.M. Subsequently (Damian Paletta and David Enrich, "FDIC Pushes Purge at Citi," June 5, 2009), the *Journal*, describing either the same or a subsequent early-morning call, wrote that Pandit, in frustration, had launched into an "obscenity-laced tirade."

7. David Enrich, Carrick Mollenkamp, Matthias Rieker, Damian Paletta, and Jon Hilsenrath, "U.S. Agrees to Rescue Struggling Citigroup," *Wall Street Journal*, November 24, 2008.

8. Liz Rappaport, Serena Ng, and Peter Lattman, "Uncertainty Over Rescue Intensifies Credit Crisis," *Wall Street Journal*, October 3, 2008.

9. Commercial paper numbers from the Federal Reserve; the higher figure was in August 2007. "Onerous terms": Rappaport, Ng, and Lattman, "Uncertainty Over Rescue Intensifies Credit Crisis." Paulson and GE: Hank Paulson, David Nason, and other interviews with the author.

10. Mary Williams Walsh, "Under Strain, Cities Are Cutting Back Projects," *New York Times*, September 30, 2008.

11. Moody's Investor Service, "Structured Finance: Special Report—Structured Finance CDO Ratings Surveillance Brief, Third Quarter 2008," October 24, 2008.

12. Ferguson, "The End of Prosperity?"

13. "Group of professors": Mark Gertler, interview with the author; "told his staff": Hank Paulson, interview with the author.

Chapter 18

1. Walter Bagehot, *Lombard Street*, quoted by Richard Fisher, President of Federal Reserve Bank of Dallas, in his speech "Historical Perspectives on the Current Economic and Financial Crisis (With Reference to Paul Volcker, Washington Irving, Walter Bagehot, Mother Caris, Rube Goldberg, and Bismarck)," Dallas, December 18, 2008.

2. The quote originated with Sam Jones, author of the *Financial Times* blog FT Alphaville.

3. Ben Bernanke, "Deflation: Making Sure 'It' Doesn't Happen Here," remarks before the National Economists Club, Washington, D.C., November 21, 2002.

4. JPMorgan, "Economic Research: The Big Fat Fed Balance Sheet," by Michael Feroli and Bruce Kasman, October 3, 2008.

5. "Ballooned 60 percent": JPMorgan, "The Big Fat Fed Balance Sheet"; "debasing": *MacroMavens*, October 3, 2008, 4–5.

6. David Nason and other interviews with the author.

7. Robert Rodriguez, FPA Capital Fund, semiannual report for period ending September 30.

8. See Brian Carney, "Bernanke Is Fighting the Last War," *Wall Street Journal*, October 18, 2008, in which the historian Anna Schwartz argued that liquidity was the basic problem in the '30s but not in 2008. Specifically, she said of the earlier debacle, "If the borrowers hadn't withdrawn cash, they [the banks] would have been in good shape." This echoed the landmark history she co-authored with Milton Friedman, *A Monetary History of the United States*.

9. Vikas Bajaj, "Panicky Sellers Darken Afternoon on Wall Street," *New York Times*, October 9, 2008.

10. "Rumors that it was running out of cash": Jeffrey Schultz, interview with the author.
11. Hank Paulson and other interviews with the author.
12. Jeffrey Schultz, interview with the author.
13. Hank Paulson and other interviews with the author. See also Jo Becker and Gretchen Morgenson, "Geithner, Member and Overseer of Finance Club," *New York Times*, April 26, 2009.
14. David Nason, interview with the author.
15. Michele Davis, interview with the author.
16. Interviews with the author and Damian Paletta, Jon Hilsenrath, and Deborah Solomon, "At Moment of Truth, U.S. Forced Big Bankers to Blink," *Wall Street Journal*, October 15, 2008, and Mark Landler and Eric Dash, "Drama Behind a Banking Deal," *New York Times*, October 15, 2008.
17. Landler and Dash, "Drama Behind a Banking Deal," and Jamie Dimon, interview with the author.
18. Robert Rodriguez, "Reaction to Treasury Plan," internal FPA e-mail, October 14, 2008.

CHAPTER 19

1. Yields for investment grade corporations peaked on October 10; junk bond yields did not peak until late November.
2. Carol Vogel, "Bleak Night at Christie's, in Both Sales and Prices," *New York Times*, November 6, 2008.
3. Mortgage debt began to fall in the second quarter of 2008 and was still falling as of the third quarter of 2009 (the last figure before this book went to press).
4. As for the three rescues of Citigroup, the U.S. invested $25 billion of TARP capital in Citigroup in October 2008. In November, it provided Citi with protection against losses of up to $249 billion, after Citi assumed the first $29 billion in losses. The government also invested more capital. Finally, in February 2009, the U.S. converted its preferred stock in Citigroup to common, thus relieving the company of the burden of dividend payments and boosting its common equity.
5. Hank Paulson, interview with the author.
6. The Fed's assets rose from $900 billion in September 2008 to more than $2 trillion a year later. The Fed purchased asset-backed securities via the Term Asset-backed Securities Loan Facility, or TALF, created in November 2008. Commercial paper holdings peaked in January 2009; after that its holdings diminished. However, its inventory of mortgage-backed securities kept growing, reaching $860 billion by September 2009.
7. As the S&P 500 is the mostly widely used barometer of stock market performance, that is the index generally relied on in this book (such as in stating that "stocks" fell 11 percent from New Year's Day to January 20). However, the *absolute level* of stocks is described in terms of the Dow Jones Industrial Index, For investors and casual market observers who may be aware of only one market number, it is mostly likely to be the level of the Dow.
8. Office market: Christina S. N. Lewis, "Office Rents Dive as Vacancies Rise," *Wall Street Journal*, October 7, 2009. Rate of bank failures: through late December 2009, 140 banks had failed.
9. Subprime and national delinquency rate: MBA. First American CoreLogic reported 15.2 million underwater mortgages at midyear; Moody's Economy.com put the number at 16 million. Later in 2009, First American revised its methodology for counting underwater

mortgages. Using its new methodology, it reported 10.7 million underwater mortgages in the third quarter.

10. On September 30, 2009, the S&P 500 closed at 1,057, 32.5 percent below its record high of 1,565 on October 9, 2007.

11. The 344,000 foreclosures in September '09 were the third-highest of any month on record.

12. "The End Is Nigh (Again)," *Economist*, October 3, 2009.

13. Edmund L. Andrews and David E. Sanger, "U.S. Is Finding Its Role in Business Hard to Unwind," *New York Times*, September 14, 2009.

14. Post-rally figure is as of September 10, 2009; Karl Russell, "Metrics," *New York Times*, September 13, 2009.

15. Roger Lowenstein, "U.S. Savings Bind," *New York Times Magazine*, October 14, 2009.

16. According to the Bureau of Labor Statistics survey of nonfarm employees, the U.S. had 130,901,000 jobs in November 2001, the month the post-dot-com bubble recession ended. Payroll employment peaked at 138,152,000 in December 2007. The recession's formal end had not been decided when this book went to press, but at midyear 2009, total employment had shrunk to just over 131 million. While that is marginally above the low of 2001, the BLS annually revises its figures as more extensive data is compiled. In October, it announced that it anticipated a reduction of 800,000 in the monthly totals for 2007–09. This would bring the total number of jobs lost during the recession to approximately 8 million, or 5.8 percent of the jobs existing at the economy's peak.

CHAPTER 20

1. House Committee on Oversight and Government Reform, October 23, 2008, hearing on "The Financial Crisis and the Role of Federal Regulators."

2. Merrill lost $39.7 billion between the third quarter of 2007 and its acquisition by Bank of America at the end of 2008, just eclipsing the $39.6 billion it had earned since 1996. Fannie's and Freddie's losses wiped out all profits in their history as publicly traded firms.

3. Stephen Mihm, "Why Capitalism Fails," *Boston Globe*, September 13, 2009. For more on Minsky and his relevance to 2008, see Robert Barbera, The Cost of Capitalism: Understanding Market Mayhem and Stabilizing Our Economic Future (New York: McGraw-Hill, 2009).

4. "Market fatigue," special report, *Economist*, October 3, 2009.

5. Money set aside by Goldman for compensation during the first nine months of 2009, most of which was during the recession, had rebounded to the level of compensation in 2007.

6. For an idea of how such a rule would work, see the author's "Thain's Original Sin Rooted in Executive Pay," Bloomberg, January 26, 2009.

7. Such firms included Goldman, Morgan Stanley, and Credit Suisse.

8. See, for instance, Joe Nocera, "Talking Business: Only a Hint of Roosevelt in Financial Overhaul," *New York Times*, June 17, 2009.

9. Ben Bernanke, speech before Greater Austin Chamber of Commerce, Austin, Texas, December 1, 2008.

10. David Moss, of Harvard Business School, recommended that banks be discouraged from becoming too big to fail.

11. Michael McKee and Scott Lanman, "Greenspan Says U.S. Should Consider Breaking Up Large Banks," Bloomberg, October 15, 2009.

12. In his reconfirmation hearing, on December 3, 2009, Bernanke told the Senate Banking Committee, "I did not anticipate a crisis of this magnitude."

13. From September 30, 2007, to September 30, 2009, leverage at Citigroup declined from 18.6 to 13.5; at Goldman from 26.8 to 13.6, and at Morgan Stanley from 33.9 to 14.8.

14. James Surowiecki, "The Financial Page: Why Banks Stay Big," *New Yorker*, November 2, 2009. The banks are Bank of America, Citigroup, JPMorgan Chase, and Wells Fargo.

15. Matt Apuzzo and Daniel Wagner, "Geithner Makes Time to Talk to Wall Street Bankers," Associated Press. The story, published October 8, 2009, in the *Boston Globe*, reported eighty such contacts in Geithner's first seven months.

16. "The Keynes books are Peter Clarke's *Keynes: The Rise, Fall, and Return of the Twentieth Century's Most Influential Economist* (New York: Bloomsbury, 2009); Robert Skidelsky's *Keynes: The Return of the Master* (New York: PublicAffairs, 2009); and Paul Davidson's *The Keynes Solution: The Path to Global Economic Prosperity* (New York: Palgrave Macmillan, 2009).

17. G20 deficits: "A Fine Balance," special report, *Economist*, October 3, 2009. U.S. deficit is for year ended September 30, 2009. Rodriguez, FPA "Client Letter Commentary," January 27, 2009.

18. See in particular Mohamed A. El-Erian, CEO of PIMCO, "Secular Outlook: A New Normal," May 2009.

19. House Committee on Banking and Financial Services, hearing on "The Financial Derivatives Supervisory Improvement Act of 1998," July 24, 1998.

20. Jeff Sommer, "In This 10-Year Race, Bonds Win by a Mile," *New York Times*, October 25, 2009. Data is through September 2009.

21. Floyd Norris, "To Rein In Pay, Rein In Wall Street," *New York Times*, October 30, 2009.

22. Bernanke's speech at the London School of Economics on January 13, 2009, for instance, referred to the "boom" four times (three times specifically to the "credit boom"). He did not mention a "bubble."

23. Lipper/Thomson Reuters. Returns are for September 30, 1984, through September 30, 2009. FPA Capital was one of 216 diversified equity funds with a twenty-five-year record. Rodriguez began running the fund slightly before, on July 1, 1984. Dated from then, through September 30, 2009, FPA Capital's return was 14.95 percent a year, compared to 10.66 percent for the S&P.

AFTERWORD

1. Mike Mayo of CLSA.

INDEX

source of bailout funds, 229
TARP and, 223, 230, 232, 236, 263, 269
Trichet, Jean-Claude, 268

UBS, 76, 183
unemployment/job loss, xxv, 100, 132, 242, 262,
    273–74, 281–82, 284
United Kingdom, 195, 222, 229, 258, 263, 294–95
United States. *See also* economy, U.S.; government,
    U.S.
    home ownership rate in, 37
    international opinion of, 235–36, 248, 295
    total relief commitment of, 282n

Viniar, David, xviii, 79–80, 129, 217
Volcker, Paul, 156n, 301

Wachovia, 78, 105, 142, 145, 227, 240–41
    acquisitions by, 69–70
    bailout and auction of, 244–47
    Ben Bernanke and, 245–46
    buyer sought by, 211, 226
    Citigroup and, 240, 241, 244, 246–47, 251–54
    FDIC and, 245–46
    Golden West and, 70, 140, 245
    government efforts to arrange a merger for, 226,
        232
    insurance (credit default swap) premiums of, 240
    losses, 132
    Merrill Lynch and, 109
    Morgan Stanley and, 226
    stock price of, 241
    acquisition by Wells Fargo, 244–45, 253–54
Wagoner, Rick, 279
Walker, George Herbert, IV, 195
Wall Street. *See also specific firms*
    bankers to, 129
    borrowing options for, 127, 130, 131, 141, 177, 234,
        236
    buyout craze on, 19
    changes in post-2008, 290–93, 295–96
    complexity, penchant for, 23, 287
    democratization of, 17, 49–50
    denial of right to fail on, 291–92
    eclipse of golden age of, xxii, 285–86, 287–88,
        295–96
    faith in, xxii, 141, 285, 295–96
    Great Recession and, 274-75
    Alan Greenspan and, 3-4, 37, 285-86
    intellectual model of, xxiii, 3–4, 37, 45–46, 223–24,
        285, 287-88
    as subject to uncertainty, 288
    jobs lost on, number of, 284

JPMorgan Chase as banker to, 129
main business of, 49–50
Main Street and, unholy alliance between, 287
mortgage bubble and, xxiii, xxiv, 5, 13–14, 22, 23,
    35–36, 41–47, 51, 55, 80, 93
new normal on, 295
panic, susceptibility to, 62, 101–02, 136
profits of, 296–97
purpose of, 297
reform of, 290–93
refutation of belief in perfection of, 235, 272, 285,
    287–88, 295–97
short-selling against. *See* short selling
short-term paper diet of, 136
statistical modeling and, 45–46
stock prices of firms on, 125, 148, 247, 265, 287–
    88. *See also specific firms*
war with hedge funds, 135, 150, 169, 175, 203–4,
    211–12, 217, 219, 225
Wall Street Journal, 105, 112, 156n, 161, 164n
Walsh, Mark, xviii, 92–93, 188
Warsh, Kevin, xix, 96, 123, 126, 160, 169, 188–89, 196,
    232, 266, 278
Washington Mutual, 211, 227, 239–40, 288–89
    bondholders, 240
    concern over, 145, 177
    JPMorgan Chase and, 133, 239–40
    lack of risk control by, 33
    leadership change at, 164
    mortgage bubble and, 107
    mortgage practices of, 32–35
    shareholders, 239
    stock price of, 177
    subprime mortgages and, 17
Weil, Gotshal & Manges, 170, 182, 189–90, 197
Weill, Sanford I. (Sandy), xix, 66, 79, 111, 141
Wells Fargo, 240, 241, 253–54
Wen Jiabao, 295
Whitney, Meredith, xix, 110
Wilkinson, Jim, 190
Willumstad, Robert, xix, 122n, 141, 154, 159, 165,
    173–74, 177, 185–86, 190, 191, 196–97, 200, 207,
    208, 209–10, 213
Wilson, Kendrick, xix, 153–54, 156, 220–21
Winkelried, Jon, 209
Winters, Bill, 225–26
WorldCom, 279
Wriston, Walter, 250

Y2K computer collapse, 101

Zandi, Mark, 47, 77
Zubrow, Barry, xix, 129, 178, 200

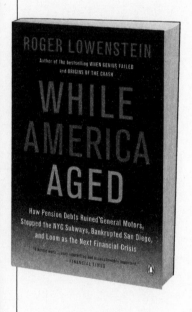

AVAILABLE FROM PENGUIN

Origins of the Crash
The Great Bubble and Its Undoing

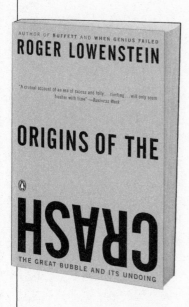

ISBN 978-0-14-303467-4

With his singular gift for turning complex financial events into eminently readable stories, Roger Lowenstein lays bare the labyrinthine events of the manic and tumultuous 1990s. In an enthralling narrative, he ties together all of the characters of the dot-com bubble and offers a unique portrait of the culture of the era. Just as John Kenneth Galbraith's *The Great Crash* was a defining text on the Great Depression, Lowenstein's *Origins of the Crash* is destined to be the book that will frame our understanding of the 1990s.

PENGUIN
BOOKS